W9-CGX-605

# SHOWCASE PRESENTS

# JUSTICE LEAGUE of AMERICA

## VOLUME THREE

**Dan DiDio** Senior VP-Executive Editor

**Mort Weisinger** Editor-original series

**Peter Hamboussi** Editor-collected edition

**Robbin Brosterman** Senior Art Director

**Paul Levitz** President & Publisher

**Georg Brewer** VP-Design & DC Direct Creative

**Richard Bruning** Senior VP-Creative Director

**Patrick Caldon** Executive VP-Finance & Operations

**Chris Caramalis** VP-Finance

**John Cunningham** VP-Marketing

**Terri Cunningham** VP-Managing Editor

**Alison Gill** VP-Manufacturing

**David Hyde** VP-Publicity

**Hank Kanalz** VP-General Manager, WildStorm

**Jim Lee** Editorial Director-WildStorm

**Paula Lowitt** Senior VP-Business & Legal Affairs

**MaryEllen McLaughlin** VP-Advertising & Custom Publishing

**John Nee** Senior VP-Business Development

**Gregory Noveck** Senior VP-Creative Affairs

**Sue Pohja** VP-Book Trade Sales

**Steve Rotterdam** Senior VP-Sales & Marketing

**Cheryl Rubin** Senior VP-Brand Management

**Jeff Trojan** VP-Business Development, DC Direct

**Bob Wayne** VP-Sales

Cover illustration by Carmine Infantino and Murphy Anderson.
Front cover colored by Drew Moore.

# TABLE OF CONTENTS

ALL STORIES WRITTEN BY **GARDNER FOX**.
ALL STORIES PENCILLED BY **MIKE SEKOWSKY** AND INKED BY **BERNARD SACHS**. ALL COVERS PENCILLED BY
**MIKE SEKOWSKY** AND INKED BY **MURPHY ANDERSON** UNLESS OTHERWISE NOTED.

UNTIL THE 1970S IT WAS NOT COMMON PRACTICE IN THE COMIC BOOK INDUSTRY TO CREDIT ALL STORIES. IN THE PREPARA-
TION OF THIS COLLECTION WE HAVE USED OUR BEST EFFORTS TO REVIEW ANY SURVIVING RECORDS AND CONSULT ANY
AVAILABLE DATABASES AND KNOWLEDGEABLE PARTIES. WE REGRET THE INNATE LIMITATIONS OF THIS PROCESS AND ANY
MISSING OR MISASSIGNED ATTRIBUTIONS THAT MAY OCCUR. ANY ADDITIONAL INFORMATION ON CREDITS
SHOULD BE DIRECTED TO: EDITOR, COLLECTED EDITIONS, C/O DC COMICS.

# JUSTICE LEAGUE of AMERICA

☆☆☆ ☆☆☆

WHERE IS THE *JUSTICE LEAGUE*, YOU WONDER? WHAT ARE THE SUPER-HEROES OF THE *JUSTICE SOCIETY* DOING ON *EARTH-ONE*? WHY ARE THEY FIGHTING THE *BAHDNISIAN HEX-THUNDERBOLT* OF THEIR FELLOW MEMBER, *JOHNNY THUNDER*? FOR THE ANSWERS TO THESE QUESTIONS, STARTLING AND STUNNING AS THEY ARE, READ ON--AND BRACE YOURSELF FOR THE AMAZING AND ASTOUNDING SITUATION THAT HAS DEVELOPED ON THE...

# EARTH-WITHOUT A JUSTICE LEAGUE!

**The ROLL CALL***

**ATOM**  **DOCTOR FATE**  **FLASH**  **GREEN LANTERN**  **HAWKMAN**  **MR. TERRIFIC**

*EDITOR'S NOTE: SINCE *EARTH-ONE* HAS BEEN DEPRIVED OF ITS *JUSTICE LEAGUE*, THIS ISSUE'S ROLL CALL CONSISTS OF MEMBERS FROM THE *JUSTICE SOCIETY OF AMERICA* OF *EARTH-TWO*!

THE VERY AIR SEEMS CHARGED WITH EXCITEMENT WHEN ONE RECEIVES A SPECIAL DELIVERY LETTER--AND SUCH PROVES THE CASE WITH *JOHNNY THUNDER* ...

WELL, IT'S ABOUT TIME! I FINALLY WAS INVITED TO ATTEND A MEETING OF THE RE-VIVED *JUSTICE SOCIETY OF AMERICA*! IT'S BEEN BURNING ME UP THE WAY THEY'VE GONE OFF ON ADVENTURES AGAIN--WITHOUT GIVING ME A TUMBLE!

I HELPED THEM OUT BEFORE AND I CAN HELP THEM OUT AGAIN! ME AND MY *THUNDER-BOLT* WILL --*OOOPS*! I FORGOT! I HAD A QUARREL WITH MY *THUNDERBOLT* AND HAVEN'T CALLED ON HIM LATELY! HOPE HE'S NOT SORE AT ME!

AS HE SPEAKS THE *BAHDNISIAN* HEX WORDS (*CEI-U*, PRONOUNCED *SAY YOU*), THE *THUNDERBOLT* THAT IS COMPELLED TO OBEY *JOHNNY THUNDER'S* COMMANDS MAKES HIS APPEARANCE ...

SAY YOU, THUNDERBOLT-- COME HERE! I APOLOGIZE ...

BOY, YOU CAUGHT ME JUST IN THE NICK OF TIME! I WAS ABOUT TO SHAKE DUST OUT OF THIS WORLD! I'M GETTING RUSTY, NOT DOING ANY-THING!

LISTEN--YOU BELONG TO ME, AND DON'T YOU FORGET IT! BESIDES, WHERE WOULD YOU GO --NO ONE ELSE HAS POWER OVER YOU!

TO *EARTH-ONE*, THAT'S WHERE! I'LL BET ITS *JOHNNY THUNDER* WOULDN'T TREAT ME THE WAY YOU DO!

HMMMM... SEEMS I *HAVE* HEARD SOME-THING ABOUT *EARTH-ONE*-- WHERE THINGS HAPPEN MORE OR LESS THE WAY THEY DO ON MY *EARTH*! I WONDER WHAT THE OTHER *JOHNNY THUNDER* LOOKS LIKE? I SURE WISH I'D COME FACE TO FACE WITH HIM!

NO SOONER SAID THAN DONE! *JOHNNY THUNDER* IS *THUNDER-BOLT*-TRANS-PORTED TO HIS *EARTH-ONE* COUNTER-PART ...

SO YOU'RE *JOHNNY THUNDER*! YOU DON'T LOOK LIKE MUCH TO ME!

I HAVE A SINKING FEELING I COMMITTED A BIG BOO-BOO BY BRINGING *JOHNNY* HERE! BUT-- HIS WISH WAS MY COMMAND!

FOR SEVERAL MOMENTS, THE TWO *JOHNNY THUNDERS* EYE EACH OTHER FROM HEAD TO TOE...

HOWEVER, I MUST ADMIT YOU'RE VERY GOOD-LOOKING-- BUT THAT'S ONLY BE-CAUSE YOU LOOK LIKE *ME!*

SAY, PAL --I REMEMBER READIN' ABOUT YOU AN' YER *T'UNDERBOLT!*

IS HE FOR REAL? DOES HE REALLY MAKE WITH THEM HOCUS-POCUS STUNTS?

OF COURSE! BUT, MY-- YOUR GRAMMAR IS *AWFUL!*

YOU LEAVE MY GRANDMA OUTTA THIS! I'M TALKIN' ABOUT YER *T'UNDERBOLT* I NEVER WAS GIVEN ONE EVEN THOUGH I WAS BROUGHT UP BY TH' *BAHDNISIANS* JUST LIKE YOU WAS-- AN' WOULD HAVE TH' POWER TO MAKE IT OBEY ME!

N-NO *THUNDER-BOLT?* I--I'M SORRY...

*ZOK!*

DON'T FEEL TOO SORRY, BO! I GOT ME AN IDEA!

AHA! TROUBLE'S STARTING-- JUST AS I ANTICIPATED!

NOW--I GOT A *T'UNDERBOLT* ALL FER MYSELF! LESSEE NOW-- HOW DO I GET HIM TO OBEY ME? WHAT'S TH' MAGIC WOIDS? *OH SAY CAN YOU SEE?* NAW--THAT'S TH' STAR-SPANGLE' BANNER! IS IT-- *YOU SEE?*

THIS ONE'S WORSE THAN THE OTHER-- AND *HE* WAS SO DUMB HE THOUGHT A *POLAR CAP* WAS SOMETHING TO KEEP YOUR HEAD WARM!

*SAY YOU!* SURE, THAT'S IT! *SAY YOU,* T'UNDERBOLT-- HOP DOWN TO TH' *UNIVERSAL TECHNICAL COMPANY* AN' SWIPE THEIR PAYROLL!

BUT THAT'S *STEALING!* ONLY *BAD* GUYS STEAL!

SO I'M A **BAD** GUY! A CROOK, SEE? WHAT MAKES YOU T'INK EVERYBODY HASTA BE A **GOOD** GUY? **EARTH-ONE** AIN'T **ALWAYS** TH' SAME AS **EARTH-TWO**! I'M AN EXCEPTION! SO GET GOIN'

MY NEW MASTER-- A SIMON LEGREE! AND I THOUGHT I WAS BAD OFF ON **EARTH-TWO**!

NEVER MIND TH' COMMENTS-- GET THE PAYROLL!

I WOULDN'T DO THIS IF I DIDN'T **HAVE** TO! BUT ORDERS IS ORDERS!

INTO THE OFFICES OF THE **UNIVERSAL TECHNICAL COMPANY** HOP-SPEEDS THE **BAHDNISIAN BOLT**...

"HOP DOWN," HE SAID! MY NEW MASTER IS SURE TOUGH ON ME!

NEXT INSTANT...

OOOPS! MISJUDGED MY SPEED! THAT'S WHAT COMES FROM BEING OUT OF PRACTICE!

THE METALLIC CLANG OF THAT IMPACT ROUSES THE ATTENTION OF BARRY (**FLASH**) ALLEN, ON HAND TO GET A SPECIAL TOOL FOR HIS SCIENTIFIC RESEARCH LABORATORY...

A LIVING LIGHTNING BOLT-- RIPPING OFF THE DOORS OF THAT SAFE!

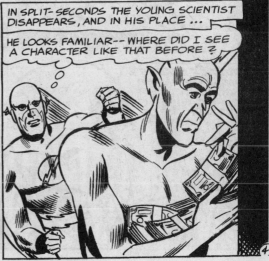

IN SPLIT-SECONDS THE YOUNG SCIENTIST DISAPPEARS, AND IN HIS PLACE ...

HE LOOKS FAMILIAR-- WHERE DID I SEE A CHARACTER LIKE THAT BEFORE?

4

SAY YOU-- NOW HEAR THIS! GO BACK IN TIME AN' DO WHATEVER YOU HAVETA DO--TO PREVENT TH' *JUSTICE LEAGUE* FROM EVER BECOMIN' SUPER-HEROES!

AYE, AYE, *MON CAPITAINE!*

INSTANTLY, THE *THUNDERBOLT* TAKES OFF ON A BACKWARD-FLIGHT THROUGH TIME, TO *CENTRAL CITY* DURING A VIOLENT ELECTRICAL STORM ...

SORRY, COUSIN! BUT I'VE GOT TO CUT YOUR JOURNEY SHORT TO THAT LABORATORY DOWN BELOW!

DEFLECTING THE LIGHTNING BOLT, THE *BAHDNISIAN* "HEX HARPOON" PREVENTS *BARRY ALLEN* FROM GETTING THE LIGHTNING-CAUSED CHEMICAL BATH WHICH ORIGINALLY TURNED HIM INTO *THE FLASH*...

I HAVE ALL THE CHEMICALS INDEXED PROPERLY, SO I MIGHT AS WELL GO HOME!

OUTWARD INTO SPACE AND TIME DARTS THE *THUNDERBOLT*, TO THE PLANET *KRYPTON* WHERE..

WHEN *KRYPTON* EXPLODED, THE *SUPERMAN-TO-BE* WAS ROCKETED AWAY FROM HIS NATIVE PLANET IN A SPACESHIP, WHILE STILL A BABY!

BUT BY CHANGING THE FISSIONABLE URANIUM CORE OF THE PLANET *KRYPTON* INTO LEAD-- I'LL PREVENT THAT EXPLOSION! THEN *SUPER-BABY* WON'T LEAVE HOME--AND *SUPERMAN* WILL NEVER EXIST ON *EARTH!*

ON HIS WAY BACK TO *EARTH-ONE*, THE *HEX-BOLT* STOPS OFF AT ANOTHER POINT IN TIME AS A SPACESHIP IS SPEEDING THROUGH THE SOLAR SYSTEM ...

BY PREVENTING THAT DEADLY YELLOW RADIATION FROM STUNNING *ABIN SUR* -- HE WILL BE ABLE TO PULL OUT OF HIS DIVE AND NEVER CRASH ON *EARTH!*

6

THERE HE GOES, STILL THE *GREEN LANTERN* OF THIS SPACE-SECTOR! TEST PILOT *HAL JORDAN* HAS MISSED HIS CHANCE TO BECOME *GREEN LANTERN!*

ONWARD INTO SPACE-TIME RACES THE *THUNDER-BOLT*--TO SHATTER A WHITE DWARF STAR-FRAGMENT THAT WOULD OTHERWISE HAVE FALLEN IN AN *IVY TOWN* MEADOW..

I'LL SMASH IT TO SPACE-DUST-- THUS PREVENTING *RAY PALMER* FROM USING IT TO MAKE HIMSELF THE *WORLD'S SMALLEST SUPER-HERO*-- THE *ATOM!*

BACK TO EARTH HE HURTLES AGAIN, TO THAT CRITICAL MOMENT WHEN *DR. ERDEL* IS ABOUT TO ACTIVATE HIS ROBOT-BRAIN INVENTION...

WHEN THE GOOD DOCTOR TURNS ON HIS ROBOT-BRAIN--IT WILL SHORT-CIRCUIT AND FAIL TO WORK!

I'VE FAILED!

YES, YOU'VE FAILED, *DR. ERDEL!* NOW *J'ONN J'ONZZ* WON'T COME TO *EARTH* AS THE *MARTIAN MAN-HUNTER!*

BZZI.. BZZ..

CLICK!

CLICK! CLICK!

INTO *GOTHAM CITY* HE SPEEDS, TO THAT INSTANT IN TIME WHEN *BATMAN* IS MAKING HIS FIRST APPEAR-ANCE AS THE *MASKED MANHUNTER*...

I HATE DOING THIS TO *BATMAN*--BUT IT'S THE ONLY WAY I CAN CUT HIS CAREER SHORT!

*EDITOR'S NOTE: "The CASE OF THE CHEMICAL SYNDICATE!"- DETECTIVE COMICS #27--MAY, 1939.

ASSISTED BY THE *THUNDERBOLT*, THE TWO CRIMINALS SLAM HEAVY FISTS INTO *BATMAN*...

*OWFF!!* WHERE'D I EVER GET THAT WILD IDEA I'D MAKE A GOOD CRIME-BUSTER? *OOOF!!* THIS IS MY FIRST AND LAST CASE! I'M GOING BACK TO BEING A PLAYBOY!

7

TO THE BOTTOM OF THE SEA, TO THE HIGH REACHES OF THE AIR, ON LAND AND IN SPACE, FLASHES THE LIVING LIGHTNING-BOLT...

NO MORE *AQUAMAN*-- NO MORE *WONDER WOMAN*-- NO MORE *GREEN ARROW*-- NO MORE *HAWKMAN*! I'VE WIPED OUT THE *JUSTICE LEAGUE*-- BY PREVENTING ITS SUPER-HERO MEMBERS FROM COMING INTO EXISTENCE!

WHEN HE RETURNS TO MAKE HIS REPORT...

MISSION ACCOMPLISHED! BUT ¡ puff! ¡ PUH-LEEZE! NO MORE JOBS LIKE THAT! I'M EXHAUSTED!

YIPPEE! NOTHIN' CAN STOP ME NOW!

YOU REALIZE, OF COURSE, SINCE THERE ARE NO MORE SUPER-POWERED CRIME-FIGHTERS HERE, THIS *EARTH* HAS BEEN ALTERED!

OKAY, SO I'LL CALL IT *EARTH-A*-- A FOR *ALTERNATE*! AN', MAN, AM I EVER GONNA GET RICH WIT' YOUR HELP!

★JUSTICE LEAGUE of AMERICA

# Earth--WITHOUT A JUSTICE LEAGUE!--

PART 2

ON *EARTH-TWO,* IN THE SECRET HEADQUARTERS WHERE THE MEMBERS OF THE REVIVED *JUSTICE SOCIETY OF AMERICA* TAKE THEIR EASE, FROWNS OF WORRY CREASE THE FOREHEADS OF THE GATHERED MEMBERS:-- *DOCTOR FATE, GREEN LANTERN, ATOM, FLASH, HAWKMAN* AND *MR. TERRIFIC.* WHERE IS *JOHNNY THUNDER*? *WHY* IS HE SO LATE? *WHAT* CAN BE DETAINING HIM?

I'M GETTING WORRIED ABOUT *JOHNNY THUNDER!* HE SHOULD HAVE BEEN HERE HOURS AGO!

MAYBE WE'D BETTER START A SEARCH FOR HIM!

I'LL SMOKE HIM OUT-- WITH MY CRYSTAL BALL!

IN THAT SECTION OF THE CLUBHOUSE WHERE HE KEEPS A SPARE CRYSTAL BALL, *DOCTOR FATE* CHARGES IT WITH MAGICAL POWER...

A *CLOUDY* CRYSTAL BALL! IT MEANS *JOHNNY THUNDER* IS NOWHERE ON *EARTH!*

THAT ONLY DEEPENS THE MYSTERY!

SUDDENLY, THE *MAGIC MASTER* GESTURES AT A GLOWING, JAGGED LINE OF FORCE IN THE CRYSTAL BALL...

LOOK! MY MAGIC HAS CONTACTED A TRAIL OF *IONIZED AIR* IN OUR ATMOSPHERE--RELATED TO *JOHNNY THUNDER* -- BECAUSE IT WAS MADE BY HIS *THUNDERBOLT!*

BY THE SPIRITS! THE TRAIL LEADS INTO -- EARTH-ONE!

WHY SHOULD HE GO THERE-- WHEN HE'S EXPECTED HERE?

THAT'S OUR JOHNNY! YOU KNOW HIM, GREEN LANTERN-- AND HIS WACKY WAY OF DOING THINGS!

CLOSE IN ON HIM, DOCTOR FATE--LET'S SEE WHAT HE'S UP TO!

AGAIN THE EERIE CONJURATIONS OF THE MASTER MAGE FLOW FORTH -- AND THE MAGICAL PROPERTIES OF THE CRYSTAL BALL CROSS THE BARRIERS OF SPACE AND TIME...

THERE HE IS-- ASLEEP!

HE WAS ROCKED ASLEEP -- BY A SOCK ON THE CHIN!

BUT WHERE'S HIS THUNDERBOLT?

FOCUSING IN ON THE THUNDER-BOLT, THE JUSTICE SOCIETY MEMBERS SEE...

OKAY, GANG, LET'S GET OUT THERE AN' ROB! REMEMBER, YOU GOT NUTHIN' TO WORRY ABOUT NOW THAT THERE AIN'T NO MORE SUPER-HEROES ON EARTH! BEST OF ALL, WE GOT TH' T-BOLT TO HELP US!

INCREDULOUS EYES LIFT FROM THE CRYSTAL BALL...

DID I HEAR RIGHT? NO SUPER-HEROES? NO ATOM? NO GREEN LANTERN-- NO JUSTICE LEAGUE?

FELLOW-MEMBERS, A NEW CASE HAS BEEN TOSSED INTO OUR LAP! AND ON OUR WAY TO LOOK FOR OUR FRIENDS, WE'LL STOP THAT CROOKED JOHNNY THUNDER AND THE THUNDERBOLT FROM COMMITTING THAT ROBBERY!

THE REAL JOHNNY THUNDER CAN WAIT! HE'S IN NO IMMINENT DANGER!

AS THEY HAVE DONE IN THE PAST, THE SUPER-HEROES OF EARTH-TWO VIBRATE INTO THE SPACE-TIME CONTINUUM OF EARTH-ONE...

IMAGINE AN EARTH WITHOUT ANY SUPER-HEROES! IT SEEMS INCREDIBLE!

BUT TRUE, APPARENTLY! WELL, THERE MAY NOT BE ANY SUPER-HEROES THERE NOW, BUT THERE WILL BE-- IN MOMENTS! EARTH-ONE, HERE WE COME!

10

AND ON *EARTH-ONE*, AS THE *THUNDERBOLT* CRACKS OPEN THE LOCKED DOORS OF A SUBURBAN CORPORATION BUILDING...

SAY YOU, T-BOLT! MY GANG'LL TAKE OVER NOW! T'ROW UP A BARRIER AROUND THIS PLACE-- SO NO COPS CAN GET IN TO STOP US!

CRACK!

I'M FORCED TO OBEY ORDERS--EVEN IF I DON'T LIKE 'EM! HOW'M I EVER GOING TO GET OUT OF THIS MESS?

THUS IT IS THAT, AS *DOCTOR FATE* AND *GREEN LANTERN* MAKE VISIBLE THE IONIZED AIR PATTERN OF THE *THUNDERBOLT*, THE *JUSTICE SOCIETY* MEMBERS CRACK THROUGH THAT BARRIER...

I FEEL A STRANGE FORCE ABOUT US--BUT IT'S TOO WEAK TO AFFECT US!

SECONDS LATER...

I ALWAYS WANTED TO BE A GANG-LEADER! NOW IT'S PAYIN' OFF AN'--:GULP!:- T-BOLT, I TOLD YA TO PUT A BARRIER AROUND THIS PLACE! WHO *ARE* THOSE GUYS?

I *DID* PUT UP A BARRIER-- BUT ONLY TO KEEP OUT *COPS*, LIKE YOU SAID! YOU GOT TO TELL ME *EXACTLY* WHAT TO DO, YOU KNOW, OR I'M ON MY OWN!

BEFORE HIS HORRIFIED EYES, *JOHNNY THUNDER* SEES THE *JUSTICE SOCIETY* MEMBERS GO INTO THEIR CRIME-BUSTING ROUTINE...

MEET *MR. TERRIFIC*--DUBBED THE "MAN OF A THOUSAND TALENTS" AND THE "DEFENDER OF *FAIR PLAY*"!

THE FLASH NEEDS NO INTRODUCTION-- I'VE BEEN ON THIS *EARTH* BEFORE!

THE ATOM'S MY NAME! I MAY BE *SMALL*-- BUT I PACK A *BIG* PUNCH!

A LITTLE FURTHER ON, A STUNNED *JOHNNY* WATCHES HELPLESSLY AS...

*GREEN LANTERN* AND I WORKED OUT THIS BIT OF TEAMWORK--

I'LL MAKE *LIGHT* WORK OF THOSE FELLOWS!

WHO *ARE* THESE COSTUMED CLOWNS? I WIPED OUT TH' *JUSTICE LEAGUE*-- AND NOW *THEY* SHOW UP! KILL 'EM OFF, *T-BOLT*!

*UH-UH!* I'M OBLIGED TO DO ANYTHING YOU COMMAND--EXCEPT *KILL!* ACCORDING TO MY *BAHDNISIAN* HEX CODE-- THAT'S *TABU!*

OKAY THEN! I'LL GIVE YA THE RIGHT ORDERS! *SAY YOU*-- SLAP THEM GUYS DOWN!

*ROGER! WILCO AND OVER!*

THE THUNDERBOLT TURNS HIMSELF PARTIALLY INTO AN ENORMOUS HAND AND....

SPLAAAT!

FAIR PLAY

(12)

DAZED BUT OTHERWISE UNHARMED, THE SUPERBLY-CONDITIONED *JUSTICE SOCIETY* MEMBERS SLOWLY RISE TO THEIR FEET...

THEY'RE GETTIN' UP! YOU DIDN'T HIT 'EM *HARD* ENOUGH! *T'UNDERBOLT--DO* SOMETHIN'!

SURE--BOSS--BUT WHAT? REMEMBER, YOU MUST TELL ME *WHAT* TO DO! I'M NO MIND-READER!

I GOTTA THINK! THIS AIN'T PANNIN' OUT TH' WAY I THOUGHT IT WOULD! WHAT TO DO? I GOT IT! *T-BOLT*--KICK 'EM OFF THE *EARTH!*

AGAIN THE *BAHDNISIAN HEX-BOLT* FLASHES OUT WITH ITS AWESOME POWERS...

THAT'S FAR ENOUGH! I KICKED THEM OFF THE *EARTH*--ABOUT TEN FEET OFF!

THAT AIN'T WHAT I MEANT-- AND YOU KNOW IT!

I KNOW FROM NOTHING-- EXCEPT TO OBEY ORDERS TO THE LETTER!

13

THEN GET MY BOYS AWAY FROM HERE--BEFORE THOSE SUPER-HEROES SLAM INTO 'EM AGAIN!

I'M ON MY WAY--WITH A *ZIP* AND A *ZAP!*

MEANWHILE, *DOCTOR FATE* IS SENDING OUT BOLTS OF HIS *CHALDEAN* MAGIC TO PROTECT HIS FELLOW *JUSTICE SOCIETY* MEMBERS...

THE THUNDER-BOLT COMING AT US AGAIN--BUT IT'S IN FOR A SHOCKING SURPRISE!

THEN THE *MYSTICAL MAGE* LEADS A COMBINED ASSAULT ON THE *BAHDNISIAN HEX-BOLT!*...

PROTECTED BY A MAGICAL SHEATHING, YOU CAN NOW FIGHT ON EVEN TERMS WITH THAT FUGITIVE FROM A THUNDERSTORM!

YIIII! HEY, *THUNDER*--BAIL ME OUT OF THIS UNEVEN FIGHT!

COME BACK, *T'UNDERBOLT!* GET *ME* AND *YOU* OUTA HERE!

whew! THAT'S A RELIEF! IT'S THE MOST SENSIBLE ORDER YOU'VE GIVEN ME ALL DAY.!

SO SWIFTLY DOES THE *HEX-BOLT* EXECUTE HIS ORDERS THAT THE SUPER-HEROES MYSTERIOUSLY FIND THEM-SELVES LEFT ALONE WITH THEIR PRISONERS! AFTER QUESTIONING THEM...

THESE CROOKS CLAIM THERE NEVER HAS BEEN AN *ATOM* OR *FLASH* OR *GREEN LANTERN* ON THIS *EARTH!*

THEN WHAT HAPPENED TO THEM, *ATOM?* MY CRYSTAL BALL SHOWED US *EARTH-ONE*--AND WE KNOW THAT THE *JUSTICE LEAGUE USED* TO EXIST HERE!

THE *JOHNNY THUNDER*-- OF *THIS EARTH*--MUST KNOW THE ANSWER TO THE MYSTERY--

HE--AND THE *EARTH-TWO THUNDERBOLT* HE'S GAINED CONTROL OF!

I SUGGEST, WHILE SOME OF US TURN THESE CROOKS OVER TO THE POLICE, OTHERS VISIT *BARRY ALLEN*--*HAL JORDAN*--*RAY PALMER* TRY TO AND DISCOVER WHAT HAPPENED!

I'LL SEE WHAT I CAN DO ABOUT REVIVING OUR *JOHNNY THUNDER*!

*S*HORTLY, IN A POLICE RESEARCH LABORATORY..

ME--THE FLASH--"THE *FASTEST MAN ON EARTH*"? YOU MUST BE PUTTING ME ON! MY FIANCÉE *IRIS WEST* ALWAYS KEEPS CALLING ME THE "*SLOWEST MAN ON EARTH*"!

AND IN A *FERRIS AIRCRAFT COMPANY* HANGAR..

I NEVER HEARD OF A *POWER RING*--OR OF ANYONE NAMED *ABIN SUR*! I'M A *TEST PILOT*-- NOT A *GREEN LANTERN*!

IT'S AS IF SOMETHING HAPPENED TO PREVENT *HAL JORDAN* FROM BECOMING THE *GREEN LANTERN* OF *EARTH-ONE*!

*I*N THE UNIVERSITY LABORATORY OF *IVY TOWN*..

ME--SHRINK MYSELF IN SIZE?! I WISH I COULD! I'VE BEEN WORKING ON THE COMPRESSION OF MATTER--BUT NEVER GOT ANYWHERE WITH IT!

AND IN *JOHNNY THUNDER'S* BOARDING HOUSE ROOM ...

THE *THUNDERBOLT* MUST HAVE PUT OUR *JOHNNY* IN A COMA--AND SINCE HIS MAGIC HAS BEEN *ACCOMPLISHED*, I CAN'T *NULLIFY* IT AND BRING *JOHNNY* OUT OF IT! THE ONLY WAY TO DO THAT IS TO CAPTURE THE OTHER *JOHNNY THUNDER* AND THE *THUNDER-BOLT*!

# Earth--WITHOUT A JUSTICE LEAGUE--

PART 3

AS THE MYSTIC MIGHT OF *GREEN LANTERN'S POWER RING* FLARES--TO MINGLE WITH THE MAGICAL WIZARDRIES OF *DOCTOR FATE*--AN ELDRITCH CHANGE COMES OVER THE MEMBERS OF THE *JUSTICE SOCIETY OF AMERICA!* FADING AWAY ARE THEIR SUPER-HERO IDENTITIES OF *EARTH-TWO!* APPEARING IN THEIR STEAD ARE THE MISSING MEMBERS OF THE *JUSTICE LEAGUE* OF *EARTH-ONE!*

LET'S GET GOING--!

WHERE DO WE FIND *JOHNNY THUNDER* AND HIS *THUNDER-BOLT?*

I'LL FIND THEM WITH MY "MAGICAL" TELESCOPIC-VISION!

IN HIS HIDEOUT, THE CRIMINAL *JOHNNY THUNDER* IS BEMOANING HIS SORRY FATE...

JUST MY LUCK TO HAVE A BUNCH OF SUPER-HEROES SHOW UP ON EARTH AFTER I'D GOTTEN RID OF TH' *JUSTICE LEAGUE!* SAY YOU, T-BOLT-- WHERE ARE THOSE CHARACTERS ANYWAY?

THEY'VE DIS-APPEARED FROM EARTH!

THAT'S TRUE ENOUGH FROM *MY* POINT OF VIEW--SINCE THEY'VE CHANGED THEMSELVES INTO THE *JUSTICE LEAGUE!*

THAT'S GREAT! IF THEY'RE GONE, I CAN GO OUT ROBBIN' AGAIN! BUT THIS TIME I WON'T BOTHER WITH A GANG! *YOU'RE* ENOUGH OF A GANG FOR ME, T-BOLT! I'VE GOT JUST TH' CAPER YOU CAN HANDLE TO A T!

17

MOMENTS LATER, *JOHNNY THUNDER* RIDES THE *THUNDER-BOLT* ACROSS THE SKY--TOWARD AN OCEAN LINER HIRED FOR A CHARITY CRUISE...

THAT SHIP IS LOADED WITH MILLIONAIRES! WE'LL MAKE A FAST HAUL AND A FASTER GETAWAY!

AS *JOHNNY* IS DEPOSITED ONTO THE DECK...

NOW LINE 'EM ALL UP FOR ME AND KEEP 'EM HELPLESS WHILE I SWIPE THEIR VALUABLES!

SUDDENLY, FROM ABOVE...

THE *J-JUSTICE LEAGUE* ALIVE--BACK IN ACTION! *HOLD IT! CANCEL ALL ORDERS!* NEW ONES COMIN' UP! DIVIDE YOURSELF INTO *SIX THUNDERBOLTS* -- AND START FIGHTIN' THEM GUYS!

HE DOESN'T KNOW IT--BUT BY DIVIDING MYSELF INTO SIX *DIFFERENT* THUNDERBOLTS--EACH OF ME IS ONLY ONE-SIXTH AS STRONG AS MY ORIGINAL SELF!

THE *MARTIAN MANHUNTER* IS THE FIRST ONE TO MAKE CONTACT WITH THE *BAHDNISIAN HEX-BOLT*...

*OWTCH!* I FELT THAT! I MUST BE EVEN WEAKER THAN I THOUGHT I'D BE!

18

SUPERMAN DIVES LIKE A CANNON-BALL, GRIPPING AND CARRYING HIS *THUNDER-BOLT* TOWARD THE SHIP'S MASSIVE ANCHOR...

THE IMPACT WON'T HURT THE *MAN OF STEEL*--BUT IT'LL JUST ABOUT FLATTEN ME!

WHILE *BATMAN* MAKES ONE OF HIS PATENTED FLYING TACKLES...

WHEN HE HITS THAT WATER-- *SHORT-CIRCUIT!*

SIMULTANEOUSLY, THE *SCARLET SPEEDSTER* FORCES HIS OPPONENT DOWNWARD WITH FEET THAT DRUM WITH ACCELERATING POWER...

WHEN WE LAND ON THAT DECK-- HE'LL BE OUT COLD!

THE *EMERALD CRUSADER* DRIVES A MIGHTY *YO-YO* DOWNWARD...

THE *THUNDER-BOLTS* CAN'T WITHSTAND OUR SIX-WAY ATTACK FOR LONG!

*SPLAT!*

THE *TINY TITAN* DOUBLES HIMSELF INTO A BALL AND LIKE A LIVING PINWHEEL--LANDS RIGHT ON TARGET...

YIII-- MY EYE!

19

AS THE **THUNDERBOLT** STREAKS ACROSS THE SKY... THEY **LOOKED** LIKE-- AND **ACTED** LIKE-- TH' **JUSTICE LEAGUE!** WERE THEY **REALLY** THEM? IF NOT, WHO WERE THEY?

THEY WERE THE **JUSTICE SOCIETY** MEMBERS OF **EARTH-TWO**--DISGUISING THEMSELVES AS THE **JUSTICE LEAGUE** MEMBERS I PREVENTED FROM EXISTING!

OHO! SO **THAT** EXPLAINS IT! TRYIN' TO TRICK ME, eh? WELL, TWO CAN PLAY AT THAT GAME! I GOT AN IDEA, **T-BOLT!** YOU'RE GOIN' TO FREE SIX OF MY BEST BOYS FROM TH' JAIL THEM **JUSTICE SOCIETY** GUYS PUT 'EM IN!

AS THE **HEX-BOLT** DEPOSITS HIS **EARTH-ONE** BOSS IN HIS BOARDING HOUSE... THEN TAKE TH' SIX OF 'EM BACK IN TIME TO TH' POINT WHERE TH' ORIGINAL **JLA** MEMBERS BECAME SUPER! BUT THIS TIME--SUBSTITUTE MY BOYS IN THEIR PLACE! HURRY IT UP--BEFORE THE "**JUSTICE SOCIETY**" TRACKS ME DOWN HERE!

SINCE I'M TRAVELING IN TIME, I'LL BE BACK IN NO TIME AT ALL!

SO IT IS THAT RACE MORRISON AND NOT BARRY ALLEN GAINS THE SUPER SPEED OF **THE FLASH,** AS IT IS BARNEY JUDSON WHO BECOMES THE SIZE-SHRINKING **ATOM...**

**EDDIE ORSON** IS GIFTED WITH THE POWERS OF THE **MARTIAN MANHUNTER!** RIPPER JONES IS SUBSTITUTED FOR **SUPERMAN!** BILL GORE IS TURNED INTO **BATMAN!** AND MONK LOOMIS WINS THE RIGHT TO BECOME **GREEN LANTERN...**

22

WHEN THE *THUNDERBOLT* RETURNS, *JOHNNY THUNDER* IS SURROUNDED BY A SUPER-GANGSTER *"JUSTICE"* LEAGUE...

REMEMBER, YOU TAKE YER ORDERS FROM ME, SEE-- OR I'LL WIPE YOU OUT! WHEN THEM *JSA* GUYS SHOW UP HERE--FIGHT 'EM WIT' YER SUPER-POWERS AND TROUNCE 'EM GOOD!

HERE THEY COME NOW!

SHORTLY, THE *JUSTICE SOCIETY* MEMBERS, STILL POSING AS *JUSTICE LEAGUE* SUPER-HEROES, THUNDER INTO *JOHNNY THUNDER'S* HIDE-OUT...

THE *JUSTICE LEAGUE*--?!

NO--THEY'RE DRESSED LIKE THE *JLA*-- BUT THEY'RE NOT--

KEERECT! THIS IS *MY* *"JUSTICE"* LEAGUE-- BAD GUYS, EACH AND EVERY ONE OF 'EM, I'M HAPPY TO SAY!

MOREOVER, I KNOW YOU'RE NOT THE REAL *JUSTICE LEAGUE* EITHER! I STOPPED *THEM* FROM EVER GETTIN' STARTED! INSTEAD OF THEM, I HAD MY OWN GANG BECOME SUPER-HEROES, AS YOU CAN SEE! I'M GONNA MAKE YOU SORRY YOU EVER BEGAN MEDDLIN' IN MY AFFAIRS!

BUT TO AVOID ANY CONFUSION--AND TO MAKE SURE I CAN FOLLER TH' ACTION WIT' OUT A SCORECARD-- T'UNDERBOLT, DO YER STUFF! CHANGE THEM GUYS INTO THEIR *REAL* COSTUMED SELVES!

23

THE *THUNDERBOLT* STRIKES -- AND IN AN INSTANT A MAGICAL TRANSFORMATION!

PRESTO! IT'S DONE!

HIS VOICE CRACKING IN TRIUMPH, *JOHNNY THUNDER* OF *EARTH-ONE* SOUNDS THE CALL TO COMBAT!...

OKAY! NOW I CAN SEE WHO'S WHO! SO -- LET TH' BATTLE BEGIN!

AT THIS CRITICAL POINT WE ARE OBLIGED TO END THIS FIRST PART OF OUR TWO-BOOK STORY ABOUT THIS CRIMINAL *JOHNNY THUNDER* OF *EARTH-ONE* AND HIS MISUSE OF THE *EARTH-TWO THUNDER-BOLT*!

THE BATTLE ROYAL WILL BEGIN IN THE FORTHCOMING (SEPTEMBER) ISSUE OF *JUSTICE LEAGUE OF AMERICA* -- IN WHICH WE WILL LEARN IF THE *JUSTICE SOCIETY* CAN DEFEAT THE CRIMINAL "JUSTICE" LEAGUE -- AND DO ANYTHING TO RETURN THE REAL *JUSTICE LEAGUE* TO LIFE!

24

# JUSTICE LEAGUE of AMERICA

☆☆☆   ☆☆☆

**THE JUSTICE SOCIETY OF EARTH-2**

ATOM

JOHNNY THUNDER

THE THUNDER-BOLT

ATOM

**THE LAWLESS LEAGUE OF EARTH-A**

DOCTOR FATE

BATMAN

FLASH

FLASH

GREEN LANTERN

GREEN LANTERN

HAWKMAN

J'ONN J'ONZZ

MR. TERRIFIC

SUPERMAN

Alarmed by the non-appearance of *JOHNNY THUNDER* at their headquarters, the members of the *JUSTICE SOCIETY OF AMERICA* of *EARTH-2* locate him in *EARTH-1*, the victim of his own double! The criminal *JOHNNY THUNDER* places the good (but slightly wacky) *JOHNNY THUNDER* in a coma and takes command of his *BAHDNISIAN MAGIC THUNDERBOLT*.

His first command to the *THUNDERBOLT* is to nullify the existence of the *JUSTIC LEAGUE OF AMERICA* of *EARTH-1* by going back into time and preventing them from ever gaining their super-powers, or by forestalling their budding careers as crime-fighters!

Now on a world without a super-hero, *JOHNNY THUNDER* fancies it is safe to rob. His security is shattered when the super-powered *JUSTICE SOCIETY OF AMERICA* crosses over into *EARTH-1* and prevents his gang from committing crimes! As a countermeasure, the criminal *JOHNNY THUNDER* uses the *THUNDERBOLT* to rob -- and is again thwarted by the sextet of *JUSTICE SOCIETY* heroes. Another inspiration prompts him to substitute his gang for the original [and now nonexistent] members of the *JUSTICE LEAGUE*! Thus -- on *EARTH-A* (for alternate,), he has a *LAWLESS LEAGUE* ready to battle and overcome the *JUSTICE SOCIETY*!

As he shouts the words, "Let the battle begin!" the stage has been set for --

CRISIS ON EARTH-A!

EVEN AS THIS STRUGGLE OF TITANS IS ABOUT TO TAKE PLACE, *JOHNNY THUNDER* ORDERS THE *THUNDERBOLT* OF HIS *EARTH-2* COUNTERPART TO TAKE HIM TO A SAFE PLACE -- AND SET UP A TELEVISION SCREEN ON THE WALL...

HEY, *T-BOLT*--NOT IN BLACK AND WHITE! I WANNA WATCH THIS IN LIVIN' COLOR!

WHY DIDN'T YOU SAY SO IN THE FIRST PLACE?

NEXT MOMENT..

THERE, THAT'S BETTER--OR IS IT? *MR. TERRIFIC* HAS TURNED THE TABLES ON MY *BATMAN!*

FAIR PLAY

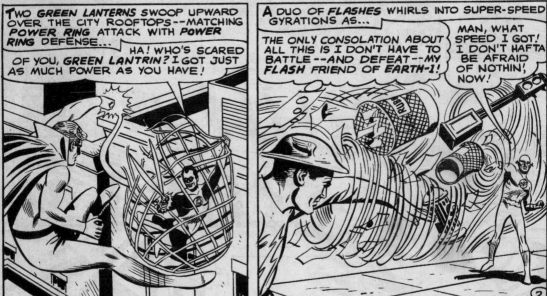

TWO *GREEN LANTERNS* SWOOP UPWARD OVER THE CITY ROOFTOPS--MATCHING *POWER RING* ATTACK WITH *POWER RING* DEFENSE...

HA! WHO'S SCARED OF YOU, *GREEN LANTRIN?* I GOT JUST AS MUCH POWER AS YOU HAVE!

A DUO OF *FLASHES* WHIRLS INTO SUPER-SPEED GYRATIONS AS...

THE ONLY CONSOLATION ABOUT ALL THIS IS I DON'T HAVE TO BATTLE--AND DEFEAT--MY *FLASH* FRIEND OF *EARTH-1!*

MAN, WHAT SPEED I GOT! I DON'T HAFTA BE AFRAID OF NOTHIN', NOW!

2

THE GANGSTER-*SUPERMAN* REACHES DOWN AND RIPS A SKELETON SKYSCRAPER LOOSE FROM ITS FOUNDATION...

I USETA DREAM I COULD DO SOMETHIN' LIKE THIS!

I NOT ONLY HAVE TO DUPLICATE THAT PHONY *SUPERMAN'S* POWERS-- I HAVE TO *TOP* THEM!

HE HURLS IT DOWN ON THE *MASTER MAGE*, TOTALLY ENGULFING HIM!

I GOT IN THE *FIRST*-- AND *LAST*--BLOW!

*CRASH!*

MEANWHILE--UPWARD FROM THE SKYSCRAPER COMES THE BLUE-AND-GOLD FORM OF *DOCTOR FATE*...

HUH? YOU AIN'T EVEN GOT A SCRATCH ON YOU?!

MY *MAGIC* PROTECTS ME, *SUPERMAN!*

BUT--NOTHING CAN PROTECT YOU FROM MY *MAGIC!*

THE CRIMINALLY-MINDED *MARTIAN MANHUNTER* APPEARS TO BE TOO MIGHTY A FOE FOR EVEN *HAWKMAN* TO HANDLE...

I GOT YOU TRAPPED IN THIS DEAD-END ALLEYWAY, *HAWKMAN!* THERE'S NO ESCAPE DOWN--UP--OR OUT!

SIMULTANEOUSLY, THE SINISTER *ATOM* PLOTS A *SIZE-SURPRISE* ATTACK ON HIS NAMESAKE FROM *EARTH-2*...

HOW CAN I FIGHT SOMETHING I CAN'T SEE?

I'LL WAIT UNTIL THE LAST MOMENT BEFORE I MAKE MYSELF BIG AND HEAVY-- SO WHEN I SOCK HIM, IT'LL TAKE HIM COMPLETELY BY SURPRISE!

3

ONLY A WIZARD-FIST COULD HIT *SUPERMAN* WITH SUCH TELLING EFFECT...

*ZOK!*

I KNOW MAGIC IS A *WEAKNESS* OF HIS-- SO I'LL DISH OUT A *REAL BIG HELPING* OF IT!

BACK AND FORTH THE *EMERALD WARRIORS* ARE STAGING A COLOSSAL COMBAT OF SUPER-WEAPONS...

I HAVE A *COUPLE* OF ADVANTAGES WORKING FOR ME! I'M *EXPERIENCED* AT POWER-WILLING WEAPONS TO FIGHT FOR ME! AND WHILE I KNOW *HIS* WEAKNESS, HE DOESN'T KNOW *MINE!*

PANIC-STRICKEN BY THE AWESOME BARRAGE HE MUST FEND OFF AS HE DESPERATELY HURLS HIS CRIMINAL-UNDERWORLD WEAPONS AT THE *EARTH-2 GREEN LANTERN,* THE EVIL *EMERALD WARRIOR* LEAVES HIMSELF WIDE OPEN FOR--

*WHAM! WHAM!*

A *YELLOW FIST*-- A COLOR HIS RING IS *POWERLESS* TO COPE WITH!

NOT FAR AWAY, UNABLE TO USE HIS WINGS, *HAWKMAN* DROPS LIKE A STONE AS...

I *MISSED* YOU--BUT I GOT YOUR *WINGS!*

I CAN'T FLY--BUT I CAN *STILL* USE MY BELT OF *NTH METAL* TO GET ME UP OR DOWN!

④

AS HE DROPS, *HAWKMAN'S* BOOTS SCRAPE HARD ALONG THE BUILDING WALL...

ONE CHANCE TO OVER-COME MY *ALMOST* INVULNERABLE FOE... USING FRICTION...

THEY CAUSE A SHOWER OF SPARKS TO FALL TOWARD A REFUSE CAN OF OIL-SOAKED RAGS...

THERE! THAT OUGHT TO RESULT IN...

...A *FIRE!* AND FIRE IS THE ONE WEAKNESS OF THAT SUPER-MARTIAN!

OHHH! MY SUPER-POWERS DRAINING OUT OF ME!

THE SPEED-DUEL BETWEEN THE *FLASHES* OF TWO WORLDS CONTINUES OUT INTO THE COUNTRY-SIDE, NEITHER ONE YIELDING AN INCH...

THE TORNADOES WE'RE WHIPPING UP ARE COUNTERBALANCING EACH OTHER! IT'S ABOUT TIME I GAVE THAT UPSTART A LESSON IN SUPER-SPEED TRICKS!

AS THAT FEARSOME FRAY RAGES--THE *FLASH* OF *EARTH-1* FEELS A TAPPING ON HIS SHOULDER...

I'M VIBRATING SO FAST HIS FIST IS PASSING RIGHT THROUGH ME! AND AT THE SAME TIME...

TAP! TAP!

5

NEXT MOMENT... DID IT--RIPPED OFF HIS CONTROLS SO HE CAN'T GET BIG AND SMALL AT THE PRESSURE OF HIS FINGERTIPS!

NOW THAT I'VE ALSO YANKED AWAY THE SIZE-AND-WEIGHT CONTROLS IN YOUR BUCKLE--YOU'RE THE UNDERDOG IN SIZE AND WEIGHT!

STARING WITH BULGING, DISBELIEVING EYES AT THE DEFEAT OF HIS SUPER-GANG IS JOHNNY THUNDER...

WHATSA MATTER WIT' THEM GUYS? EVERY ONE OF 'EM LET ME DOWN! THEY STARTED OUT OKAY-- THEN FIZZLED OUT--

THEY AREN'T USED TO WORKING WITH SUPER-POWERS! IT'S LIKE SENDING RANK AMATEURS AGAINST SEASONED PROFESSIONALS!

OH, YEAH? WELL, YOU WEREN'T SO HOT FIGHTING THEM SUPER-HEROES--AND THERE WAS SIX OF YOU!

THAT'S BECAUSE I WAS ONLY A PALE SHADOW OF MYSELF!

BAH! EXCUSES--EXCUSES! HEY-- MAYBE HE CAN STILL SAVE THE DAY FOR ME!

WE'VE BATTLED FROM ROOM TO ROOF, MR. TERRIFIC--AND IT'S BEEN A STANDOFF! BUT I'VE GOT ONE THING YOU HAVEN'T--A UTILITY BELT! I FORGOT ABOUT IT-- TILL NOW...

FAIR PLAY

7

# CRISIS on EARTH-A! PART 2

THE VICTORIOUS *JUSTICE SOCIETY* MEMBERS GATHER WITH THEIR DEFEATED FOES IN TOW. THE SCARS OF BATTLE--ROOFTOPS MARRED OR BROKEN, BUILDINGS DESTROYED, LAMPPOSTS BENT AND BROKEN, FENCES AND TREES UPROOTED--WILL ALL BE PUT BACK TO NORMAL BY *GREEN LANTERN*, EVEN AS *DOCTOR FATE* PREPARES TO PUT A SPELL OF ANCIENT CHALDEA ON THE SUPER-GANGSTERS...

GREAT WORK, FELLOW MEMBERS! I'LL PUT A MAGIC SPELL ON ALL OF THEM NOW--FORCING THEM TO TELL US HOW *THEY* BECAME EVIL COUNTERPARTS OF THE *JUSTICE LEAGUE!*

WHILE I REPAIR ALL THE DAMAGE WE DID IN OUR BATTLES!

UNDER *DOCTOR FATE'S* MAGICAL BIDDING...

*JOHNNY THUNDER* SENT THE *THUNDERBOLT* BACK INTO THE PAST! INSTEAD OF *BARRY ALLEN* BECOMING *FLASH*--I BECAME THE *SCARLET SPEEDSTER!*

YEAH, THAT'S THE WAY IT HAPPENED TO ALL OF US!

SO! THAT CLEARS UP THE MYSTERY OF THE MISSING *JUSTICE LEAGUE!* I SUGGEST WE GO BACK IN TIME, *DOCTOR FATE*-- AND UNDO THE HARM THAT *HEX-BOLT* DID!

BEFORE THE *JUSTICE SOCIETY* MEMBERS CAN SCOOT BACK INTO THE PAST, HOWEVER, *JOHNNY THUNDER* IS READYING ANOTHER ASSAULT...

THOSE GUYS BEAT ME AGAIN! BUT THIS TIME I'M AHEAD OF 'EM! I ALREADY THOUGHT UP ANOTHER WAY TO DEFEAT 'EM!

9

ANTICIPATORY TRIUMPH RASPS IN HIS THROAT AS HE CRIES OUT HIS ORDERS...

I READ ONCE THAT A HURRICANE HAS TH' FORCE OF A HUNDRED ATOM BOMBS! MAN, THAT'S ONE THING THEY CAN'T BUCK! *SAY YOU, THUNDER-BOLT*--WHIP UP A SUPER-HURRICANE AND SLAM THEM SUPER-HEROES HALFWAY AROUND THE WORLD!

*HEX-MAGIC* FLARES AGAIN--AND INSTANTLY A TITANIC HURRICANE WHIPS OUT OF NOWHERE...

NO WAY OUT OF THIS! THE MAGIC HAS BEEN *ACCOMPLISHED* AND I CAN'T NULLIFY IT! BUT I *CAN* MAKE A TRY AT PROTECTING US FROM ITS EFFECTS!

AT MAGICAL SPEED, A GONDOLA FORMS ABOUT THEM, CRADLING THEM FROM THE AWESOME FURY OF THE WHIPPING WIND! SIMULTANEOUSLY, THE *EMERALD GLADIATOR* FORMS TWIN ANCHORS...

INSIDE THIS AERIAL CAR, WE'RE RELATIVELY SAFE!

BY JOINING THE FORCE OF MY POWER RING TO *DOCTOR FATE'S* WIZARDRY--I'LL FORM ANCHORS TO HOLD US SAFELY!

GROWING MORE HYSTERICAL BY THE MOMENT, *JOHNNY THUNDER* HOWLS ANOTHER COMMAND...

AN EARTHQUAKE-- QUICK! IT'LL LOOSEN THE ANCHORS AND PREVENT THE *JSA* FROM TAKIN' LIFE EASY WHILE TH' HURRICANE WHIPS 'EM ABOUT!

10

THE SURFACE OF THE EARTH QUIVERS LIKE JELLY! THE ROCKS SPLIT OPEN! FISSURES APPEAR AND NOXIOUS GASES RISE UPWARDS...

OHHH! MY MAGIC GONDOLA PROTECTS US AGAINST THE HURRICANE--BUT NOT AGAINST THE EARTHQUAKE! ATOM--WATCH IT--!

AS THE MYSTIC MAGE REELS INTO UNCONSCIOUSNESS UNDER THAT UNCONTROLLABLE IMPACT BY THE ATOM, THE GONDOLA SPLITS APART AND...

THAT WOOD--MY NEMESIS--SLAMMING INTO ME--

~Whew!~ THREE OF US ARE KNOCKED OUT OF THE FIGHT! IT'S UP TO THE REST OF US TO DO THE RESCUE BIT!

HIS WINGS PARTIALLY SHREDDED IN THE TEETH OF THE HOWLING WIND, HAWKMAN MANAGES TO MAKE TWO DIVING CATCHES...

I GRABBED GL AND DOC FATE--BUT I DON'T KNOW HOW LONG MY WINGS WILL STAY ON! IF THEY GIVE WAY--WE'LL ALL FALL TO OUR DOOMS!

UNABLE TO SAVE THEMSELVES--ATOM, MR. TERRIFIC, AND FLASH DROP INTO THE MAW OF A MIGHTY FISSURE...

AIR CURRENTS SO TURBULENT--CAN'T WHIRL MY ARMS OR DRUM WITH MY FEET ON THE AIR--TO MAKE A SAFE LANDING...

NONE OF MY "THOUSAND TALENTS" CAN COPE AGAINST THIS ONSLAUGHT OF NATURAL FORCES!

11

LEADING THE FALL TO DOOM IS *MR. TERRIFIC*...

I'LL TRY TO GRAB HOLD OF THAT ROCK AND GET A GOOD HOLD ON IT!

THERE'S NO AIR TURBULENCE *INSIDE* THE FISSURE! NOW I CAN DRUM MY FEET ON THE AIR AND BUILD UP RESISTANCE!

THE *SCARLET SPEEDSTER* HALTS HIS AWESOME FALL-- AND AS HIS FEET AND LEGS BLUR TO BUILD UP AIR PRESSURE UNDER HIM, HE CATCHES *THE ATOM*, WHO IS STIRRING TO LIFE!...

I'M COMING AROUND, FELLAS!

JUST IN TIME, *ATOM!* GRAB *MR. TERRIFIC*-- WHILE I GET A GRIP UNDER YOUR FEET!

NEXT MOMENT ALL THREE *JUSTICE SOCIETY* MEMBERS HANG BY FINGERS FROM AN EDGE OF ROCK...

CAN YOU HOLD ON, ATOM?

FOR A WHILE! HOW ABOUT YOU, *FLASH?*

I'M GETTING READY TO GET US OUT OF HERE! JUST LET ME CATCH MY BREATH!

ABOVE THEM, DISASTER STRIKES AS THE TURBULENT GALE TEARS OFF *HAWKMAN'S* WINGS...

OHHH! WITHOUT MY WINGS I CAN ONLY GO *DOWN*-- INTO THE FISSURE! IF I GO *UP*--THOSE HIGH-VELOCITY WINDS WILL TEAR *DOCTOR FATE* AND *GREEN LANTERN* OUT OF MY GRASP!

12

THEN--UP FROM THE FISSURE COMES THE TRIO OF *JUSTICE SOCIETY* HEROES, WITH *FLASH* FURNISHING THE MOTIVE POWER WITH DRUMMING FEET...

GREAT TEAMWORK, FELLOWS! *TERRIFIC*-- YOU GRAB *GREEN LANTERN* AND *FATE!* I'LL HOLD ONTO THE *DOC'S* HANDS--AND USE MY GRAVITY POWER TO PULL YOU ALL UPWARD!

AS YOU DO-- I'LL ROTATE MY ARMS AND MANEUVER US TO SAFE AND LEVEL GROUND!

NO TEAM OF ACROBATS EVER PERFORMED SUCH A FANTASTIC FEAT AS THIS...

OKAY FOR LANDING, *FLASH!*

RIGHT! JUST AS SOON AS *FATE* AND *GREEN LANTERN* SNAP OUT OF IT--WE'LL GO AFTER *JOHNNY THUNDER* AND STOP HIM FROM BALKING OUR ATTEMPT TO REVIVE THE *JUSTICE LEAGUE!*

IN WILD DESPAIR, *JOHNNY THUNDER* SHOUTS OUT...

DIDJA HEAR THAT, *T-BOLT?* THEY'RE COMIN' AFTER ME--AND I'VE RUN OUT OF IDEAS HOW TO FIGHT 'EM! I GOTTA GO SOME PLACE WHERE I CAN THINK! A SAFE PLACE WHERE-- *THE MOON!* THEY'LL NEVER FIND ME THERE!

AS THE *THUNDERBOLT* LEAPS EAGERLY TO OBEY HIS *"SAY YOU"* COMMAND...

COOL IT, *BOLT*-- COOL IT! NOT SO FAST! YOU THINK YOU'RE GONNA TRICK ME, EH? WELL, I KNOW THERE'S NO AIR ON THE MOON--SO PUT A SPACESUIT ON ME FIRST SO I CAN BREATHE! OH, YEAH--AND DON'T LEAVE ANY TRAIL FOR TH' *JUSTICE SOCIETY* TO FOLLOW!

NEXT MOMENT, UPWARD TO THE LUNAR SATELLITE OF *EARTH-ONE* ROCKETS THE *BAHDNISIAN HEX-BOLT*...

I MIGHTA KNOWN I'D FORGET SOMETHIN'! IF THERE'S NO AIR ON THE MOON, I CAN'T GIVE ANY COMMANDS TO *T-BOLT!* WITH NO AIR, HE CAN'T HEAR 'EM!

13

NEXT MOMENT, THE CRIMINAL FINGER-SCRAWLS A COMMAND ON THE DUSTY LUNAR SURFACE...

*SAY YOU! PUT AIR ON THE MOON*

SHUCKS! I THOUGHT I HAD HIM THERE FOR A MINUTE!

THE *HEX-MAGIC* OF THE *THUNDERBOLT* STABS OUT-- AND INSTANTLY A COLUMN OF AIR SWIRLS UP OFF THE *EARTH* TO ENCOMPASS THE MOON...

THERE-- THAT'S BETTER! NOW I CAN TAKE OFF MY SPACESUIT, AND YOU CAN HEAR THE COMMANDS I GIVE YOU!

BACK ON EARTH, AFTER *GREEN LANTERN* AND *DOCTOR FATE* REPAIR THE DAMAGES CAUSED BY THE HURRICANE AND EARTHQUAKE, THE *JUSTICE SOCIETY* MEMBERS HOLD AN IMPROMPTU MEETING...

SINCE WE'VE LOST ALL TRACE OF *JOHNNY* AND HIS *THUNDERBOLT*, I VOTE WE GO AHEAD WITH OUR PLAN TO RESTORE THE REAL *JUSTICE LEAGUE!*

I'M IN FAVOR!

WE ALL ARE! COME ON, *DOCTOR FATE*-- LET'S DO SOME SPACE-TIME TRAVELING!

BUT WHEN THE *MASTER MAGE* AND *EMERALD CRUSADER* DRIVE INTO THE MISTS OF THE PAST...

JUST AS I FEARED! THIS MAGIC HAS ALREADY TAKEN PLACE! I CANNOT CHANGE IT!

NOR CAN I-- EVEN WITH ALL THE ENERGIES IN MY *POWER RING!*

14

WHEN THEY RETURN AND MAKE THEIR REPORT...

LOOKS LIKE OUR ONE HOPE IS TO FIND THE *EARTH-TWO JOHNNY THUNDER*--

--AND IN SOME WAY COMPEL HIM AND HIS *THUNDERBOLT*--

--TO RESTORE THEIR TRUE POWERS TO BARRY ALLEN, RAY PALMER, HAL JORDAN, AND THE OTHERS!

BUT HOW DO WE FIND THEM?

WHILE YOU TWO WENT INTO THE PAST, I CIRCLED THE EARTH IN SEARCH OF A CLUE TO THEIR WHEREABOUTS--AND THE ONLY HINT I CAME ACROSS WAS A MYSTERIOUS FUNNEL OF AIR WHIRLING AWAY FROM *EARTH*--

LIFTED UPWARD BY *DOCTOR FATE* AND *GREEN LANTERN*, THE *JUSTICE SOCIETY* RUSHES TO THE *NORTH POLE* WHERE...

YOU SEE? THE AIR IS RISING UPWARD HERE INTO SPACE!

YES--AND BY FOLLOWING IT WITH A CONJURATION, I CAN FOLLOW IT TO THE MOON!

OUT INTO SPACE GO THE SUPER-HEROES, BOUND TOWARD THE NATURE-MADE SATELLITE THAT ORBITS THE PLANET CALLED *EARTH-A*--AND THE HIDING PLACE OF *JOHNNY THUNDER*...

FAR AHEAD OF THEM ON THE LUNAR LANDSCAPE, THE CRIMINAL MIND OF *JOHNNY THUNDER* HAS ONE LAST TRUMP CARD YET TO PLAY...

EVERYTHING I'VE TRIED SO FAR HAS FAILED--SO I'M GOING TO FORM MY OWN PRIVATE BAND OF SUPER-BEINGS! I'LL MAKE THEM ACCORDING TO MY OWN IDEAS! *SAY YOU, T-BOLT, CREATE TH' FOLLOWIN' SUPER-CREATURES FOR ME...*

15

A FLASH OF *BAHDNISIAN HEX-MAGIC* AND...

MEDUSA-MAN! ONE LOOK AT HIS FACE WHEN TH' *BOLT* FINISHES IT-- AND WHAM! TH' VICTIM'S TURNED TO *WOOD!*

AND THE NEXT TO KNOW THE BREATH OF LIFE...

*ABSORBO-MAN*--WHO CAN ABSORB ANY SUPER-POWERS USED AGAINST HIM AND TURN THEM TO HIS OWN ADVANTAGE!

AND LAST TO TAKE SHAPE...

*REPELLO-MAN!* HE CAN REPEL ANY FORCE HURLED AGAINST HIM-- AND DIRECT IT BACK AT TH' SENDER! THAT OUGHTA COOL OFF THEM *JUSTICE SOCIETY* HOTSHOTS! AND YOU, *T-BOLT*--YOU STAND BY IN CASE OF EMERGENCY!

# JUSTICE LEAGUE of AMERICA

# CRISIS on EARTH-A!    PART 3

UPWARD ALONG THE SPIRALING FUNNEL OF BREATHABLE AIR COME THE *JUSTICE SOCIETY* MEMBERS TOWARD THEIR LUNAR RENDEZVOUS WITH DESTINY IN THE SHAPE OF THE THREE *JOHNNY THUNDER*—CREATED SUPER-VILLAINS-- MEDUSA-MAN—ABSORBO-MAN AND REPELLO-MAN...

HERE THEY COME NOW! GO GET 'EM, MEN! NOTHIN' CAN STOP YOU! YOU'RE THE GREATEST!

ATOM AND *MR. TERRIFIC* ARE THE FIRST TO SET FOOT ON THE DUSTY SURFACE OF THE LUNAR ORB! THEY LEAP FORWARD, EAGER FOR THE FRAY...

I SPOTTED ONE OF THEM--BEHIND THAT ROCK!

LET'S TAKE HIM TOGETHER, *ATOM!*

AS THE DUO RUSHES CLOSER, THE BEING WITH THE FACE OF DOOM STEPS OUT FROM BEHIND THE MOON STONE AND...

OHHH! THAT FACE--

--CHANGING US TO-- WOOD...

17

WARNED BY THE AWESOME FATE OF HIS FELLOW MEMBERS, *DOCTOR FATE* AVOIDS LOOKING UPON THE UPTURNED FACE OF *MEDUSA-MAN!* INSTEAD...

THESE RADAR-DIRECTED LIGHTNINGS WILL SEEK OUT OUR FOE'S FACE...

A BLANK GOLDEN MASK MATERIALIZES OVER THAT HORRIFIC FACE! MAGIC HAS FORMED IT! MAGIC HOLDS IT THERE AS *MEDUSA-MAN* STRIVES VAINLY TO FREE HIS FEATURES!

WHEW! IF IT HADN'T BEEN FOR *DOCTOR FATE* -- WE MIGHT BE WOOD LIKE *ATOM* AND *TERRIFIC!*

*FLASH!* ANOTHER VILLAIN UP AHEAD! I WONDER WHAT POWERS HE HAS?

LIKE A HUMAN CANOE, THE *SCARLET SPEEDSTER* PADDLES HANDFULS OF BITING MOON-DUST AT THE LOOMING FIGURE OF *REPELLO-MAN*...

AS THEY USED TO SAY IN THE OLD WESTERNS-- ANOTHER CRITTER BITES THE DUST!

FROM ABOVE, *HAWKMAN* DARTS DOWNWARD WITH HIS BATTLE MACE SLAMMING FURIOUSLY...

I'LL MAKE THIS A DOUBLE KAYO!

FOR A MOMENT, *REPELLO-MAN* STANDS STILL UNDER THAT JOINT ATTACK...

HE HASN'T MADE A MOVE TO STOP US, *FLASH!*

MAYBE IT'S BECAUSE HE CAN'T!

18

SUDDENLY THE GRIM FIGURE SHAKES ITSELF -- STIRS TO LIFE! OUTWARD FROM ITS BODY STREAM THE BITING DUST MOTES, AND OFF ITS HEAD SHOOTS THE *HAWKMAN* MACE...

THE MOON DUST-- DOING A TURN-ABOUT!

MY MACE-- COMING RIGHT BACK AT ME!

As THAT TERRIBLE LUNAR STORM HITS HIM-- DRIVEN BY *DOUBLE* THE STRENGTH WITH WHICH HE HURLED IT AT *REPELLO-MAN*, THE *SCARLET SPEEDSTER* DROPS...

OHHH! SLAMMING INTO ME LIKE A MILLION TINY FISTS!

WHILE THE *WINGED WONDER* BECOMES THE VICTIM OF HIS OWN ANCIENT WEAPON...

SPLAAT!

SILENCE FALLS ACROSS THIS SEGMENT OF THE MOON. *THE FLASH* AND *HAWKMAN* LIE INERT AS *REPELLO-MAN* STANDS MOTIONLESS, WAITING FOR THE NEXT ATTACK...

SPEEDING OVERHEAD GOES *GREEN LANTERN*, POWER BEAM STABBING A MASSIVE CHAIN AROUND *ABSORBO-MAN*...

EVERYTHING'S GOING WRONG! I'VE GOT TO STOP *ONE* OF THESE BEINGS, AT LEAST!

⑲

GREEN AND GLOWING, DRAWING THAT VIBRANT VERDANCY WITHIN ITSELF, STANDS *ABSORBO-MAN!* FRANTICALLY, THE *EMERALD CRUSADER* FIRES BOLT AFTER BOLT OF POWER RING ENERGY AT THE CREATION OF *JOHNNY THUNDER*...

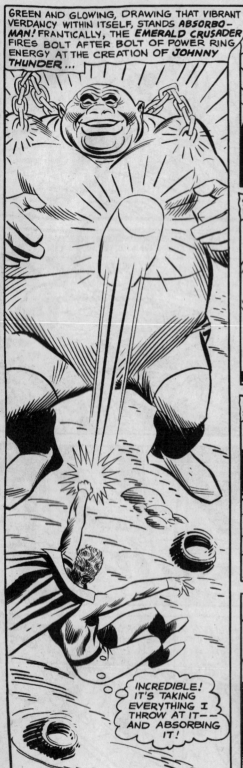

INCREDIBLE! IT'S TAKING EVERYTHING I THROW AT IT-- AND ABSORBING IT!

THEN FROM OUT OF *ABSORBO-MAN* STREAKS A MIGHTY GREEN FORCE! IT IS FORMLESS--BUT IT CONTAINS ALL THE POWER WHICH THE *EMERALD CRUSADER* HAS BEAMED AT *ABSORBO-MAN!*...

GNNNG!

SPECTATOR *JOHNNY THUNDER* GOES INTO A WILD VICTORY DANCE...

YIPPEE! I'VE WON! ONLY *DOC FATE* IS LEFT, AND WHEN HE TRIES HIS MAGIC AGAINST EITHER *REPELLO-MAN* OR *ABSORBO-MAN*--HE'LL SUFFER TH' SAME *FATE* AS TH' OTHERS!

OH-NO! LOOKS LIKE *THUNDER'S* REALLY OUT-TRICKED THE *JUSTICE SOCIETY* THIS TIME!

SINGLE-HANDEDLY, *DOCTOR FATE* SWOOPS IN ON HIS SEEMINGLY INVULNERABLE FOES...

I CAN'T BRING BACK *THE ATOM* OR *MISTER TERRIFIC*--*FLASH* OR *HAWKMAN*--BECAUSE WHAT HAPPENED IS-- ACCOMPLISHED MAGIC!

BUT I HAVE ONE SLIM THREAD OF HOPE TO CLING TO-- IN THE WOODEN PERSONS OF *ATOM* AND *MR. TERRIFIC!*

20

IN OBEDIENCE TO THE MAGIC MASTER'S SPELL, THE WOODEN SHAPES OF *THE ATOM* AND *MR. TERRIFIC* SWIRL UPWARD INTO THE AIR...

THAT "ABSORBING" MAN INGESTED THE GREAT POWERS OF *GREEN LANTERN!* I'M BANKING ON HIS HAVING ALSO INGESTED GL'S WEAKNESS--AGAINST *WOOD!*

HURLED FORWARD AT BLINDING SPEED, THE WOODEN SHAPES BANG INTO *ABSORBO-MAN!*...

THWAACK!

THUD!

THEN, BEFORE THE STUNNED EYES OF *JOHNNY THUNDER*, ABSORBO-MAN FALLS APART...

CRAAACK!

HEY! HOW'D THAT HAPPEN?

BRAVO! DOCTOR FATE HAD A TRICK IN RESERVE!

WELL, THAT SAME TRICK WON'T WORK ON *REPELLO-MAN!* AS SOON AS HE SHOOTS HIS DEADLY MAGIC AT IT--IT'LL BE FLUNG RIGHT BACK AT HIM!

HMMM... HOW'S FATE GOING TO GET OUT OF THAT TRAP? NOT EVEN I COULD DO THAT!

DOWNWARD FROM THE FINGERS OF *DOCTOR FATE* STREAMS A FLOW OF AWESOME MAGIC! STRAIGHT FOR *REPELLO-MAN* GOES THAT WIZARDRY...

*JOHNNY* IS RIGHT! REPELLO-MAN WILL REPEL MY MAGIC! BUT THAT'S WHAT I'M COUNTING ON -- TO WIN!

21

THE NECROMANTIC BOLTS CONVERGE ON *REPELLO-MAN*-- PLAY ACROSS HIS FIGURE...

WILL IT REPEL THOSE ENERGIES? IT MUST!

AS *JOHNNY THUNDER* AND THE *MASTER MAGE* WATCH--SCARCELY BREATHING--*REPELLO-MAN* SWELLS AND SWELLS...

BOY--LOOKA THAT! REPELLO-MAN IS BRACIN' HIMSELF FOR A MIGHTY REPELLIN' BLOW!

AS SOON AS HE STRIKES--IT'LL BE ALL OVER--FOR HIM!

THEN WITH AN AWESOME SURGE OF SORCERY-- *REPELLO-MAN* EXPLODES!

I FLUNG BOLTS OF *REVERSE MAGIC* AT HIM! WHEN HE TRIED TO REPEL THEM BACK AT ME--THE *REVERSE* HAPPENED--AND THEY WERE *ATTRACTED* TO HIM!

KA-ROOOOM!

A DISTRAUGHT *JOHNNY THUNDER* SCREAMS A COMMAND...

OKAY! SO IT'S MAGIC AGAINST MAGIC, NOW! *SAY YOU, T-BOLT*--GET UP THERE AND BATTLE IT OUT WITH *DOCTOR FATE!* KEEP FIGHTING TILL *YOU WIN!* THAT'S AN ORDER!

A MAGIC FINGER STABS OUT AT *DOCTOR FATE*-- WHO COUNTERATTACKS WITH A SORCEROUS METEOR AT THE *BAHONISIAN HEX-BOLT!*

22

THE MAGIC FINGER MISSES AND CRACKS INTO A LUNAR MOUNTAIN...

YIII! I'M CAUGHT IN A ROCK STORM!

EVEN AS THE LUNAR ROCKS RAIN DOWN ON HIM, THE METEOR FLUNG BY DOCTOR FATE EXPLODES IN AWESOME FURY---

I'M AN INNOCENT BYSTANDER HERE-- BUT I'M TAKIN' ALL THE PUNISHMENT!

AS THE ALL-OUT MAGICAL BATTLE RAGES OVERHEAD-- JOHNNY THUNDER IS CAUGHT IN A RIPTIDE OF INCREDIBLE MAGIC FORCES...

HAAALPP! THINGS ARE GOIN' FROM BAD TO WORSE!

MOMENTS LATER, HE IS BANGED DOWNWARD ACROSS JAGGED ROCKS...

AWWWK! WHAT A POUNDIN' I'M TAKIN'!

HE IS SMOTHERED UNDER DENSE CLOUDS OF FLYING MOON DUST...

KOFF- KOFF! I C-CAN'T TAKE ANY MORE! THEY'RE DOIN' ALL TH' F-FIGHTIN' AND I'M GETTIN' TH' WORST OF IT! ENOUGH'S ENOUGH!

23

FRUSTRATED BY HIS FAILURES-- BATTERED BY THE COLOSSAL CONFLICT ABOVE HIM--*JOHNNY THUNDER* SCREAMS HIS FINAL COMMAND...

SAY YOU, T'UNDERBOLT! *STOP!!* I WISH *NONE* OF THIS HAD *EVER* HAPPENED! I WISH EVERYTHIN' WAS BACK THE WAY IT WAS BEFORE I SAW YOU--AND THAT I NEVER SEE YOU AGAIN TH' REST OF MY LIFE! SAYS *ME!*

INSTANTLY, EVERYTHING RETURNS TO WHERE IT ORIGINALLY WAS BEFORE *JOHNNY THUNDER* OF *EARTH-TWO* DECIDED TO GO TO *EARTH-ONE!* THUS--AT *JUSTICE SOCIETY* HEADQUARTERS...

HI, FELLOW MEMBERS! GOOD TO SEE YOU AGAIN!

JOHNNY, YOU'RE RIGHT ON TIME! LET'S START THE MEETING!

AND ON *EARTH-ONE*, AT ITS REGULAR MEETING, IS THE *JUSTICE LEAGUE*...

NO UNUSUAL CRIMES REPORTED TO US, THOUGH THERE'S AN ITEM HERE ABOUT SOMEBODY NAMED *JOHNNY THUNDER*--A SMALL-TIME CROOK...

JOHNNY THUNDER? THE NAME SOUNDS FAMILIAR! NOW WHERE DID I HEAR OF IT BEFORE...?

WE KNOW WHAT HAPPENED, READER--BUT NOBODY ELSE DOES! AND I'M NOT GOING TO SHOOT OFF MY BIG MOUTH TO TELL ANYBODY--FOR WHAT THEY DON'T KNOW WON'T BOTHER THEM! HOW ABOUT *YOU*--WILL *YOU* KEEP MY SECRET?

24

END.

# JUSTICE ☆☆☆ LEAGUE of AMERICA

☆☆☆

CONSCIENCE IS MANY THINGS, SAY THE PHILOSOPHERS. HE WHO HEEDS ITS VOICE IS A VIRTUOUS MAN. WERE SOME MAN TO BUILD A MACHINE WHICH COULD COMPEL MEN TO HEED THE "STILL SMALL VOICE" OF CONSCIENCE, THEN HE MIGHT MAKE EARTH INTO A *UTOPIA* !
OR--SUFFER THE SAME TERRIBLE FATE THAT OVERTOOK *ANDREW HELM* WHEN HE ATTEMPTED TO GIVE HIS NATIVE PLANET A CONSCIENCE, AND DREW THE *JUSTICE LEAGUE OF AMERICA* INTO THE EERIE CASE OF THE ...

# INDESTRUCTIBLE CREATURES OF NIGHTMARE ISLAND!

The Roll Call

AQUAMAN

ATOM

BATMAN

FLASH

GREEN ARROW

GREEN LANTERN

HAWKMAN

J'ONN J'ONZZ

SUPERMAN

WONDER WOMAN

WE ARE CAUGHT IN THE GRIP OF INVUL-NERABLE MENACES THAT NO OTHER EYES ON EARTH CAN SEE !

## "The conscience is more wise than science" — Whewill

DEEP IN A REMOTE AREA OF HIMALAYAN TIBET IN THE YEAR 1900, THERE STOOD A GOLDEN CITY HIDDEN BEHIND AN INVISIBLE FORCE-FIELD OF KINETIC POWER..

UNKNOWINGLY APPROACHING THIS UNSEEN BARRIER WAS AN AMERICAN EXPLORER WITH HIS WIFE AND 4-YEAR-OLD SON, ANDREW HELM ...

THEN LIKE HAWKS UPON AN UNSUSPECTING PREY, MOUNTAIN BANDITS STRUCK, THEIR BULLETS FLYING SWIFTLY AND DEADLY...

HAI! MUCH LOOT!

ONLY GOOD AMERICANS-- ARE DEAD ONES!

M-MOMMY; SOB! DADDY...

IN A FEW SHORT MOMENTS, THE UGLY WORK WAS DONE. ONLY A CHILD SAT WAILING AMID THE DESTRUCTION OF THE LITTLE EXPEDITION ...

COME, CHANDRA GOPAR! WE MUST SAVE THE CHILD!

FROM A DISTANCE, THE BANDIT CHIEFTAIN *CHUNG KA* CHANCED TO TURN AROUND--AND STOOD SPELLBOUND AS THE BARRIER LIFTED MOMENTARILY...

HAI! IT IS THE FABLED GOLDEN CITY--*TA MING!* THE GREAT BRIGHTNESS!

AFTER THE CHILD WAS TAKEN BEHIND THE INVISIBLE FORCE-FIELD, *CHUNG KA* SOUGHT ALSO TO ENTER, BUT FOUND THE BARRIER IMPASSABLE ...

I SHALL COME BACK-- WITH MANY MEN, MANY GUNS! I SHALL FIND A WAY TO ENTER PAST THIS UNSEEN FENCE AND TAKE THOSE RICHES FOR MY OWN!

THE YEARS PASSED SLOWLY. THE CHILD ANDREW HELM GREW UP WITH THE LAMAS OF *TA MING*, STUDYING, FASTING, LEARNING THE MANY ARTS MASTERED BY THE ORIENTAL SAVANTS...

FOR SEVENTEEN YEARS HE STUDIED TELEPATHY AND THE ART OF ASTRAL PROJECTION IN WHICH A PERSON'S SPIRIT LEAVES HIS BODY...

FOR THE ASTRAL BODY TO BE SEPARATED TOO LONG FROM THE CORPORAL BODY WOULD BE FATAL! IN THE BRIEF TIME ALLOTTED ME, I CAN EXPLORE THE WORLD -- AS DID MY FATHER ...

AND WHAT OF *CHUNG KA* THE BANDIT? FOR THOSE SEVENTEEN YEARS HE HAS BEEN A PRISONER IN A *PEKING* JAIL..

SOMEDAY I SHALL BE FREE! THEN I SHALL GO BACK TO *TA MING* -- AND REAP MY GOLDEN HARVEST!

ALL THINGS MUST END, EVEN PRISON TERMS, AND ON A WARM DAY IN THE TIME OF THE *HSIAO SHU*\*, *CHUNG KA* HAS RETURNED TO THE GOLDEN CITY OF HIS DREAMS...

SINCE IT IS IMPOSSIBLE TO GO THROUGH OR OVER THE BARRIER, WE SHALL GO *UNDER IT! DIG!*

\* EDITOR'S NOTE: "SLIGHT HEAT," APPROXIMATELY JULY 7 AND 8.

A TUNNEL EMPTIES OUT-- AND THEN A HORDE OF RUTHLESS, CONSCIENCE-LESS OUTLAWS SWARM OVER THE GOLDEN CITY OF *TA MING!*...

SLAY THEM ALL! LET NONE SURVIVE!

POW!

POW!

3

YET WHEN THE LOOTERS COME AND GO, ONE YOUTH SURVIVES. ANDREW HELM, WOUNDED AND LEFT FOR DEAD, CRAWLS PAINFULLY THROUGH THE DEBRIS...

THOSE FOOLS! WHAT THEY STOLE WAS NOT NEARLY AS VALUABLE AS THE KNOWLEDGE THESE LAMAS WOULD SOMEDAY HAVE GIVEN THE WORLD!

WITH WHAT LITTLE STRENGTH IS LEFT HIM, HE STAGGERS OUT OF THE DEVASTATED CITY...

I SHALL CONTINUE MY STUDIES--UNTIL I CAN GIVE THE WORLD MY INHERITANCE FROM THE LAMAS, THE TREASURE OF KNOWLEDGE...

THE PAGEANT OF THE YEARS MOVES ON. NOW ANDREW HELM IS AN OLDER MAN WHO LIVES IN ISOLATION ON AN ISLAND BETWEEN NEW ZEALAND AND AUSTRALIA...

NOW AT LAST, AFTER THESE MANY YEARS, MY MACHINE IS READY--TO SAVE MANKIND FROM--ITSELF!

TO PREVENT ANYONE FROM INTERFERING WITH ME, I SURROUNDED MY ISLAND WITH THE SAME FORCE-FIELD THE LAMAS PUT AROUND *TA MING*! SINCE MY ASTRAL EXPLORATIONS HAVE SHOWN THAT *CONSCIENCE* SEEMS TO BE SUPPRESSED IN THE WORLD, I SHALL RELEASE IT WITH MY INVENTION--

--THE *CORTI-CON-SCIENCE MACHINE!*

JUST AS THE BRAIN CAN BE ELECTRICALLY STIMULATED TO CAUSE A PERSON TO FEEL HATE OR LOVE, HUNGER OR SATISFACTION, COWARDICE OR BRAVERY--SO MY *CORTI-CONSCIENCE*, BY AFFECTING THE CEREBRAL CORTEX AND THE BRAIN'S AMYGDALA PORTIONS-- WILL GOVERN THE BEHAVIOR OF A PERSON!

"THE STORY OF MAN'S INHUMANITY TO MAN IS THE HISTORY OF THE EARTH! ONE MAN ALONE HAS BEEN ABLE TO DO BUT LITTLE TO MAKE HIS FELLOW HUMANS HEAR AND OBEY THEIR *CONSCIENCES*..."

MOSES

CHRIST

CONFUCIUS

MOHAMMED

BUDDHA

WITH THIS MACHINE -- WHICH IS A SCIENTIFIC ADAPTATION OF THE DISCOVERIES OF THE LAMAS OF *TA MING* -- I SHALL STIMULATE THE "CONSCIENCE FACTORS" IN THE HUMAN BRAIN -- AND COMPEL MEN TO HEED THE MORAL LAWS!

"NO LONGER SHALL CITIZENS BE DEPRIVED OF THE RIGHT TO VOTE..."

VOTE HERE

NO LONGER SHALL JUVENILE DELINQUENTS MAKE CITY STREETS AND SUB-WAYS A PLACE OF TERROR AND PANIC..."

HIYAH!

HIYAH!

HIS HAND THROWS DOWN THE LEVER, AND THE UP-WARD-JUTTING RODS BEGIN TO GLOW, FORM-ING A GLOBE AT THEIR RADIATION POINTS! AND FROM THAT GLOBE HYPERFREQUENCIES PULSE OUTWARD AROUND THE EARTH...

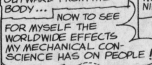

AS HE HAS BEEN TAUGHT BY THE LAMAS OF *TA MING*, ANDREW HELM PROJECTS HIS SPIRIT OUTWARD FROM HIS BODY...

NOW TO SEE FOR MYSELF THE WORLDWIDE EFFECTS MY MECHANICAL CON-SCIENCE HAS ON PEOPLE!

THERE ARE NO SPATIAL LIMITS TO THE ASTRAL FORM. "ANDREW HELM" FLASHES OUT INTO THE WORLD LIKE A LIGHT-NING BOLT...

5

WITH A BIT OF BROKEN MIRROR, THE *LORD OF THE LOOKING GLASS* FOCUSES SUNLIGHT IN A BLINDING BEAM OF BRILLIANCE..

I HAVE TO JOIN WITH *THE FLASH* AGAINST YOU, *SHARK!* HE HAS MORAL LAW ON HIS SIDE!

*MIRROR MASTER,* YOU IDIOT! WHAT'S GOT INTO YOU ANYWAY?

TO THE UTTER AMAZEMENT OF THE *SCARLET SPEEDSTER,* HIS FORMER ALLY FLINGS HIMSELF AT THE FALLING *SHARK..*

I CAN'T LET YOU GO ON FIGHTING HIM! YOU'RE IN THE WRONG, *SHARK!*

LET ME GO! NOTHING WILL STOP ME FROM MY MISSION TO PREY ON HUMAN BEINGS!

AND THEN--AS THE ASTRAL ANDREW HELM BEAMS WITH PRIDE AND TRIUMPH--THE *SHARK* OPENS HIS EYES WIDE ...

BY NEPTUNE--YOU'RE ABSOLUTELY RIGHT! I MUST HAVE BEEN OUT OF MY MIND TO DO WHAT I DID! FLASH-- I'M SORRY!

WHAT'S COME OVER THOSE TWO? THEY SEEM TO HAVE BE- COME--CON- SCIENCE STRICKEN!

ANDREW HELM HURTLES ASTRALLY ON, TOWARD AN ISLAND IN THE CARIBBEAN WHERE A DICTATOR WATCHES A GUIDED MISSILE IN THE FINAL COUNTDOWN STAGE FOR FIRING ...

"AMERICA THE BEAUTIFUL," THEY CALL IT! BUT NOT FOR LONG!

FIVE! FOUR! THREE! TWO! ONE! ZE--

THE WORD FREEZES IN HIS MOUTH--THEN A HARSH VOICE SCREAMS A COUNTERORDER AS THE *CORTI-CONSCIENCE* RADIATION TOUCHES HIS BRAIN ...

*STOP!!* I MUST BE MAD TO WANT TO KILL MY FELLOW HUMAN BEINGS! DESTROY ALL OUR ATOMIC WARHEADS AT ONCE!

EVERYTHING IS WORKING OUT AS PLANNED!

7

MANY MILES AWAY IN GOTHAM CITY, A GRIM CAPED FIGURE VAULTS FROM HIS BATMOBILE AS THE PENGUIN AND CAPTAIN COLD TURN TO FACE HIM...

SINCE A PENGUIN COMES FROM A FRIGID CLIMATE, IT WAS INEVITABLE THAT YOU AND I TEAMED UP, CAPTAIN COLD!

BETWEEN YOUR BUMBERSHOOT BLASTS AND MY COLD-GUN FLARES, WE HAVE BATMAN TRAPPED AS HE'S NEVER BEEN BEFORE!

FROM THE UMBRELLA STREAKS A SPARKLING SHOWER OF WHIRLING PROPELLERS--EVEN AS A BLOCK OF SOLID ICE ENCASES THE LEGS OF THE MASKED MANHUNTER!...

HA! HA! WHILE THAT ICE I'VE FORMED PREVENTS BATMAN FROM GETTING AWAY--THE PENGUIN'S PROPELLER WEAPONS WILL CUT HIM TO RIBBONS!

THE COWLED CRUSADER SWINGS HIS MAGNETIZED CAPE--AND IN RESPONSE TO THE POWERFUL TUG, THE PROPELLERS VEER TO ONE SIDE...

THOSE BLADES WILL ACT LIKE ICE PICKS--AND CHOP AWAY THE BLOCK THAT HOLDS ME!

EVEN AS THE WORLD'S GREATEST DETECTIVE LEAPS FREE OF HIS ICY PRISON, THE MASTER OF FOWL PLAY CRIES OUT...

WAIT, CAPTAIN COLD! STOP! WE CAN'T GANG UP ON BATMAN!

HUH? WHAT'S WITH THE PENGUIN?

WITH HIS PUDGY HANDS, THE WADDLING LITTLE CROOK GRIPS THE FRIGID FELON'S GUN WRIST...

LAY OFF WITH THAT COLD-GUN! DON'T YOU REALIZE IT'S-- ILLEGAL!

PENGUIN-- YOU'VE FLIPPED YOUR HIGH-HAT!

8

SUDDENLY--AS THE EMANATIONS FROM THE ARTIFICIAL CONSCIENCE OF THE WORLD FINALLY PENETRATE THE SINISTER BRAIN OF *CAPTAIN COLD*...

HOW RIGHT YOU ARE, *PENGUIN*! LUCKY *BATMAN* IS HERE! IT SAVES US THE TROUBLE OF TURNING OURSELVES IN!

NOW I'VE HEARD EVERY-THING!

ON THE FAR-FLUNG BATTLEFRONTS OF THE WORLD WHERE MEN HAVE RESORTED TO VIOLENCE TO SETTLE THEIR DIFFERENCES, WEAPONS ARE DISCARDED AS --

WE WERE WRONG TO ATTACK YOU!

FROM NOW ON, WE SHALL BE NEIGHBORS --AND FRIENDS!

AND THE MEMBERS OF THE *JUSTICE LEAGUE OF AMERICA*-- ENCOMPASSED BY A WORLD WITH A NEW-FOUND CON-SCIENCE, IN WHICH THERE IS NO HATRED, NO OPPRESSION, NOT EVEN ANY CRIME-- TOUCH THEIR EMERGENCY SIGNALS FOR A SPECIAL MEETING...

I'M NOT KNOCKING WHAT'S HAP-PENED--BUT THERE MUST BE A REASON FOR THIS CHANGE IN PEOPLE!

HOW WONDERFUL! PEOPLE ENDING OLD FEUDS--SETTLING GRUDGES IN FRIENDSHIP!

*WHEW*: CROOKS SURRENDERING VOLUNTARILY! MONEY POUR-ING INTO "*CONSCIENCE FUNDS*"!

IN ONE FELL SWOOP--MY WORK'S BEEN DONE!

I'M ALL AT SEA TO EXPLAIN THIS CHANGE!

THE ENTIRE EARTH--TURNED INTO A WORLD-WIDE *JUSTICE LEAGUE*!

THEY GATHER IN THE *SECRET SANCTUARY* WHERE HONORARY MEMBER *SNAPPER CARR* IS ALREADY WAITING FOR THEM...

MAN, LIKE BEND AN EAR TO THIS HAP-HAP-HAPPY NEWS!

HATE GROUPS DISBAND! UNITED STATES AND RUSSIA AGREE TO COOPERATE IN SPACE--TRAVEL! DISARMAMENT TALKS UNDER WAY...

IN AWED AMAZEMENT, THE MEMBERS LISTEN TO THE TRANSFORMATION RESULTS OF THE *CORTI-CONSCIENCE* [OF WHICH THEY ARE COMPLETELY UNAWARE]...

THE *UNITED NATIONS* HAS VOTED TO OUTLAW WAR, POVERTY AND ALL OPPRESSION!

FROM ALL IN-DICATIONS EARTH HAS BEEN TURNED INTO A *UTOPIA*!

I WANT TO CHEER-- YET SOME-HOW I HAVE A SINKING FEELING ALL THIS NEWS IS TOO GOOD TO BE TRUE!

9

AT THIS PRECISE MOMENT, ACROSS THE BROAD EXPANSE OF THE PACIFIC OCEAN, THE ASTRAL BODY OF ANDREW HELM IS SPEEDING AS FAST AS LIGHT ITSELF...

THIS IS TERRIBLE! I WAS SO FASCINATED BY WATCHING THE GOOD DEEDS OF THE WORLD-- I PAID NO ATTENTION TO THE *TIME!*

HE DROPS TOWARD AN ISLAND ONLY HE CAN SEE...

I MUST RESET THE CONTROLS OF MY *CORTI-CONSCIENCE!* TO DELAY ANY LONGER COULD VERY WELL UPSET ITS DELICATE BALANCES!

WITHOUT CONSTANT ATTENTION, THE *CORTI-CONSCIENCE* CAN GO HAYWIRE--AND EVEN I AM NOT SURE WHAT WOULD HAPPEN THEN! INSTEAD OF DOING GOOD ACROSS THE WORLD--IT MAY DO IRREPARABLE HARM!

HE HURTLES TOWARD HIS INERT BODY...

IN MY ASTRAL FORM I CANNOT TOUCH THE *CORTI-CONSCIENCE* CONTROLS! I MUST REENTER MY BODY--AND HOPE I'M NOT TOO LATE!

★ JUSTICE LEAGUE of AMERICA ★

# INDESTRUCTIBLE CREATURES of NIGHTMARE ISLAND!
## PART TWO

*"conscience warns us as a friend before it punishes as a judge"* --Stanislaus

WITHIN ONE INCH OF HIS INERT FORM, THAT ASTRAL PROJECTION WHICH IS ANDREW HELM RECOILS IN UTTER HORROR...

I *AM* TOO LATE! I CANNOT ENTER MY BODY! I WAS AWAY FROM IT TOO LONG--MY LIFE-ENERGY HAS DRAINED OUT OF IT--CONDEMNING ME TO AN ETERNAL EXISTENCE AS AN INTANGIBLE, INVISIBLE ENTITY!

IN BITTER DESPAIR, THE ASTRAL FIGURE FLINGS ITSELF AT THE CONTROLS OF THE *CORTI-CON-SCIENCE*...

MY ASTRAL HANDS CANNOT GRIP THE LEVER! AND SINCE NO ONE CAN SEE THE ISLAND OR PASS THE KINETIC BARRIER--MY *CORTI-CON-SCIENCE* MACHINE CAN NEVER BE SHUT OFF!

WHAT HAVE I DONE TO THE WORLD? AT FIRST THE RADIATIONS OF MY MACHINE INTENSIFIED MANKIND'S CON-SCIENCE! BUT NOW ITS OPERATING OUT OF CONTROL-- BUILDING UP AN OVERDOSE-- AND I FEAR THE HARMFUL RESULTS...

AS THOSE TERRIBLE RADIATIONS SWEEP OUT ACROSS THE PLANET, THE ASTRAL FORM OF ANDREW HELM WAILS IN DISMAY...

I HAVE UNLEASHED A TERRIBLE FORCE ON THE WORLD! THE VOICE OF MANKIND'S CON-SCIENCE WILL BE STILLED! THE EVIL NATURE OF MEN WILL RUN RIOT...

IN THE *JUSTICE LEAGUE* SANCTUARY...

GANG WARFARE RAGES IN THE CITY STREETS! ARMIES ARE MASSING ON THE BORDERS! NUCLEAR BOMB ULTIMATUMS...

WELL, *THAT* WAS A SHORT-LIVED PEACE! FELLOW MEMBERS, WE MUST DO SOMETHING TO STOP THIS REIGN OF CHAOS!

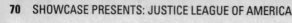

ONLY *SUPERMAN* RISES TO ANSWER THE CHALLENGE OF THE RAMPAGING *CORTI-CONSCIENCE* RADIATION...

WELL, COME ON! DON'T JUST SIT THERE WITH A WORLD CRISIS AT HAND! *FLASH*, YOU TAKE NORTH AMERICA! *AQUAMAN* CAN-- SNAP OUT OF IT! WHAT ARE YOU ALL *WAITING* FOR?

COOL IT, *SUPERMAN!* WHAT RIGHT DO *WE* HAVE TO INTERFERE WITH THE RIGHTS OF OTHER PEOPLE?

THE *MAN OF STEEL* LISTENS IN STUNNED SILENCE AS...

THAT'S TELLING HIM, *GL!* LIVE AND LET LIVE--

RIGHT! IF PEOPLE WANT TO FIGHT AND ROB AND OPPRESS OTHER PEOPLE, WE CANNOT IMPOSE OUR WILLS ON THEM! THEY HAVE RIGHTS TOO, YOU KNOW!

ANGRILY, *SUPERMAN* CRIES OUT..

WHAT'S GOT INTO YOU ALL? YOU DON'T SEEM ABLE TO TELL THE DIFFERENCE BETWEEN RIGHT AND WRONG ANYMORE!

RIGHT AND WRONG? WHO ARE *YOU* TO JUDGE WHICH IS WHICH?

EVERY HUMAN SHOULD BE MASTER OF HIS OWN DESTINY!

WHEEE--OOO! WHAT A MESS THIS HAS TURNED OUT TO BE! ONE THING'S SURE--THEY'RE NOT ACTING LIKE THEIR NORMAL SELVES--INDICATING SOME MYSTERIOUS FORCE OR RADIATION HAS *THEM* IN ITS GRIP-- BUT NOT *ME!* MAYBE I CAN USE *GREEN LANTERN'S POWER RING* TO DISPEL IT!

HE IS PREPARED TO COME TO BLOWS WITH THE *EMERALD CRUSADER* TO GAIN POSSESSION OF THE RING, WHEN...

YOU WANT MY *POWER RING?* BE MY GUEST-- TAKE IT! WHAT RIGHT DO I HAVE TO HOG IT FOR MYSELF?

OH, BROTHER!

AS HIS FINGERS CLOSE ON THE JEWELED CIRCLET, A BEAM OF AWESOME POWER STRIKES THE OTHER MEMBERS-- BATHING THEM IN ITS MYSTIC MIGHT...

;UHH; I FEEL AS IF A GREAT WEIGHT HAS BEEN LIFTED FROM ME!

ME, TOO! WHAT KIND OF GIBBERISH WAS I SPOUTING ANYHOW?

WHY ARE WE HANGING AROUND HERE--WHEN THERE'S WORK TO BE DONE!

LET'S HOP TO IT! *SUPER-MAN*, *WONDER WOMAN* AND I WILL STRAIGHTEN THINGS OUT IN THE WORLD--

WELL, THAT'S MORE LIKE IT! *FLASH*, *BATMAN*, AND *AQUAMAN* WILL TRACK DOWN THE SOURCE OF THE UNKNOWN RADIATION!

SECONDS LATER, SIX OF THE GREAT SUPER-HEROES OF THE *JUSTICE LEAGUE* CLEAVE THE AIR LIKE AVENGING SPIRITS..

TROUBLE-- HERE WE COME !

*H*ALFWAY AROUND THE WORLD, ON A DISTANT BATTLE-FIELD, THE *MAN OF STEEL* CLEAVES A FURROW IN THE GROUND, TUMBLING ARTILLERY AS IF THE MASSIVE CANNONS WERE TOYS...

BEFORE THEY CAN START SHOOTING, I'LL BURY ALL THEIR BIG GUNS !

HIS SUPER-BREATH SENDS CHARGING TROOPS REELING AND TUMBLING INTO ONE ANOTHER...

WHOOSH!

AN INSTANT AFTERWARD HE IS SCOOPING UP WEAPON ARSENALS AND DUMPING THEIR CONTENTS FAR OUT AT SEA ...

WITHOUT GUNS AND AMMUNITION, ALL THEY CAN DO NOW IS HAVE HAND-TO-HAND COMBAT !

13

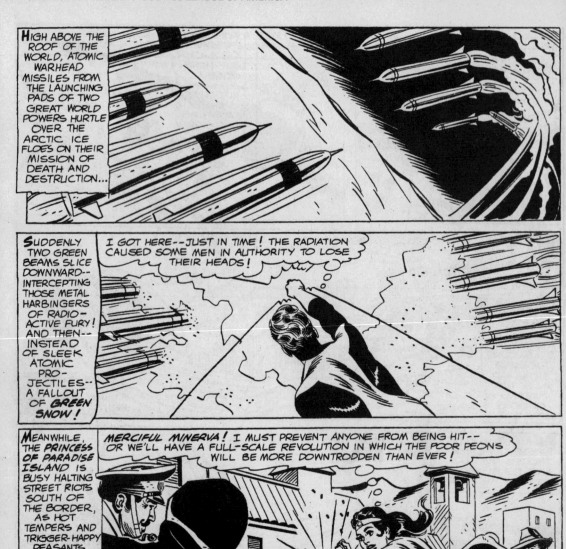

HIGH ABOVE THE ROOF OF THE WORLD, ATOMIC WARHEAD MISSILES FROM THE LAUNCHING PADS OF TWO GREAT WORLD POWERS HURTLE OVER THE ARCTIC ICE FLOES ON THEIR MISSION OF DEATH AND DESTRUCTION...

SUDDENLY TWO GREEN BEAMS SLICE DOWNWARD-- INTERCEPTING THOSE METAL HARBINGERS OF RADIO- ACTIVE FURY! AND THEN-- INSTEAD OF SLEEK ATOMIC PRO- JECTILES-- A FALLOUT OF *GREEN SNOW*!

I GOT HERE--JUST IN TIME! THE RADIATION CAUSED SOME MEN IN AUTHORITY TO LOSE THEIR HEADS!

MEANWHILE, THE *PRINCESS OF PARADISE ISLAND* IS BUSY HALTING STREET RIOTS SOUTH OF THE BORDER, AS HOT TEMPERS AND TRIGGER-HAPPY PEASANTS BATTLE THEIR DICTATORIAL POLICE...

MERCIFUL MINERVA! I MUST PREVENT ANYONE FROM BEING HIT-- OR WE'LL HAVE A FULL-SCALE REVOLUTION IN WHICH THE POOR PEONS WILL BE MORE DOWNTRODDEN THAN EVER!

HER WILD DASH CARRIES HER THROUGH TROOPS AND PEASANTS INTO THE PALACE WHERE THE GREAT DICTATOR SENDS OUT HIS CRUSH- ING TAXES AND OPPRESSIVE LAWS...

STOP HER! STOP HER!

YOU CAN STOP ME-- BY FOLLOWING SOME SIMPLE RULES!

HOLDING THE DICTATOR IN ONE HAND, WITH THE OTHER SHE WRITES IN SOLID STONE...

AND IF YOU DON'T OBEY THEM-- I'LL BE BACK!

TREAT YOUR NEIGHBOR AS **YOU** WOULD BE TREATED!

A JOB FOR **EVERY** MAN!

NO LAWS THAT AID ONLY THE RICH!

I WILL! I WILL!

IN THE **BATJET**, AIDED BY THE SCIENTIFIC INSTRUMENTS IT CONTAINS, THE **COWLED CRUSADER** AND **AQUAMAN** HOVER ABOVE A SEEMINGLY EMPTY SPOT IN THE **PACIFIC OCEAN**...

NO DOUBT OF IT! THIS IS WHERE THOSE RADIATIONS EMANATE FROM!

THERE'S BUT I DON'T SEE A THING, BATMAN!

HURTLING TOWARD THEM COMES THE **FASTEST MAN ON EARTH**, EYES SCANNING THE BROAD AND EMPTY WASTES OF THE WORLD'S MIGHTIEST OCEAN...

I HOPE **BATMAN** CAN SEE WHAT WE'RE LOOKING FOR-- BECAUSE **I** CAN'T! YET I'M SURE I'VE PINPOINTED THE SOURCE OF THE RADIATIONS TO THIS AREA!

SEE ANYTHING, **BATMAN**? OR YOU, **AQUAMAN**?

NOT A THING, **FLASH**! LET'S SEND OUT AN EMERGENCY ALERT SIGNAL TO SUMMON THE REMAINING MEMBERS! MAYBE THEY'LL HAVE BETTER LUCK!

AS THAT URGENT SIGNAL FLASHES ACROSS THE EARTH AND INTO THE REACHES OF SPACE ITSELF, OTHER **JUSTICE LEAGUE** MEMBERS REACT...

MUST BE SOMETHING MIGHTY BIG GOING ON TO DRAW ME BACK FROM MY NATIVE PLANET **THANAGAR**!

I WAS ON A SUBATOMIC WORLD!

A STRANGE RACE BENEATH THE SURFACE OF THE EARTH KEPT ME BUSY!

I WAS INVOLVED ON A CASE THAT TOOK ME TO THE MOON!

FROM NEAR-- FROM FAR-- THEY CLEAVE THE AIR OF THE IONOSPERE TO REACH THEIR DESTINATION...

ALL I SEE ARE *FLASH* AND *BATMAN* WITH *AQUAMAN* IN THE *BATJET!* WHERE'S THE RADIATION COMING FROM?

BEATS ME! NOT EVEN MY *SUPER-VISION* CAN DETECT ANYTHING HERE!

MAYBE MY *POWER RING* WILL REVEAL IT TO US!

AS THE FULL MEMBERSHIP GATHERS, THE *POWER RING* HURLS A GREAT BEAM ACROSS THE HEAVING WAVES OF THE PACIFIC...

I'M STUMPED! NOTHING APPEARS!

INSTRUMENTS SAY THE RADIATION COMES FROM HERE!

YET MY

IF WE CAN'T SEE ANY- THING TO FIGHT-- WE'RE LICKED BE- FORE WE START!

THEN WHY CAN'T WE SEE IT?

EVEN MY *MARTIAN- VISION* HAS DRAWN A BLANK!

OHH! TRY SOMETHING! DON'T GIVE UP! THERE MUST BE SOME WAY YOU CAN SEE THE ISLAND, AND UNDO THE TERRIBLE DAMAGE I'VE CAUSED! YOU *JUSTICE LEAGUE* MEMBERS ARE MY ONLY HOPE!

# INDESTRUCTIBLE CREATURES of NIGHTMARE ISLAND!

**PART THREE**

*"a wounded conscience is able to un-Paradise Paradise itself!"* --fuller

SUDDENLY *AQUAMAN* STABS A FINGER AT A SCHOOL OF PORPOISES SWIMMING IN LINE BELOW...

LOOK, THOSE POR-POISES ARE SKIRTING AROUND SOMETHING IN THE OCEAN--AN OBJECT *THEY* CAN SEE--AND *WE* CAN'T!

QUESTION THEM, *AQUAMAN!* YOU HAVE THE POWER TO COMMUNICATE WITH FISH, AS I HAVE WITH BIRDS!

THE *SEA KING* STEPS ONTO A SURFBOARD FORMED BY *GREEN LANTERN'S POWER RING* AND...

WHAT IS BLOCKING YOUR PATH, MY FINNY FRIENDS?

ISLAND THERE! BIG SUN! SAND! TREES! HOUSE!

THERE'S AN ISLAND HERE--INHABITED! THEIR LANGUAGE IS TOO LIMITED TO TELL ME MORE!

I'LL DIRECT A *POWER RING BEAM* AT THEIR MINDS--TELEVISE THEIR THOUGHTS!

SEARCHING OUT THE PORPOISE MINDS, THE *EMERALD CRUSADER* CAUSES A MENTAL PICTURE TO APPEAR BEFORE THE JLA MEMBERS...

EVIDENTLY THE ISLAND IS INVISIBLE ONLY TO *HUMAN* EYES!

THAT WOULD EXPLAIN WHY NEITHER *SUPERMAN* NOR I--EVEN WITH OUR SUPER-HUMAN VISION--WAS ABLE TO SEE IT! NOW--LET'S EXPLORE IT!

17

FILLED WITH EAGERNESS AND EXCITEMENT, THEY HURTLE FORWARD--AND RAM WITH SHOCKING ABRUPTNESS INTO THE KINETIC FORCE-FIELD WHICH SHIELDS THE ISLAND FROM DISCOVERY...

OHHH! MY IMPENETRABLE KINETIC BARRIER IS KEEPING THEM OUT OF THE ISLAND! ALL IS LOST!

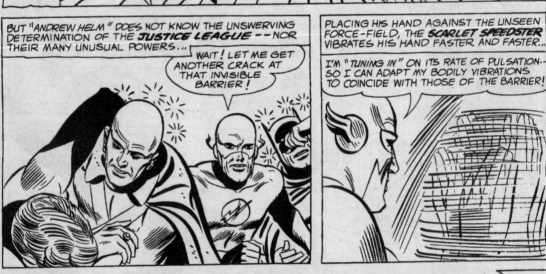

BUT "ANDREW HELM" DOES NOT KNOW THE UNSWERVING DETERMINATION OF THE *JUSTICE LEAGUE* -- NOR THEIR MANY UNUSUAL POWERS...

WAIT! LET ME GET ANOTHER CRACK AT THAT INVISIBLE BARRIER!

PLACING HIS HAND AGAINST THE UNSEEN FORCE-FIELD, THE *SCARLET SPEEDSTER* VIBRATES HIS HAND FASTER AND FASTER...

I'M "TUNING IN" ON ITS RATE OF PULSATION-- SO I CAN ADAPT MY BODILY VIBRATIONS TO COINCIDE WITH THOSE OF THE BARRIER!

MOMENTS LATER, HE STEPS INTO THE WALL ITSELF, VIBRATING IN HARMONIC RHYTHM WITH THE KINETIC FORCE-FIELD...

OKAY! MY VIBRATIONS HAVE OPENED A GAP THROUGH THE BARRIER! COME ON, MEMBERS! YOU CAN RUN RIGHT THROUGH ME JUST AS-- VIBRATING AT THIS SPEED--I CAN RUN THROUGH ANY SOLID OBJECT!

AMAZING!

THROUGH THE VIBRATIONAL GATEWAY THAT IS *THE FLASH'S* BODY, THE MEMBERS RACE ONE AFTER THE OTHER...

NOW THAT WE'RE INSIDE, WE CAN GET TO WORK SOLVING THE SECRET OF THIS PLACE!

THEY DASH BENEATH THE MIGHTY DOME OF THE KINETIC FORCE-FIELD, UNAWARE THAT THEY HAVE STEPPED FROM A NORMAL WORLD INTO A PERILOUS PHANTAS-MAGORIA!...

THEY DON'T REALIZE IT YET-- BUT THEIR PROBLEMS ARE ONLY BEGINNING ON THIS ISLAND OF NIGHTMARES!

THE FIRST MEMBER TO FEEL THE EERIE EFFECT OF THIS ISLAND IS MIGHTY *SUPERMAN* HIMSELF...

*HUH?* THAT MAGICIAN JUST POPPED OUT OF NOWHERE!

MY WAND IS GREAT, MY WAND IS FAIR! UP *SUPERMAN--* INTO THE AIR!

WHIRLED HIGH OFF THE ISLAND DUNES, THE *MAN OF STEEL* IS SWUNG AROUND AND AROUND LIKE A LIVING PIN-WHEEL!...

I CAN'T GET FREE! MY POWERS ARE USELESS AGAINST--*MAGIC!*

NOT FAR AWAY A GIGANTIC FIERY WARRIOR IS SWINGING A BLAZING BATTLE-AXE AT THE *MARTIAN MANHUNTER*..

THOSE FLAMES WEAKENING ME! I CAN'T EVEN GET CLOSE ENOUGH TO FIGHT THAT FLAMING GIANT! SOMEONE'S TUMBLED ON TO OUR WEAKNESSES...!

A GOLDEN BEAR CLOSES MASSIVE ARMS AROUND A STRUGGLING *EMERALD CRUSADER!*...

*PANT!* MY *POWER RING* IS USELESS AGAINST ANYTHING YELLOW! *PANT!* BEING SQUEEZED INTO UNCONSCIOUSNESS...

THE *TINY TITAN* IS SPUN AROUND LIKE AN ELECTRON ABOUT THE NUCLEUS OF A HELIUM ATOM!...

I--I'VE BECOME PART OF A LIVING *ATOM*--CAN'T TEAR MYSELF LOOSE!

EVEN AS *GREEN ARROW* FIRES SHAFT AFTER SHAFT AT AN ARMORED DINOSAUR FROM EARTH'S PRIMEVAL PAST...

MY MOST POWERFUL ARROWS FAIL TO DENT THE ARMOR-PLATED BODY OF THAT *STEGOSAURUS!*

AND *AQUAMAN* FALLS VICTIM TO A GIANT SEASHORE CRAB!...

HOW COME IT DOESN'T OBEY MY TELEPATHIC COMMANDS TO LET GO OF ME?

WHILE *BATMAN* REELS BEFORE THE AWESOME FISTS OF AN ANIMATED MARBLE GLADIATOR...

THIS MYSTERIOUS ISLAND MUST BE THE SPAWNING GROUND OF THE INCREDIBLE FORCE THAT HAS BEEN LET LOOSE ON EARTH!

*BATMAN* IS CLOSE TO THE TRUTH! SOME OF THE RADIATION PENETRATES THE FORCE-FIELD, BUT MOST OF IT IS HELD IN CHECK INSIDE THE BARRIER, ITS PENT-UP FORCES CAUSING THESE FRIGHTFUL MENACES!

(20)

TO CHALLENGE *WONDER WOMAN* APPEARS A FEARSOME TREE DRYAD...

I--I'VE MORE THAN MET MY MATCH!

AND *FLASH* BATTLES HIS OWN INVULNERABLE MENACE IN THE FORM OF A WHIRLING SAND-BEING...

THE FASTER I MOVE, THE MORE FIRMLY IT HOLDS ME IN ITS DIZZYING GRIP!

WHILE IN THE AIR ABOVE THE ISLAND, *HAWK-MAN* FALLS VICTIM TO A GIGANTIC BIRD OF PREY! STRUGGLING DESPERATELY, HE CRIES OUT TO A PAIR OF GREAT SEA BIRDS...

*wheet* BROTHERS OF THE AIR-- HELP ME AGAINST THIS NIGHTMARISH CREATURE!

*wheet* WHAT CREATURE, HAWKMAN? WE SEE NOTHING!

CUED BY THE BIRDS, THE GRIM TRUTH DAWNS ON THE *WINGED WONDER*...

THAT'S IT! THIS MENACE MUST BE A FIGMENT OF MY IMAGI-NATION! AND IF I REFUSE TO BELIEVE IT EXISTS-- IT'S WORKING-- THE BIRD'S BEGINNING TO FADE AWAY!

21

HIS PINIONS FLAIL THE AIR AS THE **AERIAL ACE** BELLOWS HIS DISCOVERY TO HIS FELLOW **JUSTICE LEAGUE** MEMBERS...

THOSE THINGS DON'T EXIST! EVERYTHING THAT IS TAKING PLACE HERE--IS AN **HALLUCINATION!** SOMEHOW THE RADIATION IN THE DOME HAS AFFECTED OUR MINDS!

AS **ATOM**, **SUPERMAN** AND **WONDER WOMAN** BREAK FREE OF THEIR PERILS...

NO WONDER WE COULDN'T DEFEAT THESE THINGS!

IN A SENSE WE WERE FIGHTING AGAINST...

--INDESTRUCTIBLE MENACES CONJURED UP BY OUR OWN MINDS!

IN ANSWER TO **HAWKMAN'S** WARNING, **J'ONN J'ONZZ**, **AQUAMAN**, **BATMAN** AND **GREEN ARROW** CONCENTRATE ON ELIMINATING THEIR THREATS...

JOINED BY THE **SCARLET SPEEDSTER**, THE **JUSTICE LEAGUE** MEMBERS DASH INSIDE THE LITTLE SHACK THAT WAS THE HOME AND LABORATORY OF **ANDREW HELM**...

THAT GLOWING GLOBE MUST BE THE CAUSE OF EVERYTHING THAT'S HAPPENED!

OKAY--LET'S SHUT IT OFF!

THE KEEN VISION OF *SUPERMAN* AND THE *MARTIAN MANHUNTER* QUICKLY SPOTS THE ACTIVATING LEVER AND DIALS...

LET'S HOPE THIS DOES THE TRICK!

AND THAT WE WON'T BE RELEASING A WORSE RADIATION ON THE WORLD!

FOR ONE LONG MOMENT THE GLOBE SWELLS WITH TITANIC BRILLIANCE, CATCHING EVERY MEMBER IN ITS SUPERNAL GLARE...

WHAT'S HAPPENING? IS IT EXPLODING?

I CAN'T TELL--IT'S JUST--GROWING BIGGER!

AND THEN--THE *CORTI-CONSCIENCE* GLOBE IS GONE, AND ONLY THE BLACKENED RODS THAT FORMED IT CAN BE SEEN INSIDE THE ISLAND SHACK...

;whew; IT'S ALL OVER!

HIGH TIME, TOO!

ONLY THE INERT BODY OF ANDREW HELM REMAINS TO PUZZLE THEM ...

WHO IS HE?

WE'LL PROBABLY NEVER KNOW! HE LEFT NO NOTES TO TELL US WHAT HE HOPED TO ACCOMPLISH HERE ...

EVIDENTLY IT HAD SOMETHING TO DO WITH TRYING TO GIVE THE WORLD A *CON-SCIENCE*--AT WHICH HE SUCCEEDED FOR A LITTLE WHILE --

--UNTIL DEATH OVERTOOK HIM AND HIS INVENTION WENT OUT OF CONTROL!

23

TOO BAD HE COULDN'T HAVE LIVED TO REALIZE THAT CONSCIENCE CANNOT BE FORCED ON A MAN!

IT MUST COME AS A RESULT OF UNDERSTANDING BETWEEN MEN!

AND THAT MEN MUST BE EDUCATED TO UNDERSTAND THAT ONE MAN IS VERY MUCH LIKE ANOTHER!

THE OLD SAYING THAT ALL MEN ARE BROTHERS UNDER THE SKIN IS TRUE!

BE THEY BLACK, RED, WHITE OR YELLOW, EVERY MAN WANTS HAPPINESS FOR HIMSELF, HIS FAMILY, AND HIS CHILDREN!

UNTIL THIS IS PROPERLY UNDERSTOOD, THERE WILL ALWAYS BE INJUSTICE IN THE WORLD!

TO MAKE SURE THIS NEVER HAPPENS AGAIN, I'LL RESEAL THE BARRIER AROUND THE ISLAND AND SHUT OFF MAN'S ARTIFICIAL CONSCIENCE FOREVER!

ONLY THE ASTRAL PROJECTION OF ANDREW HELM REMAINS, A LONELY, DIS-EMBODIED PHANTOM WHO MUST ETERNALLY REMAIN UNSEEN AND UNHEARD...

÷SIGH÷ I'VE LEARNED MY LESSON! NOW IF ALL OTHER PEOPLE ON EARTH COULD DO THE SAME -- I'D FEEL MY INVENTION SERVED ITS PART IN THE BETTERMENT OF MANKIND!

The END

**★JUSTICE★ LEAGUE of AMERICA**

# JUSTICE LEAGUE of AMERICA

HE FOUND THE KEY TO SUCCESS -- WEALTH -- POWER ! *SUCCESS* HE ACHIEVED BY KEY-CONTROLLING THE MINDS OF MEN ! *WEALTH* HE GAINED BY HAVING HIS *KEY-MEN* ROB WITHOUT FEAR OF DETECTION OR CAPTURE !
*POWER* HE WIELDED BY USING THE *SUPER-HEROES* OF THE *JUSTICE LEAGUE* AS HIS *SUPER-SLAVES* !
HE WAS - -

# THE KEY-MASTER OF THE WORLD!

The ROLL CALL

ATOM
~
BATMAN
~
FLASH
~
GREEN·LANTERN
~
HAWKMAN
~
J'ONN J'ONZZ
~
SNAPPER CARR
~
SUPERMAN
~
WONDER WOMAN

AT A REGULAR MEETING OF THE **JUSTICE LEAGUE OF AMERICA** IN ITS SECRET SANCTUARY, **SUPERMAN** RISES TO HIS FEET TO MAKE A DRAMATIC ANNOUNCEMENT...

FELLOW MEMBERS, AS YOU ALL MUST REALIZE BY NOW--THE MOMENT HAS COME TO BREAK UP THE **JUSTICE LEAGUE!**

IT'S ABOUT TIME!

YOU DON'T HAVE TO TALK **ME** INTO THAT!

AND SO I MAKE THE MOTION TO DISBAND THE **JUSTICE LEAGUE** FOREVER! LET US REFILL OUR CUPS AND DRINK A TOAST TO--THE **JUSTICE LEAGUE THAT WAS!**

I SECOND THE MOTION, **SUPERMAN!**

LET'S MAKE IT UNANIMOUS!

**C**RYSTAL CUPS ARE DIPPED INTO THE BIG PUNCH BOWL AND ARE RAISED AS THE MOTION TO DISBAND THE **JUSTICE LEAGUE** IS PASSED BY ACCLAMATION...

IT WAS GOOD WHILE IT LASTED--BUT ENOUGH'S ENOUGH!

YEAH, MAN! LIKE THIS IS THE LIVING END!

SNAP!

**O**NE BY ONE THE MEMBERS FILE FROM THE HEADQUARTERS WHICH HAS LED TO MONUMENTAL BATTLES ON WHICH THE FATE OF WORLDS HAS HUNG!...

OKAY, **GREEN LANTERN!** DO YOUR STUFF! GET RID OF THE PLACE! WRECK IT COMPLETELY!

HERE GOES!

A MIGHTY POWER BEAM STABS OUTWARD AND INWARD! THE CEILING OF THE SECRET SANCTUARY MELTS AND RUNS MOLTEN ROCK AND FIRE INSIDE THE COUNCIL ROOM AS THE VERY FLOORS EXPLODE AND BEGIN TO QUAKE--WRITING **FINISH** TO THE SAGA OF THE **JUSTICE LEAGUE OF AMERICA**...

VROOOM!

2

EX-JUSTICE LEAGUERS GRIP HANDS, THEN TURN AWAY TO RETURN TO THEIR HOME CITIES, NEVERMORE TO MEET AS A UNITED FRONT AGAINST THE EVIL FORCES OF CRIME AND INJUSTICE...

*WHEW! I'M GLAD THAT'S OVER, ATOM!*

*WHAT A RELIEF TO KNOW I WON'T HAVE TO DROP WHATEVER I'M DOING TO HURRY OFF TO AN EMERGENCY JLA CASE!*

CAN THIS REALLY BE THE END OF THE GREAT *JUSTICE LEAGUE OF AMERICA?* WHY HAVE THESE GREAT SUPER-HEROES DECIDED TO CALL IT QUITS AS A TEAM?

LET US FOLLOW THE FORMER HONORARY MEMBER OF THE JLA AS HE HEADS FOR HIS HOME IN *HAPPY HARBOR*...

*SNAPPER CARR* CHUGS ALONG IN HIS JALOPY THEN PULLS TO THE SIDE OF THE ROAD NEAR A PUBLIC TELEPHONE! HE DIALS A NUMBER AND...

*SNAPPER CARR REPORTING! I FOLLOWED YOUR INSTRUCTIONS-- AND THE JUSTICE LEAGUE IS GONESVILLE!*

ON THE OTHER END OF THE LINE, A GRIM FIGURE HANGS UP THE PHONE WITH A SIGH OF SATISFACTION...

*NOW THAT THAT IS TAKEN CARE OF--MY PLAN TO BE KEY-MAN ON EARTH--THE SOLAR SYSTEM--THE UNIVERSE-- CAN'T MISS!*

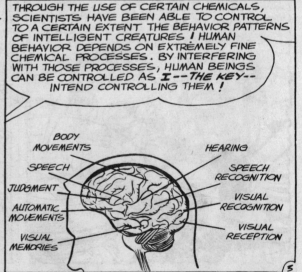

*MINE IS THE POWER AND THE ABILITY-- THROUGH THE USE OF A CERTAIN PSYCHO-CHEMICAL I DISCOVERED--TO TAKE OVER THE MINDS AND BEHAVIOR PATTERNS OF ALL MANKIND! WHAT SCIENCE HAS REGARDED AS A THEORY--I HAVE TURNED INTO AN ACCOMPLISHED FACT!*

*THROUGH THE USE OF CERTAIN CHEMICALS, SCIENTISTS HAVE BEEN ABLE TO CONTROL TO A CERTAIN EXTENT THE BEHAVIOR PATTERNS OF INTELLIGENT CREATURES! HUMAN BEHAVIOR DEPENDS ON EXTREMELY FINE CHEMICAL PROCESSES. BY INTERFERING WITH THOSE PROCESSES, HUMAN BEINGS CAN BE CONTROLLED AS I--THE KEY-- INTEND CONTROLLING THEM!*

BODY MOVEMENTS

HEARING

SPEECH

SPEECH RECOGNITION

JUDGMENT

VISUAL RECOGNITION

AUTOMATIC MOVEMENTS

VISUAL RECEPTION

VISUAL MEMORIES

FOR THE PAST SEVERAL YEARS, EVEN WHILE HE HAS BEEN PERFECTING HIS *PSYCHO-CHEMICAL,* THE KEY HAS BEEN STUDYING THE VARIOUS MEMBERS OF THE *JUSTICE LEAGUE OF AMERICA*...

*I SHALL STRIKE AT THE JUSTICE LEAGUE THROUGH ITS WEAKEST LINK-- SNAPPER CARR!*

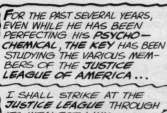

AND SO--WHILE *SNAPPER CARR* WAS ON A HIKE IN THE ROCKY HEIGHTS NORTH OF *HAPPY HARBOR*--THE KEY'S HANDS PUSHED A *KEYSTONE* OUT FROM UNDER A PILE OF ROCKS...

*THIS ROCKSLIDE I'M CAUSING WILL START THE BALL ROLLING...*

THE YOUTH WENT DOWN UNDER A SPILL OF ROLLING, THUDDING STONES--BUT THE KEY WAS THERE TO SAVE HIM ...

*I CAN'T LET ANYTHING HAPPEN TO YOU, MY YOUNG FRIEND--BECAUSE THE SUCCESS OF MY ENTIRE PLAN DEPENDS ON YOUR COOPERATION !*

MOMENTS LATER, HAVING DROPPED A FEW GRAINS OF HIS *PSYCHO-CHEMICAL* IN SNAPPER'S CANTEEN, THE KEY REVIVED HIM WITH ITS WATER ...

*FROM THIS MOMENT ON, THE PSYCHO-CHEMICAL IN THE WATER WILL ENABLE ME TO CONTROL HIS EVERY ACTION !*

LATER, IN HIS PRIVATE *KEY CLUB* HEADQUARTERS, HE STOOD BEFORE A GREAT BATTERY OF KEYS SET INTO A GIANT ELECTRONIC BRAIN...

*BY TURNING THE CORRECT KEYS, I BOMBARD SNAPPER'S BRAIN WITH THE PROPER ELECTRONIC IMPULSES--MAKING HIM SUBJECT TO MY KEY COMMANDS !*

*"FOR INSTANCE, I SHALL ORDER HIM--UNSEEN BY THE OTHER MEMBERS--TO DROP ENOUGH PSYCHO-CHEMICAL IN THEIR PUNCH BOWL TO GIVE ME CONTROL OVER THE JUSTICE LEAGUE MEMBERS THEMSELVES !"*

WITH THE NEXT STAGE OF HIS PLAN COMPLETED, HIS HANDS DARTED FROM KEY TO KEY, TURNING THEM TO ACTIVATE THE BEHAVIOR PATTERNS OF THE SUPER-HEROES...

*NOW THAT THEY'VE SIPPED THE PSYCHO-CHEMICAL PUNCH--I SHALL CHECK ITS POTENCY BY COMMANDING THEM TO DO THE MOST UNLIKELY THING I CAN THINK OF--DISBAND THE JUSTICE LEAGUE OF AMERICA !*

HAVING BEEN ASSURED BY *SNAPPER*-- AS DIRECTED-- OF THE SUCCESS OF HIS PLAN, *THE KEY* AGAIN TURNS TOWARD HIS MASSIVE KEYBOARD...

NOW THAT I HAVE ABSOLUTE PROOF I CAN COMPLETELY CONTROL THE *JUSTICE LEAGUE* MEMBERS, MY NEXT MOVE WILL BE TO ORDER THEM TO BE COMPLETELY OBLIVIOUS OF THE CRIMES AND ROBBERIES OF MY HIRELINGS--THE *KEY-MEN* I NEED TO CARRY OUT MY PLANS ...

MUCH AS I'D LIKE TO DO AWAY WITH THOSE SUPER-HEROES, I HAVE AN URGENT NEED OF THEM! IN TIME--AFTER MY *PSYCHO-CHEMICAL* PILLS ARE PROPERLY GIVEN--I SHALL SECRETLY CONTROL THE HEADS OF STATE OF ALL THE WORLD GOVERNMENTS! ALL POWER ON EARTH SHALL BE MINE!

I REALIZE THAT BEING THE POWER BEHIND EVERY NATION ON EARTH WILL BECOME BORING-- IN TIME! THEN SUPER-HEROES LIKE *SUPERMAN* AND *GREEN LANTERN* WILL CARRY ME TO OTHER PLANETS, MORE DISTANT WORLDS! THEY AND THE OTHERS-- *FLASH, WONDER WOMAN, BATMAN*-- SHALL PROTECT ME FROM ALL DANGERS--WHILE I TAKE CONTROL OF ALIEN CIVILIZATIONS!

SOON I SHALL BE THE ONE MASTER--THE SOLE RULER-- OF A CHOICE SELECTION OF PLANETS THROUGHOUT THE UNIVERSE! THE NAME OF *THE KEY* SHALL RESOUND FROM GALAXY TO GALAXY! I SHALL BE THE MONARCH OF ALL I SURVEY--AND THOSE SUPER-HEROES WILL BE MY SLAVES!

IN *GOTHAM CITY* SOME DAYS LATER-- *THE WRECKER* * AND HIS MOBSTERS RUN RIOT AT THE *COUNTY FAIR* ...

SMASH! DESTROY! WRECK! MAKE A SHAMBLES OF THE FAIR-- SO THAT WHILE EVERYONE IS BUSY TRYING TO SAVE PROPERTY-- MY MEN SHALL LOOT AND LOOT AND LOOT...

* EDITOR'S NOTE: THE WRECKER APPEARED IN *DETECTIVE COMICS #197* (JULY, 1953) IN "*THE LEAGUE AGAINST BATMAN!*"

5

BUT OUT OF THE SWIRL OF SMOKE AND THE CRIMSON FLARE OF FLAMES DART TWO DYNAMIC FIGURES! THEIR FISTS ARE STEEL HAMMERS AS THEY BLAST AND BATTER MEN OF EVIL...

GOOD THING WE ARRIVED AHEAD OF TIME FOR THE DISPLAY OF JUDO TRICKS WE WERE TO SHOW THE VACATION FUND YOUNGSTERS, ROBIN!

LET'S PUT ON OUR INTENDED SHOW FOR THESE CROOKS, BATMAN!

MIGHTY MUSCLES BULGE AS THE MASKED MAN-HUNTER SWINGS A LEG AND YANKS ON ARMS AT THE SAME TIME...

I'LL KICK OFF THE ACTION WITH THE "KNEE WHEEL" ATTACK!

AND THIS IS THE "UKI GOSHI" GRIP-- SPRING-HIP-HOLD TO YOU, FELLA!

WITHIN MOMENTS, THE WRECKER'S MEN LITTER THE GROUND AS THE COWLED CRUSADER AND BOY WONDER MOVE LIKE TWIN TORNADOES...

BIG DEAL! SO YOU KNOCKED OUT MY GANG! NOW WHAT ABOUT THOSE OTHER CROOKS -- GARBED IN THOSE KEY UNIFORMS?

THE EYES OF BATMAN AND ROBIN MOMENTARILY TURN TO SURVEY THEIR RECENT BATTLEGROUND, EVEN AS THEY POUND TOWARD THEIR INTENDED PREY!

I DON'T SEE ANYBODY WITH KEYS ON THEIR COSTUMES!

NEITHER DO I! IT'S JUST A CORNY TRICK TO TRY AND DISTRACT US SO HE CAN MAKE HIS GETAWAY!

6

SCREECHING IN ANGER AND FRUSTRATION, *THE WRECKER* GOES DOWN BEFORE THE SMASHING IMPACT OF THE DYNAMIC DUO...

WHY PICK JUST ON *ME?* YOU'RE LETTING THE OTHER GANG GET AWAY SCOT-FREE! STOP THEM TOO!

COOL IT, *WRECKER!* THERE'S NOBODY HERE BUT YOU-- AND US!

*SOK!*

IN *IVY TOWN, THE ATOM* AT THIS MOMENT IS SHOOTING UPWARD FROM THE WATERS OF AN ART GALLERY FOUNTAIN...

THE FORCE OF THESE FOUNTAIN WATERS WHERE I'VE BEEN HIDING IS TOSSING ME HIGH ENOUGH SO I CAN SEE WHAT'S GOING ON!

BELOW HIM THE SANDY SALTERS GANG--WHICH THE *TINY TITAN* HAS BEEN SHADOWING FOR SEVERAL DAYS-- IS RIFLING AN ART GALLERY WALL OF VALUABLE PAINTINGS...

I MADE MYSELF SO SMALL I COULD BREATHE IN THE TINY AIR BUBBLES IN THE WATER! NOW I'LL MAKE MYSELF LARGE ENOUGH TO GO INTO ACTION!

*CLICK!*

*CLICK!*

AT HIS CUSTOMARY HEIGHT OF *SIX INCHES* AND AT HIS FULL WEIGHT OF *180 POUNDS, THE ATOM* MOVES LIKE A HUMAN BULLET--SMACK ON TARGET!...

NOW TO MAKE THE "*PICTURE PLAY!*"

*THUD!*

THE MIGHTY MITE LANDS WITH A FOOT ON A CANVAS--WHICH GIVES UNDER HIS LESSENED WEIGHT AND HURLS HIM UPWARD AS IF IT WERE A TRAMPOLINE...

HUH?

HERE'S WHERE I PAINT YOU-- BLACK-AND-BLUE!

*BOINNG!*

7

AS HIS "MITE-Y" FIST MAKES CONTACT AND HE HEADS FOR THE REMAINING MEMBER OF THE PICTURE-LOOTING GANG ...

I'VE SAVED YOU FOR THE LAST, SANDY!

BOY, YOU SURE MUST HAVE IT IN FOR ME AND MY GANG, ATOM-- TAKING US ON WHILE THOSE OTHER CROOKS MAKE OFF WITH THE PAINTINGS!

BUT AS AN EXPERIENCED CRIME-FIGHTER, THE ATOM CONCENTRATES SOLELY ON THE BUSINESS AT HAND! ONLY AFTER HIS KNOCKOUT FIST THUDS HOME DOES HE RISK A LOOK AROUND HIM ...

I KNEW IT--NO ONE ELSE HERE! HE TRIED TO PULL THE OLDEST GAG IN THE BOOK ON ME!

SOK!

NOW TO PHONE THE POLICE TO COME AND HAUL AWAY THESE CROOKS!

WHAT'S WITH BATMAN, ROBIN AND ATOM, YOU WONDER? HOW COME--WHILE CAPTURING ONE GROUP OF CROOKS--THEY WERE COMPLETELY OBLIVIOUS TO THE PRESENCE OF OTHER KEY-GANGS COMMITTING ROBBERIES AROUND THEM? THE ANSWER'S SIMPLE--AND OMINOUS! THE KEY HAS GAINED CONTROL OF THEIR BEHAVIOR! HE PREVENTED THEM FROM SEEING WHAT OTHERS CAN SEE!

8

# JUSTICE LEAGUE of AMERICA

# KEY-MASTER OF THE WORLD.. PART 2

HIGH ABOVE *MIDWAY CITY*--WHERE THEY SERVE AS CARTER HALL, CURATOR OF THE LOCAL MUSEUM, AND HIS WIFE SHIERA--*HAWKMAN* AND *HAWKGIRL* DIVE THROUGH THOSE URBAN SKIES TO CHALLENGE THE LATEST THREAT TO LAW AND ORDER IN THAT METROPOLIS ! AN ANCIENT WAR-WEAPON SLAMS DOWNWARD--THERE IS A CLANG AND CLATTER OF BROKEN MACHINERY--AND THE AERIAL CONFLICT IS ON !

THESE *"MONARCH BUTTERFLY"* CROOKS WON'T GET FAR WITHOUT THEIR FLYING MOTORS !

I'LL COVER YOUR FLANK, HAWKMAN!

A TWISTING, KICKING MAN BEGINS THE LONG FALL EARTHWARD AS A FIST POWERS INTO A A FELLOW CRIMINAL ...

A COUPLE OF POLICE HELICOPTERS WITH A NET STRUNG BETWEEN THEM WILL CATCH THESE GUYS AS THEY DROP !

SOK!

HIS MIGHTY HANDS GRIP A BUTTERFLY WING AND AS HE RISES UPWARD ON THE LIFTING POWER OF HIS ANTI-GRAVITY BELT, THE IRIDESCENT PINION SNAPS OFF...

WITH ONLY ONE WING, THE REIGN OF THIS *"MONARCH"* IS OVER !

9

TO ONE SIDE OF HER CRIME-BUSTING MATE FIGHTS *HAWKGIRL* -- WHOSE ATTENTION IS SUDDENLY DISTRACTED BY...

THUD

WHAT'S THIS? MEN IN KEY-DECORATED UNIFORMS -- STEALING FROM A BANK BELOW!

PARKIN

AL BANK

WINGS WHIPPING THE AIR, THE *PINIONED PRINCESS* DIVES AT THE MASKED MINIONS OF *THE KEY*...

*HAWKGIRL!* HEY--SHE AIN'T SUPPOSED TO SEE US--LET ALONE *FIGHT* US!

HER ARMS SCOOP UP THE COSTUMED CRIMINALS-- AND RAM THEM HARD INTO TWO PARKED CARS...

I FIGHT ANYBODY WHO COMMITS A CRIME!

OVER THE BODIES OF HER DOWNED FOES, THE OUT-RAGED *HAWKGIRL* CRIES OUT...

YOU MIGHT AT LEAST HAVE MADE AN *ATTEMPT* TO HELP ME OVERCOME THESE KEY-MEN!

KEY-MEN? WHAT ARE YOU TALKING ABOUT? I DON'T SEE ANYONE AT ALL!

AFTER THEY TURN OVER THEIR INDIVIDUAL CAPTIVES TO THE AUTHORITIES, THE *WINGED WONDERS* FLY HOME-WARD...

*KATAR*--IF YOU AREN'T JUST PUTTING ME ON--THERE'S SOMETHING MIGHTY PECULIAR GOING ON! YOU STILL INSIST YOU COULDN'T SEE THOSE *KEY-MEN?*

NOT EVEN A SHIMMERING GLIMPSE OF THEM!

10

SHORTLY, A CONCERNED *HAWKGIRL* BROODS IN HER KITCHEN--FROM WHICH SHE WAS SUMMONED BY THE EMERGENCY CALL FROM POLICE COMMISSIONER EMMETT TO GO OUT AFTER THE BUTTERFLY MEN...

THOSE *KEY-MEN* ACTED AS IF THEY EXPECTED I WOULDN'T INTERFERE! I WONDER WHY! HMMMM--THIS GLASS HOLDS SOME OF THE MILK I USUALLY DRINK EVERY NIGHT BEFORE RETIRING...

"IF YOU RECALL, I DIDN'T DRINK THIS MILK! I GAVE IT TO THAT STRAY CAT WHO'S BEEN MOOCHING FOR FOOD LATELY..."

POOR LITTLE KITTY...

HONEY, YOU SURE ARE A SOFT TOUCH WHERE ANIMALS ARE CONCERNED!

EXCITED BY THE PROSPECT OF A POSSIBLE CLUE, THE *MARRIED MANHUNTERS* SPEND THE NEXT HOUR IN THEIR HOME LABORATORY...

AHA! MY SUSPICIONS ARE CONFIRMED! THERE'S A POWERFUL *PSYCHO-CHEMICAL* IN THE MILK!

NOW WE'RE GETTING SOMEWHERE! HAD YOU DRUNK THE MILK-- I'LL BET *YOU* WOULDN'T HAVE SEEN THE *KEY-MEN* EITHER!

SLOWLY THE GRIM TRUTH DAWNS UPON THE CRIME-FIGHTING DUO...

THERE'S ONLY ONE ANSWER! *YOU* MUST HAVE PUT THAT *PSYCHO-CHEMICAL* IN MY MILK!

UNDER ORDERS FROM SOMEONE! BUT WHO COULD HAVE GIVEN *ME* THE *PSYCHO-CHEMICAL*?

SINCE THEIR LABORATORY LACKS THE SUPER-SCIENTIFIC INSTRUMENTS AVAILABLE IN THEIR *THANAGARIAN* SPACESHIP, *HAWKMAN* DONS HIS COSTUME AGAIN AND...

OUR FIRST MOVE IS TO NEUTRALIZE THE *PSYCHO-CHEMICAL* IN MY SYSTEM!

YES...BUT REMEMBER IT'LL BE ONLY A *TEMPORARY* MEASURE! SHOULD THE *PSYCHO-CHEMICAL* BE ACTIVATED AGAIN IT WILL REMAIN IN YOU *PERMANENTLY*!

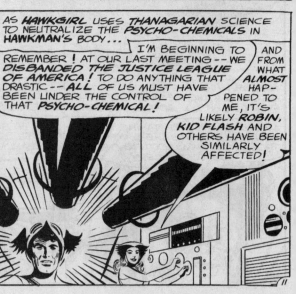

AS *HAWKGIRL* USES *THANAGARIAN* SCIENCE TO NEUTRALIZE THE *PSYCHO-CHEMICALS* IN HAWKMAN'S BODY...

REMEMBER! AT OUR LAST MEETING -- WE *DISBANDED THE JUSTICE LEAGUE OF AMERICA*! TO DO ANYTHING THAT DRASTIC -- *ALL* OF US MUST HAVE BEEN UNDER THE CONTROL OF THAT *PSYCHO-CHEMICAL*!

I'M BEGINNING TO SEE! AND FROM WHAT *ALMOST* HAPPENED TO *ME*, IT'S LIKELY *ROBIN, KID FLASH* AND OTHERS HAVE BEEN SIMILARLY AFFECTED!

11

UPWARD INTO THE AIR THE *EMERALD CRU-SADER* IS SWUNG ON EXTENDED ARMS OF PUREST ENERGY! HE HANGS THERE, HELP-LESS, STRUGGLING DESPERATELY...

YOU CAN'T HANDLE ME WITH YOUR *POWER RING BEAMS*--ANY MORE THAN YOU DID BEFORE!

LIKE A SACK OF MEAL THE CRUSADER IS FLUNG THROUGH THE AIR--TO THUD INTO A BANK WALL...!

THUD!

HE SLUMPS TO THE SIDEWALK-- UNAWARE OF THE *KEY-MEN* WHO ARE RACING OFF...

THE *INVISIBLE DESTROYER* IS COMPOSED OF PURE ENERGY! GOT TO DO SOMETHING--TO DRAIN HIM OF THAT ENERGY...

AS THE *INVISIBLE DESTROYER* CHARGES AT HIM, THE *EMERALD GLADIATOR* FORMS A MIGHTY BATTERY WITH CLAMPS THAT GRIP HIS EERIE FOE....

I'LL CHARGE THAT BATTERY WITH THE MYSTICAL ENERGY THAT GIVES HIM LIFE!

THE *INVISIBLE DESTROYER* QUIVERS AS THE *POWER-RING BATTERY* BEGINS DRAINING HIM OF HIS LIFE-FORCE--HE QUIVERS-- FIGHTS--TO NO AVAIL! MEANWHILE...

WHEW! DID YOU SEE *GL* GET THAT GUY? I SURE WOULDN'T WANT HIM AFTER *ME*!

RELAX! *THE KEY* MADE CERTAIN HE'LL NEVER BOTHER US! HE CAN'T EVEN *SEE* US!

13

THEN EACH *JUSTICE LEAGUE* MEMBER IN TURN SITS BENEATH THE NEUTRALIZING RAYS OF THE *THANAGARIAN INSTRUMENT*...

WE ALL ACCEPT THE RISK IT MEANS--THAT UNLESS WE CAPTURE THIS CRIMINAL WHO CALLS HIMSELF *THE KEY*--WE WILL BE UNDER HIS POWER FOR THE REST OF OUR LIVES!

WHEN THE MOVIES ARE SHOWN A SECOND TIME...

*GREAT HERA!* THERE THEY ARE! THEY WERE THERE ALL THE TIME!

THAT *PSYCHO-CHEMICAL* MUST BE MIGHTY POWERFUL TO AFFECT US AS IT DID! WE NEVER MEANT TO DISBAND--SO LET'S VOTE OURSELVES BACK IN BUSINESS!

AS ONE, THE VOICES OF THE RE-FORMED *JUSTICE LEAGUE* BELLOW OUT THEIR FEELINGS...

WE VOTE TO BECOME THE *JUSTICE LEAGUE* AGAIN--AND TO GO OUT AND CAPTURE *THE KEY!*

UNFORTUNATELY, I'VE BEEN UNABLE TO LEARN THE WHEREABOUTS OF *THE KEY'S* HIDEOUT! ALL I COULD DISCOVER WAS THAT THERE WAS SUCH A PERSON--THAT HE GAVE *SNAPPER* THE *PSYCHO-CHEMICAL* AND CAUSED HIM TO GIVE IT TO US!

AND AFTER THAT--I TELEPHONED HIM! SAY, MAYBE WE CAN TRACK HIM THROUGH THAT TELEPHONE NUMBER!

WITH THE COOPERATION OF THE PHONE COMPANY THEY LEARN THE ADDRESS OF THE NUMBER *SNAPPER* DIALED, BUT...

IT'S DESERTED! *THE KEY* MUST HAVE PACKED UP HIS BELONGINGS--AND MADE TRACKS SOMEWHERE ELSE!

I'VE BEEN SCANNING THE ENTIRE *EARTH* EVER SINCE WE ENTERED THIS ROOM--BUT EVEN MY *MARTIAN VISION* CAN'T LOCATE THIS CRIMINAL!

I CAN SEE ALL THE EARTH--EXCEPT *ONE SPOT*--WHICH IS PROTECTED IN SOME MANNER--INVISIBLE EVEN TO MY *SUPER-VISION!*

COULD BE THAT *THE KEY* HAS "*LOCKED*" OFF THAT AREA! BUT BEFORE WE GO THERE, LET'S QUIZ THE *KEY-MEN HAWKGIRL* CAPTURED! MAYBE WE CAN FIND OUT SOME INFORMATION THAT'LL HELP US!

(15)

IN THE PRECINCT HOUSE WHERE THE *KEY-MEN* ARE BEING HELD...

YOU'RE FIGHTING A LOSING BATTLE!

YEAH! ALL *THE KEY* HAS TO DO TO GET CONTROL OF YOU AGAIN--IS TURN A FEW KEYS ON HIS MASTER KEY-BOARD! THEN YOU'LL BE HIS PAWNS--FORCED TO DO WHAT HE ORDERS YOU TO DO!

TAUT FACES ARE TURNED TOWARD ONE ANOTHER. THEY KNOW TOO WELL THAT THE *PSYCHO-CHEMICALS* IN THEIR BODIES HAVE BEEN NEUTRALIZED-- NOT *ELIMINATED!*

WE MUST GET TO *THE KEY'S* HIDE-OUT-- AT ONCE!

THAT HIDE-OUT--AS WE ALL KNOW NOW--IS IN OUR OWN *SECRET SANCTUARY!* IT'S THE ONLY PLACE IT COULD BE--BECAUSE *GREEN LANTERN* NOW REMEMBERS WILLING HIS *POWER RING* TO CON-CEAL IT FROM US IF EVER WE WENT LOOKING FOR IT!

THAT ISN'T ALL MY *POWER RING* HAS TOLD ME! WHEN I DESTROYED THE *SECRET SANCTUARY* I UNKNOWINGLY GAVE MY RING A DELAYED ORDER--TO WAIT AN HOUR, THEN RESTORE THE HEAD-QUARTERS AND MOVE *THE KEY* AND ALL HIS MEN AND EQUIPMENT IN THERE! HE'S IN OUR HEADQUARTERS NOW--ARMED WITH HIS KEYS THAT COULD DOOM US ALL!

STORY CONTINUES ON NEXT PAGE FOLLOWING! 16

# KEY-MASTER OF THE WORLD... PART 3

IN GRIM ARRAY THE MEMBERS OF THE RE-FORMED *JUSTICE LEAGUE* HURL THEMSELVES AGAINST THE BARRIER SURROUNDING THEIR HEADQUARTERS! BEHIND THAT BARRIER IS *THE KEY!*

AND IN HIS KEYBOARD ARE LOCKED THE ELECTRONIC CONTROLS THAT CAN REACTIVATE THE TEMPORARILY NEUTRALIZED *PSYCHO-CHEMICALS*-- TURNING THESE SUPER-HEROES INTO HIS SUPER-SLAVES!

EVEN WITH ALL OUR POWERS THE *MARTIAN MANHUNTER* AND I ARE JUST BOUNCING OFF! THE *KRYPTONITE* THAT WAS MIXED IN WITH THE *PSYCHO-CHEMICAL* MADE ME WEAKER THAN I THOUGHT!

MY *POWER RING* FORMED THE BARRIER, YET NOW IT'S POWERLESS AGAINST IT!

WHOOP! I CAN'T VIBRATE MY WAY THROUGH IT!

PANTING IN REACTION TO THEIR FUTILE SUPER-EFFORTS, THE *JUSTICE LEAGUERS* TURN TO THE *EMERALD CRUSADER* AS HE HURLS *POWER RING* BEAM AFTER *POWER RING* BEAM AT THAT IMPENETRABLE OBSTRUCTION...

YOU'RE OUR ONE HOPE, *GREEN LANTERN! YOU* MUST SMASH IT DOWN!

I--I CAN'T! I MUST HAVE WHIPPED UP SO MUCH WILL POWER TO ERECT THE BARRIER-- SPURRED ON BY THE *KEY'S* CONTROL OVER ME --THAT I'LL NEED MORE TIME TO OVER- COME IT!

WE DON'T HAVE THAT KIND OF TIME! FOR ALL WE KNOW, *THE KEY* HAS SPOTTED US HERE--AND REALIZING WHAT'S HAPPENED--MAY EVEN NOW BE TURNING THE ELECTRONIC KEYS THAT WILL RENEW HIS CONTROL OVER US! THEN WE'LL *NEVER* BE FREE OF HIM!

WAIT! I'M-- GETTING AN IDEA!

17

INSIDE THE KEY-CLUB ROOM, AN ALARM SOUNDS! THE KEY LEAPS FOR THE INTRICATE ARRAY OF KEYS AND ELECTRONIC CIRCUITS...

A QUICK TURN OF THESE KEYS-- AND THEY'LL COME UNDER MY CONTROL AGAIN!

WHEEOOOO!

ONLY MY OWN BODY VIBRATIONS CAN WORK THESE LOCKS! THIS PROTECTS ME FROM ANY OF MY KEY-MEN TRYING TO DOUBLE-CROSS ME...

BUT-- HIDDEN INSIDE EACH LOCK, WITH HIS BODY PRESSED AGAINST THE ELECTRONIC TRIGGERS, IS THE WORLD'S SMALLEST SUPER-HERO!

BY PREVENTING THE KEYS FROM MAKING DIRECT CONTACT WITH THE ELECTRONIC CONTROLS-- THEY WON'T WORK AND MY FELLOW MEMBERS WILL BE SAFE!

SATISFIED THAT HE IS ONCE MORE MASTER OF THE DESTINY OF THE JUSTICE LEAGUE, THE KEY TURNS AWAY! BUT INSIDE THE GREAT KEY-BOARD...

I WONDER HOW THE KEY'LL LIKE THESE POTATOES WHEN HE FINDS OUT WHAT I'M DOING? THIS KEY-BOARD WON'T BE WORTH A COUNTERFEIT PENNY WHEN I'M THROUGH WRECKING IT!

STILL UNSUSPECTING, THE KEY WATCHES WITH ARROGANT CONFIDENCE AS THE SHAPES OF HIS FOE APPEAR ON A VIEWING SCREEN...

BOSS! THOSE SUPER-GUYS ARE COMING IN AFTER US!

TAKE IT EASY! THEY'RE ABOUT TO COME TO A DEAD STOP-- AND RACE OFF IN THE OPPOSITE DIRECTION-- WATCH!

19

ONWARD THEY COME! DESPERATELY, *THE KEY* TURNS ONCE MORE TO HIS WONDER WEAPON!

SOMETHING'S --WRONG! THE KEY-BOARD DOESN'T--FUNCTION! I HATE TO MAKE MY NEXT MOVE BECAUSE I NEED THOSE SUPER-HEROES! BUT I MUST PROTECT MYSELF ABOVE ALL!

KEY-MEN--RELEASE THE WEAPON CONTROLS! HIT THEM WITH THE FULL FORCE OF ALL THE KEY-WEAPONS I HAVE CREATED! DESTROY THE *JUSTICE LEAGUE*--TO THE LAST ONE!

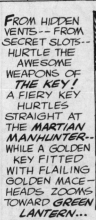

FROM HIDDEN VENTS--FROM SECRET SLOTS--HURTLE THE AWESOME WEAPONS OF *THE KEY*! A FIERY KEY HURTLES STRAIGHT AT THE *MARTIAN MANHUNTER*--WHILE A GOLDEN KEY FITTED WITH FLAILING GOLDEN MACE-HEADS ZOOMS TOWARD *GREEN LANTERN*...

OOOOH! LOSING MY SUPER-POWERS--GROWING WEAKER...

MY *POWER RING* CAN'T STOP THAT YELLOW KEY-MENACE!

A *KRYPTONITE KEY* ROCKETS TOWARD THE *MAN OF STEEL*... A FANTASTIC BLACK KEY-HOLE FLIES AT THE *FASTEST MAN ON EARTH*--A KEY-BOLA WHIRLS TOWARD *BATMAN*...

MY MUSCLES--TURNING TO WATER!

THAT BLACK KEYHOLE--LOOKS LIKE AN ENTRANCE INTO SOME EERIE DIMENSIONAL WORLD! ITS RAYS ARE GRIPPING ME--

IF THAT THING TIGHTENS AROUND ME, IT'LL CRUSH ME TO A PULP!

HAWKMAN IS THE TARGET OF A WINGED LOCK FIRING BEAMS OF TITANIC ENERGY--*WONDER WOMAN* IS MENACED BY AN ANIMATED KEY SEEKING TO CATCH HER WITH ITS LOOPED GRIP...

THE *AERIAL ACE*--WHILE DODGING THE DEADLY BEAMS FROM THE *WINGED LOCK*--FINDS THE *KRYPTONITE KEY* BELOW HIM! HE DIVES SWIFTLY AND THRUSTS IT WITH STUNNING IMPACT INTO THE ROCKY WALL!...

THESE KEY-WEAPONS SEEM TO HAVE BEEN DESIGNED FOR EACH OF US! MAYBE WE CAN DO BETTER BY SWITCHING TACTICS! I'LL TAKE ON *SUPERMAN'S* MENACE...

*SNAPPER CARR* RISKS LIFE AND LIMB IN A DESPERATE TACKLE--AS HE GRIPS AND DRAGS THE *SCARLET SPEEDSTER* FROM THE KEYHOLE WHICH IS ABOUT TO ENVELOP HIM!...

LIKE COOL, MAN! HERE'S ONE ADVENTURE I'M TAKING AN ACTIVE PART IN!

THOUGH CAUGHT BY THE LASSO-KEY, THE *AMAZON PRINCESS* COMMANDS HER OWN MAGIC LASSO TO RESCUE THE *MARTIAN MANHUNTER*...

IT'S GOOD TO BE WORKING AS A *TEAM* AGAIN!

...AND SENDS HIM LIKE A LIVING HAMMER AGAINST THE GOLDEN KEY BATTERING AWAY AT *GREEN LANTERN*...

...ENABLING THE *EMERALD WARRIOR* TO CONCENTRATE HIS ENERGIES AT THE FLAMING KEY...

MY OWN SPECIAL BRAND OF "FIRE-EATER"!

WHILE THE NOW INVIGORATED *SUPERMAN* RIPS APART THE LASSO-KEY HOLDING *WONDER WOMAN*...

SEEMS LIKE OLD TIMES, *WONDER WOMAN*-- GIVING EACH OTHER A HELPING HAND!

21

REGAINING HIS FOOTING, *THE FLASH* GRABS UP *SNAPPER* AND WHIRLS HIM ABOUT LIKE A BATON...

WITH *SNAPPER* PROVIDING THIS EXTRA SURFACE AREA, I'M WHIPPING UP A STRONG WIND-CURRENT TO KEEP THAT FLYING KEYHOLE AWAY FROM ME!

M-MAN... WH-WHAT... A... B-BLAST...

LEAPING IN, THE *MARTIAN MANHUNTER* WITH HIS SUPER-BREATH HURLS THE DIMENSIONAL KEYHOLE AND THE KEY-BOLA INTO OUTER SPACE...

VROOOOSH!

THE SPECIALIZED WEAPONS OF *THE KEY* DESTROYED, HIS *KEY-MEN* DESPERATELY TURN THEIR *KEY-GUNS* AT THE ON-CHARGING *JLA*...

*WONDER WOMAN* AND I WILL PAVE THE WAY! FOLLOW US!

SUDDENLY-- SPIKED KEYS RISE UP FROM THE VERY FLOOR OF THE HEAD-QUARTERS TUNNEL ENTRANCE-- SHARP AND DEADLY...

I'LL HANDLE THESE THINGS!

THE *MARTIAN MANHUNTER* HURLS HIMSELF FORWARD IN A ROLLING BODYBLOCK-- CLEARING A PATH FOR HIS FELLOW MEMBERS...

22

DIVING LIKE A HUNTING FALCON *HAWKMAN* SLAMS INTO TWO *KEY-MEN*...

BATMAN CLEAVES A PATH WITH FISTS THAT HIT WITH ROCK-LIKE POWER AND PRECISION...

A WHIRLING CRIMSON TORNADO REVEALS *THE FLASH* DOING HIS SPECIALTY...

OFF TO ONE SIDE, THE *TINY TITAN* CASTS OFF HIS ROLE OF "SECRET AGENT" AND DELIVERS A "KEY" BLOW OF HIS OWN...

AND FINALLY-- WITH HEAT-VISION AND *POWER-RING BEAM*-- WITH AMAZON MUSCLES AND MARTIAN MAN-POWER-- A QUARTET OF SUPER-HEROES COMPLETELY DEMOLISHES THE KEY-BOARD...

THIS IS ONE WEAPON WE DON'T DARE KEEP INTACT FOR OUR SOUVENIR ROOM!

WITH HIS KEY-MEN KNOCKED OUT-- HIS KEY-BOARD WRECKED, THE MASTER KEY TURNS HIMSELF IN...

I SUPPOSE IT'D BE TOO MUCH TO ASK YOU JUSTICE LEAGUERS HOW YOU MANAGED TO OVERCOME THE PSYCHO-CHEMICALS IN YOUR BODIES--?

OBVIOUSLY! THAT'S ONE SECRET NO KEY COULD UNLOCK!

HE KNOWS OUR EVERY WEAKNESS -- AND THE LOCATION OF OUR SECRET HEADQUARTERS! I'D BETTER WIPE THAT KNOWLEDGE FROM HIS MIND!

THEY THINK THEY'VE TRIUMPHED OVER ME -- BUT JUST BEFORE I SURRENDERED, I MANAGED TO PULL MY LAST AND GREATEST KEY TRICK!

24

AND SO AS WE TAKE LEAVE OF THE KEY, THERE REMAINS UNANSWERED THE MEANING OF HIS LAST CRYPTIC THOUGHT...

...AND UNDER WHAT DRAMATIC AND DREAD CIRCUMSTANCES THE ANSWER WILL BE REVEALED TO US-- AND THE UNWARY JUSTICE LEAGUE OF AMERICA!

The End -- AS OF NOW!

As METAMORPHO, THE ELEMENT MAN, LEAVES HIS HOUSE TO CALL UPON HIS GIRL FRIEND SAPPHIRE STAGG..

I'M ON MY WAY, SAPPHIRE, BABY. PRETTY SOON YOU AND I WILL--

HEYY! WHAT'S WRONG, YOUNGSTER?

¡SOB! EVERYBODY ON THE BLOCK B-BUT ME HAS A S-SKATEBOARD TO PLAY WITH! ¡SOB!

THEN--BEFORE THE BOY'S INCREDULOUS EYES, METAMORPHO ALTERS THE CHEMICAL STRUCTURE OF HIS BODY, WILLING THE IRON AND CARBON TO ALLOY THEMSELVES INTO...

ONE SKATEBOARD-- COMING UP! HOP ABOARD, PAL!

OH, BOY!

THE ELEMENT MAN, WHO CAN WILL THE CHEMICAL COMPONENTS OF HIS BODY TO ASSUME WHATEVER SHAPE HE WISHES, IS SOON ROLLING ALONG WITH HIS PASSENGER...

WOW! THIS IS -- FUN!

BAWW! I WANNA SKATEBOARD THAT GOES UPHILL TOO!

UNTIL, A MILE CLOSER TO THE MANSION OF SIMON STAGG, INDUSTRIALIST AND BUSINESS TYCOON...

THERE YOU ARE, KID! HOW DO YOU FEEL?

LIKE A MILLION!

AFTER DEPOSITING THE YOUNGSTER IN A TAXI TO BE DRIVEN SAFELY HOME, METAMORPHO IS ABOUT TO CONTINUE HIS JOURNEY WHEN...

HEYY! WHAT GIVES WITH MY ARMS? THEY'RE SHOOTING SKYWARD-- ON THEIR OWN!

OH, LOOK! IT'S THAT NEW SUPER-HERO METAMORPHO! I WONDER WHAT HE'S UP TO?

2

OUT OF THOSE SEEMINGLY ENCHANTED FINGERS STREAKS A CLOUD OF HYDROGEN AND CARBON GASES, FORMING A SKY-WRITING MESSAGE...

YOU ARE INVITED TO ATTEND A MEETING OF THE JUSTICE LEAGUE...

HOW ABOUT THAT! *METAMORPHO'S* WRITING HIS OWN INVITATION! THAT'S *"IN,"* BROTHER!

FOR THE PURPOSE OF DETERMINING YOUR QUALIFICATIONS TO BE A FULL-TIME MEMBER! JUST FOLLOW THE ARROW!

NO--NO! I CAN'T--!

SORRY! I GOT ME A DATE WITH THE PRETTIEST GAL IN THE WHOLE WORLD--*SAPPHIRE STAGG!* THANKS ALL THE SAME--BUT JOIN THE *JUSTICE LEAGUE?* THAT'S JUST ABOUT THE *LAST* THING I'D WANT TO DO! I'M BUZZING OFF--

FLAKE OFF, *JLA!* FUN'S FUN AND ALL THAT--BUT LEMME ALONE! IF YOU WANT A NEW MEMBER FOR THE *JUSTICE LEAGUE*--

HOLD IT, *METAMORPHO!* IF ANYBODY'S GOING TO JOIN THE *JUSTICE LEAGUE*--IT'S *ME!!*

HEY-- WHAT--?

CLANG

/3

AS THE *ELEMENT MAN* STARTS TO RESUME HIS NORMAL BODY...

WAIT, WHOEVER YOU ARE! WHY PICK ON ME? YOU GOT THINGS ALL WRONG!

CAN'T YOU GET IT THROUGH YOUR THICK SKULL I DON'T *WANT* TO BE ADMITTED TO THE *JUSTICE LEA* -- OOOPS!

SPLAT!

AND YOU *WON'T* BE, *META-MORPHO!* I'M ACCEPTING THAT INVITATION IN YOUR PLACE!

AND WHAT BETTER WAY TO DEMONSTRATE TO THE *JUSTICE LEAGUE* MY SUPERIOR QUALIFICATIONS THAN BY SHOWING YOU UP!

WHO'S ARGUING? I GOT PERSONAL REASONS FOR NOT WANTING TO JOIN THE *JUSTICE LEAGUE!* BUT YOU'RE GETTING ME *MAD!* SO LAY OFF-- OR ELSE!

IN THE SECRET HEADQUARTERS OF THE *JUSTICE LEAGUE OF AMERICA,* ITS DRAFTING COMMITTEE ON NEW MEMBERS SITS ENTHRALLED AS...

*METAMORPHO* MUST BE KIDDING! IMAGINE ANYBODY NOT WANTING TO JOIN UP WITH US!

WHAT PUZZLES ME IS-- WHO'S THE CHARACTER PLAYING BATBALL WITH HIM?

WELL, COME *ON!* WE CAN'T JUST SIT AROUND HERE AND LET *METAMORPHO* GET BANGED AROUND! HE'S IN THAT MESS ON ACCOUNT OF *US!*

RIGHT! LET'S JET OUT THERE AND GET RID OF THAT INTRUDER! WE'LL SHOW *META-MORPHO* WHAT *JLA* TEAMWORK CAN DO!

4

WITHIN MOMENTS, THE MEMBERSHIP COMMITTEE DIVES TO THE ATTACK...

I'M ALL SET TO FIGHT OUR "UNINVITED" MEMBER-- BUT WHERE IS HE?

CAN'T YOU GUYS LEAVE ME ALONE? YOU'VE GOT ME INTO ENOUGH TROUBLE AS IT IS! LET ME WORK MY OWN WAY OUT OF THIS--

SUDDENLY, FROM THE RUINS OF THE OBJECTS THE JLA'ERS HAVE DESTROYED--ERUPT ANIMATED ATOMIC PARTICLES AND "MICRO-ORGANISMS"...

THESE THINGS SPRANG TO LIFE--WHEN WE SMASHED THE WEAPONS THAT WERE BATTERING METAMORPHO!

WHATEVER THEY ARE--THEY SEEM TO HAVE AN ALIEN LIFE OF THEIR OWN!

DOESN'T MATTER TO US WHAT THEY ARE OR WHERE THEY COME FROM-- WE SHALL OVERCOME!

CALLING UPON ALL THEIR SUPER-POWERS AND SKILLS--THE JLA TEAM FINDS ITSELF EMBROILED IN A BATTLE THAT TESTS ITS EVERY RESOURCE...

NO SOONER SAID THAN--OOF!

THIS THING IS GRABBING ME--DRAGGING ME INSIDE IT!

SEE WHAT COMES OF ALL YOUR HEROICS? HOLD ON--THIS IS MY FIGHT TOO! I'LL GIVE YOU FELLOWS A HAND!

SOMEBODY SEND OUT--AN EMERGENCY SIGNAL TO-- THE REST OF THE MEMBERS! WE COULD USE HELP!

5

BUT SO OVERWHELMING IS THE ATTACK UNLEASHED UPON THE *JUSTICE LEAGUE* TEAM AND ITS CANDIDATE FOR MEMBERSHIP THAT...

GREAT KRYPTON! I CAN'T REACH MY EMERGENCY SIGNAL!

NEITHER CAN I! WE'RE GOING TO HAVE TO STOP THESE THINGS-- ON OUR OWN!

ABRUPTLY--THEIR DEADLY OPPONENTS DISAPPEAR AND THE SUPER-HEROES FIND THEMSELVES BACK INSIDE THE SECRET SANCTUARY!..

HOW'D WE GET BACK HERE?

DID OUR OPPONENTS TAKE A RUN-OUT POWDER--

--OR DID **WE?**

OKAY--NOW THAT THE PARTY'S OVER -- WILL SOMEBODY PLEASE TELL ME WHAT THIS IS ALL ABOUT?

WE WANTED TO INTERVIEW YOU AS A POSSIBLE NEW MEMBER OF THE *JUSTICE LEAGUE, METAMORPHO!* YOU'VE HAD A TASTE OF BATTLE WITH US--SO HOW ABOUT IT?

IN ONE WORD-- **NO!** YOU FELLAS JUST GOTTA UNDERSTAND THAT I *DON'T LIKE* BEING *METAMORPHO!* I JUST WANT TO GET BACK TO MY OLD SELF, *REX MASON!*

" *WHEN*--AS MY SOLDIER-OF-FORTUNE SELF-- I SET OUT WITH A REVIVED PREHISTORIC MAN-- *JAVA*--TO FIND THE *ORB OF RA* FOR SAPPHIRE'S FATHER, I NEVER IMAGINED I'D BE TRAPPED INSIDE AN EGYPTIAN PYRAMID WHERE... "

A GLOWING METEOR -- BLAZING MORE BRIGHTLY THAN AN EXPLODING SUN! I'LL BE FRIED TO A CRISP!

6

"BOMBARDED BY THE AWESOME RAYS OF THAT THROBBING METEOR, MY ENTIRE BODY AND BRAIN WERE CHANGED! I WAS NO LONGER REX MASON! I HAD BECOME AN *ELEMENT MAN*..."

THE METEOR MADE ME INTO A SUPER-BEING-- WHICH I DON'T GO FOR AT ALL! TO JOIN UP WITH YOU WOULD MEAN I'D HAVE TO KEEP BEING *METAMORPHO*--WHEN ALL I WANT IS TO BE REXY-BOY MASON--

WELL, THAT'S A SWITCH ON US SUPER-POWERED FELLOWS--!

SO THANKS FOR THE INVITE, FELLAS-- AND NO HARD FEELINGS, I HOPE!

FOR PETE'S SAKE! WE'RE ALL STANDING AROUND TALKING AS IF *NOTHING* UNUSUAL HAD HAPPENED! WHAT ABOUT THAT TOUGH FIGHT WE HAD? THE FAILURE OF OUR SIGNAL DEVICES? OUR MYSTERIOUS ATTACKER-- INVITING HIMSELF IN AS A JLA MEMBER...

BATMAN'S RIGHT! WE'VE GOT PROBLEMS-- AND NO ANSWERS...

SAY, AS LONG AS I'M HERE--MAYBE YOU CAN HELP ME OUT ON *MY* PROBLEM I'VE BEEN WAITING FOR SIMON STAGG TO FIND A WAY TO CHANGE ME BACK TO MY NORMAL SELF, BUT--

*YOU* COULD DO WHAT HE HASN'T BEEN ABLE TO, *GREEN LANTERN*--WITH YOUR *POWER RING*!

IF THAT'S YOUR CHOICE-- WHY NOT?

TURN ON THE JUICE, *GL*! I'M ANXIOUS TO GO OUT AFTER THE UNKNOWN PARTY WHO *WANTS* TO BE A *JUSTICE LEAGUE* MEMBER!

7

A VERDANT BEAM STABS OUTWARD TOWARD THE *ELEMENT MAN*...

MAN, LIKE I CAN HARDLY WAIT!

SUDDENLY THAT BEAM STOPS IN MID-AIR...

COME ON--DON'T KEEP ME IN SUSPENSE!

SOMETHING'S WRONG! I CAN'T WILL MY *POWER RING BEAM* ANY FURTHER--CAN'T GET IT TO TOUCH AND CHANGE YOU!

THEN AS EVERY EYE IS FOCUSED ON THE GREEN GLOW...

IT'S CHANGING SHAPE!

WHAT FORCE CAN POSSIBLY BE STRONG ENOUGH TO AFFECT *GREEN LANTERN'S POWER RING?*

8

# ★JUSTICE★ LEAGUE of AMERICA

# METAMORPHO SAYS NO-- PART 2

BEFORE ANY MEMBER OF THE *JUSTICE LEAGUE* CAN MOVE-- FASTER EVEN THAN *FLASH* OR *SUPERMAN* OR *METAMORPHO* CAN REACT TO THE EERIE FORM THAT SUDDENLY FASHIONS ITSELF FROM THE POWER BEAM --THE RING-ENERGY EXPLODES OUT- WARD IN A SUNBURST OF AWESOME FURY!
FROM IT STAB RAYS OF LIGHT THAT ENVELOP THE MEMBERS AND THEIR GUEST AS A TELEPATHIC VOICE ERUPTS INSIDE THEIR BRAINS!

I HAVE THE POWER AND WILL TO GAIN CONTROL OVER *GREEN LANTERN'S* POWER RING BEAM--FOR I AM --*THE UNIMAGINABLE!* THE MIND OF MAN CANNOT CONCEIVE WHAT MY TRUE SHAPE IS, FOR MAN'S EYES ARE NOT CAPABLE OF REGISTERING THAT SHAPE UPON HIS BRAIN!

"I CAME INTO EXISTENCE LONG AGO ON A PLANET SO FAR FROM YOUR *EARTH* THAT NO TELESCOPE HAS EVER SEEN ITS STAR-SUN! FOR UNTOLD EONS I LIVED, AND MY POWERS GREW AND MATURED TO ABSOLUTE PERFECTION..."

I AM WEARY OF MY WORLD. I WOULD GO OUT INTO SPACE TO OTHER STARS AND OTHER PLANETS.

"BY TAKING THOUGHT, I WAS ABLE TO RISE SPACEWARD--TO DART FROM STAR TO STAR--UNSEEN AND UNIMAGINED! MANY WERE THE STRANGE AND WONDERFUL THINGS I SAW--YET NONE SO UNUSUAL AS THE *JUSTICE LEAGUE* ITSELF..."

AMAZING--AND EXCITING--HOW THOSE BEINGS OF EARTH ARE BATTLING THE METALLIC CREATIONS OF *KRAAD THE CONQUEROR* ON THE PLANET *ARALAX!*

"SINCE I FOUND NOTHING TO EQUAL YOU CREATURES IN ALL THE EONS OF WANDERING THE STAR-PLANETS, I SECRETLY FOLLOWED YOU TO *EARTH*, WATCHING YOU PERFORM MANY MORE MARVELS..."

THEY HAVE ME ENTHRALLED! HOW WILL THEY GET OUT OF *THIS* SITUATION?

"SO IMPRESSED WAS I THAT WHEN YOU COMMITTEE MEMBERS MET TO DECIDE UPON A NEW CANDIDATE FOR ADMISSION, I WAS THERE..."

WE CERTAINLY MUST CONSIDER THE *ELONGATED MAN!*

YES--AND *ADAM STRANGE* AS WELL...

HOW ABOUT THAT NEW SUPER-HERO-- *METAMORPHO!*

METAMORPHO LOOKS LIKE A SHOO-IN TO ME...

ALL MY LIFE I'VE BEEN A "LONER"! NOW I'LL TEAM UP WITH THESE OTHER SUPER-BEINGS!...eh? THEY'RE OFFERING MEMBERSHIP TO *METAMORPHO?* I'LL HAVE TO MAKE THEM CHANGE THEIR MINDS--IN MY FAVOR!

"SWIFTLY, I MADE PLANS..."

WHAT BETTER WAY TO PROVE MY DESIRABILITY AS A MEMBER OF THE *JUSTICE LEAGUE* THAN TO SHOW I'M FAR MORE POWERFUL THAN MY RIVAL?

"WELL, YOU KNOW WHAT HAPPENED! YOU INTERFERED JUST WHEN I WAS PROVING MY SUPERIORITY OVER THE *ELEMENT MAN*..."

WHAT'S THIS? THE *JUSTICE LEAGUE* MEMBERS HAVE COME TO RESCUE *METAMORPHO*! I DON'T WANT TO FIGHT *AGAINST* THEM -- I WANT TO FIGHT *WITH* THEM!

"PREVENTING YOU FROM SIGNALING THE REST OF YOUR TEAM, I BROKE OFF THE FIGHT-- BUT IT TOOK A LITTLE TIME FOR MY ENERGIES TO FADE OUT, WHICH IS WHY YOU HAD TO GO ON FIGHT-ING! THEN I SWITCHED YOU TO YOUR HEADQUARTERS.."

SOON AS I'M AT FULL STRENGTH, I'LL REJOIN THE *JUSTICE LEAGUE*!

NOW I'M HERE TO BE ADMITTED TO MEMBER-SHIP! OF COURSE, THE VOTE WILL BE UNANIMOUS --

NOT SO FAST, *UNIMAGINABLE*! WE HARDLY KNOW ANYTHING ABOUT YOU!

AS FAR AS I'M CON-CERNED MY VOTE WILL BE-- *NO*!

SAME HERE!

FOOLS! YOU *CAN'T* TURN ME DOWN! I'M A BETTER FIGHTER THAN ALL OF YOU PUT TOGETHER-- INCLUDING YOU, *SUPERMAN*! I MAY BE *UNIMAGINABLE* -- BUT MY POWERS ARE VERY REAL! I'LL GIVE YOU ONE LAST CHANCE TO CHANGE YOUR MINDS, OR ELSE --

NEVER MIND THE *OR ELSE!* THE ANSWER IS STILL *NO!*

THEN YOU GIVE ME NO CHOICE! YOU'RE GOING TO HAVE TO FIGHT ME--AND WHEN I OVERWHELM YOU, YOU'LL BE *FORCED* TO ACCEPT ME AS YOUR NEWEST MEMBER! READY? HERE WE GO!!

INSTANTLY THE *JUSTICE LEAGUE* QUINTET--ALONG WITH CANDIDATE *METAMORPHO* --FIND THEMSELVES OUTSIDE THE SECRET SANCTUARY BATTLING STARTLING CREATURES NONE OF THEM HAS EVER SEEN BEFORE...

THIS THING SEEMS TO GROW TENTACLES AT WILL!

THIS CREEP IS STICKY AS FLY-PAPER!

GO ON--HIT ME! SEE IF I CARE! YOU CAN'T HURT THE SOLID MARBLE I'VE CHANGED MYSELF INTO!

MY FIST-- PLUNGES OFF THIS ALIEN-- WITHOUT HARMING IT!

I CAN'T DO ANY- THING AGAINST THOSE YELLOW FLAMES!

THIS LIFE-FORM IS GRIPPING ME SO HARD I MUST VIBRATE AT ULTRA-SUPER-SPEED TO TEAR FREE FROM ITS CLUTCH!

CAUGHT BY SURPRISE AT FIRST--HURLED INTO COMBAT BEFORE THEY ARE READY FOR IT--THE SUPER-HEROES RALLY TO THE FRAY...

THERE IS NO ESCAPE FROM ENTITIES SUCH AS THESE! IN ALL THE UNTOLD MILLENNIA OF THEIR EXISTENCE, ONLY I--**THE UNIMAGINABLE**--HAVE BEEN ABLE TO SUBDUE THEM!

--YOU MEAN, UP TO **NOW**!

'AT'S TELLING HIM, **SUPERMAN**!

WE'RE NOT SCARED OF ANY-THING!

WE'VE GOT A PRETTY GOOD RECORD TOO--NEVER LOST A FIGHT YET!

AND WE'RE NOT GOING TO START NOW! SO GET SET TO COUNT TO TEN OVER THESE CREATURES WHEN WE SPOIL THEIR RECORDS!

WHY SHOULD I LET MYSELF GET CLOBBERED? I'LL SIMPLY TURN INTO A **GAS**! LET'S SEE WHAT YOU CAN DO NOW, BUB!

**GREEN LANTERN'S POWER RING** FLARES TO GREEN-HOT INTENSITY! THEN..

THOSE RAYS OF YOURS WON'T BE VERY STRONG ONCE I "RAIN" YOU ALL OVER A COUPLE OF ACRES OF GOOD OLD MOTHER EARTH!

ALMOST AT THE SAME MOMENT, THE **COWLED CRUSADER** TENSES HIS MIGHTILY MUSCLED BODY--HEAVES HIS FOE...

MY FIRST LAW OF SURVIVAL IS--ALWAYS TAKE ADVANTAGE OF AN OPPORTUNITY!

**WHOOOPS!** THIS ENTITY IS YANK-ING ME INSIDE IT!

13

WHIRLING LIKE AN INDIAN DERVISH--HIS ARMS CHURNING LIKE SUPER-SWIFT PROPELLER BLADES--THE *FASTEST MAN ON EARTH* CREATES A BLAST OF AIR THAT...

UP YOU GO, MY ALIEN FOE! BUT NOW THAT I'VE GOT YOU THERE-- WHAT DO I DO WITH YOU?

JUST HOLD IT THERE, *FLASH!* I'LL WRAP THIS UP--!

THE *MAN OF STEEL* WHIPS HIS FOE FULL INTO THAT LIVING CURTAIN...

I HATE TO SAY THIS--BUT IT'S CURTAINS FOR YOU!

AS THE OVERWHELMED FOES MAKE CONTACT...

I NEVER THOUGHT I'D SEE *KARATCHOK* OR *PHENTHOL* SUFFER DEFEAT!

KA-VOOOM

THE MOMENTARY SILENCE ON THE FIELD OF BATTLE IS BROKEN WHEN *THE UNIMAGINABLE* HURLS ANOTHER THREAT...

EVEN IF YOU DEFEAT MY EVERY WARRIOR IN THIS SKIRMISH BETWEEN US-- YOU SHALL YET LOSE THE "WAR"! *NOTHING* CAN *DEFEAT ME!*

THE BLOWHARD'S GOT A POINT THERE! HOW YOU GONNA BEAT SOMETHING YOU CAN'T SEE!

SNARLING IN HIS THROAT, *SUPERMAN* HURTLES UPWARD...

I CAN'T SEE *THE UNIMAGINABLE*-- BUT I CAN SEE THAT BOWL-PAWN OF HIS! SO WHEN THE MASTER ISN'T AROUND I'LL TAKE ON THE SERVANT!

14

ACROSS INTERSTELLAR SPACE STREAKS *THE UNIMAGINABLE*...

BY DROPPING AN ATOM OFF MY BODY HERE AND THERE -- I'M LEAVING A TRAIL FOR THOSE *JUSTICE LEAGUERS* TO FOLLOW! WHEREVER *THE UNIMAGINABLE* IS HEADED -- HE'S GOING TO WIND UP WITH PLENTY OF COMPANY!

BEHIND HIM, ON THE SCORCHED BATTLEFIELD OF *EARTH*...

WELL, WE DEFEATED THE *UNIMAGINABLE'S* FIRST SHOCK TROOPS -- BUT THE WORST IS YET TO COME!

TOO BAD WE DON'T KNOW HIS HOME BASE -- SO WE CAN BRING THE FIGHT TO HIM!

HOW ABOUT THAT *METAMORPHO?* HE DUCKED OUT ON US EVEN BEFORE THE FIGHT WAS OVER!

AND WE WERE ALL SET TO ENROLL HIM IN THE *JLA!*

NEVER MIND HIM NOW! WE HAVE PROBLEMS ENOUGH WITHOUT CONCERNING OURSELVES ABOUT THE *ELEMENT MAN!*

LET'S RETURN TO HEADQUARTERS AND TALK OVER WAYS AND MEANS TO FIGHT *THE UNIMAGINABLE!*

SOON AFTERWARD, THEY FILE INTO THE SECRET SANCTUARY...

FOR IF *THE UNIMAGINABLE* EVER BEATS US -- AND WE REFUSE TO TAKE HIM INTO THE *JLA* --

--HE'LL TAKE US TO HIS WORLD AND KEEP US PRISONERS TO FIGHT FOR HIM WHEN THE MOOD STRIKES HIM!

LOOK--!

⑰

# METAMORPHO SAYS NO -- PART 3

UPWARD INTO SPACE SURGES THE SUPER-HERO QUINTET OF EARTH! AND SPANGLED ACROSS THE FIRMAMENT--VISIBLE FIRST TO THE EYES OF *SUPERMAN* AND THEN THE OTHER MEMBERS --ARE THE "SIGN-POST" ATOMS FROM *METAMORPHO'S* BODY! BLAZING LIKE JEWELS, THEY LEAD THE *FABULOUS FIVE* TOWARD THE VERY RIM OF THE UNIVERSE!

SUDDENLY, THE LINE OF ATOMS CURVES-- TOWARD A *SUPER-NOVA* IN THE THROES OF AN ERUPTION...

*THE UNIMAGINABLE* VEERED OFF HERE TO GO PAST THAT EXPLODING STAR!

WHAT POSSIBLE CONNECTION COULD THERE BE BETWEEN *THE UNIMAGINABLE* AND A *SUPER-NOVA?* *

*EDITOR'S NOTE:

A STAR WHICH EXPLODES CATA- STROPHICALLY, LIBERATING MOST OF ITS ENERGY. IT IS A THOUSAND TIMES AS BRIGHT AS AN ORDINARY NOVA, RELEASING AS MUCH ENERGY IN *ONE* SECOND AS OUR SUN DOES IN *60 YEARS!*

IT'S HARD TO BELIEVE HE ACCIDENTALLY STRAYED OFF COURSE!

COULD BE THAT HE ABSORBS THE VAST ENERGIES RELEASED BY A *SUPER-NOVA* TO GIVE HIM HIS INCREDIBLE POWERS!

I'LL LIGHT UP THOSE ENERGIES AND SEE WHERE THEY LEAD TO!

SURE ENOUGH-- THEY'RE HEAD- ING IN THE SAME DIRECTION AS THE ATOMS GIVEN OFF BY *METAMORPHO!* LOOKS LIKE *FLASH* HAS HIT THE RIGHT ANSWER!

IF *THE UNIMAGINABLE* IS GOING TO ABSORB THOSE *SUPER-NOVA* ENERGIES-- HE'S GOING TO ABSORB *US* AS WELL! I'M CHANGING YOU ALL INTO "NEGATIVE" RADIANT ENERGY SO YOU CAN BLEND WITH THE ENERGIES OF THE *SUPER-NOVA!*

AS WISPS OF COLORED LIGHT, THE *FABULOUS FIVE* FUSE WITH THE TITANIC FORCES UNLEASHED BY THE EXPLODED STAR! AS SUCH THEY ARE SWEPT ALONG THROUGH SPACE AT UN- GUESSABLE SPEEDS...

20

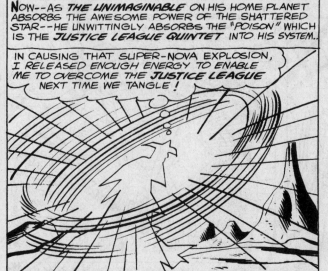

NOW--AS *THE UNIMAGINABLE* ON HIS HOME PLANET ABSORBS THE AWESOME POWER OF THE SHATTERED STAR--HE UNWITTINGLY ABSORBS THE "POISON" WHICH IS THE *JUSTICE LEAGUE QUINTET* INTO HIS SYSTEM..

IN CAUSING THAT SUPER-NOVA EXPLOSION, I RELEASED ENOUGH ENERGY TO ENABLE ME TO OVERCOME THE *JUSTICE LEAGUE* NEXT TIME WE TANGLE!

INSIDE THE UNPERCEIVABLE FORM OF THEIR FOE, THE SUPER-HEROES ARE LIKE TINY *MOTES* OF LIVING MATTER-- SWEPT ALONG BY COLOSSAL COSMIC FORCES INTO THE VERY BEING OF *THE UNIMAGINABLE*...

IT'S AS IF WE'RE BEING SWEPT ALONG THROUGH HIS "*BLOOD STREAM*"!

MUST BE BYPASSING HIS "HEART"!

THUMPA! THUMP! THUMPA! UMP!

THE ENERGIZED *SUPERMAN* AND *BATMAN* LASH OUT SAVAGELY, RELEASING SOME OF THEIR OWN RADIATIONS IN A PULSE-STUNNING ATTACK...

GOT TO KEEP PUNCHING AWAY--AND HOPE I'M MAKING CONTACT WITH SOMETHING INSIDE *THE UNIMAGINABLE'S* "BODY"!

WHAP! SOK!

WHIRLED ALONG THROUGH ANOTHER PART OF THEIR TITANIC FOE-- *FLASH* AND *GREEN LANTERN* FIND THEM-SELVES SURROUNDED BY TREMENDOUS MENTAL FORCES...

SSSSSSS! WHIRRR! ZZZZT! SSSSSSS

SOUNDS LIKE WE'RE DRIFTING THROUGH THE CREATURE'S "BRAIN"!

21

INSTANTLY THE **SCARLET SPEEDSTER** WHIRLS INTO ACTION...

LET'S SEE HOW OUR FOE STANDS UP UNDER THIS **SHOCK-WAVE** TREATMENT!

NOT FAR AWAY, **GREEN LANTERN** IS HAMMERING AWAY HIMSELF...

ENOUGH OF THESE BLOWS OUGHT TO KNOCK HIM OUT!

REDUCING HIMSELF TO ATOMIC SIZE, THE **TINY TITAN** ADDS HIS STRENGTH TO THE AWESOME BATTLE...

**THE UNIMAGINABLE** IS GOING TO END UP WITH A BODY OF MESSED-UP ATOMS!

TO AID HIS FRIENDS COMES **METAMORPHO**-- WILLING HIMSELF INTO A GREAT PROPELLER BLADE THAT CUTS AND SLASHES AS IT TRAVELS...

IF ANYTHING WILL STOP THIS THING-- OUR **SIX-WAY ATTACK** OUGHT TO DO IT!

THE REALIZATION THAT HIS DOOM IS UPON HIM OVERWHELMS **THE UNIMAGINABLE**...

SOMEHOW-- THE **JUSTICE LEAGUE** HAS FOUND THE ONE WAY TO OVERCOME ME -- BY BECOMING PART OF MY BODY! I CAN'T DESTROY THEM -- WITHOUT DESTROYING MYSELF!

22

INSIDE *THE UNIMAGINABLE, SUPERMAN* SMASHES ABOUT LIKE AN EXPLODING ATOM BOMB--*THE FLASH* ROTATES AT MULTI-LIGHT SPEEDS--*GREEN LANTERN* POWER-RINGS APPENDAGES TO INERT LIFELESSNESS--*ATOM, BATMAN* AND *METAMORPHO* BATTER AWAY AT THE DELICATE WALLS OF RADIANT ENERGY...

A LONE CRY SCREECHES ACROSS THE PLANET...

*GYARRRGH! I CANNOT BREAK FREE OF THE THINGS THAT ARE OVERWHELMING ME! THE JUSTICE LEAGUE-- HAS WON--AGAIN...*

THERE IS A GASP... A SILENCE! THEN AS THE *JLA* REGAINS ITS NORMAL SHAPE ...

WHAT'S HAPPENED TO *THE UN-IMAGINABLE?*

THERE'S NO WAY OF KNOWING!

MAYBE IT SIMPLY CEASED TO EXIST!

HEYY-- HOW ABOUT YOU GUYS GIVING ME A HAND AND GATHER UP MY ATOMS? THEY MUST BE FLOATING ALL OVER SPACE BY THIS TIME!

FASHIONING A SPACE-VACUUM CLEANER, *GREEN LANTERN* DRAWS *METAMORPHO'S* STRAY ATOMS FROM THE VOID...

WHILE YOU'RE AT IT, *GL*-- HOW ABOUT GIVING ME THE FULL TREATMENT-- CHANGING ME INTO *REX MASON*-- AS YOU WERE ABOUT TO DO BEFORE *THE UNIMAGINABLE* SO RUDELY INTERRUPTED?

23

THE ROYAL FLUSH IS THE STRONGEST HAND IN THE GAME OF POKER, JUST AS IT PROVES TO BE IN THE GAME OF LIFE-AND-DEATH WHICH THE ROYAL FLUSH GANG CHALLENGES THE JUSTICE LEAGUE OF AMERICA TO PLAY!

FOR BACKING UP THE ACE, KING, QUEEN, JACK AND TEN IS A STRANGE POWER THAT CHECKS THE SUPER-HEROES AS THE FIVE WIZARDS OF THE CARD DECK GO ABOUT COMMITTING --

# THE CARD CRIMES OF THE ROYAL FLUSH GANG!

JUSTICE LEAGUERS

SUPERMAN

BATMAN

Wonder Woman

FLASH

HAWKMAN

AND AS THE JOKER OF THE GAME -- SNAPPER CARR!

ROYAL FLUSHERS

THE ACE

THE KING

THE QUEEN

THE JACK

THE TEN

ON A MAIN BOULEVARD, AS DUSK ENFOLDS *MIDWAY CITY*, A FANTASTIC FIGURE RACES FROM A LOCAL BANK...

AS THESE COPS ARE ABOUT TO FIND OUT--THE *THREE OF CLUBS* IS THE CARD FOR *SORROW!*

NATIONAL BANK

SUDDENLY THE FLIPPED CARD ERUPTS IN A SPRAY OF BRILLIANT LIGHT...

;SOB; I FEEL SO WEEPY--AND SAD--

TEARS BLINDING ME ;SOB; CAN'T SEE TO SHOOT!

HA! HA! I'M THE ONLY ONE WHO'S *HAPPY* AROUND HERE!

IN AN EMERGENCY LIKE THIS, *MIDWAY CITY* POLICE COMMISSIONER GEORGE EMMETT HAS BUT ONE RECOURSE! HIS HURRY-CALL TO CARTER (*HAWKMAN*) HALL AND HIS WIFE SHIERA (*HAWKGIRL*) AT THE MUSEUM BRINGS INSTANT RESULTS...

THERE HE IS!

WHAT A BIZARRE GET-UP! HE LOOKS LIKE A LIVING PLAYING CARD!

OUT OF THE UNIFORM THAT CONCEALS HIS IDENTITY, THE *CLUB KNAVE* DRAWS AN ODD "CLUB" WEAPON...

YOU'RE ABOUT TO LEARN WHAT A "CARD" I REALLY AM, *HAWKMAN!*

UPWARD FLIES THAT CLUB MISSILE--TO BURST FORTH INTO A BREATHTAKING FIREWORKS DISPLAY...

IT'S TAKEN ON THE SHAPE OF THE *SEVEN OF SPADES--* THE CARD THAT FORETELLS A-- *DISAGREEMENT!*

;BRRR; I FEEL A SUDDEN CHILL...

NUMBNESS OVERCOMING ME...

2

SHAKING OFF THAT MOMENT OF INTENSE COLD, THE **WINGED WONDER** DRIVES DOWNWARD AT PULSE-STUNNING SPEED...

FUN AND GAMES IS FINE, **JACK**--BUT HERE'S WHERE I TOP YOUR PLAY WITH A "ROCKCRUSHER HAND"!

HAWKMAN--NO!

YOU'RE GOING AT IT THE WRONG WAY! YOU'LL NEVER CATCH THE **KNAVE** DOING THAT!

YOU TELL HIM, **HAWKGIRL**!

THE **SEVEN OF SPADES** IS TAKING EFFECT--MAKING THE TWO BICKER AND QUARREL ABOUT EVERYTHING THEY DO! HA!HA!

I'LL SHOW YOU HOW TO NET HIM-- THE CORRECT WAY!

YOUR TURN, **HAWKMAN**! YOU **KNOW** SHE ISN'T DOING IT THE WAY IT SHOULD BE DONE!

UNABLE TO HELP HIMSELF-- FORCED BY EMANATIONS FROM THE SEVEN OF SPADES TO QUARREL AT ANYTHING AND EVERYTHING--**HAWKMAN** REACHES OUT AND...

THAT NET IS FROM NOWHERE-- LET ME HAVE IT!

WHY, YOU-- BLUNDERING FOOL! YOU'VE SPOILED EVERYTHING!

THE ONLY HELP YOU WERE-- WAS TO AID THAT CROOK! I'D HAVE FLATTENED HIM WITH ONE PUNCH IF YOU HADN'T INTERFERED!

I'D HAVE NETTED HIM BY NOW IF YOU WEREN'T SUCH A **KNOW-IT-ALL**!

HAHAHA! WHILE THEY JAW AT EACH OTHER, I'LL MAKE MY GETAWAY!

MANY MILES AWAY IN *CENTRAL CITY*, AT THE *METROPOLITAN ART GALLERY*...

FOR THE *KING OF CLUBS*--A ROYAL TREASURE OF ART!

A TIMELY ENTRANCE--BY THE *FASTEST MAN ON EARTH*..

THOSE KAYOED GUARDS YOU LEFT AT THE ENTRANCE-- LED ME STRAIGHT TO YOU!

THANKS FOR THE NEWS-FLASH, *FLASH*! NOW I HAVE ONE FOR YOU!

THESE *FIVE DIAMONDS* MEAN UNEXPECTED NEWS--IN YOUR CASE *BAD NEWS*!

SEE SPOTS IN FRONT OF MY EYES-- WHIRLING ROUND AND ROUND...

WHEN YOUR VISION CLEARS, EVERYTHING YOU SEE FROM NOW ON--WILL LOOK LIKE *THIS*! HA! HA! HA!

4

SUDDENLY *THE FLASH* SEES THE WORLD ABOUT HIM AS A CUBIST PAINTING! ANGLES -- SHAPES -- FORMS -- BECOME A NIGHTMARE BEFORE HIM ...

WHERE'S THAT CROOK? I CAN'T PICK HIM OUT IN THIS MAD, MAD WORLD!

HE LEAPS TOWARD WHERE HE THINKS HE SEES THE *KING OF CLUBS*, BUT...

OVER HERE, FLASH!

THUMMP!

THE *SCARLET SPEEDSTER* LASHES OUT WITH A VICIOUS HOOK BUT...

CLINK!

OWWW!

HA! HA! HA! THESE CARD GIMMICKS ARE EVERY-THING *THE ACE* SAID THEY'D BE!

WHILE ON A RAISED PLATFORM AT A FASHION DISPLAY BY THE *HOUSE OF STYLE, WONDER WOMAN* -- GARBED AS *THE QUEEN OF DIAMONDS FOR A DAY* -- IS MODELING FOR CHARITY...

SO INTENT ARE ALL EYES ON THE PRETTY MODELS AND THE FASHIONS THEY DISPLAY, THAT NO ONE NOTICES ...

A *QUEEN OF CLUBS* IS BETTER THAN A *QUEEN OF DIAMONDS* ANY DAY -- AS *WONDER WOMAN* IS ABOUT TO FIND OUT!

WITH THE SWIFTNESS OF A LEAPING PANTHER, THE *CLUB QUEEN* STRIKES...

*I'LL* TAKE THAT DIAMOND CLOAK, *WONDER WOMAN!* I WARN YOU--IT'LL BE A WASTE OF TIME TRYING TO STOP ME!

*GREAT HERA!*

I'M PAYING FOR THE CAPE WITH THIS *TWO OF SPADES!* IN FORTUNE-TELLING ARGOT--IT MEANS A *REMOVAL* OR *LOSS!*

I'LL STOP YOU FAST ENOUGH WITH MY MAGIC LASSO!

THE CARD'S ENLARGING-- SHIELDING HER FROM MY ROPE!

THE *DEUCE* YOU SAY!

YOU WERE LUCKY, *WONDER WOMAN!* IF THE WHOLE CARD HAD FALLEN ON YOU, YOU'D HAVE LOST *ALL* YOUR *SUPER-POWERS!*

AS IT IS--SINCE YOU HALVED THE CARD, IT WILL ONLY DE- PRIVE YOU OF HALF YOUR GREAT ABILITIES!

IT'S CLINGING TO ME! GOT TO-- TEAR IT LOOSE!

THEN--AS THE *AMAZON PRINCESS* LEAPS FORWARD, SHE DISCOVERS TO HER HORROR...

*MERCIFUL MINERVA!* I CAN'T GET UP NEARLY ENOUGH SPEED TO CATCH HER-- AND MY MAGIC LASSO ONLY GOES *HALFWAY* TOWARD WHERE SHE'S RUNNING!

AND NOW FOR THE *TRAVEL CARD*-- THE *NINE OF DIAMONDS!* YOU'RE ON YOUR WAY TO THE *JUSTICE LEAGUE'S SECRET SANCTUARY*-- SO YOU'D BETTER ALERT YOUR FELLOW MEMBERS TO MEET YOU THERE!

OBEDIENT TO THE STRANGE POWER RADIATING FROM THE MYSTIC CARD, *WONDER WOMAN* TOUCHES THE SIGNAL DEVICE IN HER TIARA...

AN OVERWHELMING POWER--FORCING ME TO SUMMON THE *JUSTICE LEAGUE* TO AN EMERGENCY MEETING!

OH--AND ONE MORE THING--

EXIT

YOU'D BETTER STOP OFF IN *CENTRAL CITY* AND PICK UP *THE FLASH!* HE'S SO GROGGY BY THIS TIME YOU'LL HAVE TO LEAD HIM THERE BY THE HAND!

SOON AFTER-- AT THE ENTRANCE- WAY TO THE SECRET HEAD- QUARTERS OF THE *JUSTICE LEAGUE...*

WHY DON'T YOU *CARRY FLASH, WONDER WOMAN?* IF HE'S IN TROUBLE OF SOME SORT, *THAT'S* NO WAY TO HELP HIM!

WHAT'S COME OVER *HAWKMAN?* ORDINARILY, HE WOULDN'T BE TELLING *WONDER WOMAN* HOW TO HANDLE SUCH A SITUATION!

7

INSIDE THE MEETING ROOM, WHERE THEY HAVE BEEN JOINED BY *SUPERMAN* AND *SNAPPER CARR*, THE STORIES OF THE CARD-CONTROLLED TRIO ARE QUICKLY TOLD...

*WE'LL* HAVE TO DEAL WITH THESE CARD-CROOKS! THE OTHER MEMBERS ARE INVOLVED IN CRITICAL CASES OF THEIR OWN!

WHO NEEDS *THEM*? THEY'D ONLY GET IN OUR WAY!

POOR *HAWKMAN*! HE'S ALL SHOOK UP! HE JUST CAN'T HELP SQUABBLING WITH EVERYONE!

ONE THING'S CLEAR--THE MERE FACT THAT THIS NEW GANG STEERED CLEAR OF *ME* SHOWS NO *MAGIC* OR *KRYPTONITE* WAS INVOLVED!

HOW ABOUT *ME*?! IT BUGS ME THAT THEY DIDN'T EVEN THINK ENOUGH OF *BATMAN* TO TRY AND STOP HIM! MAN, THAT HURTS!

AHH, STOP COMPLAINING, *BATMAN*! THAT'S *MY* DEPARTMENT!

INSTEAD OF THINKING ABOUT OURSELVES, WE BETTER GET DOWN TO THE BUSINESS AT HAND--HOW TO CAPTURE THAT CARD GANG!

*MOAN* A BIG HELP *I'LL* BE--WHEN I CAN'T EVEN SEE STRAIGHT!

# CARD CRIMES of the ROYAL FLUSH GANG
### PART TWO

FAR FROM THE SECRET SANCTUARY ARE GATHERED FIVE FANTASTICALLY GARBED FELONS! ALONG WITH THE PREVIOUSLY SEEN *JACK, QUEEN* AND *KING* OF CLUBS ARE *THE ACE*-- MASTERMIND OF THE GROUP-- AND *TEN SPOT,* WHOSE MUSCLES BULGE WITH ALMOST INHUMAN STRENGTH!

NOW THAT WE'VE GATHERED THE *JUSTICE LEAGUE* TOGETHER--WE'RE ALL SET TO BRING ABOUT THEIR UTTER DEFEAT AND ANNIHILATION!

AS HIS EYES SURVEY HIS CARD-CLAD COHORTS, *THE ACE* RECALLS WITH SATISFACTION HOW THE *ROYAL FLUSH GANG* CAME INTO BEING...

I'VE BEEN GAMBLING ALL MY LIFE WITH CARDS! WHILE MAKING AN INTENSE STUDY OF THEM AND THE LAWS AND SCIENCE OF GAMBLING-- I STUMBLED ONTO AN AMAZING DISCOVERY--!

THERE IS A STRANGE FORCE THAT INFLUENCES CARDS AND THEIR LUCK! THAT'S WHY THEY'RE USED TO TELL FORTUNES! EVEN ASTROLOGERS MAINTAIN THAT SOMETHING ABOUT THE STARS "IMPELS" PEOPLE TO ACT AS FORETOLD IN THEIR HOROSCOPES...

"I ISOLATED THAT FORCE--WHICH I CALL *STELLARATION*-- THEN WENT TO GREECE TO CONTINUE MY RESEARCHES.."

I MUST INVENT A MACHINE TO "TRAP" THIS *STELLARATION* SO I CAN PUT IT TO USE--COMPELLING PEOPLE TO ACT IN WHATEVER MANNER I CHOOSE!

"I SPENT UNCOUNTED WEEKS PERFECTING A SPECIAL INSTRUMENT TO GATHER IN *STELLARATION* AND INTENSIFY IT..."

ONCE THE CARD HAS ABSORBED ENOUGH STAR-FORCE, I CAN RELEASE THIS *STELLARATION*-- BY FOCUSING IT ON A PERSON-- AND THROUGH AUTO-SUGGESTION INDUCED BY A FORTUNE-TELLING CARD--TO COMPEL HIM TO DO AS I SAY!

"IN MY EARLIER YEARS I HAD BEEN THE CHILDHOOD LEADER OF THREE OTHER BOYS AND A GIRL. WE'D SHARED MANY STREET FIGHTS AND THEFTS AND KNEW JUST HOW TO WORK AS A TEAM...

WE GOT AWAY WITH IT!

THANKS TO YOU, *PUDGE!* YOU ALWAYS FIGURE OUT NEAT WAYS TO STEAL AND GET AWAY SAFELY!

"AFTER CHECKING OUT MY STELLARATION CARDS-- I GOT IN TOUCH WITH MY OLD FRIENDS AND MADE THEM A PROPOSITION..."

WE'LL TEAM UP AGAIN--AS THE *ROYAL FLUSH GANG*--WITH CARD-LIKE UNIFORMS TO SUIT! *CLUBS* ARE CARDS OF BAD FORTUNE--FOR OTHERS! SO WE'LL CHOOSE IT FOR OUR UNIFORMS!

WHY BOTHER WITH UNIFORMS? WE'D DO JUST AS WELL WEARING FACE-MASKS--

10

SURE--BUT IF WE'RE GOING TO BE THE BEST GANG IN THE BUSINESS, LET'S MATCH IT--WITH THE BEST UNIFORMS!

QUEENIE'S RIGHT! BESIDES, WHEN THE LAW TRIES TO STOP US--IT'LL FIND OUT THE CARDS ARE ALWAYS STACKED AGAINST IT!

WELL? YOU SAW HOW MY STELLARATED CARDS OVERCAME HAWKMAN, FLASH AND WONDER WOMAN! ARE YOU CONVINCED? ARE YOU ALL READY TO DEAL DEATH TO THE JUSTICE LEAGUE?

LEAD THE WAY, ACE! LET'S SHUFFLE OFF!

MOMENTS LATER, THE ROYAL FLUSH GANG RACES TO ITS D-FOR-DESTRUCTION DATE WITH THE JUSTICE LEAGUE OF AMERICA...

ALWAYS REMEMBER--THE STELLARATION FORCE IS OF NO USE UNLESS IT'S FOCUSED ON ITS VICTIMS!

WE DON'T EVEN HAVE TO BLUFF 'EM-- WE HOLD ALL THE TOP CARDS!

YEAH! AND IF ANY OF THE JUSTICE LEAGUERS AREN'T ON HAND--WE'LL GET THE REST LATER ON!

IN THE SECRET SANCTUARY, HONORARY JLA MEMBER SNAPPER CARR IS MONITORING THE GREAT WORLDWIDE RADIO WHICH IS TUNED IN ON ALL POLICE AND INTERPOL CALLS, WHEN...

HEY, CATS! SLANT YOUR EAR-DRUMS IN THIS DIRECTION!

HEAR ME, JUSTICE LEAGUERS--ONE AND ALL! THIS IS THE ACE OF CLUBS-- CUTTING IN ON A POLICE BROADCAST TO CHALLENGE YOU TO A "MATCH PLAY" AGAINST MY WINNING ROYAL FLUSH COMBINATION!

HAWKMAN, FLASH AND WONDER WOMAN HAVE ALREADY SAMPLED OUR POWERS! TO THEM--AND THE REST OF THEIR TEAMMATES-- THE ACE ANNOUNCES THAT HIS OPENING LEAD WILL BE A LOOTING RAID ON THE PLATEAU CITY BANK! WILL YOU BE THERE -- OR DO YOU PREFER TO SIT THIS GAME OUT?

STAY PUT, FELLOW MEMBERS! I'LL HANDLE THIS *ROYAL FLUSH GANG* BY MYSELF! THOSE TRICK CARDS WON'T AFFECT *ME*!

DON'T BE A SUPER-HOG, *SUPERMAN*! EVERYBODY GOES OUT ON THIS CAPER! THE CHALLENGE WAS ISSUED TO THE *WHOLE JUSTICE LEAGUE*!

I GO ALONG WITH *HAWKMAN*! THIS CALLS FOR A JOINT EFFORT-- EXCLUDING *FLASH*, OF COURSE! HIS EYES--

HOLD ON! NOBODY PUTS *ME* IN A DISCARD PILE! JUST GUIDE ME OUT THERE! I CAN WHIP UP SOME TROUBLE FOR THOSE *ROYAL FOURFLUSHERS* WITH A WHIRLWIND OR TWO!

AND SO-- BY *BAT-JET* AND *ROBOT PLANE*, WITH *SUPERMAN* AND *HAWKMAN* CLEAVING THE AIR-- THE JLA QUINTET SOON ARRIVES AT THE *PLATEAU CITY BANK*...

BRACE YOURSELF, *FLASH*! YOU'RE ABOUT TO HIT PAY DIRT!

I'VE CONTACTED POLICE COMMISSIONER EMMETT TO KEEP THE POLICE OUT OF THIS! IT'S OUR GAME TO WIN, LOSE, OR DRAW!

PLATEAU CITY BANK

AS HIS FEET TOUCH TERRA FIRMA, THE *SCARLET SPEEDSTER* STARTS WHIRLING-- WHILE THE *MAN OF STEEL* RIPS UP THE VERY PAVEMENT ALONG WHICH THE *PASTEBOARD PIRATES* FLEE...

SOMEONE TELL ME HOW I'M DOIN'...!

GREAT, *FLASH*! YOU'RE BLOWING UP A STORM!

HERE'S WHERE I DRAW A HAND AGAINST THAT *ACE OF CLUBS*! I'VE BEEN SLIGHTED LONG ENOUGH!

12

WE'RE PLAYING DEALER'S CHOICE, BATMAN--AND YOU'VE DRAWN-- THE FOUR OF DIAMONDS!

YOU MUST HAVE DEALT ME A WINNING CARD! YOUR HOCUS-POCUS DIDN'T WORK ON ME!

ZOK!

MEANWHILE, CLUB QUEEN GRAPPLES WITH THE AMAZON PRINCESS...

YOU'RE NOT HALF-STRONG ENOUGH TO STOP ME, HONEY-- THANKS TO MY DEUCE OF SPADES!

I SENT YOU OFF ON ONE TRIP-- NOW YOU'RE GOING ON ANOTHER!

THUD!

TO ADD TO THAT CRASH-LANDING, WONDER WOMAN, I'M GOING TO HIT YOU WITH THE NINE OF SPADES--THE SICK-NESS CARD!

13

FLYING TO WHERE THE ACTION IS, *HAWKMAN* ZEROES IN ON THE *JACK OF CLUBS*...

I DEBATED MYSELF WHETHER TO TACKLE THE *JACK* OR *TEN*-- *YOU* LOST, *JOCKO!*

I'M CUTTIN' IN, *HAWKMAN*-- AND YOU CAN'T ARGUE ABOUT THE RESULT!

*POW!*

FROM ABOVE THE EMBATTLED CRIMINALS AND CROOK-CATCHERS COMES THE *MAN OF STEEL*..

I'VE TWISTED THIS GIRDER INTO A FIVE-WAY HANDCUFF WHICH I'LL LOOP ABOUT THOSE PASTEBOARD PUNKS TO CARRY THEM OFF TO JAIL!

BUT EVEN AS HE IS ABOUT TO "HANDCUFF" TWO OF THE CARD-GANG--

I'LL USE THE *TEN* AND *JACK* FOR OPENERS!

--*BATMAN* RAMS INTO HIM WITH FLYING FEET!

HEY! WHOSE SIDE YOU ON--?

*OOOF!* WHO HIT ME!

WHY'D YOU GANG UP ON ME, BATMAN?

I--I COULDN'T HELP IT! I GOT A DOSE OF THE FOUR OF DIAMONDS-- THE CARD OF BETRAYAL!

SO YOU GOT CARDITIS, TOO! I TOLD YOU TO LEAVE THIS GANG TO ME! JUST CLEAR OUT OF MY WAY--

BUT AS SUPERMAN PLUNGES PAST THE MASKED MAN-HUNTER...

TRIPPED ME--

--RIGHT INTO HAWKMAN--KNOCKED HIM OUT OF THE WAY AS I DID FLASH!

THUD!

ONLY ONE WAY TO STOP BATMAN FROM BETRAYING ME--KNOCK HIM OUT TOO! I'LL APOLOGIZE LATER!

ZOK!

15

OOOH--DO I FEEL AWFUL! NEVER FELT SO SICK IN MY LIFE--

ALL THE OTHERS ARE OUT OF ACTION! THAT LEAVES IT UP TO ME TO WHEEL-AND-DEAL WITH THE *ROYAL-FLUSH* CROOKS!

AS HE QUICKLY OVERTAKES HIS CARD-QUARRY...

YOU SHOULD HAVE STAYED PAT, *SUPERMAN!* NOW YOU GET MY ACE-IN-THE-HOLE CARD--THE *ACE OF SPADES!*

AND SINCE IT'S BEEN TREATED WITH *STELLARATION* FROM A *GIANT RED STAR*- IT'S STRONG ENOUGH TO WEAKEN--AND *DOOM* YOU!

FLOODED WITH WEAKNESS AS HIS SUPER-POWERS SEEP AWAY, *SUPERMAN* DROPS TO HIS KNEES...

I HAVE WON! I HAVE GAINED MY LONG SOUGHT-FOR REVENGE OVER THE *JUSTICE LEAGUE!* THEY CAN NEVER THREATEN ME AGAIN!

16

# CARD CRIMES of the ROYAL FLUSH GANG

## PART THREE

BATTERED BY THE EERIE CARD EMANATIONS OF THE *ROYAL FLUSH GANG*, THE *JUSTICE LEAGUERS* FACE UNCONDITIONAL DEFEAT. *WONDER WOMAN* IS *SICK!* *SUPERMAN* IS JUST ANOTHER HUMAN BEING! *FLASH* CANNOT SEE STRAIGHT! *BATMAN* IS UNDER A COMPULSION TO BETRAY HIS FELLOW MEMBERS! AND *HAWKMAN* FEELS CALLED UPON TO DISAGREE WITH ANYTHING AND EVERYBODY--EVEN HIMSELF!

*VICTORY,* THEN, IS VERY REMOTE ...*UNLESS...*

BATMAN--THE *BETRAYER*--THAT'S ME!

NO MATTER HOW MUCH I ARGUED WITH YOU, *BATMAN*-- I COULDN'T CONVINCE YOU YOU'RE NOT RIGHT! THESE CARDS ARE THE SOURCE OF OUR PROBLEMS...

WE'VE ALL BEEN CARD-JINXED--

I--FEEL WEAK-- BUT ONLY IN COMPARISON TO MY ACCUSTOMED SUPER-POWERS!

I GUESS IT'S JUST AS WELL I *CAN'T* SEE WHAT'S GOING ON!

MOMENTS LATER, THE MEMBERS ARE ON THEIR WAY BACK TO THEIR HEADQUARTERS...

YOU'LL HAVE TO GIVE ME A LIFT TOO, *BATMAN!*

I'LL FLY YOU BACK, *WONDER WOMAN!* MAYBE THE COOL UPPER AIR WILL DO YOU GOOD!

17

WHEN THEY ENTER THEIR SECRET SANCTUARY...

BACK SO SOON! YOU CAPTURED THE *ROYAL FLUSH GANG,* HEY?

BOY, COULD I ARGUE WITH YOU ON *THAT* SCORE!

WE FAILED, *SNAPPER!* WE WERE HOOKED BY PLAYING CARDS--

EVERYTHING THAT HAPPENED-- WAS MY FAULT!

YOU COULDN'T HELP--

*OOOPS! BATMAN-- WATCH* IT! YOU LED ME RIGHT INTO A CHAIR!

YOU SEE? I'M STILL BEING FORCED TO BETRAY YOU ALL!

IN GROWING DISMAY, *SNAPPER* LISTENS TO THEIR TALE OF WOE-- THEN SHEDS SOME LIGHT IN THE ROOM OF GLOOM...

AWW, COME ON, EVERYBODY! CHINS UP AND ALL THAT JAZZ! THERE'S GOTTA BE *SOME* WAY OUTTA THIS MESS!

YOU NAME IT, KIDDO -- AND I'LL ARGUE YOU OUT OF IT! WE'RE STOPPED COLD FROM EVERY ANGLE!

WITH DESPERATION IN HIS VOICE, THE YOUNGEST MEMBER OF THE *JUSTICE LEAGUE* APPEALS TO THE OTHERS...

*SUPERMAN? FLASH? BATMAN? WONDER WOMAN?*

I'M JUST A HAS-BEEN NOW...

I'D ONLY BETRAY EVERY-BODY...

I SEE WHAT YOU MEAN, *SNAPPER*-- BUT THAT'S *ALL* I CAN SEE...

I'M SICK... SICK... SICK...

THEN HE DELIBERATELY SWINGS ON THE *WINGED WONDER*...

YEAH! AND *HAWKMAN* HASN'T GOT THE *SENSE* TO HELP US!

WHAT'S THAT? NO SENSE? WHY, I'D HAVE *YOU* KNOW THAT *I* KNOW EVERYTHING ANY-BODY ON EARTH KNOWS-- THANKS TO MY *ABSORBASCON \*!*

*EDITOR'S NOTE: A SUPER-SCIENTIFIC DE-VICE THAT EXTRACTS ALL KNOWLEDGE FROM INTELLIGENT MINDS AND FEEDS IT TO ITS USERS!

18

MY SCHEME'S WORKING! I'VE GOT *HAWKMAN* ARGUING WITH ME!

IZZAT SO? HOW COME *YOU* COULDN'T FIGURE OUT WHAT MAKES THOSE CARDS WORK-- WHAT GIVES THEM THEIR POWER OVER YOU ALL!

I COULDN'T, HEY? I'LL SHOW YOU, BRIGHT BOY...

STUNG TO IRRITATION BY *SNAPPER'S* NEEDLING TACTICS, THE *AERIAL ACE* CONCENTRATES...

ALL KNOWLEDGE ON EARTH IS LOCKED IN MY BRAIN! ALL I HAVE TO DO IS SUMMON IT TO MY CONSCIOUS MIND! QUIET, EVERYBODY! I WANT TO SHOW THIS FUGITIVE FROM A *DISCOTHEQUE* WHAT I CAN DO!

I HAVE IT! THOSE CARDS ARE FILLED WITH A FORM OF STAR RADIATION CALLED *STELLARATION!* THAT'S WHAT MADE US THE WAY WE ARE! HOW ABOUT *THAT, SNAPPER?*

YOU'RE CLICKING ON ALL BRAIN CYLINDERS SO FAR, *HAWKMAN* --BUT--

I'LL LAY PAY *YOU* COULDN'T WORK UP SOME OF THAT *STELLARATION* AND FILL *ME* WITH IT!

BIG DEAL! I COULD DUPLICATE THAT *STELLARATION* IN THE LABORATORY DOWN BELOW-- BUT I'D RATHER STAY HERE AND DEBATE THE ISSUE WITH YOU!

CONSTANTLY CAJOLING AND NEEDLING THE *FLYING FURY,* SNAPPER PLAYS CLEVERLY UPON HIS *STELLARADIATED* BRAIN UNTIL...

OKAY, YOU'VE WON YOUR POINT! I'LL FILL YOU UP WITH *STELLARATION!*

TALK! ALL TALK! LET'S SEE SOME ACTION AROUND HERE! *DO IT!*

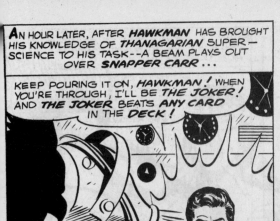

AN HOUR LATER, AFTER *HAWKMAN* HAS BROUGHT HIS KNOWLEDGE OF *THANAGARIAN* SUPER-SCIENCE TO HIS TASK--A BEAM PLAYS OUT OVER *SNAPPER CARR* ...

KEEP POURING IT ON, *HAWKMAN!* WHEN YOU'RE THROUGH, I'LL BE *THE JOKER!* AND *THE JOKER* BEATS *ANY CARD* IN THE *DECK!*

NOW AS *"THE JOKER"* I'LL TRUMP THE PLAY OF THE *ROYAL FLUSH GANG* -- LIKE THIS!

WHAT ARE YOU-- *HEYY!* SNAPPER! I'M BACK TO MY NORMAL SELF AGAIN! AND I DON'T EVEN WANT TO ARGUE ABOUT IT!

AS FAST AS HIS LEGS CAN CARRY HIM, *SNAPPER* RACES INTO THE COUNCIL ROOM AND MAKES CONTACT WITH THE CARD-STRICKEN MEMBERS...

*OHH!* MY SICKNESS HAS LEFT ME--I CAN SENSE THE RETURN OF ALL MY AMAZON POWERS!

*BATMAN*--YOUR *"BENEDICT ARNOLD"* DAYS ARE OVER!

I CAN SEE AGAIN! AND *SNAPPER*-- YOU'RE A SIGHT FOR SORE EYES!

I FEEL MYSELF BEING CHARGED WITH MY GOOD OLD SUPER-POWERS!

THE NEXT MOMENT *SNAPPER* IS CAUGHT UP IN A TORRENT OF BACK-SLAPS-- AND A *KISS!*

20

21

FLAMING SPADES STAB THE AIR IN THE NEXT ROOM, THROUGH WHICH THE **ROYAL FLUSH GANG** HAS FLED...

WATCH IT! FLAMING SPADE PIPS--

THE ACE IS SURE PLAYING A *HOT HAND* ALL RIGHT!

KEEP GOING! I'M CALLING A SPADE A SPADE-- *SUPERMAN-STYLE!*

FURTHER ON, A HUGE CHANDELIER OF DIAMOND PIPS SHOWERS DEADLY CHEMICALS DOWN ON THE *FEARSOME FOURSOME*...

I'LL HANDLE THE ACTION HERE!

I'LL KEEP THAT STUFF UP--OUT OF HARM'S WAY!

*whew!* IT'S AN *INSTANT DIS-SOLVENT!* IF IT HAD EVER TOUCHED US--!

CORNERED IN THE LAST ROOM, **THE ACE** PREPARES HIS FINAL COUP...

BY JOINING HANDS, WE'VE MADE OURSELVES A STAR-RADIATION UNIT! WE'LL HIT 'EM WITH OUR OWN *COMBINED STELLARATION*-- BLAST 'EM OUT OF EXISTENCE!

OKAY, *W.W.* AND *MR. B*-- YOU KNOW WHAT TO DO!

THIS IS THE LAST HAND, FOLKS! AND IT'S GOING TO BE A *WHAMMER!*

23

JUST AS SNAPPER'S CONTACT WITH US ELIMINATED OUR STELLARATION -- SO DID IT DO TO THE ROYAL FLUSH GANG!

QUICK HANDS UNMASK THE ROYAL FLUSHERS...

THE ACE OF CLUBS IS PROFESSOR AMOS FORTUNE -- THE MAN WE'VE DEFEATED TWICE BEFORE!*

*EDITOR'S NOTE: JLA #6: "THE WHEEL OF MISFORTUNE" AND JLA #14: "MENACE OF THE ATOM BOMB."

MY STELLARATION GIMMICK WORKED NO BETTER THAN MY STIMOLUCK WHICH ACTIVATED YOUR LUCK GLANDS-- OR MY DE-MEMORIZER!

THAT MAKES IT THREE STRIKES AND OUT, PROFESSOR!

LATER, IN THE JUSTICE LEAGUE'S HEADQUARTERS...

THIS IS GOING IN OUR SOUVENIR ROOM, SNAPPER -- AS A MEMENTO OF THE JOKER WHO DEFEATED THE ROYAL FLUSH GANG!

I--I'M SO PROUD-- I COULD BUST!

SNAP! SNAP!

The End

24

"WITH MY RING POWERLESS, I LASHED OUT WITH A FIST AIMED AT ITS HEAD -- BUT..."

EH? MISSED IT COMPLETELY!

SHADES OF GOLIATH! NO WONDER I WASN'T ON TARGET! I'VE DOUBLED IN SIZE! THAT SUITS ME -- I CAN USE MY SIZE-- ADVANTAGE TO --

THAT TAKES CARE OF IT! NOW TO COME UP WITH THE ANSWER TO THIS MYSTERY!

WHAK!

POWER RING -- WHAT CAUSED THIS INSTANT-GIANT ROUTINE?

IT WAS A DELAYED REACTION-- DUE TO YOUR BODY ABSORBING AN ANTIBODY FROM THE UNIMAGINABLE WHILE YOU AND YOUR FELLOW JUSTICE LEAGUE MEMBERS FOUGHT HIM INSIDE HIS BODY *!

* EDITOR'S NOTE: JUSTICE LEAGUE OF AMERICA #42: METAMORPHO SAYS -- NO!

"MYSTIFIED BY THE INABILITY OF THE POWER RING TO RID ME OF THE ALIEN ANTIBODY--ALTHOUGH IT COULD ENLARGE MY UNIFORM TO FIT MY NEW SIZE--I FLEW TO THE PLANET WHERE WE'D BATTLED THE UN-IMAGINABLE..."

WE NEVER DID LEARN WHAT HAPPENED TO THE UNIMAGINABLE WHEN WE OVERCAME HIM -- BUT MAYBE I CAN FIND SOMETHING HERE TO USE AS AN ANTIDOTE!

3

"WHILE I SEARCHED FOR THAT ELUSIVE SOMETHING-- SOMETHING ELSE GRABBED ME..."

GREAT GUARDIANS! I COMPLETELY FORGOT THAT THE UNIMAGINABLE HAD IMPRISONED HERE SOME OF THE MOST FEARSOME MENACES OF THE UNIVERSE! THEY'VE BROKEN LOOSE--!

"I LASHED OUT AT IT WITH A BLAST FROM MY POWER RING..."

TH-THIS TH-THING IS SHAKING M-ME TO PIECES! G-G-GOT TO S-S-STOP IT BEFORE I F-FLY APART!

"BUT TO MY AMAZEMENT, THE CREATURE SURROUNDED ITSELF WITH AN AURA LIKE A GOLDEN FOG--THROUGH WHICH MY RING-WEAPON COULD NOT GO!..."

WHAT I'D LIKE TO KNOW IS-- HOW COME I ALWAYS SEEM TO COME UP AGAINST MENACES THAT USE YELLOW WHEN I FIGHT THEM? IT'S ENOUGH TO GIVE ME A COMPLEX!

"SUDDENLY THE BEAST LET GO OF ME! SOMETHING I COULDN'T SEE HAD ATTACKED IT FROM BEHIND..."

NOW WHAT?

4

"'WE BARRELED DOWN HERE WHILE YOU WERE FIGHTING THAT CREATURE! SUPERMAN GRABBED IT--YANKED IT AWAY FROM YOU--AND YOU KNOW THE REST...'"

"AFTER COMPARING STORIES WE REALIZED THAT *FLASH* AND *ATOM* MIGHT ALSO HAVE BEEN AFFECTED-- SINCE THEY HAD BEEN INSIDE *THE UN- IMAGINABLE'S* BODY TOO! SURE ENOUGH, WHILE *FLASH* WAS IN HIS CIVILIAN IDENTITY..."

OWTCH! BUMPED MY HEAD ON THE LABORATORY CEILING! HOW--

"QUICKLY THE TRUTH DAWNED ON HIM AS IT HAD ON *BATMAN* AND ME..."

IF ANYBODY SEES ME LIKE THIS-- I'LL NEVER BE ABLE TO APPEAR AS *THE FLASH* WITHOUT REVEALING MY SECRET IDENTITY! GOT TO GET OUT OF HERE--

"AND SO THE FASTEST MAN ON EARTH VIBRATED TO INVISI- BILITY--DARTED THROUGH WALLS-- AND EMERGED IN HIS OWN HOME..."

I'LL USE THE *FLASH* UNIFORM I KEEP COMPRESSED IN THIS RING--AND THE SPARE ONES I KEEP HANDY-- TO MAKE ONE BIG ENOUGH TO FIT ME!

"JUST AS THE SCARLET SPEEDSTER WAS ABOUT TO DON HIS OUTSIZED GARMENT..."

THAT GREEN BEAM--! LIFTING ME SKYWARD--!

...AND SO WE FEEL OUR ONLY HOPE TO RESTORE YOUR *STATUS QUO* IS TO FIND AN ANTIDOTE ON THIS PLANET, PERHAPS FROM WHAT'S LEFT OF *THE UNIMAGINABLE*, IF WE CAN FIND A TRACE OF HIM!

WHERE DO WE START LOOKING?

"IT WAS BATMAN WHO YELLED A WARNING..."

WE'D BETTER START LOOKING THERE-- BECAUSE WE'RE IN FOR TROUBLE!

I KIND OF WELCOME A FIGHT! I FEEL PRETTY MEAN RIGHT NOW! I JUST REALIZED THAT CAROL FERRIS MIGHT NOT BE TOO HAPPY WITH A TWELVE-FOOT-HIGH BOY FRIEND!

THE QUINTET OF SUPER-HEROES MAY NOT NEED AN ANTIDOTE TO THE STRANGE ANTI-BODIES WHICH HAVE INCREASED THE NORMAL SIZE OF FOUR OF THEM!

FOR RACING TOWARD THEM COMES A NEW AND MIGHTY MENACE ON THIS AMAZING WORLD! UNLESS THEY DEFEAT THAT MENACE ... WELL, READ ON!

# THE PLAGUE THAT STRUCK THE JUSTICE LEAGUE-- PART 2

"GALLOPING TOWARD US CAME FIVE OF THE MEANEST-LOOKING MENACES YOU EVER TOUCHED EYEBALL TO! THESE WERE ONLY *SOME* OF THE OFF BEAT CHARACTERS THAT *THE UNIMAGINABLE* HAD ROUNDED UP FROM OTHER PLANETS AND KEPT IMPRISONED ON HIS WORLD!
AS YOU KNOW, WE HAD ALREADY FOUGHT--AND BEATEN--FIVE OF THOSE WARRIORS WHILE ON EARTH! THE SECOND FIVE LOOKED TWICE AS TOUGH AND ROUGH..."

"THE *COWLED CRUSADER* DIDN'T WAIT FOR HIS FOE TO GET TO HIM! HE THREW ONE OF HIS PATENTED PUNCHES ON THE RUN!"

HUH? MY KING-SIZED FIST DIDN'T EVEN MAKE HIM WINCE!

YAA-HHH!

MY BIGGER-THAN-USUAL SIZE MUST HAVE SAPPED MY STRENGTH!

ZOK!

9

"WITH PANTHER-LIKE FURY, *BATMAN* LEAPED UP AND CHARGED BACK..."

MY BEST BET IS TO JUDO-HANDLE HIM--TURN HIS STRENGTH AGAINST HIM!

"NEARBY, *FLASH* CIRCLED ABOUT HIS TARGET-- TYPICAL SUPER-SPEED STYLE--WHEN TO HIS DISMAY..."

I SHOULD HAVE HIM WHIRLING LIKE A TOP BY NOW--BUT THIS DOUBLE SIZE OF MINE SEEMS TO HAVE CUT MY SPEED DOWN BY HALF!

*uhh!* CAT-CREATURE STRUCK SO FAST-- I COULDN'T EVEN SEE HIM COMING!

THERE'S MORE THAN ONE WAY TO SKIN A CAT--

SKREEE--!

HERE'S WHERE I COOL HIM OFF-- IN THE WATER BELOW!

CATS FEAR WATER-- AND SO DOES THIS CAT-BEAST JUDGING BY THE PANICKY CONTORTIONS HE'S GOING THROUGH TRYING TO BREAK FREE!

"I MYSELF WAS HAVING NO PICNIC WITH MY TORNADO-- LIKE CHALLENGER..."

MY POWER RING'S GOING AT ONLY HALF BLAST! CAN'T WORK UP ENOUGH JUICE TO HOLD OFF THAT BAG OF WIND!

"UP, UP, UP I WAS LIFTED ON THE AIRY ARMS OF THAT AWESOME ANNIHILATOR..."

GOING TO WHIP ME DOWN ON THE JAGGED ROCKS BELOW? NOT BEFORE I GET ONE MORE POWER-RING-SHOT AT IT!

*"WHILE ALL THIS ROCK-AND-ROLLING WAS GOING ON-- SUPERMAN AND SUPER-ROBOT MET WITH BONE-RATTLING RAGE..."*

KLANG!

THIS THING IS JUST AS SUPER-STRONG AS I AM!

IT HITS GOOD, TOO! WELL, I'VE ONE THING GOING FOR ME IT HASN'T!

CRASH!

SOK!

I CAN FLY--AND IT CAN'T! I'M GOING TO TURN MY-SELF INTO A HUMAN MISSILE--

--ZERO DOWN ON IT--

--AND TURN THAT ROBOT INTO A BIG NOTHING!

CRASH!

13

"THEN THERE WAS QUIET, WITH ONLY OUR PANTING VOICES TO SHATTER THE SILENCE...."

WE STOPPED 'EM ALL RIGHT--BUT WE'RE NO NEARER THE SOLUTION TO OUR PROBLEM! HOW DO WE GET BACK TO NORMAL SIZE?

BY FINDING THE REMAINS OF THE UNIMAGINABLE--AND SEARCHING THROUGH THEM FOR A CLUE TO OUR CURE!

SUPERMAN-- YOU START THE SEARCH!

"CRISS-CROSSING THE PLANET WENT SUPERMAN'S TELESCOPIC VISION...."

I DON'T KNOW WHAT WE DID TO HIM-- BUT THERE'S NO SIGN OR TRACE OF THE UNIMAGINABLE ANYWHERE!

THAT MEANS WE MAY NEVER BE ABLE TO RESUME OUR NORMAL IDENTITIES!

LOOKS LIKE WE'VE REACHED A DEAD END--

PERHAPS I CAN BE OF HELP!

WHO ARE YOU?

I AM DOCTOR BENDORION! I, ALONE, OF ALL THE CREATURES THE UNIMAGINABLE SPACENAPPED ONTO HIS PLANET, AM A MAN OF PEACE, BEING A SCIENTIST AND A PHYSICIAN!

AS THE GREATEST MEDICAL MAN IN THE GALAXY, THE UNIMAGINABLE BROUGHT ME HERE TO ADMINISTER TO HIS ARMY OF WARRIORS! I AM QUITE FAMILIAR WITH THE UNIQUE ANTIBODY THAT HAS AFFECTED YOU--AND CAN CURE YOU...

14

HA! A REGULAR *BENDORION CASEY!*

I DON'T CARE WHO HE IS-- IF HE CAN CURE US, I'M HIS PATIENT!

I'LL NEED THE FACILITIES OF A WELL-EQUIPPED MEDICAL LABORATORY! PERHAPS ON YOUR HOME WORLD THERE MIGHT BE ONE AVAILABLE TO ME?

THE *JUSTICE LEAGUE* HAS ONE OF THE FINEST LABORATORIES ON EARTH IN ITS *SECRET SANCTUARY!*

GOOD! BUT I WARN YOU, TIME IS PRECIOUS! AFTER YOU FOUR ABSORBED THE ANTIBODIES FROM *THE UNIMAGINABLE,* THEY UNDERWENT AN "INCUBATION PERIOD"... AFTER WHICH YOU BECAME "ILL"...

DURING THAT INCUBATION PERIOD YOUR BODIES WERE *CARRIERS* OF THE PLAGUE WHICH YOU TRANSMITTED TO WHOMEVER YOU CAME IN CONTACT WITH! NOW FOR THE WORSE NEWS OF ALL-- UNLESS YOU ARE CURED, YOU FOUR WILL DIE IN *TEN HOURS--* TO BE FOLLOWED BY THE DEATHS OF THE OTHERS YOU HAVE TOUCHED--

I GAVE *IRIS WEST--*THE KISS OF DEATH!

*CAROL FERRIS--* IN DEADLY DANGER!

JEAN LORING-- DOOMED!!

*ROBIN!* WHAT HAVE I DONE TO YOU?

THERE'S NO TIME TO WASTE! *GREEN LANTERN,* BEAM US TO THE *SECRET SANCTUARY--* WHILE WE SIGNAL THE OTHER MEMBERS TO MEET US THERE!

AS *GREEN LANTERN* CONCLUDES HIS STORY....

THIS IS *DOCTOR BENDORION--*THE SOLE HOPE OF ALL US PLAGUE-STRICKEN PEOPLE!

PLEASE-- CAN I GO TO WORK NOW? I HAVE LESS THAN TEN HOURS TO FIND AND USE THAT CURE!

MEANWHILE, HAVING BEEN ALERTED TO *HIS* POSSIBLE DANGER BY A HURRY-UP CALL FROM THE *JLA, METAMORPHO* BURSTS INTO THE *SECRET SANCTUARY...*

I BETTER CUT OUT FROM CIVILIZATION TILL I'M CURED TOO! I WAS ALSO INSIDE *THE UNIMAGINABLE!*

THERE IS NO NEED FOR THAT! WHEN *GREEN LANTERN* VACUUMED UP YOUR UNTAINTED ATOMS FROM INTERSTELLAR SPACE AND REPLACED THEM IN YOUR BODY, THE HEALTHY ATOMS DE-STROYED THE ANTI-BODIES!

15

THEN WHAT'S THE BIG PROBLEM? ALL YOU HAVE TO DO IS ADD SOME OF MY ATOMS TO YOUR BODIES AS A CURE-ALL--

A GOOD IDEA--BUT IT WON'T WORK! YOUR ATOMS EXHAUSTED THEIR THERAPEUTIC VALUE WHEN THEY CURED YOU!

AS *METAMORPHO* LEAVES, *SUPERMAN* LEADS *DOCTOR BENDORION* INTO THE LABORATORY WHILE *WONDER WOMAN* BUSILY STITCHES...

I'LL HAVE THIS DOUBLE-SIZE UNIFORM READY FOR YOU IN A FEW MINUTES, *BATMAN!*

SUITS ME, WONDER WOMAN! BUT BE CAREFUL HOW YOU GIVE IT TO ME--I DON'T WANT TO CONTAMINATE YOU!

THEN... HERE YOU ARE, BATMAN--

LISTEN--EVERYBODY!

ATTENTION, *JUSTICE LEAGUE!* GANGS OF CROOKS HAVE STORMED INTO *SEACOAST CITY!*--WIELDING ASTONISHING POWERS AS THEY COMMIT CRIMES...

*SUPER-CROOKS* RUNNING RIOT IN *SEA-COAST CITY*--AND ONLY A NUMBER OF THE *JUSTICE LEAGUERS* WHO DARE RESPOND TO THE EMERGENCY CALL!

(16)

# JUSTICE LEAGUE of AMERICA

# THE PLAGUE THAT STRUCK THE JUSTICE LEAGUE...PART 3

THE *SECRET SANCTUARY* ERUPTS WITH A CALL TO ARMS! DANGER THREATENS FROM BANDS OF SUPER-CROOKS SWARMING ALL OVER *SEACOAST CITY*-- AND THE *JUSTICE LEAGUE* IS AT PART STRENGTH! FOUR OF ITS MEMBERS DARE NOT VENTURE OUT TO DEFEND THE CAUSE OF LAW AND ORDER FOR FEAR OF DOOMING ANYONE THEY COME IN CONTACT WITH!

POLICE UNABLE TO COPE WITH THE SUPER-POWERED THIEVES! *JUSTICE LEAGUE*--PLEASE RESPOND--

--OR WE'D SPREAD OUR TERRIBLE GROWTH-PLAGUE EVEN MORE!

JUST OUR LUCK! WE'RE IN ISOLATION! WE CAN'T GO OUT AND STOP THEM--

RELAX, YOU GUYS! YOU HAD YOUR INNINGS FIGHTING *THE UN-IMAGINABLE* AND HIS WARRIORS! *WE'RE* TAKING OVER!

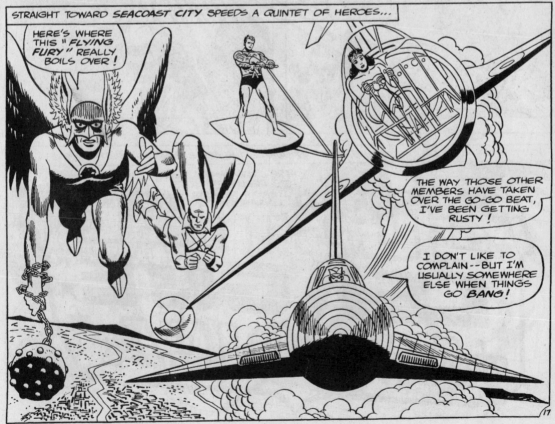

STRAIGHT TOWARD *SEACOAST CITY* SPEEDS A QUINTET OF HEROES...

HERE'S WHERE THIS "FLYING FURY" REALLY BOILS OVER!

THE WAY THOSE OTHER MEMBERS HAVE TAKEN OVER THE GO-GO BEAT, I'VE BEEN GETTING RUSTY!

I DON'T LIKE TO COMPLAIN--BUT I'M USUALLY SOMEWHERE ELSE WHEN THINGS GO *BANG!*

17

SHORTLY, OVER *SEACOAST CITY*...

HERE GOES THE OPENING SHOT AT THOSE BANK-THIEVES-- A TEAR-GAS ARROW TO TURN THEIR LAUGHTER TO TEARS!

HA! HA! WE'RE READY AND WAITING FOR YOU, *GREEN ARROW!*

SEA-COAST CITY BANK

THEY'RE RUNNING RIGHT THROUGH MY SMOKE-SCREEN --WITHOUT SHEDDING A TEAR!

HA! HA! OUR SUPER-POWERS TOOK THAT ATTACK IN STRIDE!

DOWNWARD DROPS *WONDER WOMAN*...

ONCE I GET MY MAGIC LASSO AROUND THEM, THEY'LL BE SUBJECT TO MY COMMANDS!

WONDER WOMAN-- YOU'RE ABOUT TO BECOME *BLUNDER WOMAN!*

AS ONE OF THE RACING MEN WHIRLS AND GESTURES...

WW-- YOUR MAGIC IS AS PHONY AS YOU ARE! HA! HA!

MERCIFUL MINERVA! HE FROZE MY NOOSE IN MID-AIR-- WITH A WAVE OF HIS HAND!

NOW IT IS THE TURN OF THE *"FLYING FURY"* TO SAMPLE THE EERIE POWERS OF THE THIEVES...

HERE COMES *HAWKMAN!* I'D FEEL BETTER IF I HAD A WEAPON TO HANDLE HIM!

ONE GUN COMIN' UP!

18

THE THIEF LIFTS HIS BARE HAND AND MAKES LIKE A GUN...

ALL I HAVE TO DO IS SAY--

BANG! I GOT YA, HAWKMAN!

;UHH!; AN INVISIBLE FORCE-- SLAMMING ME BACK INTO THIS BUILDING!

CRASH!

OUT OVER THE HARBOR, A LOOT-HAPPY GANG IS SPEEDING AWAY FROM A MILLIONAIRE'S YACHT WHEN...

I'LL SUMMON UP THE HARBOR FISH TO SWARM INTO THEIR SPEEDBOAT-- TOPPLE IT...

IT'S SUPER-POWER TIME, GANG!

YOU CAN'T MESS AROUND WITH US, AQUAMAN! YOU'RE ALL WASHED UP!

GREAT NEPTUNE! HE SWUNG AT EMPTY AIR-- AND KNOCKED ME OVER!

AT ANOTHER PART OF TOWN, IN A PAYROLL OFFICE...

HOLD IT! GET YOUR HANDS OFF THAT SAFE!

OKAY, MARTIAN MANHUNTER-- I'VE GOT ALL THE MONEY OUT OF IT ANYWAY--

--SO YOU CAN HAVE IT!

KLUNK

19

*SHORTLY AFTERWARD, THE FRUSTRATED JUSTICE LEAGUERS MEET TO DISCUSS THEIR STUNNING SETBACK...*

THEY TOOK US--BUT GOOD!

THEY LOOKED LIKE **COMMON CROOKS**-- BUT ACTED LIKE **SUPER-CROOKS!**

WE'VE GOT TO SOLVE THIS PUZZLER BY OURSELVES! WE CAN'T CALL ON THE OTHER MEMBERS TO HELP OUT--

THOSE CROOKS WERE WELL PREPARED FOR US--CONFIDENT THEY COULD OUTMATCH EACH OF OUR POWERS!

**SAY!** HOW ABOUT **NOT** USING OUR OWN POWERS? LET'S SWITCH 'EM AROUND...

MY BATTLEMACE FOR YOUR BOW-AND-ARROWS, G.A.!

I'LL TRANSFORM MY BODY INTO THE SHAPE OF A **BOOMERANG** --META-**MORPHO**-STYLE!

I'LL HURL THE **MARTIAN BOOMERANG** AT THOSE THUGS--SO YOU TAKE MY **MAGIC LASSO**, AQUAMAN!

*SURE ENOUGH--AS THE FEARSOME FIVE ROAR INTO BATTLE ACTION ONCE AGAIN, THEIR UNCONVENTIONAL ATTACKS TAKE THE THIEVES COMPLETELY BY SURPRISE...*

MEANWHILE, FAR TO THE NORTH, THE *AURORA BOREALIS* HAS STARTED MOVING DOWN THE COAST! DESTRUCTIVE LIGHTNINGS STAB AND DART! POWERLINES ARE DISRUPTED! DISASTER THREATENS THE ENTIRE EASTERN SEABOARD!

ZZZZT!

ZZZZT!

WHEN THE REPORT OF THE *AURORA BOREALIS* IS FLASHED TO *JUSTICE LEAGUE* HEADQUARTERS...

NOTHING IS ABLE TO HALT THE ONCOMING MENACE! *GOTHAM CITY* LIES DIRECTLY IN ITS PATH!

AND HERE WE STAND--HELPLESS! I'M ALL FOR GOING OUT TO HELP! BY THE TIME WE'RE CURED OF THE PLAGUE, THERE'LL BE NO ONE LEFT TO SAVE!

A TIMELY ENTRANCE BY *SUPERMAN* AND *DOCTOR BENDORION*...

I WAS IN THE LAB WITH *DOCTOR BENDORION* WHEN WE HEARD THAT REPORT COME IN AND HE ADVISED ME IT'S PERFECTLY SAFE FOR YOU TO GO OUT AND TACKLE THE *AURORA BOREALIS* MENACE!

I'VE MADE SUCH EXCELLENT PROGRESS--YOU NEEDN'T STAY ISOLATED ANY LONGER...

WITHIN THE HOUR--WHILE YOU'RE STOPPING THE *AURORA BOREALIS* AS IT HEADS SOUTH TO *GOTHAM CITY*-- I'LL HAVE COMPLETED MY CURE-BEAM!

GO-GO-GO!

SNAP! SNAP!

21

ON THE OUTSKIRTS OF *GOTHAM CITY* THE UNDAUNTED QUINTET OF SUPERIOR HEROES RAMS INTO THAT PULSATING VEIL OF VIRULENCE! THE HANDS OF MIGHTY *SUPERMAN* GRIP AND REND! *FLASH* USES WHAT SPEED HE CAN MUSTER UP! *BATMAN* HURLS BLACKOUT BOMBS FROM HIS UTILITY BELT! *GREEN LANTERN* CONCENTRATES ON DRAWING ELECTRICAL FURY INTO HIS *POWER RING!* *ATOM* SEEKS TO LEND WHAT AID HE CAN!

UNDER THE UNITED EFFORTS OF THE FIGHTING FIVE, THE CORUSCATING CURTAIN SHRIVELS -- LOSES ITS AWESOME ENERGIES -- SHRIVELS UP...

*FLASH,* THIS WHOLE SET-UP SMELLS -- LIKE A *RED HERRING!* YOU'RE THE BEST BET TO CHECK OUT MY SUSPICIONS!

CRUNCH!

WHAT DO YOU WANT ME TO DO, *BATMAN?*

IN THE *SECRET SANCTUARY* LABORATORY, SOMEWHAT LATER, WHEN THE *JUSTICE LEAGUE* TEAMS HAVE COMPLETED THEIR TASKS...

PERFECT TIMING! YOU'VE FINISHED YOUR WORK AND SO HAVE *I!* A SIMPLE PRESS OF THIS BUTTON -- AND MY SPECIAL RAY WILL GO OUT OVER EARTH!

BUT BEFORE I DO THAT -- YOU HAVE ONE LAST CHANCE TO RECONSIDER THE ELECTION OF *THE UNIMAGINABLE* TO THE *JUSTICE LEAGUE!* YOUR CHOICE IS CLEAR -- ACCEPT HIM -- OR DIE, ALONG WITH EVERYONE ELSE ON *EARTH!*

I WAS RIGHT! *DOCTOR BENDORION* IS A PHONY! HE'S REALLY *THE UNIMAGINABLE!*

22

NOT QUITE, *BATMAN!* AT THE MOMENT YOU WERE ON THE VERGE OF DEFEATING ME ON MY WORLD, I HURLED MYSELF INTO THE BODY OF THE *REAL DOCTOR BEN-DORION,* USURPING HIS LIFE-FORCE! LATER, WHEN YOU RETURNED TO MY PLANET, I SAW MY CHANCE TO FULFILL MY MISSION OF BECOMING A *JUSTICE LEAGUE* MEMBER!

ACTUALLY, ALL YOU HAD TO DO TO BE CURED OF THE PLAGUE WAS TO GET *ABSOLUTE REST!* SO I HAD TO COME UP WITH TWO MENACES TO KEEP YOU BUSY WHILE I PERFECTED THIS MACHINE THAT WOULD *REALLY* DOOM YOU!

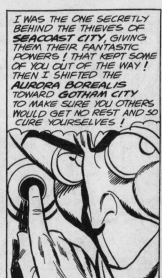

I WAS THE ONE SECRETLY BEHIND THE THIEVES OF *SEACOAST CITY,* GIVING THEM THEIR FANTASTIC POWERS! THAT KEPT SOME OF YOU OUT OF THE WAY! THEN I SHIFTED THE *AURORA BOREALIS* TOWARD *GOTHAM CITY* TO MAKE SURE YOU OTHERS WOULD GET NO REST AND SO CURE YOURSELVES!

NOW--GIVE ME YOUR ANSWER! DO YOU TAKE ME IN AS A MEMBER--OR DO I PRESS THE BUTTON THAT WILL ACTIVATE THE DEATH-RAY TO EARTH?

THE ANSWER IS STILL-- *NO!*

WE WOULDN'T HAVE YOU AT ANY PRICE!

GO AHEAD-- PRESS THE BUTTON!

THE *UNIMAGINABLE* WITH THE ENRAGED FACE OF *DOCTOR BENDORION* PRESSES THE ACTIVATION BUTTON...

FOOLS-- PREPARE TO DIE-- *GREAT STARS!* MY MACHINE ISN'T WORKING!

*SURPRISE!!*

I FIRST BECAME SUSPICIOUS OF YOU WHEN YOU USED THE EARTH-EXPRESSION *"HOURS"* TO TELL US HOW LONG IT WOULD TAKE YOU TO FIND A CURE FOR OUR PLAGUE! BUT YOU REALLY GAVE YOURSELF AWAY WHEN YOU SAID THE *AURORA BOREALIS* WAS MOVING *SOUTH* TOWARD *GOTHAM CITY!* YOU COULDN'T KNOW THAT, BECAUSE *DOCTOR BENDORION* HAD NEVER BEEN ON *EARTH* BEFORE!

SO WHEN *BATMAN* TOLD ME HIS SUS-PICIONS, I VIBRATED MYSELF TO INVISIBILITY AND I RACED HERE TO DIS-CONNECT YOUR MACHINE!

23

WHEN YOU COME TO, YOU'LL BE IN AN ESCAPE-PROOF CONTAINER--STRIPPED OF YOUR POWERS--A THREAT TO NO ONE EVER AGAIN!

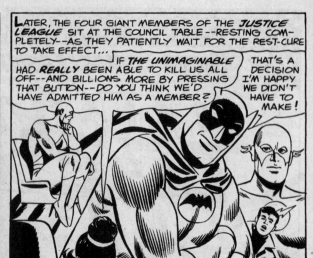

LATER, THE FOUR GIANT MEMBERS OF THE *JUSTICE LEAGUE* SIT AT THE COUNCIL TABLE--RESTING COMPLETELY--AS THEY PATIENTLY WAIT FOR THE REST-CURE TO TAKE EFFECT...

IF *THE UNIMAGINABLE* HAD *REALLY* BEEN ABLE TO KILL US ALL OFF--AND BILLIONS MORE BY PRESSING THAT BUTTON--DO YOU THINK WE'D HAVE ADMITTED HIM AS A MEMBER?

THAT'S A DECISION I'M HAPPY WE DIDN'T HAVE TO MAKE!

BATMAN--SHHHH! DON'T EVEN TALK! YOU MUST REST COMPLETELY!

UNTIL--FINALLY...

WE'RE CURED! I HAVE ALL MY SUPER-SPEED BACK!

WONDER WOMAN--WHERE'S THAT *OLD* UNIFORM OF MINE?

MY SIZE AND WEIGHT CONTROLS WORK PERFECTLY AGAIN!

MY *POWER RING* AND I ARE BACK ON THE BEAM AGAIN!

THE END

# JUSTICE ☆☆☆ LEAGUE ☆☆☆ of AMERICA

HOW'S *THIS* FOR A CHAIN REACTION OF INCREDIBLE EVENTS? THE *JUSTICE LEAGUE* ANSWERS A SUMMONS FOR HELP--TOO LATE! THE MENACE HAD ALREADY BEEN TRAPPED AND IMPRISONED! BUT BY THEIR UNTIMELY APPEARANCE, THE *JUSTICE LEAGUERS* UNWITTINGLY RELEASE THE MENACE-- AND AN ENTIRELY DIFFERENT MEANS MUST BE USED TO RE-CAPTURE IT! THEN, AFTER GREAT DIFFICULTY *THAT* IS MANAGED, A CRITICAL SITUATION ARISES THAT DEMANDS THE RE-RELEASE OF THE MENACE! AND THEN -- WHOA! THE *BEST* IS YET TO COME IN ...

## The SUPER-STRUGGLE AGAINST SHAGGY MAN!

THE ROLL CALL

ATOM
BATMAN
FLASH
GREEN ARROW
HAWKMAN
*Wonder Woman*

STORY BY:
GARDNER FOX

PENCILS BY:
MIKE SEKOWSKY

INKS BY:
FRANK GIACOIA
JOE GIELLA

FROM ALL CORNERS OF THE EARTH, MAIL ADDRESSED TO THE *JUSTICE LEAGUE OF AMERICA* POURS INTO THE SPECIAL POSTAL BOX RESERVED FOR ITS USE IN THE NATION'S CAPITAL! FROM THERE THIS MAIL IS FORWARDED TO A LOCAL POST OFFICE WHERE A MEMBER PICKS IT UP EVERY MONTH...

ON ONE OCCASION, THE PLANE CARRYING THE ACCUMULATED MAIL CRASHED INTO A MOUNTAINSIDE...

PROTECTED BY A METAL BOX, THE MAIL REMAINED UNSEEN AND UNDISCOVERED FOR TWO YEARS--UNTIL A CHANCE DISCOVERY BY A MOUNTAIN--CLIMBER...:

WHAT'S THIS--?

U.S. MAIL

FROM THERE, THE BOX FOUND ITS WAY INTO THE SECRET SANCTUARY OF THE *JUSTICE LEAGUE*...

TWO OF THE LETTERS IN HERE ARE OLDSVILLE! TOO LATE TO DO ANYTHIN' ABOUT 'EM NOW--

IT'S *NEVER* TOO LATE FOR THE *JUSTICE LEAGUE* TO ACT, *SNAPPER*-- IF SOMEONE REALLY NEEDS HELP! OPEN UP THE FIRST ONE --

*WHEEE-DOOO!* SOME BRAIN-BOY HAS WHIPPED UP A WAY-OUT INVENTION--THAT DESTROYS ANYTHING THAT *MOVES!* HE URGENTLY NEEDS--*NEEDED* OUR HELP TO DESTROY *IT*-- BEFORE IT WRECKS THE WORLD!

BUT THAT WAS TWO YEARS AGO! WHAT-EVER HAPPENED TO THAT MENACE?

*SNAP!*

WHY DON'T I GO BACK IN TIME ON MY *COSMIC TREADMILL* -- FIND OUT WHAT HAPPENED -- AND UNDO ANY DAMAGE IT --

NO, *FLASH!* HISTORY CAN'T BE CHANGED! BUT I MUST ADMIT I'D LIKE TO KNOW WHAT HAPPENED TO THE INVENTOR -- AND HIS *FRANKENSTEIN MONSTER!*

SAME HERE! IT WON'T TAKE *ME* LONG TO CHECK OUT HIS PRESENT WHEREABOUTS --

I'LL FOLLOW YOU UP -- IN MY *ARROW PLANE!*

TWO'S COMPANY -- THREE'S A TEAM! I'M JOININ' YOU!

SO GREAT IS *FLASH'S SUPER-SPEED* THAT HE RACES ONTO THE LITTLE ISLAND -- WHERE INVENTOR *ANDREW ZAGARIAN* MAINTAINS HIS HOME AND LABORATORY -- FAR AHEAD OF *GREEN ARROW* AND *HAWKMAN...*

THE ISLAND SEEMS PEACEFUL ENOUGH -- THAT MUST BE PROFESSOR ZAGARIAN -- SEEMINGLY WITHOUT A WORRY IN THE WORLD!

*FLASH!* GOOD GOSH -- DID IT TAKE *YOU* A LONG TIME TO ANSWER MY LETTER!

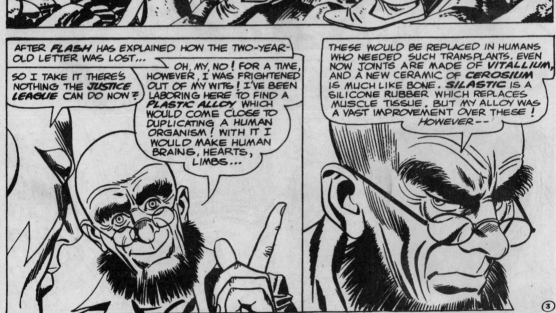

AFTER *FLASH* HAS EXPLAINED HOW THE TWO-YEAR-OLD LETTER WAS LOST...

SO I TAKE IT THERE'S NOTHING THE *JUSTICE LEAGUE* CAN DO NOW?

OH, MY, NO! FOR A TIME, HOWEVER, I WAS FRIGHTENED OUT OF MY WITS! I'VE BEEN LABORING HERE TO FIND A *PLASTIC ALLOY* WHICH WOULD COME CLOSE TO DUPLICATING A HUMAN ORGANISM! WITH IT I WOULD MAKE HUMAN BRAINS, HEARTS, LIMBS...

THESE WOULD BE REPLACED IN HUMANS WHO NEEDED SUCH TRANSPLANTS. EVEN NOW JOINTS ARE MADE OF *VITALLIUM*, AND A NEW CERAMIC OF *CEROSIUM* IS MUCH LIKE BONE. *SILASTIC* IS A SILICONE RUBBER WHICH REPLACES MUSCLE TISSUE. BUT MY ALLOY WAS A VAST IMPROVEMENT OVER THESE! HOWEVER --

3

"WHEN I TESTED OUT MY *PLASTALLOY* IN THE OVERSIZED BODY I CREATED, I MADE A WRONG POWER HOOK-UP WITH MY SMALL ATOMIC POWER GENERATOR.."

SOMETHING'S GONE HAYWIRE! MY GENERATOR IS POURING TOO MUCH VOLTAIC PRESSURE INTO THE PLAST-ALLOY BODY! THE HAIR FOLLICLES RESPONDED BY CAUSING TREMENDOUS GROWTH...

"*THE* BRAIN OF THE PLASTALLOY "MAN"—WHICH SHOULDN'T HAVE WORKED AT ALL!—BECAME DISTORTED! THE BODY RESPONDED TO THAT TERRIFYING INTAKE OF ENERGY BY ASSUMING A PSEUDO-LIFE FORM!..."

URR!

IT—IT'S ALIVE!

"PARALYZED WITH FRIGHT, I COULDN'T MOVE—AND *THAT* SAVED MY LIFE! FOR THE *SHAGGY MAN* STARTED SMASHING WHATEVER MOVED—BEGINNING WITH THE GENERATOR!.."

NO! NO! YOU'LL WRECK MY LIFE'S WORK!

URRRKK!

CRASH!

"I BARELY LIFTED A HAND IN PROTEST—WHEN THE HAIRY THING WHIRLED AND LASHED OUT WITH A CLUB-LIKE ARM..."

"I STARED HELPLESSLY AS HE WRECKED EVERYTHING THAT WAS IN MOTION!..."

HE'S INHUMAN—A MENACE TO THE WORLD—HE MUST BE DESTROYED—!

KRAK!

KRUNCH!

"SAYING THE *SHAGGY MAN* HAD TO BE DE-STROYED WAS ONE THING! FIGURING OUT HOW TO MAKE A MOVE AGAINST IT WAS ANOTHER! FROM A HIDING PLACE I TOOK A SHOT AT HIM..."

HE'S EVEN SMASHING A *TREE BRANCH* WAVING IN THE WIND, SO GREAT IS HIS URGE TO ANNIHILATE ANYTHING THAT MOVES! AH--BLASTED AWAY ONE OF HIS ARMS! THAT OUGHT TO SLOW HIM DOWN!

*BLAM!*

"TO MY AMAZEMENT--I DISCOVERED THAT *SHAGGY MAN* HAD THE PROPERTY OF REGENERATION OF TISSUE! AS I STARED, HE GREW A NEW ARM TO TAKE THE PLACE OF THE OLD ONE!..."

THE TASK IS BEYOND ME! ONLY ONE THING TO DO-- APPEAL TO THE JUSTICE LEAGUE OF AMERICA TO COME HERE AND STOP HIM--BEFORE HE LEAVES THIS ISLAND!

"WHILE WAITING FOR YOU TO RESPOND, A SEN-SATIONAL IDEA STRUCK ME! I PLACED TWO ELECTRO-MAGNETS IN A SEA-CAVE AND ARRANGED FIRES TO MELT INGOTS OF IRON..."

NOW FOR THE RISKY PART! LURE *SHAGGY MAN* INSIDE HERE WHERE I CAN SNAP MY TRAP!

"SUCCEEDING IN GETTING HIM TO PURSUE ME INTO THE CAVE, I RACED TO THE CONTROLS THAT TIPPED THE CAULDRONS OF MOLTEN IRON AND..."

THIS BETTER WORK-- OR MY OWN CREATION WILL KILL ME!

"THE CAULDRONS OF MOLTEN IRON DUMPED THEIR STEAMING CONTENTS DOWN ON *SHAGGY MAN*..."

*URRRK!*

"BUT ON HE CAME! I KEPT PUMPING FURIOUSLY--TIPPING MORE MOLTEN IRON ON HIM UNTIL HE DRIPPED BLAZING METAL ON THE FLOOR..."

EVEN IF I STOPPED PUMPING--REMAINED STOCK-STILL--IT'S PROBABLY TOO LATE! HE'S DE-TERMINED TO KILL ME!

"THEN—WITH HIS MIGHTY HANDS RAISED TO SQUASH ME—THE IRON WAS CAUGHT AND GRIPPED BY THE GREAT MAGNETS ON EITHER SIDE OF THE CAVE..."

JUST IN TIME—THE IRON ENCOMPASSING HIS BODY ENABLED THE MAGNETS TO GRIP HIM—HOLD HIM MOTIONLESS!

AS THE PROFESSOR CONCLUDES HIS HARROWING ADVENTURE...

I RAN OUT OF THE CAVE AND SEALED IT UP—AS YOU CAN SEE! *SHAGGY MAN* IS IMPRISONED IN THERE! HE CAN NEVER MOVE AGAIN!

SUDDENLY, AS IF IN DEFIANCE OF THE GOOD DOCTOR'S WORDS—A MIGHTY HAIRY HAND BASHES THROUGH THE CEMENT AND A VOICE BELLOWS IN MONSTROUS FURY...

GRUGGHH!

HE—HE'S BROKEN FREE?! BUT THERE WAS NO WAY TO REMOVE THE MAGNETIC GRIP—

*er—ONE* WAY, PROFESSOR! WHEN I RACED ONTO THIS ISLAND, THE VIBRATIONS OF MY SUPER-SPEED COULD HAVE SHATTERED THE IRON ON HIS BODY AND RELEASED HIM FROM THE MAGNETS THAT HELD HIM FAST!

JUSTICE LEAGUE of AMERICA

# SUPER-STRUGGLE AGAINST SHAGGY MAN

**PART 2**

CEMENT CRACKS! ROCKS ARE PULVERIZED! THE VERY GROUND SHUDDERS AS THE CREATED COLOSSUS CRASHES OUT OF HIS CAVERN PRISON! GONE IS THE IRON WHICH SHEATHED HIS BODY! USELESS ARE THE MAGNETS WHICH HAD GRIPPED HIS MUSCLES! MAD WITH RAGE, EAGER TO GRIP AND REND, HE SEARCHES FOR ANYTHING THAT MOVES--ON WHICH TO VENT HIS FURY!

DON'T ANYONE MOVE! SHAGGY MAN REACTS VIOLENTLY TO MOVEMENT OF ANY SORT!

NO CAN DO, PROFESSOR! WE JUSTICE LEAGUERS CAME HERE TO FIGHT IF NEED BE--AND WE HAVE TO MOVE TO DO IT!

NOTCHING A SHAFT TO HIS BOW, THE BATTLING BOWMAN SENDS IT WINGING TOWARD ITS TARGET...

GURRRKK!

I'LL KNOCK HIM OUT WITH THIS STUN-GAS ARROW!

AS FAST AS THE EYE CAN FOLLOW, THE HAIRY HUMANOID SNATCHES THAT SLIM LENGTH OF WOOD FROM THE AIR AND CRUNCHES IT!...

WOW! HE MOVED ALMOST AS FAST AS I CAN!

I'VE NEVER FIRED AN EXPLOSIVE ARROW AT A "LIVING" THING BEFORE--BUT I'LL DO IT NOW IF ONE OF YOU WILL DIVERT HIS ATTENTION...

LEAVE THAT TO ME...

7

FIRE AWAY, *G.A.*! HE'S ONLY GOT EYES FOR ME!

GROWRRR!

RIGHT ON TARGET! HIS BODY IS FLYING APART!

VA-BLAM!

THAT TAKES CARE OF HIM!

NO-NO, *GREEN ARROW*! WATCH NOW-- AND SEE WHAT HAPPENS!

BEFORE THE STUNNED EYES OF THE ON-LOOKERS, THE *SHAGGY MAN* REGENERATES HIS LOST TISSUE! ARMS, LEGS, HANDS, FEET--ALL GROW BACK WITHIN A MATTER OF MOMENTS...

TUATARAS AND *GECKOS* CAN GROW NEW TAILS WHEN THEY LOSE THEIR OLD ONES--BUT THIS IS *INCREDIBLE*!

I'M GOING TO LURE HIM BACK INSIDE THAT SEA-CAVE!

WITH THE FULLY RESTORED *SHAGGY MAN* LURCHING AT HIS HEELS, THE *SCARLET SPEEDSTER* HURTLES INTO THE SEASIDE CAVERN...

I'LL REPEAT PROF. ZAGARIAN'S MAGNETIC TRAP! WITH MY SUPER-SPEED I'LL FIRE UP THOSE CAULDRONS OF IRON--AND RE-CAPTURE HIM THE SAME WAY!

8

FRICTION BEGINS THE MELTING PROCESS OF THE IRON! STEAM RISES AS METAL TURNS MOLTEN! THE *FASTEST MAN ON EARTH* TURNS TOWARDS THE CONTROLS AS *SHAGGY MAN* COMES FOR HIM...

JUST AS I COUNTED ON! HE'S TOO "*DUMB*" TO STEER CLEAR OF THE SAME TRAP!

BUT THE HAIRY HUMANOID SHAKES HIMSELF AS DOES A DOG WHEN RIDDING HIMSELF OF WATER! RED-HOT METAL FLIES THROUGH-OUT THE CAVERN...

**SWOSSSHH!**

I--I DIDN'T COUNT ON THAT! HE'S LEARNED HOW TO *ADAPT* HIMSELF TO A PREVIOUS DANGER!

I'VE GOT TO KEEP VIBRATING TO LET THAT RED-HOT IRON PASS *THROUGH* MY BODY WITHOUT HARMING ME! WHILE I DO THAT-- I'LL LEAD *HAIRY HARRY* INTO THE OPEN!

AS THE CREATED COLOSSUS LUMBERS OUT INTO SUNLIGHT-- *FLASH* GREETS HIM WITH A BLINDING, CUTTING SAND-STORM ...

MAYBE I CAN BURY HIM UNDER TONS OF SAND...

BUT--OUT OF THAT SWIRLING, DRIVING SANDSTORM COMES A MASSIVE, HAIRY FIST WHICH ...

HAWKMAN-- CARRY ON...

**WHOP!**

9

FROM ABOVE DROPS THE *WINGED WONDER*--SWINGING A MEDIEVAL WEAPON...

DON'T MOVE, *FLASH!* THIS *TALON-PIKE* WILL GET THIS WALKING MATTRESS AWAY FROM YOU!

URRRKK!

GET GOING, *FLASH!* I'LL KEEP HIM OUT OF YOUR HAIR!

HE SAW ME WITH A WEAPON-- NOW HE WANTS ONE TOO!

TRYING TO SWEEP ME OUT OF THE SKIES...

LONG AS *HAWKMAN* KEEPS OUT OF HIS REACH, HE'LL BE OKAY! BUT WHAT CAN *WE* DO TO STOP *SHAGGY MAN?*

I HOPE THAT *SECOND LETTER* DOESN'T POSE AS MUCH OF A PROBLEM TO THE OTHER MEMBERS AS THIS ONE DID TO US!

THE SECOND LETTER FORCES A CRY OF SUR-PRISE FROM THE THROAT OF *THE ATOM* ...

IT'S FROM A MAN NAMED *ABNER MICHAELS!* HE'S AN ASTRONOMER HUNTING IN SOUTH AMERICA FOR THE REMAINS OF A *LOST MOON* OF EARTH--

*ABNER MICHAELS?* I KNOW HIM! HE USED TO TEACH AT *IVY UNIVERSITY*-- BUT HE DISAPPEARED TWO YEARS AGO, SOON AFTER THE DATE OF THAT LETTER ...

BUT WHY WOULD THE SEARCH FOR THE *"LOST MOON"* POSE A *THREAT?*

SOUNDS LIKE THE SORT OF MYSTERY I'D LIKE TO WORK ON--IF IT'S NOT TOO LATE!

WHAT ARE WE WAIT-ING FOR? LET'S GO!

AND SO, A SECOND TRIO OF SUPER-HEROES IS SOON HURTLING SOUTH-WARD BEYOND THE RAIN FORESTS OF BRAZIL, OVER THE TUNDRA COUNTRY OF NORTHERN CHILE, WHERE ...

*WONDER WOMAN--LOOK!* WHAT *IS* THAT GIGANTIC OBJECT?

I DON'T KNOW--BUT I HAVE A SNEAKY FEELING IT HAS SOMETHING TO DO WITH THAT LETTER WE RECEIVED!

ALMOST IN THE SAME MOMENT, THE *TINY TITAN* SEES...

THERE'S *ABNER MICHAELS!* WAVING TO US!

GO BACK! GO BACK! YOU'RE IN TERRIBLE DANGER! I'M BEING KEPT A PRISONER OF THE MOON--CREATURE--AND IT WON'T LET ANYONE RESCUE ME!

WON'T LET *ANYONE* RESCUE YOU? WELL, *JUSTICE LEAGUERS* ARE SOMETHING SPECIAL!

YOU DON'T KNOW ITS FRIGHTENING POWERS! FORGET ABOUT ME! SAVE YOURSELVES...

MY SKY-HOOK WILL PICK HIM UP IF WONDER WOMAN'S MAGIC LASSO DOESN'T MAKE IT!

AS THE BATPLANE TRAILS THE MAGIC LASSO THAT GRASPS THE LONG-MISSING ASTRONOMER...

IT SHOT UP A TENTACLE-- CAVING IN THE BATPLANE!

CRUNCH!

I WARNED YOU...

MERCIFUL MINERVA! BEFORE I CAN FREE MICHAELS-- THAT TENTACLE MAY CRUSH HIM!

A THIRD TENTACLE RISES UPWARD-- AND FROM ITS TIP SPURTS A COLUMN OF WATER WITH THE FORCE OF A GEYSER...

SPLOOSH!

OHHH! BEING KNOCKED SENSE- LESS...

GOT TO GRAB WONDER WOMAN'S FALLING ROPE--SAVE MICHAELS FROM A BODY- SHATTERING LANDING!

THE COWLED CRUSADER CATCHES HOLD OF THE MAGIC LASSO--JUST IN TIME....

I'LL LET YOU DOWN-- NICE AND EASY!

MEANWHILE, ATOM IS DOING HIS SHARE TO STOP THE TENTACLE- ONSLAUGHT...

WONDER WOMAN-- SNAP OUT OF IT-- WHILE I HOLD OFF THIS WATER-HOSE TENTACLE!

12

HOW YOU DOING, **WONDER WOMAN** ?

STILL ALIVE AND JUMPING ! **GREAT HERA** ! WHAT'VE WE COME UP AGAINST ?

A SUPER-INTELLIGENCE FROM THE FAR REACHES OF THE GALAXY !

FOR EONS THAT INTELLIGENCE ROAMED ALL SPACE AS A SPHERE OF METEORIC METAL. THOUSANDS OF YEARS AGO IT WAS CAUGHT BY THE GRAVITY PULL OF EARTH AND BECAME EARTH'S **SECOND MOON** ! AS TIME PASSED IT WAS DRAWN CLOSER AND CLOSER TO THE PLANET--AND BEGAN TO SHAKE APART WHEN IT PASSED **ROCHE'S LIMIT !** *

*EDITOR'S NOTE : SCIENCE BUFFS KNOW THIS IS THE DISTANCE AT WHICH A SATELLITE BREAKS UP INTO FRAGMENTS AS IT ORBITS A PLANET !

"AS THOSE METALLIC FRAGMENTS FELL FROM THE SKY, THEY RESEMBLED GREAT FIREBALLS. AS A RESULT OF ITS FIRST PASS OVER EARTH, PARTS OF THIS SHATTERED 'MOON' HAVE BEEN FOUND IN THE **ARGENTINE**-- AND HERE IN **CHILE** ON ITS SECOND PASS *... "

*EDITOR'S NOTE: AN ACCOUNT OF THIS CELESTIAL CRACK-UP APPEARED IN **NEWSWEEK**, SEPTEMBER 20, 1965.

"I CAME HERE TO STUDY THOSE FRAGMENTS, GATHERING THEM TOGETHER IN A GREAT PILE... "

ACCORDING TO CERTAIN TESTS I'VE MADE, THE MOON FELL HERE ABOUT **5800 B.C.** ...eh ? THE MOON FRAGMENTS--HEXADRITES--ARE STARTING TO **GLOW**--!

"TOO LATE, I REALIZED THAT THOSE **HEXADRITES** WERE PART OF A MIGHTY INTELLIGENCE ! THOUGH IT KEPT ME CONFINED HERE, I STILL MANAGED TO GET OFF A LETTER TO THE **JUSTICE LEAGUE**... "

I'VE MADE ARRANGEMENTS FOR A NATIVE TO PICK UP MY MAIL AND SEND IT OUT !

13

"THE MOON-THING KEPT ME PRISONER TO PREVENT ME FROM GIVING THE ALARM-- AND KEPT ME ALIVE TO PROBE MY BRAIN FOR KNOWLEDGE OF OUR WORLD..."

IT'S GATHERING ALL ITS SCATTERED PARTS TO ITSELF-- REFORMING INTO ITS ORIGINAL MASSIVE ORGANISM!

"THEN IT SENT OUT TENTACLES OF METEORIC METAL, DRIVING THEM DEEP INTO THE GROUND..."

IT'S SAPPING THE EARTH OF MINERALS-- CHEMICALS-- GASES-- OILS! IT EVEN FEEDS ON ROCKS! SOON-- EARTH WILL BE A HOLLOW SHELL -- AND FALL APART!

AS THE ASTRONOMER CONCLUDES HIS STORY...

IT WAS WITH MIXED EMOTIONS WHEN I SAW YOU ARRIVE! I'D GIVEN UP HOPE OF EVER BEING RESCUED! AND NOW I FEAR THAT NONE OF US WILL EVER LEAVE HERE ALIVE!

THE FIGHT FOR OUR LIVES IS ABOUT TO CONTINUE! HERE COMES ANOTHER TENTACLE!

WE'LL HIT IT HERE --THERE-- EVERYWHERE-- PROBING FOR ITS WEAK SPOT...

LET ME HAVE A CRACK AT IT WITH MY MAGIC LASSO! IF I CAN SNARE IT, IT'LL BE FORCED TO OBEY MY COMMANDS!

ANOTHER MASSIVE METAL APPENDAGE RISES UPWARD-- FIRING A BARRAGE OF ROCKS AT *WONDER WOMAN* EVEN AS HER LASSO IS YANKED FROM HER HAND...

HOW LONG CAN I HOLD OFF THIS ONSLAUGHT?

A BOULDER FINDS ITS MARK AND THE *AMAZON PRINCESS* DROPS AS IF POLE-AXED...

I'VE GOT TO GET HER OUT OF RANGE OF THOSE ROCKS!

GO TO IT, *BATMAN*-- WHILE I TANGLE WITH THAT TENTACLE!

*WOW!* AS IF I DIDN'T HAVE ENOUGH TROUBLE FIGHTING THIS ROCK-SHOOTING TENTACLE-- IT'S WHIPPED UP ANOTHER ONE--A *SAND-BLASTER!*

BENEATH THOSE FLAILING METAL APPENDAGES RACES *BATMAN*-- CARRYING AN INERT *WONDER WOMAN*...

INCHES TO THE LEFT OR INCHES TO THE RIGHT-- AND I'LL BE STOPPED SHORT!

AS THE *MASKED MAN-HUNTER* DEPOSITS HIS BURDEN BEYOND THE REACH OF THE TENTACLED MONSTROSITY, THE *TINY TITAN* RIDES THE WIND CURRENTS UPWARDS, LIGHTER THAN A FEATHER...

WHA--WHAT DO WE DO NOW?

I DON'T KNOW, MICHAELS! OFFHAND, I CAN'T THINK OF ANY POSSIBLE WAY TO STOP THAT CREATURE! I HOPE THE OTHER *JUSTICE LEAGUERS* ARE HAVING AN EASIER TIME OF IT THAN WE ARE!

AND SO BOTH JLA TEAMS HAVE SEEMINGLY MET THEIR MATCH!

BEFORE *SNAPPER* CAN BLINK HIS SURPRISED EYES, *FLASH* HAS JOINED THE OTHER TRIO...

JUST STANDING AROUND-- DOING NOTHING?

THERE'S NOTHING LEFT TO TRY! WE TACKLED THAT MONSTER--

--AND WERE THROWN FOR A LOSS!

AFTER THEY EXPLAIN THE SITUATION TO HIM, A DAWNING LOOK CROSSES THE FACE OF THE *SCARLET SPEEDSTER*...

DON'T GO 'WAY! I'LL BE RIGHT BACK--WITH THE ANSWER TO YOUR PROBLEM!

BEFORE THEY CAN SAY *FLASH*, THE *MODERN MERCURY* IS BACK ON THE ISLAND WHERE *SHAGGY MAN* IS FIGHTING HIS REFLECTION...

AFTER ALL THE TROUBLE I WENT TO-- TO MAKE THAT UNBREAKABLE MIRROR-- I'VE GOT TO SMASH IT!

MEETING WITH *HAWKMAN* AND *GREEN ARROW* FIRST, HE GIVES THEM CERTAIN INSTRUCTIONS...

I DON'T HAVE TIME TO EXPLAIN THE REST IN DETAIL-- BUT JUST DO AS I'VE SAID...

I'LL STRING ALONG...

--EVEN IF IT SOUNDS LIKE YOU'VE FLIPPED YOUR COSTUME, *FLASH*!

VIBRATING AT ACCELERATING SPEED, *FLASH* TRIGGERS VIBRATORY IMPULSES AT THE UN- BREAKABLE MIRROR...

NO ORDINARY FORCE COULD SMASH THIS MIRROR--BUT MY SUPER- SWIFT VIBRATIONS ARE ABLE TO SHATTER THE GLUE THAT HOLDS THE THIN SHEETS OF MIRROR METAL TOGETHER!

AACK!

CR

THEN THE *SCARLET SPEEDSTER* WHIRLS AND RACES OFF TOWARD THE WAITING *ARROWPLANE*..

SURE ENOUGH! THE *SHAGGY MAN* IS HOT ON MY HEELS! THE TRICK THEN WILL BE TO PREVENT HIM FROM SEEING ANYTHING *MOVING* WHILE HE'S INSIDE THE PLANE--OR HE'LL LEAP OUT TO DESTROY IT!

17

ONCE THE PLANE IS OFF THE GROUND, HE WON'T REALIZE IT'S MOVING AS LONG AS HE CAN'T RELATE IT TO ANYTHING ON THE *OUTSIDE*! THAT'S WHY I MUST MAKE SURE NOT TO PASS WITHIN SIGHT OF ANY MOVING OBJECTS!

AS THE *MONARCH OF MOTION* VIBRATES THROUGH THE BOTTOM OF THE PLANE, THE *HAIRY HUMANOID* LEAPS INTO IT....

NOW TO TIE A ROPE AROUND THE PLANE-- AND TURN IT INTO A BIG KITE!

EVEN BEFORE THE *SHAGGY MAN* DISCOVERS THAT THE PLANE IS EMPTY SAVE FOR HIMSELF, THE *ARROWPLANE* IS FLYING HIGH THROUGH THE SKY...

I'LL GO BY WAY OF THE *PANAMA CANAL*! THERE'S LESS CHANCE FOR HIM TO SEE ANY-THING MOVING OVER WATER! ALL HE'LL BE LOOKING AT IS A CLOUD-LESS SKY!

BEHIND HIM...

LET'S GET TO WORK!

IF *FLASH* WANTS ANOTHER *SHAGGY MAN*--WE'LL GIVE HIM ONE!

18

# SUPER-STRUGGLE AGAINST SHAGGY MAN

UPWARD FROM THE TUNDRA-LAND OF NORTHERN *CHILE* REACH THE AWESOME TENTACLES OF THE MOON CREATURE! RUSHING TO MEET THOSE METALLIC APPENDAGES COMES *SHAGGY MAN*-- TOWED ALONG BY THE *SCARLET SPEEDSTER*! HE BELLOWS WITH RAGE! HIS MUSCLES WRITHE AND DANCE WITH THE EAGERNESS TO REACH OUT AND DESTROY THIS ALIEN, MOVING OBJECT!

**PART 3**

GYAAAGGH!

SHAGGY MAN SEES THE MOON CREATURE! HERE'S WHERE THEY FIGHT IT OUT!

HAIRY HANDS PUNCH! METALLIC TENTACLES CONTRACT....

GRAGGH!

NEXT MOMENT THEY ARE LOCKED IN A TITANIC STRUGGLE FOR MASTERY OF ALL THEY SURVEY...

AARRGH!

HUD!

SHADES OF PLUTO! WILL YOU LOOK AT *THAT*?

WHO *IS* THAT HAIRY THING, *FLASH*?

WHERE'D YOU *GET* IT?

AS THE FIGHT RAGES ON, THE *SCARLET SPEEDSTER* EXPLAINS...

...AND SO I FIGURED FOR A CHANGE OF PACE I'D PUT A *VILLAIN* TO WORK FOR US! DOING A BANG-UP JOB TOO!

FEROCIOUS SCREAMS OF RAGE REND THE AIR AS THE MOON-BEING AND THE *HAIRY HUMANOID* BATTLE TO A FINISH...

GURRRK!

AAARGH!

ACCORDING TO MY COUNT, *SHAGGY MAN'S* LOST AND GROWN BACK *SEVEN ARMS, THREE FEET, FOUR HEADS* -- AND IS STILL GOING STRONG!

THE ROLE OF SPECTATOR IS AN UNUSUAL ONE FOR THE *JUSTICE LEAGUE* -- BUT THEY STRUGGLE MANFULLY TO REMAIN OUT OF THAT SUPER-STRUGGLE...

HO-HUMM!

- SIGH! -- IF ONLY ALL OUR CASES COULD GO LIKE THIS!

YOU'D GET BORED, *BATMAN*!

*HAWKMAN* AND *GREEN ARROW* ARE THE ONLY ONES IN ACTION RIGHT NOW!

HOW SO, *FLASH*?

AFTER *SHAGGY MAN* DESTROYS THE *MOON-BEING* -- HE'LL HAVE TO BE MADE HELPLESS, REMEMBER? I CAN'T USE A MIRROR ON HIM AGAIN -- HE *ADAPTS* TO ANY TRICK THAT'S ALREADY BEEN USED ON HIM! SO...

20

I TOLD *HAWKMAN* AND *GREEN ARROW* TO BUILD A *DUPLICATE SHAGGY MAN* WITH THE HELP OF THE PROFESSOR... BUT NOT TO *ACTIVATE* IT UNTIL WE NEEDED IT! HERE THEY COME NOW!

PROFESSOR ZAGARIAN WARNED US NOT TO USE HIS ELECTRONIC SIGNAL DEVICE UNTIL WE'RE ABSOLUTELY SURE THIS *SECOND SHAGGY MAN* CAN'T HARM ANYBODY BUT HIS OTHER SELF!

RIGHT YOU ARE! THAT MEANS I HAVE TO GET TO WORK!

I'D LIKE TO HELP OUT, *FLASH!*

WE'VE GOT TO MAKE THIS PIT WIDE AND DEEP!

I'LL LINE IT WITH STONES TO PREVENT ANY EARTHQUAKE FROM RELEASING THEM!

MEANTIME, THE INDESTRUCTIBLE *SHAGGY MAN*--GROWING NEW LIMBS FOR THE ONES THE MOON-BEING DESTROYS--IS SLOWLY BUT SURELY OVERCOMING HIS OPPONENT...

LOOK! THE CORE--THE VERY HEART OF THE MOON BEING--IS ROLLING AWAY TO SAFETY!

I'LL HANDLE THIS, *BATMAN!* IF YOU OR ONE OF THE OTHERS INTERFERES, *SHAGGY MAN* WILL SEE YOU AND MAY BE DISTRACTED!

*SMASH!*

BY MAKING MYSELF MICRO-SCOPICALLY SMALL AND LIGHT ENOUGH TO RIDE THE BREEZE TOWARD THAT MOON CORE, *SHAGGY MAN* WON'T SEE *ME!*

CLICK! CLICK!

SO SMALL NO HUMAN EYE CAN SEE HIM, THE 180-POUND *ATOM* PUSHES THE PULSING MOON CORE TOWARD THE PIT *FLASH* AND *WONDER WOMAN* HAVE DUG...

I HOPE *SHAGGY MAN* NOTICES THIS THING BEFORE IT ROLLS INTO THE PIT!

AS IF HIS DISTORTED BRAIN CATCHES THE THOUGHTS OF *THE ATOM*, THE *HAIRY HUMANOID* LIFTS HIS HEAD! INFLAMED EYES GLARE AS A SNARL LEAVES HIS THROAT...

*URRRKK!*

HERE HE COMES! HERE I GO!

GROWLING--SNARLING--FISTS STRIKING WITH SLEDGE-HAMMER IMPACT--*SHAGGY MAN* CLINGS TO HIS FOE...

*SOK!*

WHILE THIS BATTLE RAGES ON THE *SUR-FACE* OF THE PLANET, FAR BELOW *FLASH* AND *WONDER WOMAN* HAVE COMPLETED THEIR CHORE...

THIS JUST ABOUT DOES IT, *FLASH!* EVERYTHING'S IN READINESS FOR OUR GUESTS!

ALL IT NEEDS NOW IS...

HEADS UP DOWN THERE!!

22

LOCKED IN THEIR DEATH-STRUGGLE, **SHAGGY MAN** AND MOON-CREATURE PLUMMET OVER THE LIP OF THE PIT...

HERE THEY COME!

URRRK!

CRUNCH!

THE **AMAZON PRINCESS** AND **SCARLET SPEEDSTER** RACE UPWARD AS THE BATTLING BEHEMOTHS DROP PAST THEM...

I'LL GET THE OTHER **SHAGGY MAN** AND TOSS HIM IN!

WHILE I GATHER UP THE FRAGMENTS OF THE MOON-BEING AND DROP THEM DOWN, TOO!

SECONDS LATER...

OKAY, **HAWKMAN**-- WHEN THE INERT **SHAGGY MAN** HITS BOTTOM, TURN ON THE JUICE!

BY THAT TIME, I'LL HAVE THROWN THE REST OF THE MOON CREATURE IN AFTER HIM!

AS **FLASH** AND **WONDER WOMAN** PUT A STONE CEILING OVER THE COMBAT-CHAMBER, **HAWKMAN** PRESSES THE ACTIVATION BUTTON...

GURRK!

GYAAA!

ABOVE THE CLOSED-IN PIT...

BUT, **FLASH!** THE MOON-CREATURE MAY RECOVER IN TIME AND REASSEMBLE ITS FRAGMENTS AGAIN! WE'LL BE FACED WITH THE PROBLEM OF STOPPING THEM!

NO, WE WON'T! THAT'S THE BEAUTY OF MY IDEA!

23

"WHEN THE MOON-BEING REASSEMBLES ITSELF AND MOVES--BOTH SHAGGY MEN WILL BE DISTRACTED AND UNITE TO DESTROY IT..."

THUD! POW BLAM!

"THEN--WHEN THE SHAGGY MEN OVERCOME THE MOON-CREATURE-- THEY'LL GO BACK TO FIGHTING EACH OTHER AS LONG AS TIME WILL LAST..."

WHEN THE MEMBERS RETURN TO THE SECRET SANCTUARY, THEY FIND GREEN LANTERN AND SUPERMAN WAITING FOR THEM. AFTER THEY TELL THEIR STORY...

I WISH I COULD HAVE FINISHED MY CASE SOONER AND BEEN WITH YOU! I'D LIKE TO HAVE MATCHED MY POWER RING AGAINST THE MOON-CREATURE!

I WONDER HOW I WOULD HAVE MADE OUT AGAINST THE INVULNERABLE SHAGGY MAN?

I WONDER--COULD EITHER OF THEM HAVE WON?

WELL, THAT'S ANOTHER STORY! MAYBE SOME ISSUE OR OTHER WE'LL GIVE IT TO YOU!

THE END

As a truck hurtles at dangerous speeds along the twisting roads of *Moro Mountain*...

*Those fur hijackers won't get far! I'll soon overtake them and--oh-oh! Heavy fog rolling in!*

*Fog's become so pea-soupy, I can't see the truck at all now--but judging from the sound of its motor, I'm right over it!*

Suddenly the mist thins--and *Hawkman* sees to his amazement...

*Great Polaris! The truck is gone--and there's an armored car in its place-- firing up at me!*

BLAM! BLAM!

Dipping and darting, the *Winged Wonder* whips wisps of mist in front of him...

*Truck or armored car--those men are criminals! One thing's sure--I'm not leaving here empty-handed!*

FLAP! FLAP!

Then--like a disembodied spirit--he drives out of the mist...

*They left the car to get a better shot at me--only to give me a better shot at them!*

WWHAPPP!

THIS GUY'S JAW MAKES TOO *HAND-Y* A TARGET TO RESIST MY *PERSONAL TOUCH!*

SLOOKK!

WHEN THEY COME TO, I'LL FIND OUT HOW THEY PULLED THAT SWITCHEROO!

KLIINNK!

SOK!

ON *MORO MOUNTAIN*, ANOTHER GRIM FIGURE IS BURSTING WITH QUESTIONS AS HIS *SAND-CAR* HURTLES AFTER A FLEEING VEHICLE...

BEATS ME HOW I COULD BE CHASING AN *ARMORED CAR*-- ONLY TO HAVE IT TURN INTO A BIG *TRUCK!* MY BEST BET IS TO RUN THE TRUCK OFF THE ROAD--

ROAARR!

GET SET FOR A THRILLING TREAT, FANS! YOU'RE ABOUT TO SEE *SANDMAN*-- ONE OF THE ORIGINAL MEMBERS OF THE *JUSTICE SOCIETY OF AMERICA* (OF *EARTH-TWO*) GO INTO ACTION WITH HIS SPECIAL WEAPON-- *SAND!*

CRASH!

ACME FURS CO.

ACME FURS

SCREEECH!

I DON'T HAVE TO BE A MIND-READER TO KNOW THOSE CHARACTERS ARE CROOKS-- NO MATTER WHAT SORT OF VEHICLE THEY'RE RIDING IN! A HANDFUL OF SAND INTO THE AIR--AND...

AN ODDLY SHAPED ENERGY-ROD FLASHES A TORRENT OF HEAT AND WATER AT DRIFTING GRAINS OF MATTER...

THEIR GUNS WILL BE NO MATCH FOR MY SPECIAL WEAPON!

3

A CEMENT WALL -- FORMED LIKE MAGIC IN FRONT OF US!

HEYYY! THAT'S NOT *HAWKMAN*! WHAT KINDA DEAL HAVE WE STUMBLED INTO?

**BLAM! WHAM!**

THE CEMENT WALL CRUMBLES INTO A SANDY CURTAIN AS THE *GRAINY GLADIATOR* SURGES FORWARD...

LOOK OUT! WHOEVER HE IS -- HERE HE COMES!

I'VE BEEN OUT OF THE CROOK-CATCHING BUSINESS SO LONG-- THESE THUGS DON'T EVEN *KNOW* ME!

THIS GUY'S A WHIZ! HE TURNED THE SAND INTO -- *GLASS*!

IT'S GOT US *HANDCUFFED*!

TALK UP! HOW'D YOU CHANGE THAT ARMORED CAR INTO A HIJACKED TRUCK?

**SOCK!**

*HAWKMAN* AND *SANDMAN* ARE NOT THE ONLY CRIME-FIGHTERS WONDERING WHAT STRANGE FORCE HAS COME UPON THEIR NORMAL, ORDERLY WORLDS! FOR INSTANCE, AT THIS MOMENT ON *EARTH-TWO*....

AH! I DIAGNOSED THIS CASE AS A BANK ROBBERY! NOW I'M HERE TO OPERATE!

TROUBLE AHEAD! IT'S *DOC MID-NITE*!

(4)

OUT OF HIS MEDICAL SATCHEL, *DOCTOR MID-NITE* YANKS A SPECIALIZED WEAPON ...

WHEN I CAME OUT OF RETIREMENT, I CHANGED SOME OF MY CRIME-FIGHTING TECHNIQUES ! DEMONSTRATION NUMBER ONE-- MY *CYROTUBER* !

THE WEAPON QUIVERS AND HUMS--AND SHOCKED NERVES REACT TO ITS STABBING POWER...

NOW I DON'T HAVE TO RELY SO MUCH ON MY OLD-FASHIONED *BLACKOUT BOMB* !

⸮ULP⸮ ALL OF A SUDDEN...I'M DOIN' A CRAZY *WATUSI* !

THE NERVES OF THE HUMAN BODY CONTROL ALL ITS ACTIONS AND REACTIONS. BY STIMULATING THEM IN A CERTAIN WAY--I CAN CONTROL WHAT THESE THUGS DO !

THEN--FROM THE OPEN BANK VAULT OFF TO ONE SIDE OF THE CHAMBER, A THIRD GUN-MAN FIRES...

ANOTHER ONE ! I'VE GOT A SPECIAL TREATMENT FOR HIM !

FROM ANOTHER ANODE OF HIS MEDICAL WEAPON THE *MAN OF MIDNIGHT* TRIGGERS A BLAST OF POWER ...

MY HAND-- FROZEN SOLID!

JUST AS A *CYRO-PROBE* CAN CHANGE WARM FLESH TO SOLID ICE WITH LIQUID NITROGEN DURING AN OPERATION-- SO ALSO CAN MY *CYROTUBER!*

5

As the CRIME CRUSADER leaps forward to round up his captors-- he finds himself whirled around and around--violently and incredibly...

WHA-WHAT'S HAPPENING TO ME? I FEEL LIKE A TOP WITH LEGS!

Suddenly hands reach out to grip and stop him as...

DOCTOR MID-NITE!? WHERE'D YOU COME FROM? I WAS JUST ABOUT TO PULL A WHIRLABOUT CAPTURE OF SOME BANK ROBBERS WHEN THEY DISAPPEARED AND I NABBED YOU!

I WAS DOING THE SAME THING--WHEN I FOUND MYSELF SPUN OUT OF MY EARTH-TWO-- AND INTO YOUR EARTH-ONE!

Elsewhere on EARTH-ONE, under cover of a tear-gas bomb from his UTILITY BELT-- BATMAN blasts through at some jewel thieves...

I'LL WRAP THIS UP SO FAST, THESE CROOKS WON'T BE CLEARY-EYED TILL THEY SEE THEMSELVES IN JAIL!

WHAPPP! CLUNK!

There is an abrupt moment of intense cold, of dizziness-- and out of nowhere comes a flying fist...

WHEW! THAT PUNCH HAD KNOCKOUT DROP PLASTERED ALL OVER IT!

THUDD!

For a few moments--before the last wisps of the tear-gas bomb disappear and they can recognize each other, two crime-crusaders exchange powerhouse punches...

HOLD IT! WHAT AM I DOING BATTLING BATMAN?

WILDCAT! HOW'D YOU GET MIXED UP IN THIS?

ZAPPP! POWW!

EXERT ALL HIS TITANIC ENERGIES AS HE WILL--THE **GHOSTLY GUARDIAN** CANNOT WITHSTAND THE OVERWHELMING PRESSURES THAT DRAW HIM OUT OF THIS COSMIC UNIVERSE...

I FEEL LIKE SMOKE -- DRAWN BY A STRONG SUCTION! WHERE IS IT TAKING ME?

NOT FAR AWAY--IN A STRIPED PRISON--GLOBE OF MYSTIC ENERGIES --THE MARSHLAND MONSTER KNOWN AS **SOLOMON GRUNDY** FEELS AN ALIEN POWER SURGING INTO HIS BODY...

AAARRGGHH!

HURLED OUT OF ORBIT--BATTERED BY THE FANTASTIC FORCES THAT HAVE AFFECTED OTHERS ON **EARTH-ONE** AND **EARTH-TWO** -- THE PRISON IN WHICH **DOCTOR FATE** AND **GREEN LANTERN** PLACED THE **MACABRE MAN-THING** HURTLES EARTHWARD...

GYYAAGHHH!

WHAT'S GOING ON--AND OFF-- **EARTHS ONE** AND **TWO?**

ONLY TIME AND THE MYSTERIES OF SPACE ITSELF HOLD THE ANSWER!

READ ON FOR THE STARTLING DEVELOPMENTS THAT BUILD TO A SMASHING, AWE-INSPIRING CLIMAX!

(8)

# CRISIS BETWEEN EARTH-ONE AND EARTH-TWO!

**PART TWO**

TO FACE A DESPERATE CHALLENGE FROM SOME UNKNOWN FORCE OR ADVERSARY--THE DISPLACED MEMBERS OF THE *JUSTICE SOCIETY* GATHER WITH THE INVOLVED *JUSTICE LEAGUERS* IN THE *EARTH-ONE* SECRET SANCTUARY!
DISBELIEF AND GRIM DETERMINATION ETCH THEIR FACES WITH FURROWED FURY AS THE REALIZATION BURSTS ON THEM THAT THEY HAVE NO CLUES AT ALL TO THE SOLUTION OF THIS MYSTERIOUS MENACE!

IT'S ABSOLUTELY INCREDIBLE! MEN AND WOMEN OF BOTH *EARTHS*--TRANSFERRED BACK AND FORTH AT RANDOM IN MADCAP FASHION!

HERE COMES *GREEN LANTERN* AND--WHAT A PLEASANT SURPRISE--*BLACK CANARY!*

HAS ANYBODY LEARNED WHAT'S BEHIND THIS? *GREEN LANTERN* TRIED TO SEND ME BACK TO *EARTH-TWO*--BUT WAS POWERLESS TO DO SO!

I WONDER IF THE TROUBLE SPOT WE'RE HUNTING IS ON MY NATIVE *EARTH-TWO?*

EVEN IF IT WERE--HOW'D WE GET THERE? MY *POWER RING* COULDN'T SEND *BLACK CANARY* BACK--

AND DON'T COUNT ON MY SUPER-SPEED VIBRATIONS TO DO IT! I'VE ALREADY TRIED--AND NO CAN DO!

THEN--FOR AWHILE AT LEAST-- WE'RE STUCK HERE ON *EARTH-ONE!*

WHILE DIAGNOSING OUR TROUBLES-- WE'D LIKE TO OFFER OUR SERVICES AS SUBSTITUTES FOR ANY OF YOUR MEMBERS WHO WERE TELE-PORTED TO *EARTH-TWO!*

OFFER ACCEPTED!

HOLD IT! A NEWS FLASH COMING IN ON OUR INTER-NATIONAL RADIO--!

ELSEWHERE ON *EARTH-ONE,* THE HULKING HUMANOID KNOWN AS *SOLOMON GRUNDY* HAS MADE A LANDING FROM HIS ORBITING PRISON GLOBE AND...

GYAGGHH! ME FIND *GREEN LANTERN!* ME KILL HIM DEAD!

DEMENTED RAGE SPARKLES IN HIS BESTIAL EYES! HOT BLOOD SURGES THROUGH HIS VEINS WITH PRIMITIVE KILL-LUST! ONE THOUGHT ALONE OBSESSES HIS SUBHUMAN BRAIN...

ME HATE *GREEN LANTERN!* ME KILL HIM DEAD!

CALL THE POLICE! A MONSTER'S ON THE LOOSE!

FROM COUNTRYSIDE TO CITY STREET THE *MARSHLAND MONSTER* TURNS HIS TITANIC STRENGTH TO SENSELESS DESTRUCTION AS...

*GREEN LANTERN* COME HERE! THEN--ME *KILL!*

CRA SH!

HOLD ON! *SOLOMON GRUNDY* IS NOT THE *ONLY* AWESOME ATAVAR BEING FREED FROM AN IMPRISONING SLEEP! FOR IN *GOTHAM CITY'S ALFRED MEMORIAL FOUNDATION* AT THIS MOMENT-- IN A LABORATORY WHERE UNLEASHED POWER IS RUNNING WILD...

THE *BLOCKBUSTER* IS BREAKING LOOSE --DISAPPEARING BEFORE MY EYES --!

ZZZ ZZTT!

10

THE EERIE ENERGIES THAT HAVE DISPLACED PEOPLE FROM *EARTH-ONE* TO *EARTH-TWO*-- NOW DISPLACE *BLOCKBUSTER!* JUST AS *SOLOMON GRUNDY* WAS SWITCHED ONTO *EARTH-ONE*, THE BRUTE BEHEMOTH HAS BEEN TRANSFERRED TO *EARTH-TWO!*

**GYARRGH!**

THUS OUR SUPER-HEROES OF *EARTH-ONE* ARE ABOUT TO BE CHALLENGED BY ONLY *ONE MAMMOTH MONSTER*-- BUT WHAT AN ADVERSARY *SOLOMON GRUNDY* IS GOING TO BE!

FOR--IMPRISONED IN THE GLOBE OF STRIPED MAGIC YELLOW BANDS AND POWER RING GREEN BANDS-- HE HAS ABSORBED SOME OF *DOCTOR FATE'S* POWERS AS WELL AS THOSE OF *GREEN LANTERN* *...

* *EDITOR'S NOTE!* IF YOU HAVEN'T READ IT, YOU'RE OUT OF LUCK-- BUT IF YOU CAN BEG, BORROW OR BUY A COPY OF *SHOWCASE #55*, YOU CAN STILL THRILL TO **"SOLOMON GRUNDY GOES ON A RAMPAGE!"**

BUT--BEFORE WE GET TO THAT PULSE-STUNNING, POWER-PACKED BATTLE BETWEEN *SOLOMON GRUNDY* AND THE *JUSTICE* MEMBERS-- WE WANT YOU TO PEEK IN ON A CERTAIN LABORATORY IN *IVY TOWN* ...

MY EMERGENCY *JUSTICE LEAGUE* SIGNAL BUZZING LIKE MAD--BUT THE SIZE-AND-WEIGHT CONTROLS OF MY INVISIBLE *ATOM* UNIFORM WON'T FUNCTION!

THOUGH HE HAS BEEN HELPING HIS ITALIAN EXCHANGE-SCIENTIST ASSISTANT, *ENRICHETTA NEGRINI*, IN HER GREATEST EXPERIMENT, RAY PALMER QUICKLY LOSES INTEREST, SINCE...

I CAN'T HELP MY FELLOW MEMBERS ON WHATEVER CASE IT IS THAT OCCUPIES THEM! I'M STUCK HERE-- AS RAY PALMER!

OKAY, NOW WE'RE READY! THE SEETHING HATE IN THE BRAIN OF *SOLOMON GRUNDY* ALLOWS HIM ONLY ONE THOUGHT: SEEK OUT AND DESTROY *GREEN LANTERN!* AND AS THE MEMBERS OF THE *JUSTICE* GROUPS SURGE FORWARD-- HE HEARS THAT NAME CRIED OUT...

GREEN LANTERN-- LOOK! IT'S *SOLOMON GRUNDY!*

GREEN LANTERN? GYAARRGH!!! ME *KILL* HIM!

11

As the GIRL GLADIATOR drops, the SCARLET SPEEDSTER rockets forward...

I'LL WINDMILL THAT STUFF AWAY FROM BLACK CANARY-- WHILE WHIPPING UP A STORM OF OBJECTS AT SOLOMON GRUNDY--TO DISTRACT HIM UNTIL I CAN COME TO GRIPS WITH HIM!

Then--as FLASH super-speeds at the MARSHLAND MONSTER...

ARRRGGH! ME STOP YOU! ME SEND YOU BACK!

HEYY! I--I'M NOT MOVING FORWARD! I'VE BEEN STOPPED DEAD IN MY TRACKS!

Unable to stop his progress in reverse, the SCARLET SPEEDSTER races backward around the world...

I STILL HAVE ALL MY SPEED--BUT FOR SOME STRANGE REASON I'M NOT ABLE TO CONTROL IT! BUT MAYBE THIS WON'T BE A TOTAL LOSS--IF I CAN SLAM INTO SOLOMON GRUNDY FROM THE REAR!

Straight to his starting point he back-dashes...

WHEN I WHAM INTO HIM AT THIS SPEED--THAT SWAMP-LAND SAVAGE IS GOING TO BE BANGED GALLEY-WEST!

OOOPS! WHETHER SOLOMON GRUNDY IS DOING THIS WITH THE MAGIC OF DOCTOR FATE OR THE POWER RING ENERGY OF EARTH-TWO'S GREEN LANTERN MAKES NO DIF-FERENCE! BROTHER, HE IS DOING IT!

ARRGGGH! KILL! KILL!

RISING INTO THE AIR-- UP AND AWAY FROM HIM!

DRAWN BETWEEN WORLDS -- ON THE BORDERLAND OF EVERYWHERE AND NOWHERE -- THE *DISEMBODIED DETECTIVE* COMES FACE TO FACE WITH THE TERRIFYING CHALLENGE OF... *THE UNKNOWN!*

WHAT IS THAT THING? AN INTELLIGENT BEING -- OR SOME MANIFESTATION OF UNGUESSABLE NATURAL FORCES IN THIS SPACE SECTOR? IT'S GIVING OFF -- AN ODD GLOW THAT'S WEAKENING ME!

WITH MY SPECTRAL POWERS I CAN SENSE THAT IT COMES FROM AN *ANTI-MATTER UNIVERSE!* IF IT COMES IN CONTACT WITH SOLID MATTER OF MY UNIVERSE -- *INSTANT DESTRUCTION!*

SINCE I AM A SPIRIT I AM NOT COMPOSED OF POSITIVE MATTER! I MUST FIGHT AND DEFEAT THIS *UNKNOWN* BEFORE IT CROSSES OVER THE BORDERLAND ONTO *EARTH* ITSELF!

WHUPP!

**SHEEESH!**

Is *SPECTRE* EVER IN FOR A SHOCK! IF YOU ARE BRAVE ENOUGH -- GO ON READING! BUT IF YOU CAN'T STAND THRILLS AND DANGERS, SURPRISES AND CATASTROPHES -- STOP NOW AND PLAY IT SAFE!

# JUSTICE LEAGUE of AMERICA

# CRISIS BETWEEN EARTH-ONE AND EARTH-TWO!

**PART THREE**

IN THE EERIE REALM BETWEEN *EARTHS* -- BETWEEN SPACE AND NON-SPACE -- ON THE VERY RIM OF TIME ITSELF -- THAT BORDERS OUR MATTER UNIVERSE AND THE ANTI-MATTER UNIVERSE WHICH IS THE OPPOSITE OF OUR OWN WORLD -- THE *GHOSTLY GUARDIAN* ENGAGES IN ONE OF THE MOST FRIGHTENING FIGHTS EVER KNOWN !

THOUGH *THE SPECTRE* IS NOT COMPOSED OF MATTER, THE ALIEN ENERGIES SEETHING INSIDE HIS ANTI-MATTER OPPONENT TAKE THEIR OWN TOLL OF THE *SPIRIT SLEUTH* !

MY ARM SHRANK TO A THIRD OF ITS FORMER SIZE ! AND ⸴ OHH ⸴ MY BATTERED HEAD !

ZWAAK

MY HEAD--SWELLING UP LIKE A BALLOON ! EVERY TIME I COME INTO CONTACT WITH THE *ANTI-MATTER MAN* -- SOMETHING *TERRIBLE* HAPPENS TO ME !

As the *DISCARNATE DETECTIVE* desperately seeks to rally his ebbing powers...

I'LL SUSPEND TIME ITSELF SO I CAN--! TOO LATE! HE'S HIT ME SO HARD HE'S DRIVEN MY LEGS UP INTO MY BODY!

**BOP**

DISTORTED AND DEFORMED, DAZED AND SHOCKED BY CONTACT WITH ANTI-MATTER, *THE SPECTRE* IS HELPLESS TO MOVE...

AT LEAST MY SPIRIT SENSES ARE STILL FUNCTIONING! AND THEY TELL ME THAT *ANTI-MATTER MAN* IS ON HIS WAY TO EARTH! THE INSTANT HE SETS HIS ANTI-MATTER FOOT ON *EARTH*--THEY'LL BOTH BLOW UP LIKE AN EXPLODING NOVA!!

THREAT BUILDS UPON THREAT AS *THE SPECTRE* SEES...

*EARTH-ONE* AND --*EARTH-TWO*-- ON A COLLISION COURSE! EVEN IF *ANTI-MATTER MAN* NEVER STEPS ON EITHER OF THEM--THEY ARE DOOMED TO MEET--AND BLOW UP ANYWAY!

QUIETLY BUT DESPERATELY HE FIGHTS A LONE BATTLE--EXERTING EVERY EFFORT TO COMMAND HIS SPIRIT SHAPE TO ITS NORMAL FORM--RISING UPWARD AND OUTWARD TOWARD THE TWIN EARTHS...

I AM THE ONLY ONE IN ALL THE UNIVERSES WHO KNOWS ABOUT THE ONCOMING DOOM OF *EARTH-ONE* AND *EARTH-TWO*! IT'S UP TO *ME* TO PREVENT IT!

AND THEN--OUTDOING THE LEGENDARY *ATLAS* WITH THE WORLD UPON HIS SHOULDERS--THE *GHOSTLY GUARDIAN* HOLDS OFF ONE EARTH WITH HIS HANDS, THE OTHER WITH HIS FEET!...

THERE! FOR A WHILE AT LEAST THERE WILL BE NO COLLISION! BUT--HOW LONG CAN I MAINTAIN THIS POSITION?

18

AT THIS CRITICAL MOMENT LET US RETURN TO *BATMAN* AND THE MEMBERS OF THE *JUSTICE SOCIETY* ON *EARTH-TWO!* SHORT HOURS BEFORE-- IN THE SECRET SANCTUARY...

HOW ABOUT IT, *DOCTOR FATE*-- "*MAGIC*" ME BACK TO *EARTH-ONE!*

THAT'S NOT GOING TO BE AS EASY AS IT SOUNDS, *BATMAN!* I'VE BEEN CHECKING INTO MY CRYSTAL BALL HERE-- AND I CAN'T SEE *ANYTHING* OF *EARTH-ONE!* IF I CAN'T *SEE* IT-- I CAN'T *SEND* YOU THERE!

AS LONG AS YOU'RE STUCK HERE, YOU CAN HELP US CLEAR UP THIS MESS...

HOLD IT! LISTEN TO WHAT'S COMING IN OVER THE RADIO--

A PRIMITIVE THROWBACK TO THE DAYS OF THE CAVEMAN IS RUNNING WILD IN *PINETREE CITY!* THE POLICE ARE UNABLE TO COPE WITH HIM--

I WONDER IF THAT CAVEMAN CHARACTER IS CONNECTED WITH THE FANTASTIC DISPLACEMENTS THAT HAVE BEEN OCCURING BETWEEN *EARTH-ONE* AND *EARTH-TWO?*

LET'S GO FIND OUT!

AND SO-- UNAWARE OF THE DOOM THAT THREATENS BOTH THEIR EARTHS-- *BATMAN* WITH THE *JUSTICE SOCIETY* MEMBERS RACE DOWN UPON...

GOOD GOSH-- IT'S THE *BLOCKBUSTER!* I'VE NEVER BEEN ABLE TO STOP HIM AS *BATMAN*-- ONLY AS *BRUCE WAYNE*, BECAUSE I ONCE SAVED HIS LIFE!

INSTANTLY THE *MASKED MANHUNTER* YANKS OFF HIS DISGUISE-- BUT NOT BEFORE *WILDCAT* DRIVES TO THE ATTACK...

NOBODY HAS EVER STOOD UP YET TO THE PUNCH THAT MADE ME UNDEFEATED CHAMPION OF *EARTH-TWO!*

*WHAP!!*

BLOCKBUSTER DOES NOT BLINK-- EVEN UNDER THAT FRIGHTFUL BLOW! INSTEAD...

WAIT! I'M THE ONLY ONE WHO CAN HANDLE HIM--

ZOKK

AS THE BATTERED WILDCAT RAMS INTO BATMAN...

THWAAK!

THE COWLED CRUSADER LIES WITH HIS FACE PRESSED INTO THE GROUND--UNCONSCIOUS-- AS...

I'LL TAKE CARE OF HIM-- WITH UNBREAKABLE GLASS FASHIONED FROM THIS SPECIAL SAND AND A BLAST FROM MY SAND-GUN!

GOT HIM LOCKED UP INSIDE SHATTER-PROOF GLASS--HARMLESS AS A GLASS STATUE!

PETRIFIED BY THE HARD SHEATH, THE BRUTISH BEHEMOTH STANDS RIGID... UNTIL--WITH A MAD BELLOW OF BERSERK FEROCITY...

AARRGGH

IN--CREDIBLE! HE SMASHED HIS WAY OUT!...

KRAAK

20

FORWARD DARTS THE *MASTER OF MAGIC*...

GOT TO CHANGE THAT DEADLY GLASS TO WATER--MAKE IT SPLASH HARMLESSLY OVER *SANDMAN*...

SPLASH!

SPLASH!

THEN HE TURNS HIS ATTENTION TO THE *CAVEMAN COLOSSUS*..

I'LL LIFT HIM UP INTO THE AIR AS A HUMAN BALLOON--WHERE HE CAN'T DO ANY HARM...

*BUT*--EVEN AS *BLOCKBUSTER* RISES UPWARD--OUT OF HIS MIGHTY BODY FLOW THE ELECTRICAL IMPULSES IT ABSORBED IN THE *ALFRED MEMORIAL FOUNDATION*...

AMAZING! HE HAS THE POWER TO CONVERT MY MAGIC-KINETIC ENERGIES--INTO SOME TYPE OF POWER THAT HE HIMSELF CAN UTILIZE!

R/IP!

ZZZZZ!

OVERPOWERING ME--WITH MY OWN MAGIC AURA!

CAN'T MOVE! MY BODY SEEMS CAUGHT IN A *SPELL!*

GYAAGGH!

INTO THE AIR *BLOCKBUSTER* SWINGS HIS VICTIM...

GYAAGHH!

DAZEDLY BRUCE WAYNE LIFTS HIMSELF UP ON ONE KNEE. HIS HAND FLASHES OUTWARD, PALM UP...

ACROSS THE *BLOCKBUSTER'S* MISSHAPEN FACE PASSES A STRANGE LOOK AS HE SEES THE FACE OF THE MAN WHO ONCE BEFRIENDED HIM...

AAAGGH!

I'M *BRUCE WAYNE!* YOU RE-MEMBER ME! I SAVED YOUR LIFE IN A QUICKSAND BOG!

THEN WITH A HAPPY SHOUT HE DROPS *DOCTOR FATE* AND CATCHES HOLD OF HIS FRIEND, HIS PAL, HIS BUDDY!...

GYAAA! GYAAGH!

OHH, BOY! EVEN WHEN HE LIKES YOU -- HE'S SO STRONG HE HURTS YOU!

21

AND WHEN THE *JUSTICE SOCIETY* MEMBERS COME TO...

HE WILL OBEY ME -- IN MY CIVILIAN IDENTITY! I AM THE ONLY ONE -- BESIDES HIS BROTHER -- WHOM HE WILL LISTEN TO...

YOU'VE REVEALED YOUR TRUE FACE TO US! WELL -- IT DOESN'T MATTER, SINCE WE'RE ON *EARTH-TWO* AND YOU'RE FROM *EARTH-ONE*!

THUMPA! THUMPA!

YOUR SECRET WILL BE SAFE WITH US!

BUT THIS DOESN'T SOLVE OUR IMMEDIATE PROBLEM! YOU CAN'T GO ON BABY-SITTING FOR THAT BRUTE, *BATMAN!* WHAT ARE WE GOING TO DO WITH HIM?

WHAT INDEED CAN *BATMAN* AND THE *JUSTICE SOCIETY* MEMBERS DO WITH THE *BLOCKBUSTER?* HOW CAN THEY PREVENT HIS GOING ON ANOTHER RAMPAGE? AND OVER ON *EARTH-ONE* -- CAN FLASH, GREEN LANTERN, DR. MID-NITE, BLACK CANARY AND HAWKMAN EVER BE *REALLY* SURE THAT *SOLOMON GRUNDY* WON'T BURST OUT OF HIS MOUNTAIN PRISON?

ON *EARTH-ONE*, RAY (ATOM) PALMER STILL CANNOT GET HIS SIZE-AND-WEIGHT CONTROL DEVICE TO WORKING...

I BELIEVE I AM SUCCEEDING, RAY! I AM DOING WHAT I SET OUT TO DO! OH, IT'S SO EXCITING!

I WISH I COULD SUCCEED IN WHAT *I'M* TRYING TO DO!

AND DON'T FORGET *ANTI-MATTER MAN* WHO IS APPROACH-ING EARTH AS HE STRIDES ACROSS THE EERIE REALM BETWEEN WORLDS...

FINALLY, WHAT OF *SPECTRE* -- AND THE CRISIS HE'S TRYING TO STAVE OFF BETWEEN *EARTH-ONE* AND *EARTH-TWO*?

23

OUT ON THE VERY RIM OF EXISTENCE WHERE NO-WHERE BECOMES SOME-WHERE, AND TIME MERGES INTO SPACE ITSELF...

STRANGE OVERWHELMING FORCES ARE HURLING THE TWO *EARTHS* TOGETHER! I--CANNOT--RESIST THEM MUCH LONGER...

THE NON-MATTER FORM OF THE *DISEMBODIED DETECTIVE* SHRINKS! SMALLER HE BECOMES AND STILL SMALLER...

YOU DO NOT *DARE* MISS THE CONCLUDING CHAPTERS TO THIS TALE OF TERRIFIC FORCES WHICH PIT SUPER-HEROES AGAINST THE GRIM GIANTS OF *EARTH-ONE* AND *EARTH-TWO*-- AGAINST THE DREAD DANGER OF *ANTI-MATTER MAN*--AGAINST THE COMING CRASH OF TWO WORLDS WHICH WILL MEAN THE UTTER DESTRUCTION OF MANKIND!

IS THERE ANYTHING THE *JUSTICE LEAGUE* AND *JUSTICE SOCIETY* MEMBERS CAN DO TO PREVENT THE ABSOLUTE END OF *EVERYTHING?*

AMAZING ANSWERS NEXT ISSUE!

24

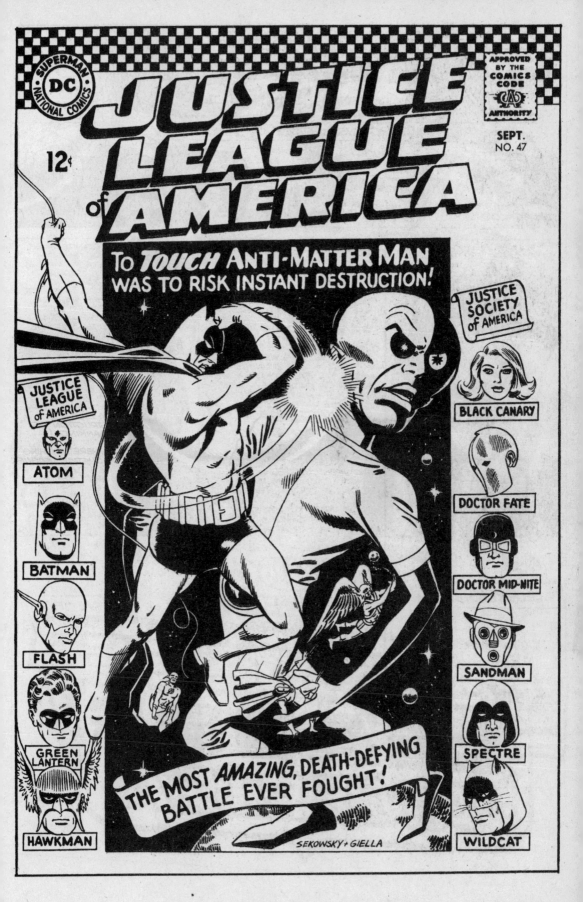

STORY BY GARDNER FOX

# JUSTICE LEAGUE of AMERICA ☆☆☆

ART BY MIKE SEKOWSKY & SID GREENE

## JUSTICE SOCIETY OF AMERICA

BLACK CANARY

SANDMAN

WILDCAT

DR. MID-NITE

SPECTRE

DR. FATE

FOR YOU JOHNNY-COME-LATELIES WHO MISSED THE FIRST HALF OF THIS EXTRAVAGANZA -- WE'LL CLUE YOU IN THAT CERTAIN PEOPLE AND SUPER-HEROES HAVE BEEN MYSTERIOUSLY SWITCHED FROM *EARTH-ONE* TO *EARTH-TWO* AND VICEY VERSEY!

INCLUDED AMONG THE DIS-PLACED VICTIMS WERE *BLOCK-BUSTER* -- NOW RUNNING AMUCK ON *EARTH-TWO*, AND *SOLOMON GRUNDY* -- NOW STALKING *EARTH-ONE* FOR HIS HATED FOE, *GREEN LANTERN!*

FINALLY, *THE SPECTRE* HAD EXTENDED HIMSELF BETWEEN BOTH *EARTHS* TO PREVENT AN ONRUSHING COLLISION BETWEEN THEM, ONLY TO START LOSING HIS GRIP BECAUSE OF THE NEARBY PRESENCE OF A WANDERER FROM THE ANTI-MATTER UNIVERSE! NOW THAT THESE DIRE EVENTS HAVE YOU ALL SHOOK UP, HOW CAN YOU RESIST READING...

## THE BRIDGE BETWEEN EARTHS!

THE BLOCKBUSTER

SOLOMON GRUNDY

JUSTICE LEAGUE OF AMERICA

HAWKMAN

GREEN LANTERN

FLASH

BATMAN

ATOM

1

IN A LABORATORY AT *IVY UNIVERSITY,* ENRICHETTA NEGRINI CHECKS HER SPACE-WARPING MACHINE-- AS RAY (*ATOM*) PALMER DESPERATELY TRIES TO GET HIS SIZE-AND-WEIGHT CONTROLS WORKING...

I THINK I'M ACTUALLY GETTING SOMEWHERE SHRINKING THE SPACE BETWEEN PLANETS...

AND I'M GETTING *NOWHERE* WITH MY SIZE-SHRINKING...

ALL MY LIFE I'VE DREAMED OF WARPING SPACE --SO MAN WON'T NEED SPACE-SHIPS TO TRAVEL TO THE DISTANT PLANETS! NOW WITH MY MACHINE, MAN WILL BE ABLE TO STEP OFF *EARTH* DIRECTLY ONTO *MARS* OR *VENUS!*

I'LL TAKE A BREAK TO EAT NOW! THE MACHINE WILL CONTINUE TO RUN BY ITSELF...

ODD! MY PALMS ARE-- *BURNING HOT!*

IT'S AS IF MY SIZE-AND-WEIGHT CONTROLS WERE GETTING AN OVERLOAD OF POWER--THE WAY AN ENGINE GETS HOT AND BREAKS DOWN FROM A SUDDEN INFLUX OF TOO MUCH POWER!

THE SPACE-WARPER'S THE ONLY THING AROUND HERE THAT COULD CAUSE THIS TO HAPPEN! BETTER SWITCH IT OFF --

*CLICK!*

÷WHEW!÷ MY CONTROLS ARE BACK TO NORMAL --I'M GETTING SMALLER!

2

SIMULTANEOUSLY ON *EARTH-TWO*, ANOTHER SURPRISING EFFECT CAUSED BY THE SWITCHING OFF OF THE SPACE-WARPING MACHINE...

YOU CAN'T GO ON BABYSITTING *BLOCK-BUSTER* THE REST OF YOUR LIFE, *BATMAN* !

MAYBE HE WON'T HAVE TO ! LOOK-- *BLOCK-BUSTER* IS DISAPPEAR-ING !

THEN, BEFORE THE BULGING EYES OF THE CRIME-FIGHTERS...

HE'S TURNED INTO-- *SOLOMON GRUNDY* !

OR IN SOME MYSTERIOUS MANNER-- *SOLOMON GRUNDY* WAS SUBSTITUTED IN PLACE OF-- *BLOCKBUSTER* !

ZZAAPP!

YOU-- *GREEN LANTERN* ! I KILL !

*GRUNDY'S* FLIPPED HIS EYE-BALLS ! HE THINKS *WILDCAT* IS *GREEN LANTERN* !

YOU-- *GREEN LANTERN* TOO ! I KILL !

I'LL GIVE HIM SOMETHING TO BELLOW AT-- A PILE OF CEMENT BLOCKS !

THUMP!

THUMP!

STRANGE ! I--I SENSE THAT MY MAGIC GLOBE IN *JUSTICE SOCIETY* HEAD-QUARTERS IS GLOWING--ALERTING ME TO A WORLDWIDE DANGER !

KRUNCH!

3

AND ON *EARTH-ONE*--THE GROUND SHAKES AS AN OMINOUS RUMBLING FILLS THE MOUNTAIN WHERE *SOLOMON GRUNDY* HAD BEEN IMPRISONED...

LISTEN! WE WEREN'T SURE WHETHER THE MOUNTAIN COULD HOLD *SOLOMON GRUNDY*-- AND IT CAN'T!

HE'S BREAKING LOOSE!

RUMMMMBLLLLL!

TO THE AMAZEMENT OF THE COMBINED *JUSTICE-LEAGUE-SOCIETY* MEMBERS...

HUH! THAT ISN'T *SOLOMON GRUNDY*!

WHO IS HE? I'VE NEVER SEEN HIM BEFORE!

WHOEVER HE IS--HE SPELLS *TROUBLE*!

IN THE WARPED MIND OF THE *BLOCK-BUSTER*, ANYONE WHO IS NOT BRUCE WAYNE OR HIS BROTHER, ROLAND DESMOND, IS A HATED FOE...

;WHEW; HIS HAND-GRIP IS SO STRONG IT FEELS LIKE A METAL CLAMP!

GYAAA!

WHEN THIS PELLET FROM MY AMULET SMASHES INTO HIM, ITS LIQUID CONTENTS WILL SPLASH OVER HIS BODY AND DEEP-FREEZE HIM!

5

FILLED WITH THE ENERGIES FROM THE *ALFRED MEMORIAL LABORATORY*--THE *CAVEMAN COLOSSUS* EYE-BLASTS THAT PELLET AS...

GYAAA!

THE BIG BABOON'S SHOWING ME AN EYEFUL! OKAY--I'LL GIVE HIM A HANDFULL OF *BLONDE DYNAMITE!*

I'LL JUDO-THROW YOU LIKE A ⸓ PUFF ⸓ ⸓ PANT ⸓ LIKE A ...

GYAAA? GYAA?

FOUR FEARFUL FIGHTING MEN RALLY FROM BLOWS THAT WOULD KAYO ORDINARY MORTALS...

COP OUT, LADY BIRD! WE'LL BOWL OVER THIS ODDBALL!

I'LL OPERATE ON HIM WITH MY *CYROTUBER!*

BUT THEY FIND THAT THEIR SUPER-POWERED ATTACK ONLY ROUSES THE *BLOCK-BUSTER* TO WHIP UP A FIRE-WORKS DISPLAY THAT ROCKS THEM BACK ON THEIR HEELS...

KA-BOOM!

VROOOSH!

ZOOM

LOW ME!

EEEOOO

6

WHILE THE SUPER-STARS ARE TAKING THEIR LUMPS ON *EARTH-ONE* -- ON *EARTH-TWO DOCTOR FATE* IS EYEING HIS CRYSTAL ORB...

IT REVEALS *THE SPECTRE* IN WARP-SPACE -- KEEPING *EARTH-ONE* FROM COLLIDING WITH *EARTH-TWO!* THOUGH HE'S WEAKENING FAST, HE WAS ABLE TO CONTACT ME FOR HELP THROUGH MY CRYSTAL BALL!

EVEN MORE OMINOUS -- I SEE A BEING FROM THE *ANTI-MATTER UNIVERSE* ADVANCING TOWARD *EARTH-TWO* -- ALONG *SPECTRE'S* BODY! IF HE TOUCHES *EARTH* WITH HIS ANTI-MATTER BODY -- BOTH HE AND THE PLANET WILL SUFFER INSTANT ANNIHILATION!

HE MUST NEVER BE ALLOWED TO SET HIS DISASTER-FOOT ON EARTH! I'LL NEED ALL THE HELP I CAN GET FROM MY FELLOW MEMBERS!

WHA-- WHAT'S HAPPENING?

ANOTHER TRICK OF OUR OPPONENT!

SOME STRANGE POWER IS DRAWING US SPACEWARD!

NO! MY *POWER RING* TELLS ME -- WE'VE BEEN CAUGHT UP BY *DOCTOR FATE'S* MAGIC! HE MUST NEED US -- FOR A MISSION EVEN MORE IMPORTANT THAN STOPPING THAT BELLOWING BRUTE BELOW!

# THE BRIDGE BETWEEN EARTHS!
## PART TWO

GREAT GUARDIANS! THERE'S THE SPECTRE-- FORMING A BRIDGE--BETWEEN THE TWO EARTHS!

SPECTRE'S KEEPING EARTH-ONE AND EARTH-TWO FROM COLLIDING-- THANKS TO THE MAGIC BOOSTER SHOT I GAVE HIM! NOW IT'S UP TO US TO PREVENT ANTI-MATTER MAN FROM SETTING FOOT ON EITHER EARTH!

THANKS TO DR. FATE'S MAGIC RING, WE THREE ARE IN POSITION TO FIGHT OUR FOE AROUND HIS MID-SECTION...

...WHILE WE THREE DO OUR FIGHTING ATOP SPECTRE'S BODY--AIMING AT ANTI-MATTER MAN'S FEET!

**GIGANTIC! COLOSSAL! TITANIC!** A TOWERING FIGURE OF CONTRA-MATTER! A LIVING, WALKING, WORLD-WRECKING BOMB! THE SAFETY OF *TWO EARTHS* DEPENDS ON EACH OF THE NINE SUPER-HEROES DOING HIS UTMOST TO OVERCOME THE INCREDIBLE ANTI-MATTER MAN!

19

*HOO-HAH! IS ANTI-MATTER MAN EVER IN TROUBLE! YOU BET HE IS -- BUT HE CAN DISH IT OUT AS WELL AS TAKE IT! AS A FOR INSTANCE -- HIS EERIE ENERGIES SURGE OUT IN A FLOW OF FURIOUS FORCE! WHEEEEE!!! -- AND LOOK WHAT HAPPENS ...*

MY WINGS -- COILING ABOUT ME -- GETTING TIGHTER -- **TIGHTER!**

I'VE BEEN TRAPPED IN MY OWN MAGICAL LIGHTNINGS!

MY OWN **POWER-HAND** -- CRUSHING ME!

MY FEET -- SO BIG, SO HEAVY -- I CAN'T MOVE 'EM!

WHATEVER ODD POWERS ANTI-MATTER MAN HAS -- HE SURE KNOWS HOW TO USE THEM! HE'S PUT US OUT OF ACTION!

**WILDCAT --** WE'RE STUCK TOGETHER -- BACK TO BACK!

*EEEE!* MY HAIR'S GROWN SO LONG ... I'M TRIPPING OVER IT!

I'M SO -- C-COLD I C-C-CAN HARDLY MOVE! MY **C-CYROTUBER'S** G-GONE H-H-HAYWIRE!

I'M -- BEING -- BURIED -- IN MY OWN SAND!

WHAT A MISERABLE MESS! BUT DANGER SERVES TO BRING OUT THE BEST IN OUR SUPER-HEROES I KNOCKED DOWN, STOMPED ON BY ADVERSITY--THEY RALLY ROUND EACH OTHER TO DO BY TEAMWORK WHAT MIGHT BE--Ahem--A BIT DIFFICULT AS INDIVIDUALS!..

THANKS FOR THE ASSIST, GL! MY PINIONS ARE NO LONGER PINNING ME DOWN!

I WISH I COULD HELP YOU, DOCTOR FATE-- BUT THOSE MAGICAL CAGE-BARS OF YOURS ARE YELLOW AND MY RING IS POWERLESS AGAINST--

MY CAGE-- STARTING TO-- FALL!

MAYBE MY FEET CAN'T MOVE--BUT MY ARMS SURE CAN! GET READY TO GO OVER THE "TOP," BATMAN AND WILDCAT!

FALLING FASTER--!

AT LEAST I CAN USE MY LONG HAIR TO TIE UP HIS ANKLES-- SO HE CAN'T GO ANY FURTHER!

GRAB HOLD, DR. MID-NITE! I'VE FORMED A GLASS RESCUE ROD TO PULL YOURSELF OUT OF THAT REFRIGERATION UNIT YOU'RE IN!

SPECTRE IS MAKING MY FALL EASY-- TURNING HIMSELF SOFT AT THIS POINT OF HIS BODY!

12

THE GHOSTLY GUARDIAN IS DOING MORE THAN THAT! HE MAKES HIS BODY BEND-- GIVE TO THE WEIGHT OF THE CAGE-- THEN BOUNCES IT UPWARD-- SWIFTLY THROUGH THE AIR...

NICE GOING, SPECTRE! YOU'RE JOINING IN ON THE FUN!

HE'S SHIFTING MY PILE OF SAND AROUND THE ANTI-- MATTER MAN'S ANKLES!

AND THERE GO MY FRIGID AIR COILS--TO MAKE THE SAND AND BLACK CANARY'S HAIR SOLID AS A CEMENT-- BUILDING FOUNDATION!

UP--UP--UP GOES DOCTOR FATE IN HIS MAGIC CAGE, FLUNG HIGH BY THE RIPPLING, BOUNCING BODY OF THE SPIRIT SLEUTH!...

WHAKK! POW!

IT'S A REAL SPINNER-WINNER, FLASH!

WHAT DO YOU THINK OF MY SOCKO-GO-ROUND, DOCTOR FATE?

UNTIL HE ARRIVES BACK WHERE HE STARTED AND...

OKAY, PALS--DON'T SPARE THE HORSES! YOU KNOW WHAT TO DO!

13

MIGHTY HANDS FASTEN ON THE MAGICAL BARS-- SLAM THE CAGE WITH KNOCK-OUT FORCE AGAINST THE ANTI-MATTER JAW...

BLAAAP!

--THE MENTAL KIND!

THAT OUGHT TO MAKE HIM SEE STARS--

AS THE ANTI-MATTER MAN MOMENTARILY LOSES CONSCIOUSNESS, HIS ALIEN ENERGIES FADE OUT-- RELEASING THE SUPER-HEROES FROM HIS POWERS...

WHAMP! WHAMP! WHOMP! SOK!

EVEN AS THEY LOCK HIS FEET INSIDE THE FROZEN MOUND OF HAIR AND CEMENT, THE LOW HEROES ON THE ANTI-MATTER TOTEM POLE MAKE ABSOLUTELY CERTAIN OF THEIR FOE...

LONG HAIR WENT OUT OF FASHION YEARS AGO! HERE'S WHERE I GET RID OF MINE!

JUST A LITTLE MORE-- AND THAT GUY'LL GIVE UP WALKING FOR EXERCISE!

YEAH-- YEAH-- YEAH! HIS FEET DO SEEM A BIT CRAMPED!

OUT INTO SPACE PLUNGE THE SUPER-HEROES TO RESUME THE BATTLE WITH THE ALIEN EXPLORER WHO MUST BE DENIED ENTRANCE TO *EARTH-ONE* OR *EARTH-TWO*! SOK! BAM! ZOWIE! LOOK AT 'EM GO!..

BUT WAIT! THIS CONTRA-CAT IS A CLAW-HAPPY FIGHTER WHO RELISHES A BANG-UP ROCK 'EM SOCK 'EM RHUBARB! HE HITS OUT AND--TUCK BACK YOUR EYEBALLS, READERS--THIS IS A MOMENT OF TRUTH! THE *JUSTICE LEAGUE* AND THE *JUSTICE SOCIETY* BOYS ARE REALLY CATCHING IT!...

HOLD IT, GUYS AND GALS! TIME OUT FOR A BREATHER--AS WE BACK-CHECK ON *THE ATOM*...

16

IN HIS *IVY UNIVERSITY* LABORATORY, WHERE THE *TINY TITAN* HAS BEEN INVESTIGATING ENRICHETTA NEGRINI'S SPACE-WARP MACHINE...

BY TURNING THIS DIAL, I FIND I CAN FOCUS THROUGH THE HELIX AND INTO WARP-SPACE--*eh?* THAT'S *THE SPECTRE* BETWEEN TWO EARTHS!

THE TWO PLANETS ARE MOVING TOGETHER--AND DESPITE ALL *SPECTRE'S* EFFORTS, HE CAN'T STOP THEM! SHOULD THOSE EARTHS MEET--THEY'LL EXPLODE! I'VE GOT TO HELP HIM--

ARMED WITH A DUPLICATE OF HIS SIZE-AND-WEIGHT CONTROLS, HE DIVES INTO THE ENERGY CURTAIN OF THE WARP-SCREEN...

BY MAKING MYSELF SMALL AS A MOLECULE, I'LL GO RIGHT THROUGH THE ENERGY-SCREEN INTO WARP-SPACE! IF MY CALCULATIONS ARE CORRECT...

...I OUGHT TO LAND SOME-WHERE NEAR *THE SPECTRE*--

*ATOM*--JUST IN THE NICK OF TIME! THE MAGIC *DOCTOR FATE* PUT INSIDE ME TO HELP HOLD THE EARTHS APART... IS FADING OUT!

*SPECTRE*--I WANT TO SHRINK YOU TO AN INCH IN HEIGHT--THEN EXPAND YOU! HOWEVER, I MUST WARN YOU--THAT WHEN YOU EXPAND AGAIN-- THE CHANCES ARE YOU'LL BLOW UP--MIGHT BE DESTROYED! BUT THAT'S THE ONLY WAY I CAN SEE HOW TO SAVE BOTH EARTHS! THE DECISION IS *YOURS!*

17

DO IT, *ATOM*--AND FAST! I WILL WILLINGLY SACRIFICE MY EXISTENCE FOR THAT OF TWO *EARTHS'*!

OKAY! I'M GOING TO SHRINK DOWN INTO THE SUBATOMIC UNIVERSE TO AVOID THE BLAST OF YOUR EXPLOSION! SEND ME A MENTAL COMMAND WHEN TO SWITCH ON THE CONTROLS!

THEN--AS THE *TINY TITAN* PLACES HIS SPARE SIZE-AND-WEIGHT CONTROL DEVICE ON THE *GHOSTLY GUARDIAN*...

THERE! NOW YOU'RE WITHIN RANGE OF THE CONTROL DEVICE! I'M GOING *DOWN*--!

CLICK!

CLICK

SWIFTLY SHRINKS THE *SPECTRE!* CLOSER AND CLOSER COME THE GREAT PLANETS!...

FORTUNATELY, THESE APPROACHING EARTHS ARE IN WARP-SPACE--OR THEIR GRAVITATIONAL ATTRACTION FOR EACH OTHER WOULD DESTROY THEM ANYHOW!

*THE ATOM* TOO HAS BECOME INFINITELY SMALLER...

THANKS TO THE ATMOSPHERE WHICH *DOCTOR FATE* PUT AROUND THE SPECTRE, THIS OXYGEN ATOM I'VE SHRUNK INTO WILL ENABLE ME TO BREATHE IN PERFECT COMFORT!

SUDDENLY... A *SPECTRAL* MESSAGE...

NOW, ATOM! SWITCH ON--!

CLICK!

CLICK!

18

A FLARING, COLOSSAL EXPLOSION BLOSSOMS UPWARD AND OUTWARD! THERE IS NO SOUND IN SPACE TO HERALD THIS SUPER-BROBDINGNAGIAN DETONATION-- ONLY THAT TITANIC BLAZE THAT SIGNALS THE BLOWING APART OF *THE SPECTRE!*...

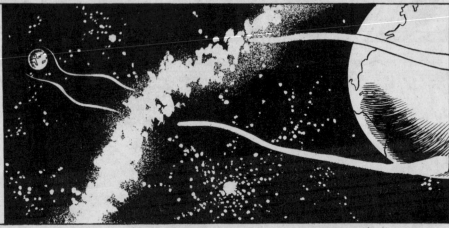

AND AS THAT AWESOME EXPLOSION SENDS ITS SHOCK-WAVES OUT ACROSS WARP-SPACE-- IT FLINGS *EARTH-ONE* AND *EARTH-TWO* APART-- BACK INTO THEIR NORMAL ORBITS FROM WHICH ENRICHETTA NEGRINI'S SPACE-WARPING MACHINE FIRST DREW THEM...

EVEN INSIDE HIS SUBATOMIC HAVEN, THE *TINY TITAN* FEELS AND SHUDDERS TO THAT FRIGHTFUL BLAST..

THAR SHE BLOWS! WELL, THIS WAS THE ONLY WAY TO DO IT! EVEN SHUTTING OFF ENRICHETTA'S MACHINE COULDN'T SEND THOSE EARTHS BACK WHERE THEY BELONGED! ONCE IN MOTION-- *THIS* WAS THE ONLY WAY TO STOP THEM!

MOMENTS LATER...

I GUESS IT'S SAFE NOW TO COME OUT OF HIDING! *SIGH*-- POOR *SPECTRE!* HE SURE WAS A HERO. HE GAVE HIS EXISTENCE TO SAVE-- *GREAT GALAXY! IS THAT THE SPECTRE--?!*

YES, *ATOM*-- I'M GETTING BACK INTO SHAPE! THOUGH THE PSYCHO-MATTER OF MY SPIRIT BODY WAS EXPLOSIVELY FLUNG TO ALL CORNERS OF THIS WARPED UNIVERSE-- I STILL MAINTAINED CONTROL OF ITS ELEMENTS!

19

JUST BEFORE I EXPLODED TO SMITHEREENS, I IMBUED MY BODY WITH SPIRITUAL-MAGNETIC ATTRACTION--SO THAT NO MATTER HOW FAR APART IT WAS FLUNG, IT WOULD BE DRAWN BACK TO NORMAL AFTER A WHILE!

SPECTRE-ACULAR!

SHORTLY, *SPECTRE* AND *ATOM* SPEED TOWARD ANTI-MATTER MAN AND THEIR SUPER-HERO FRIENDS...

WE'RE MOVING SO FAST WE'VE ALMOST CAUGHT UP TO THE SHOCK-WAVES FLUNG OUT BY MY EXPLOSION!

SLIP INSIDE MY PROTECTIVE CLOAK, *ATOM!* YOU'RE GOING TO HAVE A RINGSIDE VIEW OF WHAT HAPPENS NEXT! I'VE ALREADY ALERTED *DOCTOR FATE* AND *GREEN LANTERN* OF WHAT'S IN STORE!

A STARTLING SURPRISE--A WONDROUS WIND-UP TO THE STORY--ON THE NEXT PAGE FOLLOWING!

20

THE BRIDGE BETWEEN EARTHS!
PART THREE
THERE GOES ANTI-MATTER MAN ! THE SHOCK-WAVES FROM MY EXPLODING BODY HAVE FINALLY ARRIVED HERE AND--ARE BLASTING HIM BACK INTO HIS OWN UNIVERSE !
WITH NOT A MOMENT TO SPARE, SPECTRE !
HE HAD US IN A BAD SPOT-- BUT YOU WERE THE CLEANING FLUID THAT RUBBED IT OUT !
21

WE AREN'T FINISHED YET! WE STILL HAVE *SOLOMON GRUNDY* AND *BLOCKBUSTER* TO TAKE CARE OF!

I JUST HOPE THEY HAVEN'T DESTROYED TOO MUCH PROPERTY--OR HURT ANYONE IN THEIR SENSELESS RAGES!

OH, YOU NEEDN'T WORRY TOO MUCH ABOUT *BLOCK-BUSTER* AND *SOLOMON GRUNDY*--

JUST BEFORE *DOCTOR FATE* WHISKED US OFF OUR EARTHS-- I WILLED MY *POWER RING* TO BRING *SOLOMON GRUNDY* AND *BLOCKBUSTER* TOGETHER! FROM WHAT YOU'D TOLD ME, *SOLOMON GRUNDY* THOUGHT *EVERYBODY* WAS *GREEN LANTERN*-- AND *BLOCK-BUSTER* HATED EVERYONE BUT HIS BROTHER AND BRUCE WAYNE...

"AND SO--LOCKED IN TITANIC STRUGGLE-- THE TWO HATE-FULL BRUTES HAVE BEEN TRADING BATTERING BLOWS..."

THE SUPER-HEROES ARRIVE AT THE FIGHT ARENA JUST IN TIME TO SEE...

ZOKKO

KROWW!

THEY KNOCKED EACH OTHER OUT!

GET SET FOR MORE FIREWORKS WHEN THEY COME TO!

BLOCKBUSTER STIRS-- HIS EYES POP AT THE SIGHT OF HIS FALLEN FOE..

GYYA?

SOLOMON GRUNDY STARES WIDE-MOUTHED AT THE TITANIC TERROR...

YOU GOOD MAN! ME NOT HATE YOU NO MORE!

THEY LUNGE AT EACH OTHER-- BUT NO LONGER IN HATE AND RAGE! INSTEAD THEY LAUGH, THEIR EYES SPARKLING WITH FRIENDSHIP...

US BE FRIENDS!

GYAAAA!

GYAAA!

WHAT'S GOT INTO THOSE EX-BITTER ENEMIES?!

THUMP!

SLAP!

THUD!

THUMP!

THE SURPRISES ARE NOT DONE WITH YET! THE LONG ARMS OF FRIENDSHIP REACH OUT TO ENGULF THE SUPER-HEROES...

YOU GOOD GUYS, TOO! NOT HATE YOU EITHER!

OKAY! YOU LIKE US! BUT DON'T HUG SO HARD!

THEY KNOCKED THE HATE OUT OF EACH OTHER!

IF ONLY WE COULD GET PEOPLE AND NATIONS TO KNOCK HATE OUT OF EACH OTHER WITHOUT GOING TO WAR!

LIKE PEACE, MAN! REAL PEACE!

23

AND SO, WITH A REFORMED, FRIENDLY *SOLOMON GRUNDY*, THE *JUSTICE SOCIETY* MEMBERS RETURN HOMEWARD--ALONG WITH ALL THE OTHER DISPLACED PEOPLE OF *EARTH-TWO*..

WE'LL TALK THINGS OVER AT OUR SECRET HEADQUARTERS--

--DECIDE WHAT TO DO WITH *SOLOMON GRUNDY*, FRIEND OF THE PEOPLE!

WHILE *BLOCK-BUSTER* AND THE *JUSTICE LEAGUE* MEMBERS--ALONG WITH THE DISPLACED EARTH-PEOPLE--RETURN TO *EARTH-ONE*...

THE ALFRED FOUNDATION WILL STILL STUDY *BLOCKBUSTER*-- THOUGH I DON'T BELIEVE HE'LL GIVE US ANY MORE TROUBLE!

WHAT ABOUT ENRICHETTA NEGRINI? DO YOU THINK WE SHOULD ASK HER TO GIVE UP HER SPACE-WARP EXPERIMENTS?

NO, *ATOM! RISK* IS A NECESSARY--AND CALCULATED RISK--OF ALL SCIENTIFIC RESEARCH!

IN HER PARTICULAR CASE, ENRICHETTA NEGRINI NEVER REALIZED SHE WAS TAMPERING WITH THE FORCES OF NATURE!

BESIDES--WE SUPER-HEROES ARE ALWAYS AROUND TO MAKE THE WORLD SAFE! RIGHT, EVERYBODY?

AND WE ALL ECHO-- RIGHT!

24

STORY BY GARDNER FOX

# JUSTICE ✦✦✦ LEAGUE ☆☆☆ of AMERICA

ART BY MIKE SEKOWSKY & SID GREENE

HOW COULD THE JUSTICE LEAGUERS HOPE TO FIGURE OUT WHICH OF TWO FELIX FAUSTS WAS REAL AND UNREAL -- WHEN NOT EVEN THE SORCERERS THEMSELVES KNEW?
WITH THE CLOCK OF UNIVERSAL DOOM ALMOST AT ZERO HOUR, THE SUPER-HEROES TAKE OFF ON THEIR TOUGHEST CASE --

# THREAT of the TRUE-OR-FALSE SORCERER!

THE ROLL CALL

BATMAN

FLASH

GREEN LANTERN

SUPERMAN

AND A LAST-MINUTE DRAMATIC APPEAR-ANCE BY SNAPPER CARR

UNLESS YOU CAN TELL WHICH OF US IS THE REAL FELIX FAUST AND WHICH IS THE FALSE --

THE ENTIRE UNIVERSE AND EVERY LIVING THING ON IT WILL BLOW UP! HA! HA! HA!

IN A FEDERAL PENITENTIARY, A SMIRKING PRISONER LIFTS THE LID OF A CIGAR BOX FILLED WITH ODDS AND ENDS COLLECTED OVER A PERIOD OF MONTHS...

SOAP SHAVINGS, USED TEA LEAVES, BURNED MATCHSTICK, WORTHLESS LITTLE THINGS, ALL OF THEM! BUT THEY'LL SERVE TO GET ME OUT OF THIS JAIL CELL!

THIS MAN IS *FELIX FAUST,* MASTER MAGICIAN, NEFARIOUS NECROMANCER, WIZARD OF OF THE WEIRD ARTS...

YES, I SHALL ESCAPE -- AND I DEFY ANYONE -- ESPECIALLY THE *JUSTICE LEAGUE OF AMERICA*-- TO STOP ME!

TEALEAF--SPINACH-- GOLD OFF AN ELL, SEED FROM A PLANT AND TOLLING BELL! BIT OF SOAP AND BLOT OF INK, BURNING MATCH WITHOUT A KINK! AS BUTTERFLY FLITS, AS ACORN FALLS, *NOW HELP ME TO ESCAPE THESE WALLS!*

THE NEXT INSTANT OF THAUMATURGIC TIME, IN FAUST'S DEN OF DEMONOLOGY...

MY CONJURATION DID IT--SPRUNG ME OUT OF JAIL!

MY CONJURATION DID IT--SPRUNG ME OUT OF JAIL!

HUH? AN ECHO HERE--*NO!* IT'S ANOTHER PERSON-- LOOKING LIKE *ME!*

WHO ARE YOU?

I'M *FELIX FAUST,* OF COURSE! WHAT ARE *YOU* DOING HERE, YOU IMPOSTOR!

IMPOSTOR!? ME?! I'M FELIX FAUST, THE WORLD'S GREATEST SORCERER! YOU'RE NOT GOOD ENOUGH TO STAND IN MY SHOES!

BY THE TIME I'M THROUGH WITH YOU, YOU WON'T EVEN BE STANDING!

WHAP!

KWOK!

DISCOVERING QUICKLY ENOUGH THAT FISTICUFFS CANNOT SOLVE THEIR PERPLEXING PROBLEM, THE DUPLICATE DEMONOLOGISTS DELVE INTO MUSTY VOLUMES OF SORCEROUS LORE...

PERHAPS I MISUSED A WORD-- OMITTED A VITAL ELEMENT OF THE CON- JURATION...?

EVIDENTLY IN ESCAPING FROM PRISON, I CREATED A DUPLICATE OF MYSELF! I'VE GOT TO RECTIFY THAT BLUNDER!

DONNING CABALISTIC CLOTHES, THE TWIN FELIX FAUST CONJURES UP THE DEMON ABADDON...

NOT EVEN I WHO HAVE SERVED YOU BEFORE CAN DETERMINE WHO IS WHO! BUT THIS I DO KNOW... THE FALSE FELIX FAUST WILL FADE AWAY WHEN THE SPELL WHICH CREATED HIM WEARS OFF-- AND WHEN THAT HAPPENS...

...THE RESULTANT EX- PLOSION OF HIS DIS- APPEARANCE WILL DESTROY THIS ENTIRE UNIVERSE AND EVERY LIVING THING IN IT! FELIX FAUST--WHO- EVER YOU ARE--THERE'S ONLY ONE WAY TO SAVE YOURSELF--AND THE UNIVERSE! CONJURE THE UNREAL ONE OUT OF EXISTENCE BEFORE HE FADES AWAY!...

GOOD ENOUGH! I'LL TAKE CARE OF THAT RIGHT NOW!

WAIT! YOU'RE SURE YOU ARE THE REAL FAUST--BUT SO AM I! SHOULD THE FALSE ONE DESTROY THE TRUE ONE, HE WILL EVENTUALLY FADE AWAY--AND DESTROY THE UNIVERSE! A MISTAKE IN IDENTITY WOULD BE FATAL FOR BOTH OF US!

IT'S IMPOSSIBLE FOR US TO SOLVE THE DILEMMA --BUT I KNOW SOMEONE WHO CAN--THE JUSTICE LEAGUE OF AMERICA!

AGREED! LET US CAST A SPELL AND SUMMON THEM TO AN EMERGENCY MEETING!

3

AND SO— SHORTLY AFTERWARD— THE TWIN MAGICIANS MATERIALIZE IN JUSTICE LEAGUE HEAD-QUARTERS...

A FELIX FAUST-- IN DUPLICATE! WHAT KIND OF DOUBLE TROUBLE IS HE PLANNING?

MAYBE THIS HAS SOMETHING TO DO WITH THE REASON WHY ONLY FOUR OF US SHOWED UP AT THIS MEETING!

THE COUNTERFEIT DOUBLE MUST BE RESPONSIBLE FOR IT! HE KNOWS NO MATTER WHAT HAPPENS, HE WON'T EXIST MUCH LONGER-- SO HE CAST A MAGICAL SPELL ON THE REST OF THE JUSTICE LEAGUERS TO IMMOBILIZE THEM-- AND BRINGS DOOM TO ALL OF US!

THIS WAS YOUR DOING, YOU PHONY! I'M GOING TO FREE THEM...

TIME'S TOO VALUABLE TO WASTE DOING THAT! WE DON'T KNOW HOW MUCH LONGER BEFORE EITHER OF US FADES OUT AND DESTROYS THE UNIVERSE! WE'LL HAVE TO RELY ON THESE FOUR--

DESTROY THE UNIVERSE? SAY, WHAT'S THIS ALL ABOUT?

SWIFTLY, THE STORY POURS FROM THE LIPS OF THE TROUBLED THAUMATURGISTS...

IT'S SIMPLE TO DESTROY THE MAGICAL FELIX FAUST! THE TROUBLE IS-- WE DON'T DARE RISK IT TILL WE KNOW WHICH ONE IS REAL AND WHICH IS FALSE!

I'VE BEEN TRYING TO FIND THAT OUT WITH MY POWER RING-- BUT CAN'T!

THIS IS THE TOUGHEST PROBLEM WE'VE EVER TACKLED! ANYONE HAVE AN IDEA HOW TO START--?

WHAT ABOUT THIS IDEA? WE'LL CREATE MENACING SITUATIONS FOR YOU TO DEAL WITH--THE HANDLING OF WHICH WE HOPE-- SOMEHOW-- WILL ENABLE YOU TO DETERMINE WHICH OF US IS THE REAL FELIX FAUST!

# THREAT OF THE TRUE-OR-FALSE SORCERER-- PART 2

BY WIND, BY RAIN, BY SEA, BY STAR-- I SEND THEE ON A JOURNEY FAR!

GET SET, *BATMAN!* YOU AND *GREEN LANTERN* ARE ABOUT TO BE DISPATCHED ON YOUR QUEST!

I KNOW THIS ISN'T A *TRICK* BECAUSE I PROBED THEIR MINDS WHILE TRYING TO LEARN WHO WAS WHO! THERE REALLY ARE *TWO* FELIX FAUSTS-- BUT WHO'S THE *REAL* ONE?

SCARCELY HAVE THE TWO TROUBLE-SHOOTERS DRAWN A DEEP BREATH WHEN...

WHAT A COMEDOWN! WE'VE BEEN TRANSPORTED TO AN ORDINARY RAILROAD SIDING -- WHERE SOME FUGITIVE FROM A FREAK SHOW HAS BROKEN INTO ONE OF THE CARS!

DON'T KNOCK MAGIC, *FLASH!* I'M *VULNERABLE* TO IT-- SO I HAVE A GREAT RESPECT FOR IT! LET ME HAVE FIRST CRACK AT THAT *TROLL* ...

U.S. MAIL

5

MMPFFF! IF THERE'S ONE THING I DIDN'T NEED TODAY--IT'S A FACIAL TREATMENT!

WATCH OUT BELOW!

SIG O'KOWS

Perfumes INC.

THEY CRASH THROUGH THE ROOF OF A PARKED DELIVERY TRUCK...

CRASH!

HE LOST HIS STRENGTH AGAIN! NOW I THINK I KNOW WHY--!

YEOWWWP!

SOON'S I BELT HIM INTO DREAMLAND, I'LL FIND FLASH AND TELL HIM WHAT I'VE FOUND OUT...

WHUNNK!

DELUXE SOAP

DELUXE SOAP

THE SCARLET SPEEDSTER HAS NOT BEEN IDLE! OH, NO! FOR JUST AS SUPERMAN TOOK OFF INTO THE AIR WITH THE TROLL...

YOU'RRRE NOT GOING ANYWHERRRE, FRRRIEND!

HUH?!

I'M SEEING THINGS! A--LEPRECHAUN?!

RRRIGHT! AND GIFTED WITH MAGIC, I MIGHT ADD! AHH! I SEE YOU DON'T BELIEVE ME...

VERRRY WELL, YOU'LL GET A DEMONSTRRRATION! THE HAND IS FASTERRR THAN THE EYE, FLASH-- EVEN YOURRR SUPER-FAST EYE! YOU SEE MY HANDS AND YET...

FOURRR HANDS ARE BETTERRR THAN TWO, FLASH! HO, HO, HO!

HIS MAGICAL HANDS HOLDING ME SO TIGHTLY-- I CAN'T MOVE!

WHILE MY EXTRRRA HANDS HEAVE TO, I'LL LEAN TO...

DON'T FRRRET, FLASH! WHEN THIS IS OVERRR, I'LL SELL YOU SOME HEADACHE PILLS!

BUT--THE FASTEST MAN ALIVE CAN WORK A SPEED MAGIC OF HIS OWN! AS HIS HEAD TOUCHES THE BUILDING WALL...

BY VIBRATING AT SUPER-SPEED, I PIERCED THE WALL WITHOUT HARM! NOW TO MAKE A CHUMP OUT OF THAT IMP!

BY WINDMILLING MY ARMS, I CAN GENERATE MORE POWER THAN THE STRONGEST AIR-PLANE PROPELLER-- ENABLING ME TO --

--SHOW HIM A TRICKY "FEAT" OF MY OWN!

IS THIS OAK TREE OK WITH YOU, LEPPY OLD BOY?

ZWUKK!

# THREAT OF THE TRUE-OR-FALSE SORCERER-- PART 3

MAGICALLY WAFTED THROUGH THE AIR, *BATMAN* AND *GREEN LANTERN* BECOME TARGETS FOR AMAZING ATTACKS! FROM CLOUDS IN THE SKY, PRETTY *SYLPHIDES* COMMAND WISPY FINGERS TO ENSNARE THE *EMERALD GLADIATOR* -- WHILE THEIR EQUALLY CHARMING COUSINS, THE TREE-SPIRIT *DRYADS*, WORK WIZARDLY WEAPONS TO ENTRAP THE *CAPED CRUSADER*!

HOW CAN OUR DAUNTLESS DUO EXPECT TO FIGHT OFF *FEMALE FOES?!*

DOWN FROM THEIR CLOUD HOME SWOOP THE WINGED WOMEN...

TAG -- YOU'RE *IT!* : *tee-hee* : WE'VE NEVER HAD A REAL LIVE SUPER-HERO TO PLAY GAMES WITH BEFORE!

LOOK, KIDS -- I MEAN YOUNG LADIES! THIS CASE I'M ON IS NO LAUGHING MATTER!

13

SUDDENLY, THE GRIPPING CLOUD HANDS BEGIN TO PULL AND STRETCH THE *GREEN GLADIATOR* ...

LOOK NOW-- I'LL BE FORCED TO DO A BIT OF SPANKING-- UNLESS YOU ACT YOUR AGE!

OOOH! LET'S PLAY JUMP ROPE, EVERYBODY!

THIS IS *HUMILIATING!* I DON'T WANT TO USE MY *POWER RING* AGAINST GIRLS-- BUT THEY'RE NOT GIVING ME ANY OTHER CHOICE!

EIGHT-- NINE-- TEN--!

;*tee-hee*; ISN'T THAT *CUTE!* HE'S USING A *POWER RING* TO TRY AND BLOW AWAY THAT CLOUD!

HOW SILLY! WE'RE *MAGIC*-- AND UNLESS HE KNOWS THE MAGIC FORMULA THAT GIVES US LIFE-- HIS *POWER RING* CAN'T DO A THING AGAINST US!

ON THE GROUND BELOW-- A PILE OF BURNING LEAVES ... BY WHIPPING UP A LARGE ENOUGH FIRE WITH THESE POWER-BELLOWS, I'LL CAUSE THE HEATED AIR TO RISE UP BENEATH THE CLOUD AND BLOW IT AWAY!

BUT INSTEAD...

;*KOFF*; ;*KOFF*; THE SMOKE'S SKIRTING AROUND THE SYLPHIDES AND CONCENTRATING ON ME ;*KOFF*; ;*KOFF*; GETTING IT IN MY EYES AND LUNGS! ;*KOFF*; ;*KOFF*;

14

BUT, FINALLY THE HEAT DISSIPATES THE CLOUDY GRIP ON *GREEN LANTERN*...

I'M COMING BACK TOGETHER AGAIN!

OH, MY... HE'S SPOILING ALL OUR FUN!

WELL, LET'S NOT JUST STAND AROUND, DEARIE! LET'S SEE WHAT ELSE WE CAN DO!

SN-AP!

BOING

ALL AROUND THE WITCHBERRY BUSH, POOR GREEN LANTERN!

*-UHH-:* I'M BEING TUGGED BACK AND FORTH BY FORCES I CAN'T SEE! GOT TO--STOP THESE FUN-TIME GIRLS SOME-HOW--OR THEY'LL MAKE A WRECK OUT OF ME!

HOW DOES A SUPER-HE-MAN HERO *"FIGHT"* GIRLS? WELL, LOOK HOW *GREEN LANTERN* TACKLES THIS TICKLISH SITUATION!...

EEEEK! ALICE!!

SORRY, GIRLS! I HATE TO DO THIS, BUT AFTER ALL-- YOU ARE HELP-ING FELIX FAUST!

NO CLUE YET TO TELL ME WHO IS THE REAL--OR--FALSE FAUST!

*THEN--* LEAPING FROM BREEZE TO GALE, HOPPING ACROSS THE UPPER ROOF OF THE WORLD COMES *BOREAS,* MASTER OF WINDS, LORD OF AIR, WHOSE MEREST WHIM, HURRICANES AND CYCLONES MUST OBEY!...

HOLD, *GREEN LANTERN!* PLAY YOUR TRICKS ON *ME--* GREAT BOREAS--NOT ON MY RELATIVES, THE *SYLPHIDES!*

WHY, YOU BIG BAG OF WIND! I'LL BE *HAPPY* TO TAKE YOU ON!

FAR BELOW, *BATMAN* HAS BEEN CAUGHT AND GRIPPED BY THE ANIMATED BRANCHES OF ENTRANCED TREES...

AS *ROBIN* WOULD SAY-- *HOLY OAK!* SOMETHING LIKE THIS *WOOD* HAPPEN!

I'M BEGINNING TO FEEL LIKE A SCATTER RUG HUNG ON THE LINE FOR CLEANING!

THE BRILLIANT FLARE OF HIS UTILITY-BELT *LASER-GUN* DOES NOTHING AGAINST THE MAGIC OF THE ATTACKING TREES...

THAT SUDDEN GUST OF WIND ISN'T ANY HELP, EITHER! IT'S BLOWING SO HARD-- I CAN HARDLY GET MY BREATH!

*KLUNK!*

AS IF ENDOWED WITH WINGS BY THE WIND BLOWING ACROSS THIS NECROMANTIC LAND--A DISCARDED NEWSPAPER ADDS TO THE DISCOMFORT OF THE *CAPED CRUSADER*...

*MMMPPFF!*

AS IF I HAVEN'T GOT ENOUGH TROUBLES! NOW I GET PERSONAL DELIVERY OF A NEWSPAPER!

Daily Star SPORTS
R HOMERS!

GO PEDDLE YOURSELF SOMEPLACE ELSE!

AS HIS HAND LIFTS TO WARD OFF A LASHING BRANCH...

GOT TO KEEP THAT BRANCH AWAY FROM-- *HEYY!* ALL OF A SUDDEN IT LOST ITS ZING! THE BRANCHES ABOUT ME ARE LOOSENING TOO! STRANGE--BUT MAYBE *NOT*...

GOT TO HANG ON--FIGHT HIM OFF--TILL I CAN MANEUVER HIM INTO A CERTAIN POSITION...

ZWAAK!

AT LAST--A FIELD OF *GOLDENRODS!* IF MY THEORY IS CORRECT, *CERNUNNOS* OUGHT TO BE GETTING WEAK RIGHT ABOUT NOW-- AND HE IS!

KA-WHAM!

HE'S OUT COLD! THE *GOLD* IN THE GOLDEN-RODS... THE *INK* IN THE NEWSPAPER-- ALL FORM A DEFINITE PATTERN!

THE *GOLD* AND THE *INK* WERE PARTS OF THE *CONJURATION* WHICH BROUGHT THE *FALSE FELIX FAUST* INTO EXISTENCE! SINCE THOSE THINGS WEAKENED THE MENACES THE MASTER MAGE SUMMONED UP--THEY'LL WEAKEN THE *FALSE FAUST* AS WELL!

FROM ABOVE, *GREEN LANTERN* CRIES OUT TRIUMPHANTLY...

I'VE SOLVED THE PROBLEM, *BATMAN!* A *BUTTERFLY* AND A *BELL* WERE PART OF THE SPELL WHICH CREATED THE FAKE FELIX FAUST--

SO WERE *GOLD* AND *INK!* WE'VE DISCOVERED THE WAY TO REVEAL THE PHONY *FELIX FAUST!*

GRIPPING THEIR COUNTERS TO MAGIC, THE SUPER-HEROES RACE BACK TO THE MASTER MAGICIAN...

BACK ALREADY--WITH THE EVIDENCE TO EXPOSE MY IMPOSTOR--

--OR YOU, FELIX FAUST! WE'LL KNOW WHO YOU REALLY ARE IN A MOMENT!

AND ELSE-WHERE AT THIS INSTANT, ANOTHER CONFRONTATION IS TAKING PLACE...

THE TROLL WEAKENED NEAR FACTORY SMOKE FILLED WITH PHOSPHORUS SESQUISULPHIDE, GLUE, POTASSIUM CHLORATE AND SULPHUR--ELEMENTS USED ON THE HEAD OF A MATCH! AND WHEN I KNOCKED OUT THE TROLL, IT WAS IN THE PRESENCE OF SOAP--ALSO A PART OF THE CONJURATION!

AS WERE THE OAK ACORN AND THE SEED OF THIS FLOWER PLANT!

THIS IS YOUR MOMENT OF TRUTH, FELIX FAUST!

SOON AS WE DETERMINE WHO YOU ARE, WE'RE GOING BACK TO HEADQUARTERS!

LOOKS AS IF EVERYTHING'S ABOUT TO BE CLEARED UP, DOESN'T IT? WELL, LET'S LOOK INTO THE JUSTICE LEAGUE HEADQUARTERS--AND SEE HOW THINGS CAN BE MUDDLED UP! THE SURPRISING CLIMAX BEGINS ON THE NEXT PAGE FOLLOWING!

JUSTICE LEAGUE of AMERICA

# THREAT OF THE TRUE-OR-FALSE SORCERER-- PART 4

I WAS SO SURE WE WERE RIGHT! THOSE INCANTATION ITEMS WORKED PERFECTLY!

MAYBE BY USING THE SPELL, THE REAL FELIX FAUST ALSO MADE HIMSELF WEAK TO THOSE CHARMS?

GUESSING WON'T GET US ANYWHERE--

RIGHT! WE'VE GOT TO THINK THIS OUT!

WELL--HURRY IT UP! THE WHOLE UNIVERSE IS LIABLE TO GO BANG ANY MOMENT!

THINK! THINK! WHICH OF US IS THE REAL SORCERER? WHICH ONE IS THE FAKE?

SHUT UP WILL YOU? HOW CAN ANYBODY CONCENTRATE WITH YOU YAPPING AROUND LIKE THAT?

A REIGN OF SILENCE-- TILL SNAPPER CARR APPEARS WITH THE JUSTICE LEAGUE MAIL...

HEYY--WHAT'S WITH THESE TWO FELIX FAUSTS? & HOW'D THOSE PHONY-BALONIES GET HERE?

MAIL

ARE YOU IMPLYING THESE FAUSTS ARE FAKES?

YOU'RE SURE--NEITHER ONE OF THEM IS THE REAL THING?

OF COURSE! WHY, WHAT'S THE BIG MYSTERY?

DO YOU MEAN TO STAND THERE WITH YOUR BARE FACE HANGING OUT AND TELL US THAT AFTER ALL WE WENT THROUGH--YOU CAN COME IN--GLANCE AT THOSE TWO FELIX FAUSTS--AND KNOW THEY'RE NOT FOR REAL?

IT WAS A-- SNAP!

SNAP!

ALL RIGHT, SNAPPER-- WHAT DO YOU KNOW THAT WE DON'T?

TALK-- --SPILL IT!

A REPORTER FRIEND OF MINE IS WRITING AN ARTICLE ON PRISONS--AND I WENT WITH HIM TODAY TO THE FEDERAL PEN WHILE HE WAS DOING SOME RESEARCH! I SAW FELIX FAUST THERE, AND HE SAID TO TELL YOU THAT WHILE HIS MAGIC ESCAPE-SPELL FAILED HIM ...

...HE WAS GOING TO KEEP ON TRYING AND...HEY, FELLAS! ARE YOU LISTENING?

WE'VE HEARD ENOUGH, SNAPPER! THANKS!

WE'VE GOT TO GET TO THE PENITENTIARY WITH THESE TWO FAUSTS--FAST!

SHORTLY, OUTSIDE FELIX FAUST'S CELL...

YOU MEAN TO TELL ME I CONJURED UP *TWO* COPIES OF MYSELF WHEN I TRIED TO GET FREE? THAT THEY HAD THE RUN OF THE WORLD WHILE *I* WAS STUCK IN JAIL?

NEVER MIND THE TEMPER TANTRUM, FELIX! GET RID OF THEM!

DOUBLE ONE AND DOUBLE TWO, LISTEN AS I SEND YOU TO THE REALM FROM WHICH YOU CAME, AND--NEVERMORE BE SEEN ON LAND!

THE SAME SPELL WILL AUTOMATICALLY ALSO FREE YOUR FELLOW MEMBERS FROM THE MAGIC THOSE SPURIOUS SORCERERS PERFORMED! BUT I WARN YOU--I'M STILL GOING TO TRY AND ESCAPE!

SINCE *BOTH* THOSE FAUSTS WERE PHONIES, WHO IMPRISONED THE OTHER JLA MEMBERS?

MY GUESS IS--THEY *BOTH* DID! THEIR EVIL *SUBCONSCIOUS MINDS* FORCED THEM TO DO IT, WITHOUT THEIR *CONSCIOUS MINDS* BEING AWARE OF IT!

I'M GLAD THEY MANAGED TO LEAVE *FOUR* OF US FREE TO WORK ON THE PROBLEM-- EVEN IF IT TOOK *SNAPPER* TO SOLVE THE CASE FOR US!

FEDERAL PENITENTIARY

THE END

24

STORY BY GARDNER FOX

JUSTICE ☆☆☆ LEAGUE ☆☆☆ of AMERICA

ART BY MIKE SEKOWSKY & SID GREENE

THE *LORD OF TIME* POSSESSED THE GREATEST ARRAY OF WAR WEAPONS SINCE THE BEGINNING AND END OF TIME! WEAPONS SO AMAZING AND POWERFUL THAT EVEN THE *JUSTICE LEAGUE OF AMERICA* MUST FALL PREY TO THEM!

# THE LORD OF TIME ATTACKS THE 20th CENTURY!

I'VE GOT TO SAVE THE *JUSTICE LEAGUE* MEMBERS FROM TOTAL DESTRUCTION-- BY HURLING MYSELF INTO THE LETHAL BEAM OF THE *TIME LORD'S* WEAPON!

THE ROLL CALL

AQUAMAN

BATMAN

FLASH

GREEN ARROW

WONDER WOMAN

SNAPPER CARR

AND AS SPECIAL GUEST STAR:

ROBIN, THE BOY WONDER

ZAP!

SOMEWHERE IN THE CENTRAL HIGHLANDS OF *VIET NAM*, AN AUTOMATIC RIFLE CHATTERS IN FLAMING FURY...

THIS IS AS FAR AS YOU GET, *V-C's!*

VATTA-VATTA!

BEHIND SERGEANT EDDIE BRENT--OF SPECIAL SERVICES, A WEARER OF THE *GREEN BERET*--A LINE OF WOUNDED AMERICAN SOLDIERS MAKE ITS WAY ACROSS A JUNGLE BRIDGE...

IT'S *DEAD END BRIDGE* FOR YOU!

RAT-A-TAT-RAT-A-TAT

THE *ROMANS* HAD THE LEGENDARY *HORATIO*--THE *GREEN BERETS* HAVE *EDDIE BRENT* AT THEIR BRIDGE..

THA-PA-A-THAPPA!

TWO MONTHS LATER IN *GOTHAM CITY, U.S.A.* YOUNG JOEY BRENT AND HIS SCHOOL CHUM DICK GRAYSON THRILL TO THE SOUND OF MARTIAL MUSIC...

OUR HERO EDDIE BRENT

I CAN'T BELIEVE IT, DICK! A PARADE JUST FOR MY BROTHER EDDIE!

THE WHOLE TOWN'S TURNED OUT, JOEY! EDDIE'S OUR HERO! TOMORROW HE GETS THE *CONGRESSIONAL MEDAL OF HONOR* FROM THE PRESIDENT HIMSELF!

INSTRUMENTS BLAST OUT A HEARTFELT WELCOME AS THE TRAIN CARRYING THE MILITARY HERO STOPS. BUT THEN...

HOLD EVERYTHING! SERGEANT BRENT ISN'T WITH US! HE SUDDENLY WENT BERSERK--KNOCKED OUT THE MAIL CLERK AND SECURITY GUARD IN THE BAGGAGE CAR--

WH-AAAT?!

--GRABBED UP A SACK OF MONEY AND JUMPED OFF THE GOTHAM CITY BRIDGE! IT WAS A CLEAN GETAWAY!

I--I DON'T BELIEVE IT! MY BROTHER WOULDN'T DO SUCH A THING!

AS YOUNG DICK (ROBIN) GRAY-SON PUTS A SYMPATHETIC HAND ON THE SHOULDER OF HIS PAL, HIS KEEN EYES SEARCH OUT THE MUSCULAR BULK OF BRUCE (BATMAN) WAYNE...

MY B-BROTHER'S A HERO -SOB- NOT A HOOD!

BRUCE SEES ME TRYING TO CATCH HIS EYE! HE KNOWS THIS IS A CASE FOR-- BATMAN AND ROBIN!

-SOB- MY EDWARD IS A -- A GOOD BOY!

EVERYTHING WILL BE ALL RIGHT, DEAR! THERE MUST BE AN EXPLANATION FOR ALL THIS...

MOMENTS LATER, A SPORTS CAR RACES TOWARD WAYNE MANOR...

I CAN'T IMAGINE WHAT GOT INTO EDDIE, DICK--BUT WE MUST HELP HIM SNAP OUT OF IT!

I KEEP SEEING JOEY'S FACE! THIS'LL KILL HIS MOM AND DAD!

IN AND OUT OF THE BATCAVE AND THEIR UNIFORMS IN SPLIT SECONDS! THEN THE POWERFUL BATMOBILE STREAKS FOR THE GOTHAM CITY BRIDGE...

SINCE HE DIVED OFF THE BRIDGE--

--WE MAY BE ABLE TO PICK UP HIS TRACKS ALONG THE RIVER BANK!

TRAINED EYES SCAN THE SHEER RIVER BLUFFS...

HERE IT IS-- A STILL-DAMP FOOTPRINT! IT SHOWS WHERE HE CLIMBED UP!

OUT WITH THE BAT-ROPES, ROBIN! WE'RE FOLLOWING THE TRAIL!

SHUCKS, THE FOOTPRINTS PETER OUT UP HERE...

ONLY TO OUR NAKED EYES, ROBIN!

3

*BAT-TECTORS* IN THEIR HANDS, THE *DYNAMIC DUO* CLOSES IN ON AN ABANDONED HOUSE A MILE FROM *GOTHAM RIVER*...

REMEMBER, *ROBIN*-- EDDIE BRENT IS NOT A THIEF BY NATURE! LET'S TAKE HIM-- WITHOUT HARM-- IF WE CAN!

YOU BET! WE'VE GOT TO MAKE HIM UNDERSTAND WE WANT TO HELP HIM--

A MASSIVE SHOULDER SPLITS WOOD AS...

ALL RIGHT, EDDIE! WHAT-EVER GAME YOU'RE PLAYING-- IS OVER!

*BATMAN!* I WAS WARNED I WOULD HAVE TO TANGLE WITH YOU SOONER OR LATER! NOW I'M WARNING *YOU*-- CLEAR OUT OF HERE-- LEAVE ME ALONE...

CR A ASH!

BEHIND THE TENSED SER-GEANT A REAR DOOR SLOWLY OPENS...

I DON'T WANT TO HURT YOU, *BAT-MAN!* BUT IF YOU INTER-FERE, I'LL SHOOT--

NEVER SAW A WEAPON LIKE *THAT* BEFORE!

THE *MASKED MANHUNTER* MAKES A STEALTHY GESTURE-- AND IN ANSWER TO THAT SIGNAL...

MY SURPRISE ATTACK WILL ENABLE *BATMAN* TO DISARM EDDIE!

TO THE SHOCKED AMAZE-MENT OF THE *BOY WONDER*...

YIIIII! THAT ROD BENT BACK-- FIRED AT ME-- AND I'M BEING HURLED STRAIGHT AT *BATMAN!*

I FIGURED *YOU'D* BE SOMEWHERE AROUND, *ROBIN*-- SO I KEPT MY EYES ON THAT CRACKED MIRROR NEAR *BATMAN!*

TOSSED LIKE A LEAF IN A GALE BY A POWERFUL WIND-WHIRLPOOL, *ROBIN* THUDS HARD INTO THE STUNNED *CAPED CRUSADER*...

*GWO MP!*

*HA! HA! HA!* MY WEAPONS HAVE ONLY ONE CHARGE IN THEM-- BUT THE DAMAGE THAT ONE FIRING DOES IS *TERRIFIC!* MIGHT AS WELL DISCARD THIS BURNED-OUT ROD WEAPON AND PREPARE TO USE THIS PROPELLER ONE!

BEHIND HIS HARSH LAUGHTER, THE HEART OF SERGEANT EDDIE BRENT IS BREAKING! HIS EYES ARE GLAZED WITH AGONY, HIS LIPS CONTORTED IN GRO-TESQUE MIRTH...

I--I DON'T WANT TO DO THESE TERRIBLE THINGS! I--I'M TRY-ING TO STOP MYSELF FROM HURTING *BAT-MAN* AND *ROBIN*-- BUT I *CAN'T!* I'VE BEEN ORDERED TO OBEY--AND OBEY I MUST!

AS THE *DYNAMIC DUO* RECOVERS ITS FOOTING, THE EERIE PROPELLER SPINS AND...

OBJECTS IN THE ROOM-- BEING PROPELLED AT US--

*ROBIN'S* BEEN KNOCKED COLD! THIS HAS GONE TOO FAR! I'VE GOT TO STOP EDDIE ANY WAY I CAN!

*ZAAK!*

*WOPP!*

GASPING FOR BREATH, BATTERED AND PUMMELED, EVEN THE HARD-AS-ROCKS WEARER OF THE *GREEN BERET* KNOWS A MOMENT OF INTENSE RELIEF...

YOU'VE DONE WELL, SERGEANT! VERY WELL DONE, INDEED!

*YOU--* AGAIN!

INSTANTLY, THE PAST FEW NIGHTMARE HOURS FLASH THROUGH EDDIE BRENT'S MIND AS HE ENVISIONS HIMSELF INSIDE THE TRAIN SPEEDING HIM TO *GOTHAM CITY*...

A MOMENT AGO THE SEAT ALONGSIDE ME WAS EMPTY! SUDDENLY THIS CHARACTER IN THAT ODD GET-UP APPEARED HERE! BUT NOBODY BUT ME SEEMS TO SEE HIM! I--I'M TRYING TO ASK WHO HE IS -- BUT MY TONGUE WON'T MOVE!

NO NEED TO ASK, SERGEANT! BESIDES, *I'LL* DO ALL THE TALKING!

I AM THE *LORD OF TIME*, TELE-PATHING MY THOUGHTS TO YOU BECAUSE I HAVE SELECTED *YOU* TO BE MY PERSONAL SOLDIER AND I WANT NO ONE ELSE BUT YOU TO KNOW! SOME TIME AGO THE *JUSTICE LEAGUE* CAPTURED AND IMPRISONED ME *--USING THEIR SUPER-POWERS TO PREVENT ME FROM EVER FIRING ANOTHER WEAPON...

* *JUSTICE LEAGUE OF AMERICA #11: "ONE HOUR TO DOOMSDAY!"*

"HOWEVER, I HAD BEEN FORESIGHTED ENOUGH TO ARRANGE FOR A TIME-WARPING MACHINE TO AUTO-MATICALLY EXTRICATE ME FROM ANY DIFFICULT SITUATION..."

;GASP; I'M FREE--BACK IN MY OWN TIME-ERA! BUT I'VE LOST THE POWER TO WORK MY SUPER-WEAPONS...

YET MY AMBITION AND RESOLVE TO LOOT THE *20TH CENTURY* IS STILL STRONG WITHIN ME! I NEED SOMEONE TO--ACT FOR ME--BE MY WARRIOR AND USE MY ARRAY OF WEAPONS AS I COMMAND!

YOU ARE THE HERO OF THE HOUR TO YOUR PEOPLE, EDWARD BRENT! AS YOU SERVED THEM, SO SHALL YOU SERVE ME! IT AMUSES ME TO SELECT *YOU*, TO TURN ONE OF THEIR OWN HEROES AGAINST THEM! I NOW TAKE COMPLETE CONTROL OF YOU --BODY AND MIND!

7

AS YOUR FIRST ASSIGNMENT, YOU SHALL STEAL SOME MONEY FROM THE BAGGAGE CAR-- AS A TEST OF MY CONTROL OVER YOU! FOLLOWING THAT THEFT, YOU SHALL PROCEED TO AN ABANDONED HOUSE WHERE I HAVE LEFT A UNIFORM FOR YOU TO DON! THESE TWO WEAPONS WILL ENABLE YOU TO OVERCOME ANY INTERFERENCE!

THE *LORD OF TIME* GRINS MOCKINGLY AS...

YOU'VE EXCEEDED MY FONDEST HOPES! YOU KNOCKED *BATMAN* AND *ROBIN* UNCONSCIOUS! NOW YOU ARE READY TO GO OUT ON THE SPECIAL ASSIGNMENT FOR WHICH I CHOSE YOU!

BUT-- BUT I'M NO LAW-BREAKER! I...DON'T WANT TO HELP YOU--

WHO CARES WHAT *YOU* WANT? IF I TELL YOU TO BE A THIEF-- YOU'LL BE A THIEF! YOU SHALL STEAL AND BRING TO ME THE *TWO OBJECTS* ON EARTH THAT HAVE THE POWER TO FIRE MY WEAPONS! YOUR ORDERS ARE TO FETCH ME THE GEARS OF THE *TIME LOCK* IN THE *GOTHAM CITY BANK* VAULT-- AND THE UNAGING FOSSIL IN THE *SOUTH STATE MUSEUM!* DON YOUR SPECIAL UNIFORM--AND *GO!*

I HEAR YOU! I OBEY!

SHOULD IT PROVE NECESSARY, *YOU* WILL FIGHT THE *JUSTICE LEAGUE* WITH MY WEAPONS IN YOUR BELT-- BECAUSE I CAN'T! TO GUARANTEE YOUR SAFETY, I'LL PROTECT YOU FROM ATTACK BY A SPECIAL DEFENSE MECHANISM IN YOUR BODY! NOTHING CAN HARM YOU NOW! SO LET'S GET ON WITH MY ATTACK ON THE 20th CENTURY!

*Slowly THE LONG MOMENTS PASS. A POWERFUL BODY STIRS, SITS UP. THEN...*

ROBIN-- YOU OKAY?

I--I GUESS--SO! WOW! NO WONDER THE SERGEANT WON A MEDAL! HE SURE IS SOME FIGHTER!

8

**As ROBIN speaks, the mightily thewed BATMAN tenses...**

QUIET, ROBIN! LISTEN! JUST BEFORE COMING INTO THE HOUSE I SWITCHED ON MY TAPE-RECORDER TO NOTE WHAT EDDIE SAID, IN ORDER TO STUDY IT LATER! I THINK WE'VE CAUGHT SOMETHING...

**THE VOICES OF THE LORD OF TIME AND OF EDDIE BRENT COME TO LIFE IN THE WRECKED ROOM...**

HOLY PLAY-BLACK! SO THAT'S WHO'S BEHIND EDDIE'S ODD BEHAVIOR!

THE LORD OF TIME! THAT MAKES THIS A CASE FOR THE JUSTICE LEAGUE! I'LL SEND OUT AN EMERGENCY MEETING SIGNAL BEFORE TAKING YOU HOME!

TAKE ME HOME? YOU'VE GOT TO BE KIDDING! I HAVE A STAKE IN THIS TOO! JOEY IS EDDIE'S BROTHER-- AND ONE OF MY BEST BUDDIES! AND I HAVE A PERSONAL SCORE TO SETTLE WITH THAT LORD OF TIME--

ALL RIGHT, YOU'VE MADE YOUR POINT! WE'LL GO BACK FOR THE BAT-PLANE, THEN BE OFF TO-GETHER!

**SHORTLY, IN THE JUSTICE LEAGUE HEADQUARTERS...**

EVIDENTLY THE OTHER MEMBERS ARE BUSY ON CASES-- AND COULDN'T RESPOND...

GIVE ME FIVE, ROBIN! I'M SURE GLAD TO MEET YOU AT LAST! I'VE ENVIED YOU FOR A LONG TIME!

YOU'VE ENVIED ME?! COLOR ME GREEN, SNAPPER-- I'M JEALOUS OF YOUR BEING "IN" WITH THE JUSTICE LEAGUERS...

YEAH-YEAH-YEAH! BUT YOU'RE ON THE GO-GO WITH THE CAPED CRUSADER AGAINST VILLAINS LIKE THE JOKER, PENGUIN-- RIDDLER--

# The LORD of TIME ATTACKS the 20th CENTURY— PART 2

ACROSS THE INTERVENING MILES BETWEEN THE *JUSTICE LEAGUE* HEADQUARTERS AND THE *GOTHAM CITY BANK* SPEED *BATPLANE* AND *ROBOT PLANE* ! FOOT-FALLS DRUM ECHOES FROM THE INTERIOR OF THE BANK AS THE TERRIFIC TRIO CLOSES IN ON THE WARRIOR OF THE *TIME LORD* ! FISTS CLENCHED, MAGIC LASSO IN HAND, GOOD PREPARES TO HURL ITSELF ON EVIL !

WELL, WELL ! *BATMAN* AND *ROBIN* AGAIN ! I SEE THAT THIS TIME YOU BROUGHT ALONG A LADY FRIEND TO HELP YOU OUT !

WE KNOW IT ISN'T REALLY *YOU* SAYING THAT, EDDIE--SO WE'RE GOING TO MAKE THIS AS EASY ON YOU AS WE CAN !

I'M NOT HITTING *YOU* -- I'M REALLY LASHING OUT AT THE *LORD OF TIME* !

BUT--INCREDIBLY--IT IS NOT EDDIE BRENT--BUT ROBIN WHO SUFFERS THE IMPACT OF BATMAN'S BLOW!

YAAMPOFF!

ROBIN! WHAT'S WRONG?

I'LL TELL YOU WHAT'S WRONG, BATMAN!

THE LORD OF TIME IMMUNIZED ME FROM ALL HARM! WHATEVER HARM YOU TRY TO INFLICT ON ME, I CAN MAKE IT BACKFIRE ON YOU--OR ROBIN--OR WONDER WOMAN!

THAT STUNT WON'T WORK AGAINST MY MAGIC LASSO!

DON'T BET ON IT, WONDER WOMAN! LOOK AT WHAT'S HAPPENING TO YOU!

MERCIFUL MINERVA! I'M A PRISONER OF MY OWN LARIAT!

I SHORT-CIRCUIT THE ENERGIES YOU HIT ME WITH--BEFORE THEY CAN HARM MY NERVOUS SYSTEM--THEN RE-DIRECT THEM AT ANY ONE OF MY ENEMIES I CHOOSE!

THE LORD OF TIME MAKES ME DO IT! I'VE BEEN CHOSEN TO FIGHT FOR EVIL, BECAUSE I USED TO FIGHT AGAINST EVIL!

SEE IF YOU CAN BREAK OUT OF THIS GRIP, WISE GUY!

YOU'RE ON, BATMAN--

12

THEN WITH SAVAGE SWIFTNESS...

BATMAN--ROBIN--I'M SORRY BUT I CAN'T--HELP MYSELF--!

ZA-WHAAK!

BY PLAYING MY FINGERS OVER THIS REMOTE-CONTROL GADGET--I CAN USE YOU LIKE A PUPPET WEAPON, *WONDER WOMAN!*

ZWAPP!

AGAIN AND AGAIN THAT LIVING CLUB WHICH IS THE *AMAZING AMAZON* THUDS HER AGAINST HER COMPANIONS...

CAN'T--FIGHT BACK AT *WONDER WOMAN!* SHE ISN'T DOING THIS ON HER OWN--

JUST AS EDDIE-- IS LIKE A PUPPET IN THE HANDS OF-- THE *LORD OF TIME!*

SUDDENLY INSPIRATION COMES TO THE *MASKED MANHUNTER* AS...

QUICK, *ROBIN!* GRAB HOLD OF HER ! THEN FOLLOW MY LEAD !

HEADS LOWERED, SINEWY FINGERS GRIPPING THE *MIGHTY MAID,* THE *DYNAMIC DUO* THUNDERS FORWARD...

I NOTICED SOMETHING! I JUST HOPE IT WORKS--!

I GET IT! THE BRIGHT SPARKS *WONDER WOMAN* IS GIVING OFF! YOU THINK ...

SMART, *BATMAN*--TO NOTICE THOSE SPARKS! I WAS HOPING YOU'D DO THAT WHEN I PLAYED *WONDER WOMAN* AGAINST YOU LIKE A CLUB!

KRUNCH!

BUT I'VE GOT TO FIGHT BACK! I'M UNDER THE COMPULSION OF THE *LORD OF TIME* TO KEEP BATTLING... OVERCOME MY FOES...

DISCARDING HIS LAST USED WEAPON, THE *TIME LORD'S* WARRIOR LIFTS ANOTHER, AIMING IT WITH DEADLY ACCURACY...

BATMAN-- GUARD YOURSELF! HE'S WHIPPED OUT ANOTHER OF THOSE WEAPONS AND...OHHH!

I--I CAN'T! THE LENS OF THAT THING IS--DOING SOMETHING ODD--TO ME!

AS THE EERIE LIGHT SPREADS ACROSS THEIR BODIES...

WE'RE STUCK UP HERE--

LIKE RUNAWAY BALLOONS!

HA! HA! HA! BY FILLING YOU WITH ANTI-GRAVITY RADIATION-- I'VE MADE YOU AS LIGHT AS HELIUM! YOUR BODIES WILL EVENTUALLY RETURN TO NORMAL-- BUT BY THAT TIME--I'LL HAVE SAFELY GOTTEN AWAY WITH THE TIME-LOCK GEAR!

15

FAR TO THE SOUTH OF *GOTHAM CITY*, IN A GREAT NATIONAL MUSEUM...

IS *THAT* WHAT ALL THE FUSS IS ABOUT? AN ANCIENT RELIC--

THIS FOSSIL HAPPENS TO BE *UNIQUE!* ANCIENT OBJECTS CAN BE DATED BY THE AMOUNT OF RADIOACTIVE DECAY THEY GIVE OFF, AS IN THE *CARBON-14* TEST...

BUT THIS FOSSIL *DOES NOT DECAY!* IT IS JUST AS IT ORIGINALLY WAS-- FILLED WITH A STRANGE FORM OF RADIOACTIVITY THAT HAS NEVER CHANGED IN ALL THE MILLIONS OF YEARS IT HAS EXISTED! MY HUNCH IS THE *LORD OF TIME* NEEDS TO ABSORB THIS CHANGELESS RADIATION...

...SO THAT BY USING IT IN CONJUNCTION WITH THE TIME-LOCK GEAR, HE CAN OVER- COME THE HANDICAP WE PUT ON HIM FROM EVER FIRING A WEAPON!

LET ME HAVE IT, *FLASH!* I'LL HIDE IT IN THE OCEAN BEFORE HE GETS HERE! THE OCEAN'S A MIGHTY BIG PLACE TO LOOK FOR SUCH A SMALL OBJECT!

SOME TIME AFTER THE *SEA KING* HAS TAKEN OFF WITH THE CURIOUS FOSSIL...

THE *LORD OF TIME* GAVE ME THIS HAND-TELEPORTER TO SPEED ME TO MY DESTINATION AND-- *ehh?!* FLASH AND *GREEN ARROW*-- WAITING HERE FOR ME!

LOOK! HE STOLE THE TIME-LOCK GEAR-- AND THERE'S NOT A MARK ON HIM! HE MUST HAVE OVERCOME *BATMAN, WONDER WOMAN* AND *ROBIN!*

BUT HE WON'T GET AWAY FROM MY *SUNBURST* ARROW!

NOR FROM MY *SUPER-SPEED!*

/16

AS THE ARROW THUNKS INTO THE WARRIOR OF THE *LORD OF TIME*...

NOW TO SPIN HIM SO FAST HE'LL THINK HE'S ON A RUNAWAY MERRY GO-ROUND!

SUDDENLY AN AMAZING TURNABOUT...

I CAN'T SEE! THE SUNBURST ARROW HIT EDDIE BRENT-- BUT *I'M* THE ONE FEELING ITS EFFECTS!

I'M GOING AROUND AND AROUND-- BUT NOT UNDER MY OWN POWER! MY SPEED'S OUT OF CONTROL!

THOUGH UNABLE TO STOP HIS WILD CAREENING, THE *SCARLET SPEEDSTER* MANAGES TO REACH OUT AND GRABS THE BOWMAN..

LOAD UP YOUR ARROWS, G.A.! FIRE WHEN I SAY SO!

I GET THE MESSAGE, *FLASH!*

THOUGH UNABLE TO SEE, THE *ACE ARCHER* PUMPS ARROW AFTER ARROW AT THEIR FOE, AS *FLASH* ACTS AS HIS EYES...

FIRE!--FIRE!--FIRE!

MY DEFENSE COATING DOESN'T ACT FAST ENOUGH TO THROW OFF THE EFFECTS OF ALL THOSE RAPID-FIRE ARROWS! I'VE--GOT TO--GIVE THEM A DOSE OF ANOTHER WEAPON!

BOMBARDING THEM WITH THESE MUSEUM PIECES WILL KNOCK THEM OUT QUICKLY ENOUGH! I NOTICED THE FOSSIL I NEED ISN'T HERE! WHEREVER IT'S HIDDEN, I'LL FIND IT!

FAR FROM THE MUSEUM--IN AN UNDERSEA CAVERN...

HERE THE FOSSIL WILL REMAIN HIDDEN FOR *CENTURIES*--

NOT EVEN FOR A *MOMENT, AQUAMAN!*

THE FOSSIL GIVES OFF A TIME-RADIATION WHICH I WAS EASILY ABLE TO TRACK WITH A DEVICE GIVEN ME BY THE *LORD OF TIME!* NOW HAND IT OVER, *AQUAMAN*--OR YOU'LL GET A DOSE OF THE SAME MEDICINE I GAVE YOUR *JUSTICE LEAGUE* PALS!

AT THE *SEA KING'S* TELEPATHIC COMMAND...

HERE'S MY ANSWER, EDDIE BRENT! CREATURES OF THE SEA -- ATTACK!

ELECTRIC EELS--RAYS--SKATES--ALL THE SUBMARINE DENIZENS WHOSE BODIES GIVE OFF ELECTRICITY!

I--I CAN FEEL THOSE ELECTRICAL CHARGES! *MY* PROTECTIVE COATING IS GETTING WEAKER-- STARTING TO WEAR OFF!

FOR A LONG MOMENT, THE *TIME LORD'S* TROOPER STANDS FRAMED IN A DIAPASON OF DEADLY RAYS...

18

THEN... ÷ Whew ÷ IT'S WORKING AGAIN! IT JUST TOOK LONGER THAN USUAL TO GET GOING! I'M GLAD THIS IS MY LAST ASSIGNMENT!

EEEAGHHH!

I HAVE THE FOSSIL AND THE TIME-LOCK GEAR! NOW TO TELEPORT MYSELF TO THE *LORD OF TIME* AND GET OUT OF THIS MESS!

AS HE LAPSES INTO UNCONSCIOUSNESS, *AQUAMAN* HURLS OUT ONE LAST MENTAL COMMAND--AND IN ANSWER TO THAT CALL...

IF THAT GIANT CRAB CAN GRIP HIM--IT'LL SO OVERLOAD HIS TELEPORTER WHICH IS GEARED TO TRANSPORT ONLY HIS BODY--THE DEVICE WILL SHORT-- CIRCUIT!

WITHOUT WAITING TO TEST HIS ERRATIC PROTECTIVE DEVICE, EDDIE BRENT YANKS AT ANOTHER WEAPON IN HIS BELT AND...

I'M COMPELLED TO TAKE WHATEVER MEASURES I CAN TO BREAK FREE!

THE NEXT MOMENT... TURNED ITS CLAWS TO PUTTY--BREAKING ITS GRIP ON ME! NOW TO MAKE MY GETAWAY!

19

SOMEWHAT LATER, AT THE *SOUTH STATES MUSEUM,* WHERE *BATMAN* AND *ROBIN* HAVE JOINED THE KAYOED *GREEN ARROW* AND *FLASH...*

HOW YOU DOING, *G.A.?*

OKAY NOW-- BUT WHAT A TROUNCING THAT EDDIE BRENT GAVE US--

--THANKS TO THE *TIME LORD'S* WEAPONS--

BUT JUST BEFORE EDDIE OVERCAME US, I NOTICED AN UNUSUAL SPARKLING AROUND THE ROCKS THAT WERE PELTING US!

YOU NOTICED THAT TOO? IT MUST BE A SPECIAL EFFECT OF THE WEAPONS EDDIE WAS USING! PERHAPS SOME OF THAT ODD RADIATION IS STILL CLINGING TO THEM!

*WONDER WOMAN* WENT TO LOOK FOR *AQUAMAN* WHEN WE DIDN'T FIND HIM HERE WITH YOU! MAYBE BY THE TIME SHE GETS BACK--

--YOU FELLOWS CAN WHIP UP SOME SORT OF GADGET TO DETECT AND FOLLOW THAT WEAPON-RADIATION!

RIGHT! LET'S GET TO WORK!

*STORY CONTINUES ON NEXT PAGE FOLLOWING!* 20

★ JUSTICE ★
LEAGUE
of AMERICA

# The LORD OF TIME ATTACKS THE 20th CENTURY PART 3

IN THE MUSEUM WORKSHOP, WITH ALL ITS FACILITIES AT THEIR DISPOSAL, *BATMAN* AND *FLASH* QUICKLY GET TO WORK CONSTRUCTING A RADIATION DETECTOR-- WHEN...

HERE COME *WONDER WOMAN* AND *AQUAMAN!*

I SPOTTED THE *SEA KING* ON HIS WAY HERE, RIDING A DOLPHIN'S BACK! TO SAVE TIME, I BROUGHT HIM WITH ME IN MY *ROBOT PLANE!*

THEN... ALL FINISHED... LET'S GET GOING!

ONCE THE DETECTOR PICKS UP THE EMANATIONS STILL CLINGING TO THOSE WEAPONS EDDIE USED-- IT'LL LEAD US TO HIS SECRET RENDEZVOUS WITH THE *LORD OF TIME!*

21

IN HIS SANCTUARY, THE *LORD OF TIME* BATHES IN THE CHRONAL ENERGIES GENERATED BY THE INTERACTION OF THE TIME-LOCK GEARS AND THE UNAGING FOSSIL...

YOU'VE DONE WELL, SOLDIER! I'LL SOON BE ABLE TO USE MY TERRIFIC WEAPONS--SO HAND THEM OVER TO ME! ONCE YOU DO SO, I'LL REMOVE YOUR COMPULSIONS TO OBEY ME!

WELL--AREN'T YOU GOING TO MAKE A RUN FOR IT? I'M LOOKING FORWARD TO CUTTING YOU DOWN! I'M RUTHLESS, YOU SEE... YOU'VE SERVED MY PURPOSES--AND I HAVE NO FURTHER USE FOR YOU!

*CLICK!*

WHAT'S THIS? THE *JUSTICE LEAGUE*--STILL ITCHING FOR A FIGHT? WELL--I WON'T FIGHT YOU-- I'LL SIMPLY *DESTROY* YOU!

THAT WEAPON--FAR TOO POWERFUL EVEN FOR THE *JLA!* ONLY ONE WAY TO SAVE THEM--AND I'VE GOT TO RISK IT!

DESPERATELY, SGT. EDDIE BRENT HURLS HIMSELF FULL INTO THE FORCE OF THE WEAPON...

*EHH?!* THE BEAM ISN'T HURTING ME--BUT NEITHER IS IT HURTING THE *LORD OF TIME!*

HIT THE FLOOR, EDDIE! WE'LL TAKE CARE OF HIM!

*ZAAAP!*

WH-WHAT WENT WRONG? THE WEAPON HAD TO *DESTROY ME*-- OR THE TIME LORD!

22

IN A TIDAL WAVE OF CRASHING KNUCKLES AND FEROCIOUS FISTS THE *JUSTICE LEAGUERS* SLAM HOME AGAINST THEIR FOE...

WH-APPP!

ZLOKK!

SNOTT!

ONCE WE DETERMINED THE VIBRATION RATE OF THE *TIME LORD'S* WEAPONS--I *DUPLICATED THAT VIBRATION WITH MY BODY*--THUS NULLIFYING THE DISASTROUS EFFECTS OF HIS WEAPONS!

As THE *TIME TYRANT* DROPS UNCONSCIOUS...

IT'S YOUR--ER--DUTY TO ARREST ME NOW FOR WHAT I'VE DONE! DON'T WORRY, I WON'T PUT UP THE FIGHT I DID WHEN I WAS UNDER THE COMPULSION OF THE *TIME LORD!*

WE KNOW THAT, EDDIE! WHAT TOUCHES US MOST IS--YOU WERE WILLING TO SACRIFICE YOURSELF TO SAVE OUR LIVES!

YOU'RE STILL A *HERO* IN MY BOOK!

WE-ELL, TO TELL THE TRUTH--I WAS HOPING I HAD JUST ENOUGH STRENGTH LEFT IN THAT PROTECTIVE COATING WHICH SAVED ME FROM YOU--TO TURN THE *TIME LORD'S* LETHAL BLAST BACK AT *HIM!*

WHEN HE *"RELEASED"* ME, HE NEGLECTED TO REMOVE THAT PROTECTIVE COATING! MAYBE HE FORGOT ABOUT IT, OR MAYBE HE FIGURED IT HAD WORN OFF! ANYHOW--I HOPED TO DESTROY HIM IN THE VERY ACT BY WHICH HE INTENDED TO DESTROY YOU!

AND IF THE COATING HAD WORN OFF--YOU'D HAVE GIVEN YOUR LIFE FOR OURS! YOU'RE A REAL HERO, ALL RIGHT!

AND HOW!

23

IN THE NATION'S CAPITAL--AFTER THE STOLEN TIME-LOCK AND UNAGING FOSSIL HAVE BEEN RETURNED--AND AFTER THE LORD OF TIME HAS AGAIN BEEN IMPRISONED (WITHOUT ANY DEVICE TO FREE HIM THIS TIME)...
SERGEANT BRENT, YOU DESERVE TWO MEDALS--BUT YOU'LL HAVE TO SETTLE FOR THIS ONE! YOUR OTHER MEDAL IS ENGRAVED ON THE HEARTS OF YOUR COUNTRYMEN!
The END

**STORY BY GARDNER FOX**

**JUSTICE ☆☆☆ LEAGUE ☆☆☆ of AMERICA**

**ART BY MIKE SEKOWSKY & SID GREENE**

FOR MOST OF HER YOUNG LIFE, *ZATANNA* HAS BEEN HUNTING ON EARTH AS WELL AS ON DIMENSIONAL AND MAGICAL WORLDS FOR HER MISSING MAGICIAN FATHER *ZATARA!* NOW AT LAST SHE DISCOVERS WHERE HE IS -- ONLY TO BECOME WHEN SHE GOES THERE THE TARGET OF AWESOME MAGICAL FORCES THAT THREATEN HER VERY LIFE!

# Z--AS IN ZATANNA--and ZERO HOUR!

THE ROLL CALL

ATOM

BATMAN

GREEN LANTERN

HAWKMAN

AND--

GUEST STARRING--ELONGATED MAN!

IN THE *JUSTICE LEAGUE* HEADQUARTERS -- EMPTY SAVE FOR A CRYSTAL BALL FROM WHICH BACKWARD WORDS ARE MAGICALLY SPOKEN...

I NOMMUS NEERG NRETNAL! I LLAC NO MOTA DNA NAMTAB! NAMKWAH DNA EHT DETAGNOLE NAM!

AND IN RESPONSE TO THE IRRESISTIBLE COMMANDS...

WHAT BROUGHT ME HERE?

THERE WAS NO EMERGENCY SIGNAL!

*ATOM!* DID YOU FEEL THE SAME THING I DID?

MEANT THAT MOMENTARY DIZZINESS-- I SURE DID!

IF YOU

IT ISN'T TIME FOR A REGULAR MEET-ING, EITHER! WHAT ARE WE ALL DOING HERE?

THAT'S WHAT I'D LIKE TO KNOW! I-- THE *ELONGATED MAN*-- AM NOT EVEN A MEMBER OF THE JLA!

I BROUGHT YOU ALL HERE TO THANK YOU PERSONALLY FOR HELPING ME FIND MY FATHER, *ZATARA!*

THERE'S SOME MISTAKE! SOME OF US AT ONE TIME OR ANOTHER HELPED *ZATANNA LOOK* FOR HER FATHER--

...BUT WE FAILED!

HUH? IT'S *ZATANNA!*

SWIFTLY THE *MAID OF MAGIC*, WHO HAS SPENT MOST OF HER LIFE SEARCHING FOR HER LONG-LOST FATHER-- GROWS AND GROWS UNTIL...

YOU FAILED THE *FIRST* TIME! BUT ON THE SECOND ATTEMPT-- YOU SUCCEEDED GLORIOUSLY!

WE *DID?!*

IF YOU'RE IN-CLUDING ME, TOO, *ZATANNA*-- I HAVE NO RECOLLECTION OF EVER *MEETING* YOU, LET ALONE *HELPING* YOU!

BUT YOU *DID*, DARLINGS-- ALL FIVE OF YOU! AND I THANK YOU SO MUCH!

2

BELIEVE ME, I WOULD NEVER HAVE FOUND DADDY WITHOUT YOUR SUPER-HEROIC HELP-- OR EVEN BE ALIVE TO TELL YOU ABOUT IT!

HOLD IT, ZATANNA! WHAT DO YOU KNOW THAT WE DON'T?

ALL I RE-CALL WAS SAVING YOUR LIFE IN CHINA*--

WHILE I ACCOMPANIED YOU TO THE LAND OF THE DRUID...*

I HELPED YOU FIGHT THE WARLOCK IN DIS...*

I HAPPENED TO MEET YOU JUST ONCE IN A THEATRICAL PROP SHOP...*

*HAWKMAN #4: "THE GIRL WHO SPLIT IN TWO!"

*ATOM #19: "WORLD OF THE MAGIC ATOM!"

*GREEN LANTERN #42: "THE OTHER SIDE OF THE WORLD!"

*DETECTIVE COMICS #355: "TANTALIZING TROUBLES OF THE TRIPOD THIEVES!"

WHILE I NEVER HAD THE PLEASURE OF MEETING YOU-- UNTIL NOW!

"YOU ARE MYSTIFIED --AS YOU HAVE A RIGHT TO BE! BUT LISTEN TO MY STORY--AND MY CRYPTIC STATEMENTS WILL BECOME CLEAR... AS YOU ALL KNOW, I HAVE BEEN HUNTING FOR MY FATHER ZATARA EVER SINCE HE MYSTERIOUSLY VANISHED FROM EARTH! SOME MONTHS AGO IN AN ANTIQUE SHOP IN VIENNA... "

THE SWORD OF PARACELSUS -- WILL THIS BE THE CLUE THAT WILL LEAD ME TO MY FATHER?

"PARACELSUS WAS A FAMOUS PHYSICIAN OF THE MIDDLE AGES WHO DABBLED IN BLACK MAGIC! FINDING HIS SWORD WAS MARVELOUS-- BUT EVEN MORE MARVELOUS WAS THE DISCOVERY THAT.."

I SENSE AN EMANATION FROM THE SWORD--MY FATHER'S PERSONAL AURA! YES! HE HAS BEEN IN CONTACT WITH THIS WEAPON!

DROWS-- LLET EM TAHW UOY WONK FO ARATAZ!

ZATARA USED THIS BLADE WHEN HE FOUGHT HIS LAST AND GREATEST FOE--THE ONE WHO DOOMED HIM TO ROAM FOREVER AWAY FROM EARTH!

3

I AM *ALLURA*-- AN *ELE-MENTAL* WHO LIVES IN THE SWORD, WHICH SERVES AS A HOST BODY TO SHELTER ME! IF YOU RELEASED ME, *YOU* COULD ACT AS MY HOST-- AND I WOULD BE ABLE TO TAKE YOU TO YOUR FATHER!

WHAT MUST I DO?

"ACCORDING TO *ALLURA*, I NEEDED THE BOOK *I CHING* AND THE *TING TRIPOD* TO MAKE THE INCANTATION THAT WOULD SAFELY ALLOW HER TO LEAVE THE SWORD! IN SECURING THESE, I CAME IN CONTACT WITH THE *ELONGATED MAN*..."

"THEN--COINCIDENTALLY ENOUGH-- ON LAST *HALLOWEEN EVE*, I PER-FORMED THE SPECIAL SPELL ..."

I AM NOW IN A GASEOUS FORM, *ZATANNA!* BREATHE ME INTO YOUR BODY!

"INSTANTLY AS I FELT THE PRESENCE OF THE *ELEMENTAL* INSIDE ME, THE WALLS OF THE ROOM RECEDED AND ..."

I AM TAKING YOU TO THE LAND OF *KHARMA*-- THE LAST REFUGE OF *ZATARA!*

"WELL! SCARCELY HAD MY FEET TOUCHED THE GROUND OF *KHARMA* THAN ..."

A--FRIENDLY RECEPTION COMMITTEE?!

*NO!* THEY'RE THE EVIL BEAST-MEN OF *BELPHAGOR!* QUICKLY-- *ZATANNA*-- FIGHT THEM WITH YOUR MAGIC!

4

SEERT PIRG YM SEOF! SKCOR RETTAB MEHT!

"AND IN A MAGICAL SPLIT-SECOND..."

ZWOKK!

KLINNNK!

THUDD!

"MOMENTARILY OVERCOME BY SURPRISE, THOSE TERRIBLE ANIMAL CREATURES QUICKLY FOUGHT BACK!..."

KRAKK!

RIIIP

BONGG!

BONGGG!

DNIWLRIHW WOLB YAWA ESOHT STSAEB!

"UNKNOWN TO ME AT THIS MOMENT OF DANGER--ELSEWHERE ON THIS WORLD, MAGICAL FINGERS WERE WEAVING NECROMANTIC SPELLS AGAINST ME..."

I MUST STOP ZATANNA IN HER QUEST--OR ALL IS LOST!

"NOW--AS A RESULT OF THAT ADDED CONJURATION..."

THEY'RE BREAKING THROUGH! ZATANNA-- THOSE AWESOME BELL SOUNDS ARE STABBING THROUGH YOU--WEAKENING ME! IF I GET TOO WEAK YOU'LL HAVE TO LEAVE THIS LAND! DO SOMETHING ELSE--

BUT WHAT? WHAT?

BONG! BONG!

"IT WAS THEN THAT I THOUGHT OF YOU, HAWKMAN--AND ATOM--AND GREEN LANTERN..."

THOSE SUPER-HEROES HELPED ME ONCE--WHY NOT AGAIN? I'VE BEEN IN CONTACT WITH THEM SO I HAVE MAGICAL RAPPORT WITH THEM!

MOTA! NAMKWAH! NEERG NRETNAL, RAEPPA DNA THGIF ROF EM!

HUH? MY POWER RING DOESN'T WORK!

I'LL HANDLE THIS COWBOY'S NIGHTMARE!

BONG! BONG!

HIT HIM IN TIME--SO HE MERELY BRUSHED *ZATANNA'S* SIDE!

ZOKK!

BONG! BONG!

GREAT GUARDIANS! IN DESPERATION I DIRECTED MY *POWER RING* AT THOSE OTHER BULL-MEN--AND THIS TIME IT WORKED!

WHUPP!

KRUKK!

"OH, IT WAS SO GOOD TO SEE YOU FELLOWS DO YOUR STUFF ON THOSE CREATURES! YOU, FOR INSTANCE, *HAWKMAN*..."

THWUPP!

7

"*OH, YOU TOOK SOME SAVAGE BLOWS IN RETURN! FOR ONE LONG BREATHLESS MOMENT I BECAME TERROR-STRICKEN AS YOU REELED BACK FROM THE OVERWHELMING OCCULT ONSLAUGHT...*"

"*AHHH! BUT YOU RESPONDED AS ONLY YOU TRULY WONDERFUL HEROES CAN! YOU SCORNED YOUR HURTS! YOU FOUGHT BACK WITH SAVAGE INTENSITY...*"

WRAK!

SWAK!

YOU'VE TRIUMPHED! OH, WHAT A WONDERFUL INSPIRATION IT WAS TO CAUSE YOU *MAGICAL* COUNTERPARTS OF THE *REAL HAWKMAN, GREEN LANTERN* AND *ATOM* TO COME HERE! YOU'RE ALL SO EXACTLY LIKE THE ORIGINAL SUPER-HEROES--I COULDN'T TELL THE DIFFERENCE IF I DIDN'T KNOW!

ZZZT!

COME NOW! WE MUST FIND *ZATARA*! WITH YOU SUPER-HEROES ALONGSIDE ME, I SHALL NOT FAIL!

"SECRETLY, AHEAD OF US WAS-- *ZATARA* HIMSELF! BUT A *ZATARA* I MIGHT NOT HAVE RECOGNIZED HAD I SEEN HIM THEN! FOR HE WAS MAKING MAGIC --TO BE USED AGAINST ME-- HIS OWN DAUGHTER!!!... "

I MUST DEFEAT *ZATANNA* IN HER ATTEMPT TO REACH ME! IF I FAIL -- BUT I MUST NOT PERMIT MYSELF TO THINK OF -- *THAT DISASTER!*

**WHY** IS *ZATARA* FIGHTING THE DAUGHTER HE LOVES? **WHAT** STRANGE MOTIVATION COULD POSSESS HIM TO HURL THE MIGHTY MAGIC OF WHICH HE IS THE MASTER AT HIS OWN FLESH AND BLOOD? *THE STORY CONTINUES ON THE NEXT PAGE FOLLOWING.*

# Z AS IN ZATANNA--AND ZERO HOUR! PART 2

"FROM THE REALM OF SHADE AND SHADOW ZATARA SUMMONED UP HIS ANCIENT ENEMY--AMEN-HOTEP, NECROMANCER FROM THE LAND OF THE NILE, EVIL EGYPTIAN WIZARD WHOM LONG AGO ZATARA DEFEATED..."

JUST AS MY DAUGHTER FASHIONED UP HER *JUSTICE LEAGUE* SUPER-HERO FRIENDS TO HELP HER--SO SHALL I DRAW ASSISTANCE FROM AN OLD FOE!

AMEN-HOTEP WAKES FROM THE LONG SLEEP! HE STIRS! HE COMES IN ANSWER TO YOUR CALL, O MIGHTY ZATARA!

OG HTROF OT OD TAHW TSUM EB ENOD OT TLAH ANNATAZ! RUOY TNEICNA STNEMHCRAP LLAHS EB RUOY SNOPAEW!

I HEAR YOU, ZATARA! I SHALL OBEY!

"AS WE ADVANCED--THE SKY SUDDENLY DARKENED WITH THE SUPER-GIGANTIC FIGURE OF THE MAGICAL AMEN-HOTEP.."

WHAT MANNER OF MENACE IS THREATENING US NOW?

IF HIS SIZE IS MEANT TO PANIC US--

--WE'LL SHOW HIM UP AS A BIG NOTHING!

"WITH A RUSTLE OF ANCIENT, YELLOWED PARCHMENT, AMEN-HOTEP SHOOK OUT HIS SCROLLS..."

FIGURES PAINTED, FIGURES REAL! FIGURES FROM THIS PARCHMENT STEAL! FIGHT THESE THREE, YOUR NEW-FOUND FOES! BRING THEM LOSS AND BRING THEM WOES!

"WITH BATED BREATH I STARED AT THESE AWESOME NEW OPPONENTS! LIVING CHARIOTS! WINGED BAS! SOLDIERS OF THE PHARAOH! JACKALS! ALL THE ARMED AND MYSTIC MIGHT OF ANCIENT EGYPT-- LAND OF WIZARDRY!-- WERE ARRAYED AGAINST US!..."

I'LL HANDLE THAT CHARIOT!

12

"BUT MORE AND MORE OF THOSE PAINTED ADVERSARIES TUMBLED FROM THE PARCHMENTS AS AMEN-HOTEP SHOOK THEM OUT-- UNTIL I FEARED THEIR VERY NUMBERS WOULD OVER-WHELM YOU..."

HOW LONG CAN THIS GO ON?

NOT MUCH LONGER! YOUR HEROES ARE ABOUT TO CAVE UNDER--!

"TO MAKE MATTERS WORSE, AMEN-HOTEP NOW HURLED SOME OF THOSE VERY PARCH-MENTS DOWN AT ME! THEY FLEW LIKE EERIE BIRDS, THEIR PAPYRUS SHEETS FLAPPING LIKE WINGS..."

ZATANNA! SAVE YOURSELF! SAVE ME! I'M GETTING WEAKER AND WEAKER AS THIS PARCHMENT WRAPS ABOUT YOU!

BUT WHAT CAN I DO, ALLURA? IF ONLY I COULD REACH OUT AND RIP THOSE EVIL PARCHMENTS FROM THAT EGYPTIAN WIZARD I'D-- OHHH! REACH OUT? OF COURSE!

I HAD BEEN IN CONTACT WITH THE ELON-GATED MAN AT A THEATRICAL PROP SHOP--AND WITH BATMAN IN GOTHAM CITY, SO...

DETAGNOLE NAM DNA NAMTAB EMOC OT EM!

AT THIS CRITICAL MOMENT, THE SHARP VOICE OF BATMAN CUTS ACROSS ZATANNA'S ENTHRALLING NARRATIVE...

HOLD IT RIGHT THERE, ZATANNA! YOU AND I HAVE NEVER BEEN NEAR EACH OTHER UNTIL TODAY-- LET ALONE "IN CONTACT"!

OH YES WE HAVE, BATMAN! DO YOU RECALL THE ADVENTURE YOU HAD WITH THE WITCH WHO SERVED THE OUTSIDER?

"WHEN SUDDENLY, BATMAN--WHO THINKS EVEN WHILE HIS FIST IS GETTING IN ITS AWESOME WORK--CRIED OUT SHARPLY..."

HOLD IT, EVERYONE! I JUST THOUGHT OF SOMETHING!

KRAGG!

BREAK IT UP! NO MORE FIGHTING! WE HAVE THIS ALL WRONG! NOBODY IS TRYING TO HARM ZATANNA!

HEY, GREEN LANTERN-- GIVE ME A HAND WITH THE CAPED CRUSADER! HE'S FLIPPED HIS FACEMASK!

LET GO OF ME! I'M OKAY, I TELL YOU! I'VE JUST TUMBLED TO THE TRUTH! WE MUST LET THOSE EGYPTIAN MAGIC-MEN CAPTURE ZATANNA!

IT'S BEEN TOO MUCH OF A STRAIN FOR BATMAN!

POOR FELLOW! AND HE WAS ALWAYS SO SMART, TOO! I ALMOST ENVIED HIM THAT KEEN, ANALYTICAL MIND OF HIS!

HEAR ME OUT, WILL YOU? YOU REMEMBER THE BELLS ON THAT BULL-MAN ZATANNA TOLD US ABOUT?

DON'T STRETCH SO FAST, ELONGATED MAN! I LOSE GROUND EVERY STEP I TAKE!... SURE, WE REMEMBER THAT, BATMAN!

AND THE PARCHMENTS THAT CAME IN CONTACT WITH ZATANNA WHICH I RIPPED OFF? THEN KEEPING IN MIND THOSE BULL-HORN BELLS AND THE PARCH-MENTS--OR BOOK-- TAKE A LOOK AT WHAT PASSES FOR THE "SUN" OF THIS MAGICAL WORLD!

17

IT'S A -- CANDLE -- A MAGICAL ONE THAT GIVES THIS LAND OF **KHARMA** HEAT AND LIGHT !

BELL -- BOOK -- CANDLE --

-- THE RITE BY WHICH DEMONS ARE **EXORCISED** OUT OF A PERSON'S BODY ! THEN THERE MUST BE A **DEMON** INSIDE **ZATANNA** !

"NOT HAVING HEARD YOUR DISCUSSION, I THOUGHT AT THE TIME.."

HELP ME ! WHY ARE YOU ABANDONING ME ?

I SURE HOPE YOU'RE RIGHT, **BATMAN** !

YOU WILL BE -- IF THEY BRING HER TO THAT CANDLE !

IF YOU'RE WRONG -- WE'VE DOOMED **ZATANNA** !

**BATMAN** CORRECT IN HIS DEDUCTIONS ? HAS HIS TRAINED MIND ARRIVED AT THE **RIGHT** ANSWER -- OR THE **WRONG** ONE ? STORY CONTINUES ON THE NEXT PAGE FOLLOWING ! 18

JUSTICE LEAGUE of AMERICA

# Z AS IN ZATANNA--AND ZERO HOUR! PART 3

CURSE I GAVE, I NOW TAKE BACK! CURSE ONCE GIVEN NOW SHALL LACK A VICTIM! I SWEAR BY BEAL! THE CURSE IS GONE--BE WELL!

"THEN--AT LONG LAST!--I SAW MY FATHER! FOR THE FIRST TIME IN TWENTY LONG AND LONELY YEARS I SAW HIS FACE BEFORE ME!..."

DADDY--OHHH, DADDY!

MY CHILD, MY LITTLE GIRL! MY--ZATANNA!

"OH, HOW GOOD IT WAS TO BE WRAPPED IN HIS SHELTERING ARMS! I'M AFRAID I CRIED A LITTLE--JUST AS I'M DOING NOW, TELLING THIS TO YOU..."

FORGIVE ME FOR SENDING THOSE CREATURES AT YOU--BUT IT WAS THE ONLY WAY TO DEFEAT ALLURA...

"HIS STORY CAME OUT, TOLD BY A MAN AT PEACE WITH THE WORLD..."

ALLURA

WAS MY ENEMY! THE STORY SHE TOLD YOU ABOUT MY USING THE SWORD AND HER HELPING ME WAS--FALSE! ACTUALLY, I FOUGHT AND DEFEATED HER-- ONLY TO BE CURSED BY HER WHILE I IMPRISONED HER IN THE SWORD OF PARACELSUS!

OG OTN! DROWS!

FROM HENCE YOU SHALL NOT SEE YOUR KIN, NOR SPEAK TO HER-- LET CURSE BEGIN! NO SIGHT, NO SOUND SHALL YOU THEN HAVE, ELSE CURSE SHALL TAKE YOU TO THE GRAVE!

I NO LONGER DARED RE-MAIN ON EARTH LEST BY CHANCE I SEE YOU OR YOU SEE ME! NOR COULD I WARN YOU DIRECTLY OR EVEN INDIRECTLY! IF I SHOULD, I WOULD DOOM US BOTH TO DEATH!

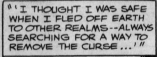

"'I THOUGHT I WAS SAFE WHEN I FLED OFF EARTH TO OTHER REALMS--ALWAYS SEARCHING FOR A WAY TO REMOVE THE CURSE...'"

SOMEWHERE THERE IS A GOOD DOUBLE OF ALLURA! IF I CAN FIND HER, IF SHE WILL AGREE TO FIGHT AND OVERCOME THE EVIL ALLURA--THE CURSE MAY BE REMOVED!

21

"'UNTIL AT LAST IN THIS WORLD OF *KHARMA*, I CAME UPON THE GOOD *ALLURA*...'"

GLADLY WILL I FIGHT THE WICKED *ALLURA*--BUT I CANNOT LEAVE THIS LAND!

THEN I HAVE FAILED--FOR I DARE NOT GO TO *EARTH* AND BRING THE SWORD WITH THE EVIL *ALLURA* IN IT TO *KHARMA*!

"'IMAGINE THEN MY SURPRISE WHEN MY MAGICAL FAMILIARS WHISPERED TO ME THAT *ALLURA* HAD COME TO *KHARMA*--INSIDE THE BODY OF MY ONLY DAUGHTER!...'"

*ALLURA* LURED *ZATANNA* HERE TO FIND ME--KNOWING IT WOULD KILL US BOTH! I MUST FIND A WAY TO STOP HER!

"'AND SO I FOUGHT YOU WITH MY MAGIC--HOPING TO EXORCISE *ALLURA* OUT OF YOUR BODY--BY *BELL*, *BOOK* AND *CANDLE*...'"

IF I CAN MAKE CONTACT WITH *ZATANNA* WITH THESE THREE OBJECTS--I CAN COMPEL *ALLURA* TO LEAVE *ZATANNA'S* BODY!

"'I FEARED I WOULD NEVER SUCCEED WHEN YOU BROUGHT IN THE *JUSTICE LEAGUE* MEMBERS--BUT WHEN *BATMAN* DEDUCED WHAT WAS GOING ON, I KNEW HOPE ONCE MORE..'"

DO YOU THINK *BATMAN* CAN CONVINCE THE OTHERS, *ALLURA*?

WE CAN ONLY HOPE!

"'THEN WHEN I REALIZED WHAT THE *JUSTICE LEAGUE* MEMBERS INTENDED...'"

OG, ARULLA! OG DNA TAEFED EHT DEKCIW ARULLA!

OH, YES, *ZATARA*! AND I SHALL FIGHT AS NEVER BEFORE!

22

"*GREEN LANTERN*, YOU HAD LISTENED AS FASCINATED AS THE REST OF US TO MY FATHER'S RECITAL. NOW YOU SPOKE ... "

I KNOW MY *POWER RING* COULDN'T HARM THE PARCHMENT CREATURES BECAUSE THE PAPYRUS OFF WHICH THEY CAME WAS *YELLOW* WITH AGE, AND MY RING IS POWERLESS AGAINST YELLOW ! BUT...

WHY DID MY RING WORK SOMETIMES AND THEN *NOT* WORK DURING OUR *FIRST* FIGHT ?

ALL LIGHT IS OF AN ENERGY FREQUENCY! THE BONGING OF THE BULL-MAN'S HORN BELLS WAS OF SUCH A FREQUENCY THAT IT PREVENTED CERTAIN LIGHT-RADIATIONS FROM FORMING!

HMMM ! COLOR IS MERELY A REFLECTION OF LIGHT OFF AN OBJECT ! WHEN THE BELLS VIBRATED AT THE SAME FREQUENCY AS *YELLOW*-- MY RING DIDN'T WORK ! WHEN THE BELLS WERE SILENT--IT DID WORK !

AND NOW YOU KNOW WHY I INSISTED ON THANKING YOU FOR HELPING ME FIND MY FATHER !

WELL ! THAT CERTAINLY WAS THE MOST UNUSUAL CASE WE WERE EVER-- er--INVOLVED IN !

STILL-- IT WAS JUST AS MUCH A VICTORY AS ANY OF OUR OTHER REAL ADVENTURES !

I'VE NEVER MET YOUR DAD, *ZATANNA*! PERHAPS SOME TIME --

NO TIME LIKE THE PRESENT ! *REHTAF REAPPA* !

I'M GLAD TO ADD MY PERSONAL THANKS TO THAT OF MY DAUGHTER'S !

TELL US, *ZATARA*. WHAT ARE YOUR PLANS, NOW THAT YOU AND *ZATANNA* HAVE BEEN REUNITED ?

WELL, FOR A WHILE, WE'RE JUST GOING TO GET ACQUAINTED !

PERHAPS SOME DAY.. SOME TIME... WE SHALL ALL MEET AGAIN ! WHO KNOWS ?

*The End*
23

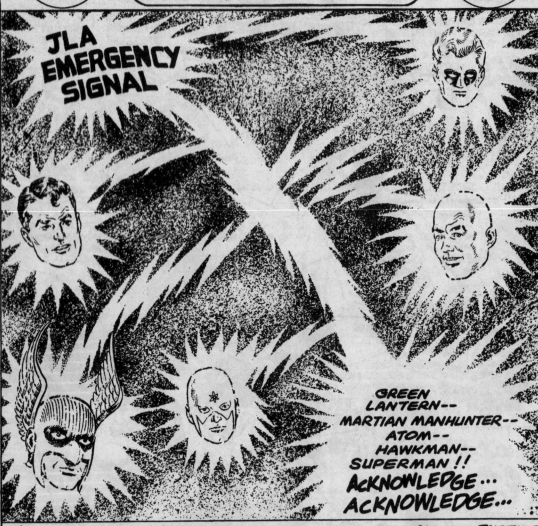

IN THE *JUSTICE LEAGUE OF AMERICA SECRET SANCTUARY*, HONOR MEMBER *SNAPPER CARR* SORTS THROUGH THE MAIL ...

ANOTHER BATCH OF LETTERS ASKING HOW COME ALL TEN MEMBERS OF THE *JLA* DON'T PARTICIPATE IN EVERY CASE! THAT'S AN EASY ONE TO ANSWER--*THEY'RE NOT OBLIGED TO!*

IF IT'S A REGULAR SCHEDULED MEETING--OR EVEN AN EMERGENCY CALL--THEY MAY BE INVOLVED ON SUCH CRITICAL CASES OF THEIR OWN THAT THEY CAN'T RISK ABANDONING THEM! FOR INSTANCE, IN ONE OF THEIR MOST RECENT CASES ...

U.S. MAIL!

... *GREEN LANTERN, ATOM, MARTIAN MANHUNTER, SUPERMAN* AND *HAWKMAN* FAILED TO SHOW UP TO BATTLE THE *LORD OF TIME**! AS REQUIRED, THEY LATER TAPED FOR THE RECORD THE REASONS FOR THEIR ABSENCES--SO LET'S START OFF WITH THE *WINGED WONDER*...

CLICK

* *JUSTICE LEAGUE OF AMERICA #50:* "The LORD OF TIME ATTACKS THE 20th CENTURY!"

"*HAWKMAN* SPEAKING. AS YOU KNOW, MY WIFE--*HAWKGIRL*--AND I ARE ON LEAVE FROM OUR PLANET *THANAGAR*, TO STUDY EARTH-POLICE METHODS. ONE EVENING AS WE WERE CLOSING IN ON A CRIMINAL MASTERMIND..."

ALL CLUES POINT TO THIS OLD ABANDONED MINE AS THE SECRET HIDE-OUT OF *FACELESS!*

WE CAN EXPECT A TOUGH FIGHT--BUT IT'LL BE TO *HIS* FINISH!

THERE'S *FACELESS* TRYING TO BOW OUT OF THE PICTURE!

YOU GO AFTER HIM, *HAWKMAN!* I'LL TAKE ON THE *EASY* ASSIGNMENT ROUNDING UP THOSE THREE THUGS OF HIS!

YOU'RE NOT GIVING ME THE SLIP THAT EASILY, *FACELESS!*

2

"HEMMED IN BY THE SWINGING DOOR, THERE WAS NO WAY FOR ME TO AVOID *FACELESS'* FIST-GREETING..."

: GROAN :

I WAS NEVER HIT SO *HARD* IN MY LIFE!

*SWOTT*

"DAZED THOUGH I WAS, I MANAGED TO SWING MY BATTLE MACE AT HIM..."

EVEN A MAN AS STRONG AS HE WON'T BE ABLE TO STAND UP TO *THIS* BLOW!

"TO MY UTTER ASTONISHMENT, AS THAT SOLID METAL GLOBE MADE CONTACT..."

HA, HA, HA! IS THAT THE BEST YOU CAN DO, *HAWKMAN?*

*THUNG!*

"THEN--FINGERS LIKE STEEL CLAWS GRIPPED AND SWUNG ME AS IF I WERE A TOY..."

ALL *I* NEED IS *SHEER STRENGTH* TO DO YOU IN!

*KLANG!*

*HAWKGIRL* WAS ONLY HALF-RIGHT! IT'S A TOUGH FIGHT--BUT IT'S TURNING INTO *MY* FINISH!

*WHUNK!*

3

*"DESPERATELY I DROVE BACK AT HIM, FLAILING WITH MY MACE..."*

MAYBE I CAN SOFTEN HIM UP-- WITH REPEATED BLOWS...

WHAT--THAT MACE AGAIN?

*"BUT IT WAS I WHO SUFFERED A MENTAL BLOW WHEN..."*

GREAT POLARIS! HIS FINGERS ARE SINKING INTO THE METAL MACE-HEAD AS IF IT WERE MADE OF SOFT CLAY--RIPPING IT IN TWO!

CRUNCH

YOUR MACE MAKES A GOOD PAIR OF CYMBALS, HAWKMAN! LET'S HEAR HOW THEY SOUND AGAINST YOUR HEAD!

*"WITH MY LAST OUNCE OF STRENGTH--I REARED BACK! A METALLIC THUNDER-CLAP EXPLODED UNDER MY CHIN! WHITE-HOT SPARKS SHOWERED ABOUT ME..."*

KLAAP!

THOSE HOT SPARKS--HITTING MY WING FEATHERS-- SETTING THEM AFLAME! NOW I'M REALLY BLAZING MAD!

BRUKK

4

ZWAAK!

WELL, IT'S ABOUT TIME! *FACELESS* IS BEGINNING TO FEEL MY PUNCHES!

THAT *KAYO* IS *OKAY* BY ME! I DON'T MIND ADMITTING--THAT'S HOW I THOUGHT *I'D* END UP!

WHHOOOM

"AFTER SNUFFING OUT MY FLAMING WINGS..."

NOW TO UNMASK THE MYSTERIOUS *FACELESS*...

**WH--AAT?!** THE *MARTIAN MANHUNTER!?!* NO WONDER I HAD SUCH A TERRIBLE TIME WITH HIM-- UNTIL MY WINGS CAUGHT FIRE! *FIRE* IS HIS *WEAKNESS!* BUT... BUT... WHAT EVER MADE HIM TURN INTO ONE OF THE WORLD'S MOST DANGEROUS CRIMINALS?

"AFTER ALERTING *HAWK-GIRL* TO THIS UNEXPECTED COMPLICATION AND IN-STRUCTING HER TO TAKE THE GANGSTERS OFF TO JAIL, I RETURNED TO FIND..."

WHAT AM *I* DOING IN THIS GARB-- *HAWKMAN!* WHERE'D *YOU* COME FROM-- WAIT! I REMEMBER GOING AFTER *FACELESS*-- MY ARCH-ENEMY-- BY MASQUERADING AS HIM--

5

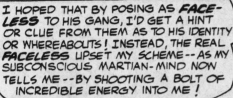

I HOPED THAT BY POSING AS *FACELESS* TO HIS GANG, I'D GET A HINT OR CLUE FROM THEM AS TO HIS IDENTITY OR WHEREABOUTS! INSTEAD, THE REAL *FACELESS* UPSET MY SCHEME--AS MY SUBCONSCIOUS MARTIAN-MIND NOW TELLS ME--BY SHOOTING A BOLT OF INCREDIBLE ENERGY INTO ME!

IT TEMPORARILY PARALYZED MY *MARTIAN* MEMORY--CAUSED ME TO BELIEVE I WAS REALLY *FACELESS*! GREAT PHOBOS! AS *FACELESS*--I PLANNED A SERIES OF CRIMES FOR "MY" MOBSTERS TO PULL OFF THIS VERY NIGHT!

CHANGE BACK TO YOUR *MARTIAN MANHUNTER* SELF--AND LET'S *BOTH* STOP THEM!

"*IT* WAS DURING THIS CRITICAL TIME THAT.."

HOW *FACELESS* MUST BE LAUGHING AT ME-- UHH! THE *JUSTICE LEAGUE EMERGENCY SIGNAL*!

WE CAN'T DROP THIS NOW TO ANSWER THE CALL! STOPPING THIS CRIME-WAVE TAKES PRIORITY! OUR BYLAWS STATE SO!

"SINCE *MARTIAN MANHUNTER*--AS *FACELESS*--HAD PLANNED THE CRIMES, HE KNEW WHEN AND WHERE THEY WERE TO OCCUR..."

I MUST UNDO WHAT I'VE UNWITTINGLY CAUSED! THE GANG IS SET TO MAKE IT AN ALL-NIGHT ROBBERY! IF WE CAN STOP THE FIRST ONE--WE'LL STOP THEM ALL!

"OUR DESTINATION WAS THE DISPLAY OF PRICELESS HISTORIC SCROLLS AND PARCHMENTS AT *MANUSCRIPT MANSION* WHERE ..."

LET'S PUT THE PRESSURE ON THOSE CROOKS, *MM*!

*SUPER*-PRESSURE, IN MY CASE, *HAWKMAN*!

6

FACELESS WARNED US YOU TWO GUYS WOULD SHOW UP--

BANG! BANG! BANG!

BUT HE NEGLECTED TO SAY IT'D BE TO SHOW *YOU* UP!

SPEAKING OF UP-- LET'S GO!

BANG BLAM

KAA-RAACK!

"*BELOW ME, THE MARTIAN MANHUNTER* WAS HAVING HIS OWN HANDS-FULL ..."

IF THAT ANCIENT SCROLL HITS ME-- IT'LL SHATTER! IT'S TOO VALUABLE TO BE DESTROYED, SO --

ZOK

--I'LL KNOCK THAT THUG OUT FROM UNDER THE SCROLL--AND CATCH IT BEFORE IT HITS THE FLOOR!

THUD!

7

# MISSING IN ACTION--5 JUSTICE LEAGUERS!

**PART 2**

TO ANSWER *MARTIAN MANHUNTER'S* QUESTION, HERE IS *GREEN LANTERN* COMING UP NEXT ON OUR TAPE RECORDING...

"*AS I WAS RECHARGING MY RING AT THE POWER BATTERY...*"

IN BRIGHTEST DAY, IN BLACKEST NIGHT, NO EVIL SHALL ESCAPE MY SIGHT! LET THOSE WHO WORSHIP EVIL'S MIGHT BEWARE MY POWER-- GREEN LANTERN'S LIGHT!

BUT HOW CAN *THAT* BE--UNLESS SOMEONE ELSE IS USING THE *POWER BATTERY* ENERGY--FOR HIS OWN EVIL ENDS! GOT TO SEE WHAT'S HAPPENING TO IT...

THE GLOW OF POWER-- BRIGHTER THAN USUAL-- AND FULL OF *EVIL* !

CLICK!

THAT'S A BREAK! AS THE ENERGY-FORCE STREAKED THROUGH THE AIR, IT LEFT TRACES BEHIND--WHICH MY *POWER RING* PICKED UP!

"*CAREFULLY I FOLLOWED THAT SPLASH OF FORCE ACROSS THE SKY UNTIL ...*"

I'VE DIRECTED THE RING TO PINPOINT ANY PLACE WHERE IT DETECTS THE PRESENCE OF THE STOLEN ENERGY AND--THAT GLOW-ING FARMHOUSE! IT'S BEEN TAINTED!

9

"AS I PIERCED THE FARMHOUSE, I FOUND PEOPLE BARRICADED INSIDE..."

:SOB: :SOB:

BOBBY, I MUST KILL *JEFF*! IT'S THE ONLY WAY TO STOP --

NO, NO, DADDY! PLEASE DON'T!

OH MY GOODNESS! *GREEN LANTERN*!

OH, BOY! AM I EVER GLAD *YOU'RE* HERE! YOU CAN SAVE MY DOG *JEFF*!

WHAT'S THE MATTER WITH *JEFF*?

WE WERE OUT PAINTING THE WELL-HOUSE WHEN ALL OF A SUDDEN SOMETHING HAPPENED TO BOBBY'S HOUND DOG! HE GREW BIGGER AND BIGGER--AND TURNED VICIOUS!

"'WE LEGGED IT TO THE SAFETY OF THE HOUSE WITH *JEFF* GROWLING AND SNARLING AT OUR HEELS...'"

WHAT'S GOT INTO THE ANIMAL?

DON'T TALK! JUST RUN!

GGRR/ONRR!

"'FROM THE SAFETY OF THE HOUSE WE WATCHED AS...'"

HE'S TEARING THE TRACTOR APART!

GRR/OWRR

10

"EVEN AS FARMER EDWARDS FINISHED HIS TALE, I SPOTTED THE GIGANTIC DOG RACING PAST THE FARM-HOUSE..."

OH MY GOLLY! HE'S AFTER THE COWS NOW!

GREEN LANTERN--CAN YOU STOP HIM--WITHOUT HURTING HIM?

THAT SHOULDN'T BE ANY TROUBLE--WITH MY *POWER RING!*

GREAT GUARDIANS! AS SOON AS MY *POWER RING* ENERGY TOUCHED HIM--HE GREW TWICE AS BIG AS BEFORE! AND--AND EVEN MORE *VIOLENT!*

GROWRRR!

*JEFF* MUST HAVE ABSORBED SOME OF THE BATTERY'S EVIL-FILLED ENERGY AS IT FLASHED BY HERE--INCREASING HIM IN SIZE AND FEROCITY! MY *POWER BEAM* HEIGHTENED THE EFFECT! I DON'T DARE USE IT AGAINST HIM AGAIN!

GRO... WRR!

THAT SOCK ON THE SNOUT OUGHT TO KNOCK HIM OUT!

ZW VOWP!

"FAR FROM BEING STOPPED, THE MASSIVE HOUND CONTINUED ON TO..."

YEOWP! HE'S SNAPPED HIS JAWS ON MY LEG!

"BACK AND FORTH THE DOG SHOOK ME AS IF I WERE A RODENT--WHEN..."

HA! SOME TIMING! THE *JUSTICE LEAGUE EMERGENCY SIGNAL* WOULD HAVE TO COME IN RIGHT NOW! WELL, IT'S A CINCH I CAN'T GO TO ANY MEETING!

A COUPLE MORE WHACKS LIKE THIS AND I WON'T BE IN ANY POSITION TO CARE WHAT HAPPENS NEXT!

"RAMMING MY FEET HARD INTO A FENCE POST, I USED IT AS A SPRINGBOARD TO..."

I THOUGHT SURE THIS EXTRA PUSH BEHIND MY PUNCH WOULD DO THE TRICK--BUT IT'S LIKE HITTING HIM WITH A FEATHER!

THWAPP!

WHAKK!

AT LEAST--THAT BLOW--KNOCKED SOME SENSE INTO MY HEAD! *NOW* I KNOW HOW TO HANDLE THAT DOG!

"ELUDING JEFF, I RACED FOR THE FARM-WELL..."

THE FARMER WAS PAINTING THE WELL-HOUSE WHEN THE DOG STARTED GROWING WITH HIS ABSORBED POWER BATTERY ENERGY...

BY IMMERSING MY HANDS IN THIS *YELLOW* PAINT, I'LL BE ABLE TO HIT *JEFF*--AND MAKE IT HURT! *YELLOW* IS THE SOLE WEAKNESS OF MY POWER ENERGY...

NOW WHEN I HIT HIM--HE REALLY FEELS IT!

ZWWAPP!

"I GAVE JEFF NO CHANCE TO RECOVER AND STRUCK BACK! I HIT HIM FROM ALL ANGLES--HARD!"

IT'S FOR YOUR OWN GOOD, FELLA!

THUNK!

"AND WHEN THE BIG HOUND WAS KNOCKED COLD..."

POOR JEFF! -SOB-

HE'LL BE HIMSELF AGAIN, BOBBY-- AS SOON AS THE POWER FORCE THAT CAUSED ALL THIS WEARS OFF!

"TAKING TO THE AIR AGAIN, I FOLLOWED THE ENERGY TRAIL DIRECTLY TO THE MARTIAN MANHUNTER!..."

ANY IDEA WHY THIS TRAIL LEADS TO YOU, MARTIAN MANHUNTER?

I CAN GUESS! SOMEHOW, FACELESS MANAGED TO TAP YOUR POWER BATTERY AND CREATE A FORCE STRONG ENOUGH TO MAKE ME LOSE MY MARTIAN MEMORY AND BELIEVE I WAS HIM!

"AFTER TURNING FACELESS' GANG OVER TO THE LAW..."

I'LL HAVE TO PUT A SPECIAL AURA OF POWER AROUND MY BATTERY TO PREVENT ANYTHING LIKE THAT FROM HAPPENING AGAIN!

GUESS WE'RE TOO LATE TO JOIN IN ON THE EMERGENCY JUSTICE LEAGUE CASE--BUT LET'S GET OVER TO HEADQUARTERS AND FIND OUT WHAT WE MISSED!

# MISSING IN ACTION -- 5 JUSTICE LEAGUERS! PART 3

NOW-- HERE'S WHERE **ATOM** SPEAKS HIS PIECE EXPLAINING HIS FAILURE TO ANSWER THE EMERGENCY SIGNAL...

"I WAS OUT OF TOUCH -- AND *TIME* -- BECAUSE I HAD GONE INTO THE *TIME POOL* TO THE YEAR *1783* -- WHERE I SAVED THE LIFE OF *BENJAMIN FRANKLIN* *..."

* THE ATOM #27: "STOWAWAY ON A HOT-AIR BALLOON!"

THAT LEAVES ONLY **SUPERMAN** UNACCOUNTED FOR! AND WHAT A YARN *HE* HAS TO TELL!...

"SEVERAL DAYS BEFORE I RECEIVED THE EMERGENCY SIGNAL I WAS UNABLE TO ANSWER, *BATMAN* AND I HAD COMPLETED A CASE IN *METROPOLIS*..."

SO LONG, *BATMAN* -- EH? THE *ENERGIMOMETER* NEEDLE ON YOUR GAUGE --!

IT'D TAKE AN OVERWHELMING FORCE TO MOVE IT THAT WAY! HOLD ON, *SUPERMAN* -- I'M NOT LEAVING *METROPOLIS* YET!

15

"AS *BATMAN* SET HIS DIRECTIONAL CONTROLS, I TRAILED THE *BATMOBILE* DOWN THE STREET UNTIL ..."

RI-I-I-P!

THOSE CUBIST CREATURES MUST HAVE RIPPED AN OPENING IN THE SPACE-TIME CONTINUUM! IT WAS THE TERRIFIC ENERGIES NEEDED FOR SUCH A FEAT THAT REGISTERED ON MY *ENERGIMOMETER!*

"AS I DROVE DOWN TOWARD THE ALIEN BEINGS, ONE OF THEM PULLED A CUBE OUT OF ITS BODY AND ... "

GOING TO USE PART OF ITSELF AS A *WEAPON*?!

"EXPLODING ON CONTACT DIDN'T BOTHER MY INVULNERABLE BODY IN THE LEAST..."

THESE CUBISTS ARE "*SQUARES*"! THEY DON'T KNOW ONLY *KRYPTONITE* OR *MAGIC*-- OR THE RAYS OF A *RED* OR *GREEN* SUN-- CAN WEAKEN ME!

ZZZ-SST

MY *FISTS* SERVE AS MY WEAPONS--

EH? IT DIDN'T BOTHER THE CUBIST AT ALL!

SWAK!

ZOWIE! IF THE *MAN OF STEEL'S* PUNCHES DON'T FLATTEN THOSE THINGS-- HOW CAN *I* DO ANY BETTER?

16

"THEN, BEFORE I COULD MOVE TO TAKE ON ANOTHER CUBIST.."

GREAT SCOTT! IT'S PARTS ARE FLYING BACK--JOINING THEMSELVES TOGETHER!

CLICK! SNAP! CLANG! CLANK!

SUPERMAN--KEEP UP THAT HEAVY BARRAGE! I JUST NOTICED SOME'THING!

WHACK!

"MY FIST WAS A MIGHTY PISTON, POKING PULVERIZING PUNCHES RIGHT AND LEFT.."

ANYTHING TO OBLIGE, BATMAN! I THINK I SPOTTED SOMETHING ODD MYSELF!

SPANG! BLATT!

THWUM!

SURE--THAT EXPLAINS IT! THEIR NERVOUS SYSTEM IS DIFFERENT FROM OURS!

18

WHEN AN EARTH CREATURE IS HIT, THE PART THAT'S STRUCK--HURTS! IT ALSO SWELLS UP! BUT THESE CUBISTS HAVE NERVOUS SYSTEMS THAT *DETOUR* ANY PAIN THEY MIGHT FEEL AT THE POINT OF IMPACT--TO A TOE-CUBE ON THEIR FEET!

THE TOE-CUBE *SWELLS* AS IT *ANESTHETIZES* ALL PAIN AND SENSATION! BECAUSE IT FEELS NO PAIN, IT CAN GO ON FIGHTING INDEFINITELY--ALWAYS BRINGING ITSELF BACK TOGETHER AGAIN IF SHATTERED! WHAT A CRAZY, MIXED-UP NERVOUS SYSTEM!

NOW LET'S SEE WHAT DEVELOPS WHEN IT HAS NO *TOE!*

*HIT HIM AGAIN, SUPERMAN--HARDER! HARDER!!*

SN AP!

I NOTICED THAT TOE SWELLING TOO! IF *BATMAN* HADN'T YANKED AWAY THAT TOE-CUBE, I WOULD HAVE!

ZZWUKK!

WITHOUT THE TOE-CUBE TO ABSORB THE PAIN, IT WAS KNOCKED *SENSELESS!*

RIGHT... AND UNLIKE *HUMPTY DUMPTY* WE'LL PUT IT BACK TOGETHER AGAIN--ONCE WE HAVE IT SAFELY LOCKED UP!

19

"BUT WITHIN THE NEXT SPLIT-SECOND, THE TWO UNHARMED CUBE-BEINGS GATHERED UP THE PIECES OF THE SHATTERED CUBE-CREATURE AND..."

THEY'RE ESCAPING THROUGH THE GAP IN THE SPACE-TIME CONTINUUM!

LET 'EM GO! NOW THAT WE KNOW THEIR WEAKNESS, THEY WON'T BE BACK--THAT'S FOR SURE!

"ONE WEEK LATER, WHILE IN THE **FORTRESS OF SOLITUDE**..."

I--I FEEL SO STRANGE, AS IF MY BODY WERE BEING TUGGED BY SOME TITANIC FORCE!

"NEXT THING I KNEW I WAS A PRISONER IN A VAST LABORATORY OF..."

WHAT A TIME FOR THE **JUSTICE LEAGUE** EMERGENCY SIGNAL TO REACH ME!

THE CUBE-CREATURES!

YES, **SUPERMAN**! ONCE YOU AND **BATMAN** LEARNED OUR WEAKNESS, WE REALIZED WE COULD NEVER INVADE AND CONQUER YOUR WORLD--

--NOT UNLESS WE COULD MAKE AN ANDROID ARMY OF INVULNERABLE **SUPERMEN**! SO WE BROUGHT YOU HERE TO STUDY YOU-- DISCOVER THE SECRET OF YOUR STRENGTH!

OUR FIRST TEST WILL BE A SIMPLE ONE-- A WOODEN RAP AGAINST THE SKULL THAT ENCLOSES YOUR BRAIN!

SW-O-TT

I--I KNOCKED HIM OUT! INCREDIBLE! IN HIS OWN WORLD WE HIT HIM WITH A *PROCLEONIC CUBE*-- AND HE DIDN'T FEEL A THING!

HE MUST BE FAKING! AROUSE HIM!

ALL RIGHT-- CONFESS YOUR TRICKERY...

I--I'VE LOST MY *SUPER-POWERS!* I'M JUST AN ORDINARY HUMAN BEING! BUT--WHY? THERE'S NO *KRYPTONITE* AROUND! I'D KNOW IT IF THERE WERE!

WE MUST LEARN HOW HE CAN TURN HIS INVUL- NERABILITY ON AND OFF! IT IS OF THE UTMOST IM- PORTANCE TO OUR PLAN!

NOR IS ANYONE USING *MAGIC!* THAT LEAVES ONLY ONE POSSIBLE EXPLANATION-- THE *SUN* OF THIS WORLD MUST BE EITHER *RED* OR *GREEN!*

THEY SUCCEEDED IN PULLING ME THROUGH THE TIME-SPACE WARP BY USING *GREEN SOLAR RADIATION*-- WHICH MADE ME A NORMAL PER- SON! THE *DOMINANT* RAYS OF A GREEN SUN MASK OUT THE YELLOW SOLAR RAYS WHICH GIVE ME SUPER-POWERS!

I'LL PLAY ALONG-- PRETEND TO COOPERATE WITH THEM!

WAIT! NO NEED TO HIT ME AGAIN! I'LL TELL YOU HOW TO DUPLICATE MY POWERS!

A VERY WISE DECISION!

21

I'LL NEED *SILICA* AND *SODA*, *BORAX*, *MAGNESIUM OXIDE*...

THESE THINGS WILL BE BROUGHT TO YOU AT ONCE...

"*THE CUBISTS WERE MY UNWITTING ASSISTANTS AS I MADE A LARGE FILTERING LENS IN THEIR LABORATORY FURNACES...*"

NOW I'LL HOLD THE LENS OVER MY HEAD!

AS THE SOLAR RADIATION INSIDE THIS LAB PASSES THROUGH IT--IT WILL FILTER OUT THE GREEN RAYS THAT DEPRIVE ME OF MY SUPER-POWERS!

"*AS THE LENS FILTERED OUT THE STRENGTH-SAPPING SOLAR RADIATION...*"

NOW I'M BEING BATHED ONLY BY *YELLOW SOLAR RADIATION*!

I'M MY SUPER-SELF AGAIN!

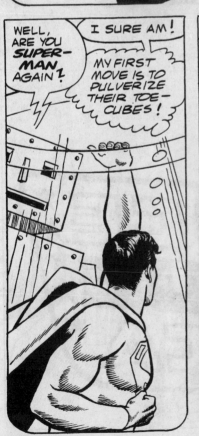

WELL, ARE YOU *SUPERMAN* AGAIN!

I SURE AM!

MY FIRST MOVE IS TO PULVERIZE THEIR TOE-CUBES!

"*AFTER THAT, I WENT INTO MY KNOCKOUT ROUTINE...*"

THAT'S THE LAST OF THEM! NEXT TIME I SEE *BATMAN* I'LL HAVE TO TELL HIM ABOUT THIS SURPRISING SEQUEL TO OUR ADVENTURE!

*"AFTER DEMOLISHING THEIR TIME-SPACE CONTINUUM APPARATUS, I CAME DIRECTLY HERE TO THE JUSTICE LEAGUE HEADQUARTERS -- TOO LATE TO HELP FIGHT THE LORD OF TIME BUT IN TIME TO MEET WITH ALL THE ASSEMBLED MEMBERS..."*

NOW THAT SUPERMAN HAS JOINED US, I'LL EXPLAIN WHAT THE EMERGENCY SIGNAL CASE WAS ALL ABOUT!

MAKE IT FAST, FLASH! THE ENTIRE JUSTICE LEAGUE IS DUE TO MAKE AN APPEARANCE IN WASHINGTON-- TO HONOR SERGEANT EDDIE BRENT AS HE RECEIVES A MEDAL OF HONOR!

WELL, THAT ENDS THE STORY-- AND JUST IN TIME TOO! HERE COME THE JUSTICE LEAGUERS NOW-- FOR THEIR NEXT MEETING!

CLICK

THE END

23

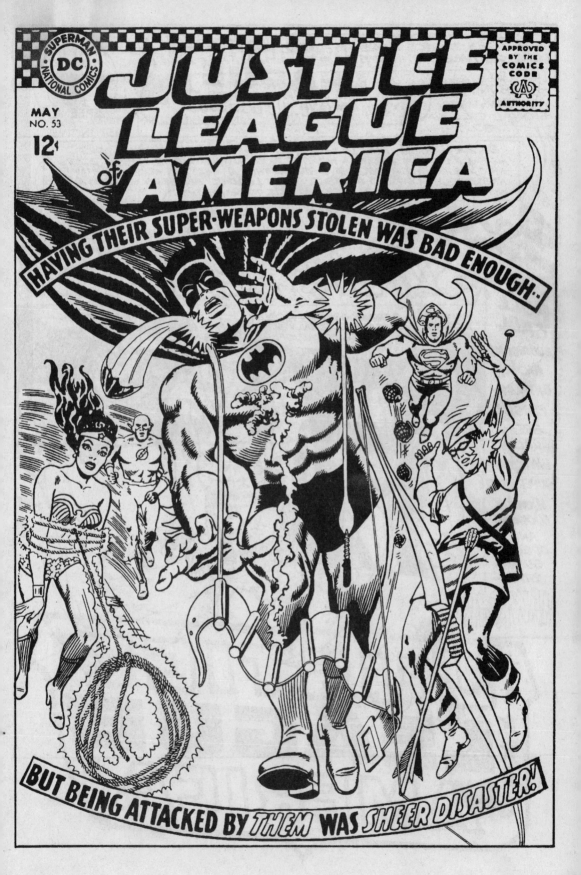

IN THE *MIDWAY CITY MUSEUM*, WHERE CARTER (*HAWKMAN*) HALL SERVES AS CURATOR AND HIS WIFE SHIERA (*HAWKGIRL*) AS HIS ASSISTANT...

KATAR-- BEFORE YOU LEAVE FOR YOUR *JUSTICE LEAGUE* MEETING-- TAKE A LOOK AT *THIS!*

WHAT IS IT? SOMETHING URGENT?

WHILE TAKING INVENTORY, I DISCOVERED THAT OUR RARE *YEHUD* COIN FROM ANCIENT ISRAEL HAS BEEN STOLEN-- AND THIS COUNTERFEIT DUPLICATE LEFT IN ITS PLACE!

SINCE WE ALONE CARRY THE SPECIAL DEVICE TO SHUT OFF OUR ALARM-- NO THIEF COULD POSSIBLY HAVE *OPENED* THE COIN'S DISPLAY CASE!

IT'S STRUCK US TOO? BUT WHEN WE READ ABOUT THE AMAZING THEFTS THAT HAVE BEEN PLAGUING ART GALLERIES AND MUSEUMS ALL ACROSS THE COUNTRY-- WE INSTALLED OUR OWN BURGLAR-PROOF *THANAGARIAN* ALARM SYSTEM!

THE DISPLAY CASE WAS *NOT* OPENED! YET THE REAL COIN WAS STOLEN! AND HERE'S AN EVEN MORE BAFFLING POINT TO CONSIDER-- THE DUPLICATE'S REVERSE SIDE IS *BLANK!* SO-- HOW *WAS* THE REAL COIN STOLEN?

I DON'T KNOW-- BUT MAYBE THIS *THANAGARIAN* DETECTOR CAN GIVE US A CLUE...

SEE-- THE SUBSTITUTE COIN GIVES OFF A FAINT AMOUNT OF UNKNOWN RADIATION! UNFORTUNATELY THE DETECTOR MUST *ABSORB* SOME OF THAT RADIOACTIVITY TO FUNCTION-- WHICH DOESN'T LEAVE ENOUGH LEFT TO ENABLE US TO TRACK IT TO ITS SOURCE!

ORIGINALLY WE THEORIZED THAT THOSE OTHER ART THEFTS WERE THE WORK OF AN ART FORGER! NOW WE KNOW SOME SUPER-SCIENTIFIC CRIMINAL IS RESPONSIBLE! NOTHING WE CAN DO ABOUT IT NOW-- SO I MIGHT AS WELL GO ON TO THE *JLA* MEETING!

:SIGH: I WISH SOMEDAY I COULD TAKE AN *ACTIVE* PART IN ONE OF THEIR ADVENTURES!

2

AT THE SECRET SANCTUARY OF THE *JUSTICE LEAGUE OF AMERICA*, GREEN ARROW SERVES AS ROTATING CHAIRMAN FOR THE REGULARLY SCHEDULED MEETING...

SINCE NO ONE HAS ANY URGENT BUSINESS FOR US TO CONSIDER, LET'S DEAL WITH THE MAIL! SNAPPER--?

NOT A SINGLE REQUEST FOR HELP, *GREEN ARROW*! BUT *GREEN LANTERN* AND *MARTIAN MANHUNTER* SENT WORD THEY WON'T BE HERE! THEY'RE OUT IN SPACE ON CASES!

IN THAT CASE, *I'D* LIKE TO BRING UP SOMETHING THAT FITS INTO OUR *"DEPARTMENT OF ODD COMPLAINTS"*! EARLIER TODAY-- AS I CORNERED A COUPLE OF ARMED BANDITS-- I FIRED A NET-ARROW OVER THEM, TO EFFECT A QUICK CAPTURE!

"BUT TO MY SURPRISE AND DISMAY..."

eh? THE NET DIDN'T OPEN! *THAT* NEVER HAPPENED BEFORE!

THUNK!

"AS BULLETS STARTED FLYING AT ME, I DUCKED FOR COVER BEHIND THE *ARROW-CAR*..."

MY FOLLOW-UP ARROWS DIDN'T WORK EITHER! I BETTER TAKE A CLOSER LOOK AT THE REST OF THEM!

"WHEN AN EXAMINATION REVEALED MY QUIVER WAS FILLED WITH ARROWS THAT ONLY *LOOKED* LIKE MINE, I ARROWED *MYSELF* AT THE CROOKS..."

WHO MADE THE SUBSTITUTION? HOW--WHY--?

WHAM!

3

NEXT, WONDER WOMAN RISES IN HER SEAT..

I WASN'T GOING TO MENTION IT--BUT A SIMILAR THING HAPPENED TO ME! I WAS FOLLOWING THREE SABOTAGE AGENTS...

"I HAD JUST CRASHED THROUGH A STONE WALL BETWEEN ME AND MY FLEEING QUARRY--AND WAS ABOUT TO HURL MY MAGIC LASSO AT THEM ..."

ONCE I GET THE LASSO AROUND THEM, THEY'LL BE COMPELLED TO TELL ME THE NAMES OF THEIR FELLOW--CONSPIRATORS!

WHUP!

"I CAUGHT THEM IN THE LARIAT'S NOOSE EASILY ENOUGH, BUT..."

WE'RE TELLIN' YOU NUTHIN', WONDER WOMAN!

INCREDIBLE! THIS CAN'T BE MY MAGIC LASSO--OR THOSE MEN WOULD BE FORCED TO OBEY MY COMMAND!

THERE IT IS--JUST A LENGTH OF GLOWING ROPE THAT MERELY RESEMBLES MINE! HOW THE SWITCH WAS MADE I CAN'T IMAGINE!

SUPER-WEAPONS SUBSTITUTED? WOULDN'T IT BE SOMETHING IF THE SAME THING--UNKNOWINGLY--HAPPENED TO MY UTILITY BELT?

MY LASER-TORCH--FIRING A RED BEAM--THAT DOESN'T EVEN RAISE A PUFF OF SMOKE IN THE CAVERN WALL!

NO TEAR GAS IN THAT PELLET! I'VE BEEN VICTIMIZED TOO!

POP!

IT'S MY TURN NOW! I HAVE A HUNCH MY EXPERIENCE WITH THE FACSIMILE COIN IS RELATED TO WHAT HAPPENED TO BATMAN, WONDER WOMAN AND GREEN ARROW!

AFTER THE *WINGED WONDER* HAS RELATED THE THEFT OF THE *YEHUP* COIN...

MY DETECTOR SHOWS THE *UTILITY BELT* HAS *NO RADIATION* IN IT AT ALL! BUT I STILL SAY THERE'S A TIE-IN BETWEEN THE *"SUPER-CRIMINAL"* AND THE WEAPONS THIEF!

THE REST OF US DON'T USE WEAPONS--SO THERE WAS NOTHING TO STEAL--AND SUBSTITUTE!

*SO!* WE DIDN'T THINK WE HAD *ANYTHING* URGENT TO DISCUSS--NOW WE'RE CONFRONTED BY A SERIES OF INCREDIBLE CRIMES TO SOLVE!

WHAT STUMPS ME IS--*WHO* WOULD WANT TO STEAL THE *UTILITY BELT-- MAGIC LASSO--* AND *ARROWS?*

LET'S FIND OUT!

JUST LIKE *THAT,* BATMAN? HOW?!

BY ROUNDING UP ALL THE *COUNTERFEIT OBJECTS* THAT WERE SUBSTITUTED FOR THE *REAL* STOLEN TREASURES! LUMPED TOGETHER, THEY MIGHT EMIT ENOUGH RADIATION FOR *HAWKMAN'S* DETECTOR TO LEAD US TO THE CULPRIT!

WHAT ARE WE WAITING FOR? LET'S GET GOING!

NO, *ATOM*--IF YOU DON'T MIND! SINCE *BATMAN, HAWKMAN, WONDER WOMAN* AND *I* ARE PERSONALLY INVOLVED, I THINK WE FOUR VICTIMS SHOULD HAVE FIRST CRACK AT SOLVING THIS--

I GO ALONG WITH THAT-- BUT AT LEAST LET *SUPERMAN* AND ME HELP YOU GET *STARTED!*

RIGHT! *FLASH* AND I COULD USE OUR SUPER-SPEED TO GET THOSE FAKE TREASURES BACK HERE WITHOUT WASTING ANY MORE VALUABLE TIME!

5

**NO SOONER SAID THAN--**

SWOOOOSH!

LIKE *WOW!* THERE GO THE TWO FASTEST MEN ON EARTH! SOMEDAY I'D LIKE TO SEE A RACE BETWEEN THEM-- TO SETTLE ONCE AND FOR ALL WHO IS *FASTER!*

**--DONE !!...** VROOOOM!

MAYBE THE FIRST ONE BACK WILL SHOW WHO'S FASTER-- :ULP: HERE THEY COME, NECK AND NECK !

**MOMENTS LATER...**

IT WORKED! I HAVE A *FIX* ON THE ODD RADIATION! NOW I CAN TRACK IT TO ITS SOURCE!

I'LL BET *GREEN LANTERN* AND *MARTIAN MANHUNTER* WILL BE SORRY THEY WEREN'T IN ON THIS CASE! I HAVE A FEELING IT'S GOING TO BE A *BLAST!*

HOW RIGHT *BATMAN* IS ! SO BRACE YOURSELF FOR ACTION, SHOCKS, THRILLS AND SURPRISES AS THE STORY CONTINUES ON THE NEXT PAGE FOLLOWING !

JUSTICE LEAGUE of AMERICA

MY PRESENT EXPERIMENTS HAVE BEEN DE-VOTED TO ANIMATING INANIMATE THINGS! EVENTUALLY, BY COMBINING THIS *ANIMATOR* WITH MY *TRANSPORTER*, I SHALL ACHIEVE MY ULTIMATE TRIUMPH!

I SHUDDER WHEN I THINK OF THE CLOSE CALL I HAD THE FIRST TIME I WAS ABOUT TO ACTIVATE THE *TELEPORTER*! I ACCIDENTALLY DIS-COVERED--JUST IN TIME--THAT IT HAS A DISASTROUS SIDE EFFECT ON ANYONE WITHIN ITS PRESENCE! I HAVE SAFEGUARDED MYSELF AGAINST IT--

SUDDENLY THE MASTER THIEF'S REVERIE IS ENDED BY...

WHAT'S THIS? *WONDER WOMAN? BATMAN? GREEN ARROW? HAWK-MAN?* HA HA! THEY DOOMED THEMSELVES-- THE MOMENT THEY ENTERED MY TREASURE-- CAVERN!

THE RADIATION TRAIL LEADS HERE--

BUT UNTIL THEIR DOOM STRIKES, I MUST AVOID CAPTURE--BY ANIMATING THESE STOLEN STATUES OF FOLKLORE--*PAUL BUNYAN AND HIS BLUE OX--THE RING-TAILED ROARER--THE DOODANG-- THE MONSTER OF LEEDS--* INTO SNARLING BATTLE-FURY!

B

UNDER THE ANIMATED CONTROL OF THEIR MASTER, THE *DOODANG* ★ GALLOPS WITH SUCH BLINDING SPEED AT THE *AMAZON PRINCESS* THAT...

★ EDITOR'S NOTE: THE *DOODANG* WAS A NIGHTMARE CREATURE OUT OF THE FAMOUS *UNCLE REMUS* TALES OF *JOEL CHANDLER HARRIS.* WANTING TO SWIM AND FLY, IT GREW BOTH SCALES AND WINGS -- AND AS A RESULT COULD DO *NEITHER!*

GREAT *HERA!* IT NABBED ME BEFORE I COULD MAKE A MOVE!

PLANNING TO MAKE ME A *MOUTHFUL MORSEL..?*

HANDS THAT CAN RIP SHEETS OF SOLID STEEL DART OUTWARD! FINGERS GRIP AND HOLD -- AS *WONDER WOMAN* DOES A HANDSTAND, PERCHED UPON A LIVING DEATH-TRAP...

THAT'LL HOLD IT OFF TILL I GET SET FOR MY NEXT MOVE...

WITH A SUDDEN EXPLOSION OF MUSCLE, SHE WHIPS INTO A SOMERSAULT AND...

I HAVE A SPLIT-SECOND TO WORK THIS -- WITH A MAGIC-LESS LASSO!

THE NOOSE OF THE PSEUDO-LASSO TIGHTENS AROUND A STALACTITE -- JUST AS...

THIS DOODANG WOULDN'T HAVE BEEN SUCH A PROBLEM IF I HAD MY REAL LASSO -- BUT THIS ROPE CAME IN HANDY JUST THE SAME!

SWINGING DOWN THE ROPE, THE GIRL GLADIATOR DOES SOME FANCY FOOTWORK...

THWAACK!

KNOCKED OFF ITS FEET, THE DOODANG DROPS INTO A GREAT CREVASSE IN THE CAVERN FLOOR WHERE...

THIS IS LIKE WEDGING A CORK IN A BOTTLE! THE DOODANG WILL FIT IN HERE SO TIGHTLY -- IT WON'T BE ABLE TO WIGGLE OUT!

10

HIGH OVERHEAD, THE *MONSTER OF LEEDS** SNAPS ITS TALONS ON *HAWKMAN* AND...

SLAMMING ME INTO THIS *STALACTITE*-- SO FURIOUSLY-- I'VE BROKEN OFF A CHUNK OF IT--

\* EDITOR'S NOTE :

IN THE MID-*18th* CENTURY, THE *MONSTER OF LEEDS*-- OR THE *JERSEY DEVIL*, AS IT CAME TO BE KNOWN --WAS BE-LIEVED TO CAUSE STORMS, FIRE AND OTHER DISASTERS ALONG THE ATLANTIC COASTLINE ! EXORCISED BY A CLERGYMAN IN THE 19th CENTURY, IT WAS LAID TO REST AND NEVER BOTHERED ANYONE AGAIN-- UNTIL *NOW*--AS THE STOLEN AND ANIMATED STATUE OF THE CRIMINAL COLLECTOR !

--WHICH I CAN TURN INTO A WEAPON--SEEING AS I DIDN'T BRING ANY OF MY OWN WEAPONS WITH ME !

I'M NOT SURE HOW TO KAYO AN ANIMATED STATUE, BUT I'VE GOT TO START SOMEWHERE !

UNABLE TO FEEL THE EFFECT OF *HAWKMAN'S* BLOW, THE *JERSEY DEVIL* RAMS INTO ITS WINGED FOE AND...

KR-UN-NK !

WOOOOF ! MANAGED TO FOLD MY WINGS BEHIND ME--IN TIME TO CUSHION THE IMPACT AGAINST THE WALL !

11

WITH A STRENGTH BORN OF DESPERATION, *HAWKMAN* LASHES OUT WITH HIS FEET..

I'VE GOT--ONE SLIM CHANCE--TO OVERCOME IT--IF IT DOESN'T SUSPECT WHAT I'M UP TO--!

RIDING THE FALLING STATUE DOWNWARD, THE *AERIAL ACE* TURNS HIS GRAVITY BELT TO FULL POWER...

IT'S DOING WHAT I EXPECTED--SPREADING ITS WINGS TO SLOW ITS FALL!

WITH A RENDING CRACK, THE STATUED WINGS OF THE *MONSTER OF LEEDS* ARE IMPALED ON SHARP STALAGMITES...

PAAN AANG

BEING ONLY A STATUE--IT CAN'T FEEL ANYTHING! THOSE LIMESTONE SPEARS WILL HOLD IT PRISONER WHILE I GO AFTER ITS CONTROLLER!

EVEN AS *WONDER WOMAN* AND *HAWKMAN* HAVE BEEN STRUGGLING FOR THEIR VERY LIVES--SO TOO HAS *GREEN ARROW* AGAINST THE *RING-TAILED ROARER* *...

SWOT!

*EDITOR'S NOTE: THE *RING-TAILED ROARER* WAS HALF-HORSE, HALF-ALLIGATOR. IT COULD SHOOT LIGHTNING OUT OF ITS LEFT EYE AND BREATHE FIRE LIKE A DRAGON! *DAVY CROCKETT,* THE GREAT FRONTIERSMAN, USED TO "BRAG LIKE A RING-TAILED ROARER," HE WAS FOND OF SAYING!

I'VE READ TALES OF THE *RING-TAILED ROARER*--BUT I NEVER THOUGHT I'D SEE--LET ALONE FIGHT--ONE!

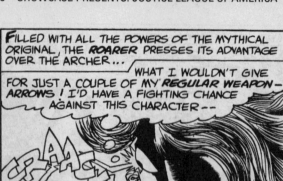

FILLED WITH ALL THE POWERS OF THE MYTHICAL ORIGINAL, THE *ROARER* PRESSES ITS ADVANTAGE OVER THE ARCHER...

WHAT I WOULDN'T GIVE FOR JUST A COUPLE OF MY *REGULAR WEAPON-ARROWS!* I'D HAVE A FIGHTING CHANCE AGAINST THIS CHARACTER--

BUT AS THE MARINES SAY-- *THE DIFFICULT WE DO AT ONCE, THE IMPOSSIBLE TAKES A LITTLE LONGER!*

*ZOKK!*

*WHOOPS!* THAT TAIL WILL END MY TALE MIGHTY SOON--UNLESS I COME UP QUICK WITH A *COUNTERWEAPON!*

BACKING UP, HE DRAWS OUT A HANDFUL OF THE PSEUDO-ARROWS...

THESE SHAFTS CAN'T DO SUPER-STUNTS LIKE MY REGULAR ONES--BUT THEY'RE *WOOD* AND...

THEY'LL *BURN!* THE *RING-TAILED ROARER* IS USED TO SEEING FIRE FROM ITS OWN NOSTRILS--BUT NOT FROM ANY *OTHER* SOURCE! HE SHOULD REACT AS ANY ANIMAL WOULD TO *FIRE!*

13

DRIVEN HEADLONG BY ITS NATURAL FEAR OF FLAMES, THE *ROARER* CRASHES SO HARD INTO A CAVERN WALL THAT...

IT FELL APART! NOW TO NAB THAT MASTER THIEF!

WHIINK

WHILE THE AIR SINGS WITH CONFLICT ALL AROUND HIM, *BATMAN* IS RUSHED BY THE STATUED *PAUL BUNYAN* AND HIS BLUE OX, *BABE\**...

SMAKK

\* *EDITOR'S NOTE:* THE REAL *PAUL BUNYAN* WAS A FRENCH-CANADIAN LOGGER NOTED FOR HIS FABULOUS STRENGTH! HE WAS ADOPTED AS A FOLK HERO BY AMERICAN LUMBER-JACKS ABOUT THE YEAR 1860, AND TALL TALES WERE SO REPEATEDLY TOLD ABOUT HIS STRENGTH THAT HE EVENTUALLY BECAME A CREATURE OF FOLKLORE! *BABE* WAS HIS BLUE OX COMPANION!

I'LL HAVE TO GET OUT OF THIS-- WITH A "LEGENDARY" ESCAPE!

IN *CRETE* DURING THE TIME OF THE *MINOTAUR*-- YOUNG MEN AND WOMEN USED TO ENGAGE IN "BULL LEAPING"--

--BUT I'LL ADD A LITTLE WRINKLE OF MY OWN-- THIS *HAND-STAND* ON ITS HORNS!

14

THE VERY CAVERN SHUDDERS AS...

BABE'S RAMMED ITS HORNS TOO DEEP INTO THE WALL FOR IT TO PULL OUT--LEAVING ME FREE TO TACKLE ITS MASTER!

HA! HA! HO! HO! I'M THE STRONGEST MAN WHO EVER LIVED, BATMAN! YOU'RE GOOD--BUT YOU'RE ONLY HUMAN!

WHEN I CONNECT--YOU'LL BE BATTERED TO A PULP!

I--BELIEVE IT, PAUL BUNYAN--BUT YOUR FIGHTING STYLE IS OUT OF DATE!

WHEN YOU WERE IN YOUR GLORY-- YOU DIDN'T HAVE TO TANGLE WITH A JUDO EXPERT!

HANDS LIKE STEEL CABLES GRIP THE STATUED WRIST! A BACK THAT IS HEAVY WITH MUSCLE BENDS-- TWISTS--ERUPTS AND...

IT'S A LITTLE LATE TO TEACH AN OLD LOGGER NEW TRICKS!

FLYING THROUGH THE AIR LIKE A MASSIVE BALLOON, THE MIGHTY PAUL BUNYAN CRASHES INTO HIS IMPRISONED BLUE OX AND...

KA-RAACK

NOW TO GRAB THE VILLAIN BEHIND ALL THIS!

15

DISBELIEF HAS DEEPENED TO DESPAIR ON THE FACE OF THE CRIMINAL MASTERMIND AS HE HAS SEEN HIS ANIMATED STATUES FALL BEFORE THE FIGHTING FURY OF THE *JUSTICE LEAGUERS*...

GOT TO KEEP OUT OF THEIR CLUTCHES--TILL THE *DOOM* STRIKES THEM...

THEY'RE CLOSING IN ON ME--! WELL, THEY MAY CAPTURE ME--BUT AT LEAST I'LL HAVE THE SATISFACTION OF KNOWING THAT *THEY* WILL SUFFER THE DREADFUL CONSEQUENCES-- NOT TOO LONG FROM NOW!

AND WHEN THE *JLA* OVERTAKES ITS QUARRY OUTSIDE THE CAVERN...

HE MUST HAVE TRIPPED AND FALLEN--KNOCKING HIMSELF OUT!

THIS MUST BE THE DEVICE WHICH HE USED TO STEAL THOSE TREASURES! HE HOPED TO GET AWAY WITH IT SO HE COULD GO ON ROBBING!

AFTER TURNING THE THIEF AND HIS STOLEN TREASURES OVER TO THE AUTHORITIES, THE FOURSOME RETURNS TO THE SECRET SANCTUARY WHERE, AFTER THEY HAVE RELATED THEIR ADVENTURES...

BUT WHAT'S THE CRIMINAL'S CONNECTION WITH YOUR STOLEN WEAPONS--*GREAT KRYPTON!* WHAT'S HAPPENING--

HAWKMAN--WONDER WOMAN--BATMAN-- GREEN ARROW--

THEY SLUMPED FORWARD...

...AND ARE DISAPPEARING!

16

THEY'RE STILL HERE! I CAN FEEL *HAWKMAN'S* BODY! IT'S *WARM*, HE'S BREATHING--SO HE'S STILL *ALIVE!*

MAYBE THEY'VE ABSORBED SOME OF THAT UNKNOWN *RADIATION...*

COULD BE! IF IT HAD THE POWER TO BEND LIGHT RAYS AROUND THEIR BODIES-- IT'D MAKE THEM INVISIBLE TO OUR EYES!

WHY DON'T WE USE THE DEVICE THEY BROUGHT BACK AND TRY TO NEUTRALIZE THE RADIATION THAT'S IN THEM!

I THOUGHT OF THAT TOO, *SUPERMAN!* BUT I'VE BEEN EXAMINING IT AND--IT'S JUST A HEAP OF *JUNK!* IT'S--*WORTHLESS!*

*FLASH* IS RIGHT! HOWEVER THE THIEF STOLE HIS TREASURES-- HE NEVER USED *THAT* TO DO IT!

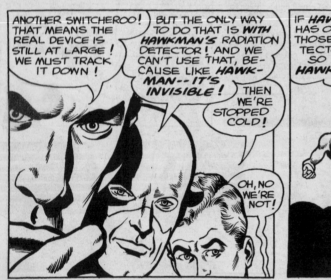

ANOTHER SWITCHEROO! THAT MEANS THE REAL DEVICE IS STILL AT LARGE! WE MUST TRACK IT DOWN!

BUT THE ONLY WAY TO DO THAT IS *WITH HAWKMAN'S* RADIATION DETECTOR! AND WE CAN'T USE THAT, BECAUSE LIKE *HAWKMAN--IT'S INVISIBLE!*

THEN WE'RE STOPPED COLD!

OH, NO WE'RE NOT!

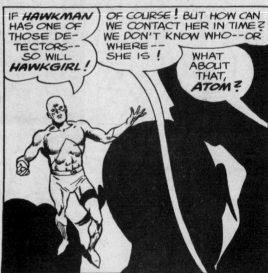

IF *HAWKMAN* HAS ONE OF THOSE DETECTORS-- SO WILL *HAWKGIRL!*

OF COURSE! BUT HOW CAN WE CONTACT HER IN TIME? WE DON'T KNOW WHO--OR WHERE-- SHE IS!

WHAT ABOUT THAT, *ATOM?*

I KNOW *HAWKGIRL'S* EARTH-IDENTITY!*

*FLASH* AND I WILL RUSH YOU TO HER, *ATOM!*

*AQUAMAN,* YOU'D BETTER REMAIN HERE IN CASE OUR STRICKEN MEMBERS RECOVER CONSCIOUSNESS! YOU CAN TELL THEM WHAT WE'RE GOING TO DO--AND CHEER THEM UP A LITTLE!

*EDITOR'S NOTE: AS REVEALED IN *HAWKMAN* #9!

SECONDS LATER, IN THE *MIDWAY CITY MUSEUM...*

*FLASH--SUPERMAN*--AND MY FRIEND, *THE ATOM!*

*SHIERA*--THIS IS NO TIME TO STAND ON CEREMONY! WE NEED YOUR HELP AS *HAWKGIRL!*

17

QUICKLY, *ATOM*, *FLASH* AND *SUPERMAN* MAKE KNOWN TO *HAWKGIRL* THE DREAD FATE THAT HAS BEFALLEN *HAWKMAN* AND THE OTHERS...

OF COURSE I'LL HELP! AND HERE'S A DUPLICATE OF THE DEVICE *HAWKMAN* USED TO TRACK DOWN THAT RADIATION!

I LEFT THE RADIO-ACTIVE ARTICLES IN THE NEXT ROOM...

MOMENTS AFTERWARD...

THERE! I HAVE A "FIX" ON THE POWER SOURCE OF THE MYSTERIOUS RADIATION EMITTED BY THESE COUNTER-FEIT TREASURES! BUT I'M GOING WITH YOU -- AS *HAWKGIRL*!

SURE THING!

WE HAVE TO HURRY! THE LIVES OF *HAWKMAN*, *BATMAN*, *WONDER WOMAN* AND *GREEN ARROW* MAY DEPEND ON HOW FAST WE DO OUR JOB!

18

# SECRET BEHIND THE STOLEN *SUPER-WEAPONS!*
## PART 3

AS *HAWKGIRL* LEADS THE *JUSTICE LEAGUERS* ON THE RADIATION TRAIL, LET US LOOK IN ON THE HIDEOUT OF GANGLAND BOSS JOHNNY MARBLES AND HIS HOODS...

I GOTTA ADMIT I'M A SMART OPERATOR--SNATCHIN' THIS GADGET RIGHT OUT FROM UNDER THE NOSES OF THEM FOUR *JUSTICE LEAGUERS!*

WHEN I FIRST READ ABOUT THOSE STRANGE TREASURE THEFTS, I KNEW QUICK AS A FLASH--*OOPS,* HOW I HATE THAT WORD!--THAT SOMEBODY HAD COME UP WITH THE PERFECT WAY TO COMMIT A PERFECT CRIME!

MAN, I WAS EATING MY HEART OUT WITH JEALOUSY! BUT WHEN I TRIED TO DIS-COVER *WHO* WAS ROBBING AND *HOW*--I DREW A BLANK! SO THEN I TOLD MY-SELF, THE *JUSTICE LEAGUE* COULD FIND THAT OUT! TO GET THEM TO DO IT, WE SWITCHED THEIR WEAPONS, PUTTIN' PHONY ONES IN THEIR PLACE--JUST LIKE WAS DONE WHEN THOSE TREASURES WERE STOLEN...

HERE THEY ARE, BOSS! *BATMAN'S* UTILITY BELT--*WONDER WOMAN'S* LASSO--AND SOUPED-UP ARROWS OF *GREEN ARROW!*

TERRIFIC! NOW ALL THE *JLA* HAS TO DO IS FIGURE THE TREASURE-THIEF WAS ALSO BEHIND THIS--AND TRACK HIM DOWN FOR US!

"*NATCH,* SOME OF THE BOYS GOT CAUGHT--BUT WE ACCOM-PLISHED OUR OBJECTIVE, AS THE MILITARY BUFFS ARE FOND OF SAYIN'..."

"WE ALSO MANAGED TO PLANT A BUGGING DEVICE ON *WONDER WOMAN'S* TIARA--SO WE COULD FOLLOW HER! THE TRAIL LED TO A CAVE..."

HERE COMES THE *MASTERMIND* NOW! THAT GADGET HE'S CLUTCHIN' HAS GOTTA BE THE GIMMICK THAT WORKS HIS ROBBERIES! KNOCK HIM OUT--AND PUT THIS PHONY GADGET WE BROUGHT ALONG TO SUBSTITUTE FOR THE REAL ONE!

19

LUCKILY, THE *JLA* DIDN'T KNOW WHAT THE *REAL* GIMMICK LOOKED LIKE--ANY MORE THAN WE DID!

I'VE BEEN TINKERING AROUND WITH IT--AND I'VE LEARNED HOW TO DO SOME TRICKY THINGS WITH IT! WATCH AS I AIM IT AT THE DOOR...

AT THIS CRITICAL MOMENT--FATE PLAYS A CRUEL TRICK ON *HAWKGIRL* AND THE *JUSTICE LEAGUERS*--AS THEY BURST INTO THE HIDEOUT...

THE JLA! AND THEY'VE RUNG IN *HAWKGIRL* ON US!

SO WHAT! THEY WON'T BOTHER US-- *THEY'RE* GETTING THE TREATMENT I WAS GONNA WORK ON THE DOOR!

TURNED INTO STATUESQUE FIGURES, THE *JUSTICE LEAGUE* MEMBERS AND *HAWK-GIRL* ARE IMMOBILIZED...

*SUPERMAN*-- YOU MAKE A GOOD STATUE! I THINK I'LL KEEP YOU IN MY DEN AS A REMINDER OF...

NEVER MIND *SUPERMAN*! COME ON-- WE GOT A LOT OF WORK TO DO! CLEAR THE AREA HERE!

20

I'M NOT GONNA WASTE ANY TIME MAKIN' MYSELF THE KINGPIN OF CRIME! I'M GONNA TELEPORT *ALL THE GOLD IN FORT KNOX* INTO THIS ROOM-- AND WE'LL NEED PLENTY OF SPACE TO HOLD IT! CLEAR THE ROOM--

OKAY! I'VE GOT A LONGITUDE-LATITUDE FIX ON *FORT KNOX*! GET SET FOR THE *GOLD RUSH OF 1967*!

CLICK!

SUDDENLY--OUT OF THE EMPTY AIR COMES A SWIRLING METAL BALL...

WHA--!? HOW DID *HAWKGIRL*--

CLANG!

WE GRABBED HER, BOSS! DO YOUR STUFF ON HER AGAIN!

SINCE THE RADIATION DIDN'T WORK ON *HAWKGIRL* FOR SOME REASON--I'LL USE SOMETHING THAT *WILL*!

I'LL PULVERIZE HER WITH *GREEN ARROW'S* BOMB SHAFT!

SORRY, BOYS! DUTY CALLS-- AND I ALWAYS OBEY!

21

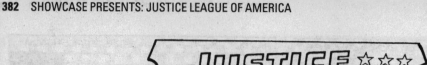

# JUSTICE ☆☆☆ LEAGUE ☆☆☆ of AMERICA

UNLESS YOU'RE AN AUTHORITY ON PLAYING CARDS, YOU'RE IN FOR A DECK-FULL OF SHOCKING SURPRISES, EERIE EXCITEMENT AND TERRIFIC THRILLS WHEN YOU ARE DEALT THE PASTEBOARD PUZZLE OF THE --

# HISTORY-MAKING COSTUMES OF THE ROYAL-FLUSH GANG!

BATMAN

FLASH

WONDER WOMAN

ATOM

MARTIAN MANHUNTER

STORY BY GARDNER FOX

ART BY MIKE SEKOWSKY & SID GREENE

ALEXANDER THE GREAT

SERPENT MAN

QUEEN ELIZABETH

JUDGE DUFFY

SIR LAUNCELOT

LATE ONE EVENING IN A BOOK STORE OF *CAPE CITY, U.S.A.* ....

SEMPER LIBER!

YOU'VE GIVEN ME THE CORRECT PASSWORD--SO THIS MAILING TUBE IS YOURS!

HARDLY HAS THE STRANGER STEPPED FROM THE BOOK STORE, WHEN ...

GOT THE MAP! I'LL SLUG HIM!

I TOLD *IRENE MARLEY* TO MEET ME HERE--SO I CAN TURN THIS OVER TO HER ...

HE'S

HALF HIDDEN AROUND THE CORNER, A GIRL GOES RIGID IN SUDDEN TERROR...

OHH!

I--I'VE GOT TO SEE IF I CAN HELP THAT POOR MAN!

SOON AFTER, IN *CENTRAL CITY,* POLICE RESEARCH SCIENTIST BARRY *(FLASH)* ALLEN ALSO STIFFENS IN SHOCKED SURPRISE AS...

THIRTY MINUTES AGO IN *CAPE CITY* A MAN IDENTIFIED AS *HAL JORDAN* WAS STRUCK DOWN BY AN UNKNOWN ASSAILANT...CRITICAL CONDITION IN *GENERAL HOSPITAL*...

HAL JORDAN! COULD THAT BE MY FRIEND-- GREEN LANTERN?

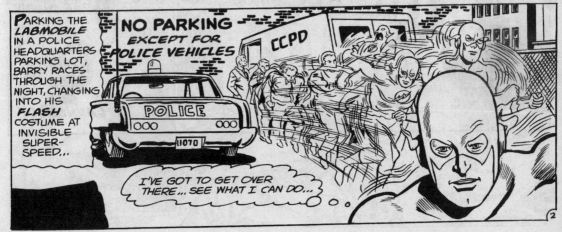

PARKING THE *LABMOBILE* IN A POLICE HEADQUARTERS PARKING LOT, BARRY RACES THROUGH THE NIGHT, CHANGING INTO HIS *FLASH* COSTUME AT INVISIBLE SUPER-SPEED...

NO PARKING EXCEPT FOR POLICE VEHICLES

CCPD

POLICE

11070

I'VE GOT TO GET OVER THERE...SEE WHAT I CAN DO...

2

SECONDS LATER, IN A HOSPITAL ROOM IN *CAPE CITY*...

OOOOH-- *THE FLASH!* WH-WHAT BRINGS *YOU* HERE?

THIS MAN IS--A FRIEND OF MINE! WHAT'S HIS CONDITION?

H-HE'S SINKING FAST...

...NOT EXPECTED TO LIVE THROUGH THE NIGHT... THE *POWER RING* WHICH HAL ALWAYS WEARS ON HIS FINGER--INVISIBLE-- IS PROTECTING HIM FROM MORTAL HARM! BUT WHEN THE RING'S 24-HOUR-LONG CHARGE EXPIRES--SO WILL *GREEN LANTERN!*

AS IF IN SYMPATHY, *FLASH* GRIPS HAL JORDAN'S HAND. ACTUALLY-- HE IS TOUCHING THE *POWER RING* AND BY SHEER WILL POWER COMMANDING IT TO ...

TELEPATH TO ME WHAT HAPPENED TO YOUR RING-WEARER...

I MAY BE ABLE TO SAVE THE LIFE OF THE MAN IN THAT WRECK!

"SEVERAL DAYS AGO, WHILE DRIVING ALONG A MOUNTAIN ROAD, HE SAW A CAR BELOW HIM THAT HAD SMASHED THROUGH A GUARD RAIL ... "

"BUT WHEN HE REACHED THE ROCKS BELOW... "

TOO LATE TO HELP ME...BUT I MUST TRUST YOU... TO HELP MY DAUGHTER, IRENE! MY NAME...ALVIN MARLEY... EXPLORER... HAVE BEEN SEARCHING FOR...

...GREATEST TREASURE IN THE WORLD! FOUND IT AFTER... MANY YEARS... MARKED LOCATION ON MAP...MAILED MAP TO MY GOOD FRIEND OLEG KOR- MANN... BOOK STORE OWNER IN *CAPE CITY*... TO PREVENT ITS BEING STOLEN... WHILE I WAS... RETURNING HOME...

3

TELL OLEG WHAT HAPPENED TO ME! PASSWORD HE AND I AGREED ON IN CASE SOMETHING LIKE THIS HAPPENED IS... *SEMPER LIBER!* HE WILL TURN OVER TREASURE MAP TO YOU... PLEASE GIVE IT TO MY DAUGHTER IRENE.. LIVING OUTSKIRTS OF *CAPE CITY*... GASP!

HE'S DONE FOR!

*"BEFORE LEAVING FOR CAPE CITY, MY WEARER PHONED IRENE MARLEY..."*

--AND YOU WANT ME TO MEET YOU AT THE BOOKSTORE TO GIVE ME THE MAP? VERY WELL, MR. JORDAN! I'LL BE THERE...

SUDDENLY... THE RING'S RUN OUT OF POWER! NOW HAL HASN'T EVEN *THAT* SAFEGUARD TO KEEP HIM FROM DYING! ONLY ONE THING TO DO-- SIGNAL THE *JUSTICE LEAGUE* TO MEET ME HERE!

SOON, *BAT-PLANE* AND *ROBOT PLANE* LAND AT THE *CAPE CITY* AIRPORT...

*WONDER WOMAN!* I HOPE WE CAN DO SOMETHING!

IF WE CAN HELP AT ALL--WE WILL, *BATMAN!* WE'VE GOT TO KEEP TELLING OURSELVES THAT!

WHILE IN HAL'S HOSPITAL ROOM...

*GREEN LANTERN* ON THE VERGE OF DEATH! WHAT HAPPENED?

I TOOK THE QUICKEST WAY HERE, *FLASH*-- THROUGH THE TELEPHONE!

AS SOON AS *BATMAN* AND *WONDER WOMAN* JOIN THE GROUP, THE *SCARLET SPEEDSTER* REPEATS WHAT THE *POWER RING* HAS TOLD HIM...

AS A STARTER, I SUGGEST *FLASH* AND I SEARCH FOR CLUES AT THE PLACE WHERE HE WAS ATTACKED!

*ATOM* AND I WILL STAND BY HERE IN CASE OTHER MEMBERS SHOW UP!

I'M GOING TO BRING DR. CLAY ROCKWELL HERE-- THE WORLD'S NUMBER ONE BRAIN SURGEON!

NOT LONG AFTERWARD, AT THE *CAPE CITY* BOOK STORE...

AS I WAS LOWERING THE BLINDS, I HEARD A THUD, BUT I SAW NOTHING EXCEPT THE GIRL WHO WAS STARING AT WHAT HAD HAPPENED!

DO YOU KNOW THIS EYE-- WITNESS?

YES--SHE'S *IRENE MARLEY*--THE DAUGHTER OF PROF. ALVIN MARLEY! I CAN GIVE YOU HER ADDRESS...

AS *BATMAN* AND *FLASH* RACE TO MISS MARLEY'S HOME...

THAT GIRL--FITS THE DESCRIPTION WE WERE GIVEN!

HELP!

FORCIBLY BEING TAKEN AWAY BY MEN DRESSED LIKE A KNIGHT--AND A GREEK WARRIOR

EVEN AS THE GREAT CRIME-FIGHTERS LEAP FORWARD-- THE COSTUMED CRIMINALS RELEASE IRENE MARLEY TO WHIP OUT ODD WEAPONS...

NO ONE INTERFERES WITH THE PLANS OF *SIR LAUNCELOT!*

THE MIGHTY WEAPONS OF *ALEXANDER THE GREAT* WILL PROVE YOUR UN-DOING!

THOSE RED RAYS DRIVING INTO ME-- LIKE KNIVES!

*WHEW!* THAT ARROW IS STIRRING UP A GALE, AS IF HUNDREDS OF ARROWS WERE WHIPPING THROUGH THE AIR AT ME!

5

CATCHING THE ALTERNATING RED--YELLOW--AND GREEN TINTS OF THE OVERHANGING TRAFFIC LIGHT, THE SWORD OF *ALEXANDER THE GREAT* HURLS ITS ENERGIES AT THE *FASTEST MAN ON EARTH.*

BUT NOW THAT I KNOW WHAT I'M UP AGAINST, I'LL VIBRATE AT ULTRA-- LIGHT SPEED...

MEANWHILE, THE *COWLED CRUSADER* HAS BEEN BATTLING THE EERIE EFFECTS OF THE ARROW-WEAPON...

AAAAOOOOOOO WWWW

...SO THOSE GREEN POINTS GO HARMLESSLY THROUGH ME! NOW TO NAB MY FANTASTIC FOE--

NOT WITH THIS *ORB* TO PRO- TECT ME, *FLASH!*

OOOH! NOW IT'S LIKE BEING HIT WITH THE FLAT OF THE BLADE! THE LIGHT-BEAMS TRAVELED WITH THE SPEED OF LIGHT--AND CAUGHT ME UNPREPARED!

AS THE ORB PULSES, A DAZED, GLASSY LOOK COMES INTO THE EYES OF THE *SCARLET SPEEDSTER*...

I--I'M BEING-- HYPNOTIZED--BY--THAT--GLOBE--

THE *ARROW-GALE* IS JUST ONE OF THE MANY THINGS MY WEAPON CAN DO, *BAT- MAN!* OBSERVE WHAT HAPPENS AS I TWIRL IT ABOVE MY HEAD...

6

FASTER WHIRLS THE ARROW--LOUDER GROWS THE SOUND OF ITS ROTATION UNTIL ...

THE SOUND--SO RAUCOUS-- GIVING ME THE *SHAKES*!

EEEWWEE OOOWW EEEOOO WWWWW WWWWW

HIS BOOTED FOOT LIFTS--THRUSTS OUT...

CLUNNNKK! SPAAANG CLAVAANGG

JUST AS I HOPED! THE CLANGOR OF THE GARBAGE CANS -- NULLIFYING THE SHOCK WAVES OF THAT ARROW SOUND! THIS GIVES ME A CHANCE TO--

--DO SOME STRIKING OUT ON MY OWN!

FZWWOTT

YOU WON'T DO *THAT* AGAIN-- NOT WITH THE AIR-PRESSURE BARRIER I'M WHIPPING UP WITH MY ARROW!

OWWPFF!

AS THE AIR-PRESSURE BARRIER SLAMS INTO THE *MASKED MANHUNTER*--AND THE *SCARLET SPEEDSTER* FEELS HIS SENSES LEAVING HIM UNDER THE HYPNOTIC INFLUENCE OF THE EERIE ORB...

*FLASH* LOOKS IN WORSE SHAPE THAN I AM! GOT TO HELP HIM!

I THOUGHT *I* WAS BAD OFF--BUT *BATMAN* IS BEING HAMMERED TO HELPLESSNESS BY THAT ARROW-ENERGY! HAVE TO RID MYSELF OF THIS HYPNOTIC TRANCE--AND SAVE HIM!

7

*BATMAN* BUMPS INTO *FLASH,* UPSETTING THE HYPNOTIC RAYS OF THE ORB-- WHILE *FLASH* VIBRATES, DISSIPATING THE AIR-- PRESSURE BARRIER...

THANKS, *BATMAN!* THAT BUMP WAS ALL I NEEDED TO SHAKE FREE OF THAT HYPNOTIC SPELL!

AND YOUR VIBRATIONS SAVED ME FROM THAT WALL OF AIR PRESSURE!

BUT WHEN THE *CAPED CRUSADER* AND *SCARLET SPEEDSTER* REACH OUT FOR THEIR QUARRY...

WHIRLING AROUND IN THEIR TRACKS--

IS THIS ANOTHER TRICK?

NEXT MOMENT...

THEY'VE WHIRLED OUT OF SIGHT!

AT LEAST WE SAVED THE GIRL FROM THEM! LET'S RUSH HER OVER TO THE HOSPITAL-- HOPING SHE CAN TELL US SOMETHING ABOUT THESE ODDLY COSTUMED MEN!

*POP!*

*POP!*

IN THE HOSPITAL ROOM, SHORT MOMENTS BEFORE...

*HAWKMAN* IS ON *THANAGAR* AND THE OTHERS ARE BUSY ON CASES THAT-- OH, COME IN, DOCTORS!

WH-WHAT ARE YOU *JUSTICE LEAGUE MEMBERS* DOING HERE?

OFF WITH OUR DOCTOR DISGUISES!

WE CAME HERE TO GET *HAL JORDAN--* AND YOU CAN'T STOP US!

*ATOM* AND I ARE GOING TO GIVE IT A GOOD TRY!

8

YOU MADE IT A LOT EASIER FOR ME TO SMASH YOU, *ATOM*-- LEAPING AT ME LIKE THAT!

YOU'VE GOT TO LAY A HAND ON ME FIRST-- *SERPENT-MAN!*

PRESSING HIS SIZE-AND-WEIGHT CONTROLS IN THE PALMS OF HIS GLOVES, THE *TINY TITAN* SHRINKS HIMSELF FROM SIGHT..

UH? HE'S GONE!

CLICK

CLICK

THEN--LIKE A BOLT OUT OF THE BLUE...

NOW THAT I MANEUVERED MYSELF BEHIND THIS CHARACTER--I CLICK MYSELF TO 6-INCH *ATOM* SIZE AND 180-POUND RAY PALMER WEIGHT--AND--

POW!

CLICK!

CLICK!

BUT THE SINISTER *SNAKE-MAN* COUNTERS THAT BLUDGEONING BLOW WITH A COUNTER-CRUSHER OF HIS OWN!

NOTHING CAN SURVIVE THIS POISON GAS ATTACK, *ATOM!*

G-GOT TO HOLD OFF BREATHING--LONG AS I CAN!

MEANWHILE, THE *MARTIAN MANHUNTER* IS IN A DEADLY BATTLE OF HIS OWN--AGAINST THE AMAZING POWERS OF THE COSTUMED JUDGE...

HOW ABOUT SOME WATER TO DROWN YOU, *MARTIAN MANHUNTER?*

YOU DON'T EXPECT ME TO BELIEVE --

ELEMENTS OF LAW

WATER

AS A TIDAL WAVE OF WATER SLAMS INTO THE CRUSADER FROM *MARS*...

OOOOOPS! I--*BELIEVE*--!

SPLASH.

BEFORE HE CAN RECOVER, A FOLLOW-UP ONSLAUGHT BY ROCKS AND SAND...

EARTH

FIRST *WATER*--AND NOW *EARTH*! AS IF THAT JUDGE WERE FIGHTING ME WITH THE FOUR "*ELEMENTS*"! THAT MEANS THE NEXT ELEMENT WILL BE--

*FIRE*! AND--FIRE IS THE ONE WEAKNESS OF MY MARTIAN BODY! GOT TO GET IN AT LEAST ONE BLOW BEFORE IT OVERCOMES ME--

FIRE

PUNCH--HAD-- NO POWER-- BEHIND IT...

AS HE COLLAPSES, THE *MARTIAN MANHUNTER* MANAGES TO GET IN A TIMELY ASSIST FOR *ATOM*...

AT LEAST I STILL HAVE ENOUGH BREATH IN ME--TO RID THE *TINY TITAN* OF THE GASES THAT ARE CHOKING HIM TO DEATH!

WHOOOSH!

BORNE ALOFT BY THE AIR CURRENT...

NICE GOING, *MARTIAN MANHUNTER*! NOW IT'S MY TURN TO "FIRE AWAY" AT THE JUDGE!

TO MAKE SURE, I'M CLOSING THE BOOK ON YOU!

AWMPPP!

CASE DIS-MISSED, YOUR HONOR!

BREAKING FREE, THE "JUDGE" TOSSES HIS CLOAK ABOUT HIMSELF WITH A HAUGHTY SNEER...

I HAVE BEEN HUMILIATED ENOUGH! I'M RETIRING --

NOT SO FAST, MR. MAGISTRATE! I HAVEN'T PASSED SENTENCE ON YOU YET!

FIST POISED FOR A KNOCK-OUT BLOW, THE *TINY TITAN* FINDS ONLY A COLLAPSING CLOAK TO TANGLE WITH!...

AFTER THE "JUDGE" TAKES HIS RUN-OUT POWDER...

WHEN THE JUDGE DISAPPEARED --HIS FLAMES DIED OUT AND MY MARTIAN SUPER-STRENGTH RETURNED ! AT LEAST I CAN CAPTURE OUR SERPENTINE FOE BEFORE HE COMES TO...

NOW TO HOLD HIM TIGHT --

THEN --TO THE STUNNED AMAZEMENT OF THE JUSTICE LEAGUER FROM MARS...

HE --BROKE INTO PIECES --JUST AS CERTAIN REPTILES CAN CAST OFF THEIR TAILS !

WH-WHAT KIND OF AMAZING CREATURES WERE WE FIGHTING ?

ACROSS THE COUNTRY FROM CAPE CITY, WONDER WOMAN DASHES INTO THE HOME OF DR. CLAY ROCKWELL...

GREAT HERA ! THAT WOMAN --DRESSED LIKE QUEEN ELIZABETH THE FIRST-- WAVING A FLOWER UNDER THE NOSE OF DR. ROCKWELL...

AH--*WONDER WOMAN*--THE *AMAZON PRINCESS!* I'VE BEEN WAITING A LONG TIME TO HAVE ANOTHER CRACK AT YOU!

SHE KNOWS ME? BUT I'VE NEVER SEEN HER BEFORE!

FLORAL GREETINGS TO YOU, *WONDER WOMAN!*

THOSE PETALS ARE LIKE DEADLY PROPELLER BLADES! MY ONLY CHANCE TO WARD THEM OFF IS TO PLAY *"BULLETS AND BRACELETS"* WITH THEM!

*PING! PING!*

YOU MAY GUARD YOURSELF FROM THE PETALS--BUT THE TINY SEEDS FROM MY FLOWER-WEAPON WILL PROVE TOO MUCH FOR YOU!

BUT THE *MAGIC LASSO* DEFTLY DEFLECTS THE SEEDS...

I'LL GIVE YOU A TASTE OF YOUR OWN MEDICINE, *"GOOD"* QUEEN BESS!

*OHHH!*

AND WHEN THE *ENCHANTED ROPE* FALLS ABOUT THE *QUEEN*...

IT GRABBED *EMPTY AIR!*

13

SOON, IN THE HOSPITAL ROOM WHERE HAL JORDAN IS SINKING FAST... LESS THAN 100 TO 1! I'VE GOT TO OPERATE AT ONCE!

WHAT ARE HIS CHANCES, DR. ROCKWELL?

APPREHENSIVE, FEARFUL FOR THE LIFE OF HAL (*GREEN LANTERN*) JORDAN, THE *JUSTICE LEAGUERS* PACE THE HOSPITAL CORRIDORS...

YOU KNOW, SOMETHING'S BEEN TROUBLING ME ABOUT THOSE COSTUMED CHARACTERS WE JUST FOUGHT! THERE'S SOMETHING *FAMILIAR* ABOUT THEM --

THAT FAKE QUEEN ELIZABETH *DID* SAY SHE WAS HAPPY TO HAVE *ANOTHER* CRACK AT ME!

BUT WE'VE NEVER SEEN ANY OF THEM BEFORE! OR--HAVE WE!

OPERATING ROOM

WHO ARE THE MYSTERIOUS ANTAGONISTS WHO MASQUERADE AS *ALEXANDER THE GREAT* AND *SIR LAUNCELOT*, A *SERPENT-MAN*, A *JUDGE* AND *QUEEN ELIZABETH*?

STORY CONTINUES ON THE *NEXT* PAGE FOLLOWING!

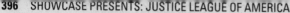

IT'S JUST STRUCK ME! WE'VE BEEN BATTLING OUR OLD FOES, THE *ROYAL FLUSH GANG*! ACCORDING TO THE HISTORY OF CARDS, THE *KING OF CLUBS* WAS DERIVED FROM *ALEXANDER THE GREAT*, THE CLUB QUEEN FROM *QUEEN ELIZABETH I* OF ENGLAND--WHILE THE JACK WAS INSPIRED BY *SIR LAUNCELOT*! THE ACE IS CALLED A *SERPENT* IN SPANISH! IN POKER, THREE TENS IS KNOWN AS A--*JUDGE DUFFY*...

BUT HOW DID THE *ROYAL FLUSHERS* GET MIXED UP WITH HAL JORDAN?

I HOPE HE CAN TELL US AFTER THE OPERATION IS OVER...

MEANWHILE, THE *CARD GANG* HAS THE STOLEN MAP--AND WE DON'T EVEN KNOW WHERE THEY'VE GONE OR WHAT THEY'RE AFTER!

OPERA NG ROO

AT THIS VERY MOMENT, IN AN UNDERGROUND LABORATORY FAR FROM *CAPE CITY*...

LUCKY WE GOT AWAY BEFORE THE *JUSTICE LEAGUE* CAPTURED US! WHAT'S OUR NEXT MOVE?

TO GO AFTER THE TREASURE ALVIN MARLEY FOUND--

BUT YOU SAID WE NEEDED IRENE MARLEY AND HAL JORDAN TO INTERPRET THE MYSTERIOUS WORDS ON THE MAP FOR US!

IT WOULD HAVE BEEN HELPFUL! WHEN I TUMBLED TO THE FACT THAT MARLEY HAD DISCOVERED THE LOCATION OF THE GREATEST TREASURE IN THE WORLD-- WE WAITED FOR HIM TO RETURN TO *CAPE CITY*!

WE EVEN BUGGED HIS DAUGHTER'S TELEPHONE, FIGURING HE'D CALL HER! THEN TO OUR HORROR, WE LEARNED MARLEY HAD BEEN KILLED IN AN AUTO ACCIDENT--

OUR ONLY LEAD WAS THE MAN WHO FOUND HIM-- *HAL JORDAN*! WE FOLLOWED HIM--AND WHEN HE OBTAINED POSSESSION OF THE MAP--TOOK IT FROM HIM...

WHILE THE MAP REVEALS WHERE THE TREASURE IS BURIED, WE COULD NOT UNDERSTAND THE CRYPTIC WORDS ON IT--

15

SO I SENT TWO OF YOU TO FETCH THE MARLEY GIRL, HOPING *SHE* COULD INTERPRET THEM! I WENT WITH THE JUDGE TO GRAB HAL JORDAN IN CASE ALVIN MARLEY HAD TOLD HIM WHAT THEY MEANT...

...WHILE I WENT TO GET DOCTOR ROCKWELL TO BRING HAL JORDAN OUT OF HIS COMA!

UNFORTUNATELY-- AND FOR A REASON I CAN'T IMAGINE-- THE *JUSTICE LEAGUE OF AMERICA* HAS INTERESTED IT- SELF IN THE CASE!

I DIDN'T EXPECT THAT--BUT IT WON'T STOP US! I'M NOT GOING TO LET THE CRYP- TIC WRITING DELAY US ANY LONGER! WE'RE FLYING TO *ASIA MINOR*-- AND THE TREASURE!

SO OFF WITH THESE HISTORICAL COSTUMES AND ON WITH OUR ORIGINAL *ROYAL FLUSH* UNIFORMS!

I NEVER COULD UNDER- STAND WHY WE HAD TO WEAR THESE OTHER COSTUMES!

IT'S ON ACCOUNT OF THE *STELLAR- ATION ENERGY* THE BOSS DIS- COVERED, *TEN!**

*STELLARATION ENERGY* IS THE STRANGE FORCE WHICH INFLUENCES CARDS AND WHICH EMANATES FROM THE STARS! IT ALSO ENABLES US TO UTILIZE UNUSUAL WEAPONS AND POWERS! BUT TO MAKE THEM WORK, THE USER HAD TO BE CLAD AS A CARD-- AN *ORIGINAL* OF A CARD, LIKE *QUEEN ELIZABETH!*

*JUSTICE LEAGUE OF AMERICA # 43: "CARD CRIMES OF THE ROYAL FLUSH GANG!"

IN THEIR PRIVATE PLANE THE CARD- CRIMINALS ARE SOON HIGH ABOVE THE ATLANTIC OCEAN...

ANY IDEA WHAT THIS TREASURE IS THAT ALVIN MARLEY FOUND?

SOMETHING SO TREMENDOUS THAT IT'S ALMOST BEYOND OUR WILDEST DREAMS! CENTURIES AGO A MAN NAMED *SASSANOS* AMASSED MANY OF THE WORKS FORMERLY CONTAINED IN THE *LOST LIBRARIES* OF THE WORLD--

16

"SCROLLS AND MANUSCRIPTS FROM THE BURNED LIBRARY OF *ALEXANDRIA*, FROM THE LOST LIBRARIES OF *PERGAMO* AND *PISISTRATUS* IN *ATHENS*, OF THE *TEMPLE* IN *JERUSALEM*, OF *PTAH* IN *MEMPHIS*-- THE BOOKS THAT SURVIVED THE BOOK-BURNING ORDERED BY THE *EMPEROR CHOU HOUANG TI* IN 213 B.C.--WERE BROUGHT TOGETHER IN ONE PLACE BY *SASSANOS*, WHO HOPED FROM THEIR WRITINGS --TO RULE THE WORLD!"

NOBODY CAN EVEN GUESS AT THE LONG-LOST KNOWLEDGE IN THOSE VOLUMES! WHY DO YOU KNOW THE ANCIENTS HAD VACCINES AND ANESTHESIA? A SUBMARINE USED BY ALEXANDER THE GREAT? MARVELS OF METALLURGY? THAT *COLUMBUS* USED A GREEK VOLUME WHICH TOLD OF A WORLD TO BE DISCOVERED IN FUTURE CENTURIES?

THOSE ARE ONLY *SOME* OF THE MARVELS WE *KNOW* ABOUT! WHAT OTHER WONDERS ARE HIDDEN IN THOSE BOOKS? HISTORY TELLS US NOTHING OF WHAT TO EXPECT--YET *SASSANOS* EXPECTED TO USE THAT WISDOM-- TO CONQUER THE WORLD!

TO CONQUER THE WORLD-- WITH *BOOKS?*

NOT MERELY WITH BOOKS! THERE ARE ALSO THREE WEAPONS OF THE ANCIENT WORLD IN THE LOST LIBRARY--AWESOME WEAPONS HISTORY TELLS US ABOUT--BUT DOES NOT REVEAL THEIR TRUE NATURE!

WHAT HISTORICAL WEAPONS ARE YOU REFERRING TO?

THE WEAPONS--ALONG WITH THE BOOKS--ARE BEHIND THESE BRONZE DOORS! THEY ADD UP TO A FORTUNE SO PRICELESS--THERE ISN'T ENOUGH MONEY IN THE WORLD TO BUY THEM! AND WE SHALL NOT SELL THEM!

WE'LL KEEP THEM OURSELVES-- ABSORB ALL THEIR HIDDEN WISDOM--AND WITH THEM-- DOMINATE THE WORLD!

MEANWHILE, IN A HOSPITAL CORRIDOR IN *CAPE CITY*, HAL JORDAN IS WHEELED OUT OF SURGERY...

IS HE--OR ISN'T HE...

WILL HE LIVE...

...BE ABLE TO TELL US ABOUT HIS ATTACKER AND THAT MAP?

DR. ROCKWELL GATHERS THE MEMBERS ABOUT HIM...

MR. JORDAN NEEDS ABSOLUTE QUIET! NO QUESTIONS-- FOR AT LEAST TEN HOURS!

TEN HOURS? IN THAT TIME THE *ROYAL FLUSH GANG* WILL HAVE THE TREASURE-- HIDE IT AND.... IRENE! ARE YOU SURE YOU CAN'T TELL US ANYTHING TO HELP US OUT?

BUT I'VE ALREADY EXPLAINED-- I KNOW NOTHING! I'M SORRY. DADDY WAS SO SECRETIVE...

WAIT! I THINK THERE IS ANOTHER WAY TO FIND OUT WHERE THE *ROYAL FLUSHERS* HAVE GONE!

YOU *DO?* WELL-- SPILL IT, *BATMAN!* DON'T KEEP US IN SUSPENSE!

THERE COULD BE ONE OTHER PERSON BESIDES ALVIN MARLEY AND HAL JORDAN WHO SAW THAT MAP!

WHAT? WHO-- *GREAT PHOBOS!* OF COURSE! THE MAN WHO OWNS THAT BOOKSTORE! MARLEY MAILED THE MAP TO HIM!

SHORTLY...

TELL US--DID YOU SEE THE MAP ALVIN MARLEY ENTRUSTED TO YOU?

WHY, N-NO! I--I DON'T PRY INTO OTHER PEOPLE'S AFFAIRS!

PLEASE, SIR! THERE IS TOO MUCH AT STAKE! ISN'T IT POSSIBLE YOU WERE *CURIOUS* ENOUGH TO HAVE UNROLLED THE MAP--

WELL, YES-- I DID TAKE A BIT OF A PEEK! BUT I CAN'T REMEMBER ANY DETAILS...

MAKES NO DIFFERENCE! WITH MY *MARTIAN-VISION* I CAN PROBE INTO YOUR BRAIN--SEE THE MAP AS YOU SAW IT! THEN I'LL DRAW IT FOR MY FELLOW MEMBERS!

18

THERE IT IS! BUT WHAT'S THAT CRYPTIC WRITING ON IT?

WHY, THAT'S IN THE ANCIENT *MINOAN* LANGUAGE! WHOEVER DREW THE MAP MUST HAVE BEEN A MARVELOUS SCHOLAR!

WHAT DOES IT SAY? CAN YOU TRANSLATE IT, IRENE?

AS BEST I CAN MAKE OUT IT SAYS TO "TAKE CARE WITH THE SEALED-OFF VOLUMES OF FORGOTTEN LORE! IF THEY ARE EXPOSED TO AIR, THE ANCIENT BOOKS WILL "--I GUESS THE WORD IS "*CRUMBLE*"! OH, MY! IF THE *ROYAL FLUSH GANG* DOESN'T KNOW ABOUT THIS--THEY'LL RUIN THOSE PRICELESS SCROLLS!

IN ASIA MINOR, BRONZE GATES CLANG OPEN AS THE *ACE OF CLUBS* LEADS HIS CARD-CRIMINALS INTO THE VAULT THAT HOLDS THE TREASURES OF UN-COUNTED CENTURIES...

HERE THEY ARE! THE WISDOM OF THE AGES-- STORED HERE JUST FOR US!

HURRY! LET'S LEARN HOW THOSE ANCIENT WEAPONS WORK!

THEN--AS THE *ACE OF CLUBS* HASTILY SCANS THE PRECIOUS VOLUMES...

YES--HERE IS THE SECRET OF THE WEAPONS!

SHORTLY... *ACE!* THE *JUSTICE LEAGUE*--COMING THIS WAY!

SOMEHOW THEY LEARNED WHERE THE LOST LIBRARIES ARE HIDDEN--AND FOLLOWED US!

LET THEM COME! WITH OUR KNOWHOW OF THE ANCIENT WEAPONS, WE'LL CRUMBLE THEM!

19

SWIFTLY, THE *ACE OF CLUBS* HANDS OUT THE WONDER WEAPONS OF THE PAST...

THE GREAT *MIRRORS OF ARCHIMEDES* WITH WHICH HE DESTROYED THE SPARTAN FLEET BY SETTING FIRE TO THEIR SHIPS!

THE *TRUMPET JOSHUA* SOUNDED TO BLAST THE WALLS OF *JERICHO!*

THE *MAGICAL TRIPOD* THAT HELPED THE *DELPHIC ORACLE* MAKE HER PROPHECIES!

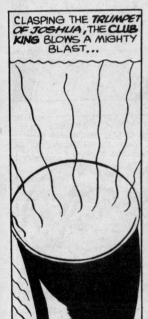

CLASPING THE *TRUMPET OF JOSHUA*, THE *CLUB KING* BLOWS A MIGHTY BLAST...

OHHH! THAT AWESOME SOUND IS -- BRINGING THE VAULT DOWN ON US!

UPWARD LEAPS THE *MARTIAN MANHUNTER* -- EVEN AS *ACE OF CLUBS* LEVELS THE *ARCHIMEDEAN MIRRORS*...

*ARCHIMEDES* CAUSED HEAT FROM SOLAR ENERGY WITH THESE MIRRORS! SO WILL I!

ONLY TEAMWORK CAN WIN THIS BATTLE! I MUST SHIELD MY FELLOW MEMBERS FROM THESE FALLING ROCKS!

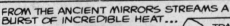

FROM THE ANCIENT MIRRORS STREAMS A BURST OF INCREDIBLE HEAT...

THAT HEAT -- CAUSING FIRES -- WEAKENING ME!

INTENSE HEAT -- DISRUPTING MY SIZE-CHANGING CONTROLS...

TRAPPED IN THESE FLAMES...

THE *MAGICAL TRIPOD OF DELPHI* IS LIFTED -- AND MAGICALLY THE ROCKY FLOOR TURNS TO LOOSE MUD INTO WHICH THE MEMBERS SINK...

GRAB HOLD OF ME, *WONDER WOMAN!* USE ME AS AN ATOMIC MISSILE TO --

20

THE AMAZONIAN MUSCLES OF THE *PEERLESS PRINCESS* RIPPLE AS SHE CATCHES THE *TINY TITAN* AND...

HOPE SHE THREW A PERFECT STRIKE-- OR WE'LL ALL SINK THROUGH THE FLOOR--AND BE ENTOMBED BELOW!

THAT TRUMPS THE *ACE OF CLUBS'* PLAY!

*CRASH!*

GRAB HOLD OF MY ARMS! USE THEM TO PROPEL YOURSELVES OUT OF THIS MUD!

NOW THAT THOSE MIRRORS ARE GONE-- MY STRENGTH IS RETURNING...

IT'S A SHAME TO SMASH THESE MARVELOUS OLD WEAPONS--BUT IT'S OUR ONLY CHANCE TO SAVE OURSELVES!

I'LL BORROW *WONDER WOMAN'S* MAGIC LARIAT-- USE IT TO WHIP MYSELF UP AND OUT OF THIS MAGICAL MORASS!

I CAN'T VIBRATE MYSELF OUT OF THIS OOZE BECAUSE THE MAGIC THAT CREATED IT IS SLOWING ME DOWN!

*SPROGG!*

HOLD ON, *FLASH*-- RESCUE PARTY'S ON THE WAY!

21

THIS IS ONE TIME WHERE *FIVE BEATS TEN* -- MY *KNUCKLES* OVER YOUR *TEN CARD-SPOTS*!

WOK!

BUT THE *TEN OF CLUBS* REFUSES TO KNUCKLE UNDER AND...

-- *WHEWW*! HE NOT ONLY "*CALLED*"ME--BUT "*RAISED*" ME!

THWUMM!

REGAINING HIS FOOTING, THE *COWLED CRUSADER* REACHES OUT MUSCULAR HANDS AND...

NO CARD IN THE PACK KNOWS *JUDO*-- SO HERE'S WHERE I WIPE THE "*DECK*" WITH YOU!

*FREED* FROM THE *HAND-CLUBBING* OF THE *TEN OF CLUBS*, THE *FASTEST MAN ON EARTH* ROTATES HIS ARMS AT *WHIRL-WIND* SPEED...

SORRY ABOUT THAT, *MARTIAN MANHUNTER* -- BUT YOU WERE THE ONE CLOSEST TO THAT *MAGIC TRIPOD*!

FEEL FREE, *FLASH*-- ANY TIME!

OOOPPF!

*THEN*, WHEN *FLASH* HAS BEEN DRAWN FROM THE MORASS WHICH QUICKLY SOLIDIFIES AFTER THE DESTRUCTION OF THE *MAGIC TRIPOD*...

EASY, *LIZ*-- OR I'LL "*CLUB*" YOU ONE!

WHAT A LOSS! THE ANCIENT WISDOM IN ALL THESE VOLUMES--GONE BECAUSE *AMOS FORTUNE*-- THE *ACE OF CLUBS*--DIDN'T KNOW THE MEANING OF THE CRYPTIC WORDS!

AND THESE WEAPONS! WHAT *HISTORICAL FINDS*! MAYBE WE CAN PUT THEM TOGETHER AGAIN--BUT IN SUCH A WAY THEY WON'T FUNCTION--AND DONATE THEM TO AN *HISTORICAL SOCIETY*!

22

IN HAL JORDAN'S HOSPITAL ROOM, THE NEXT DAY...

I'M SURE GRATEFUL TO YOU *JUSTICE LEAGUE* MEMBERS FOR TAKING A HAND IN MY AFFAIRS-- BUT I'M SORRY YOU DIDN'T SAVE SOME OF THOSE SCROLLS FOR IRENE!

MAYBE IT'S JUST AS WELL, HAL! YOU SEE, I'VE WONDERED IF IT WAS RIGHT FOR US TO TAKE THE KNOWLEDGE FROM THOSE OLD SCROLLS BECAUSE NOBODY GETS ANY-THING-- WITHOUT PAYING A PRICE!

23

ODD YOU SHOULD SAY THAT, IRENE! I WAS THINKING THAT IF WE *HAD* OBTAINED THE KNOWLEDGE OF THE OLD CIVILIZATIONS, WE MIGHT UNWITTINGLY RE-PEAT THEIR MISTAKES! PERHAPS SOMETHING DREADFUL WOULD HAVE HAPPENED--WHICH WOULD BE *OUR* PRICE TO PAY! IT MUST BE A BLESSING IN DISGUISE THAT THE BOOKS WERE BURNED AND THE WEAPONS DESTROYED!

LATER, WHEN HAL JORDAN IS DISCHARGED FROM THE HOSPITAL...

WHERE WILL YOU BE HEAD-ING TO NOW, HAL?

TO RECHARGE MY *POWER RING!* AND BE READY FOR ANY DUTIES I'LL BE NEEDED FOR-- AS *GREEN LANTERN!*

THE END

The JUSTICE LEAGUE

SUPERMAN

FLASH

GREEN LANTERN

GREEN ARROW

JUSTICE ★★★ LEAGUE ★★★ of AMERICA

The JUSTICE SOCIETY

HOURMAN

JOHNNY THUNDER

WONDER WOMAN

MR. TERRIFIC

WILDCAT

HAWKMAN

ROBIN

ART BY: SEKOWSKY & GREENE

STORY BY: GARDNER FOX

FOUR ORDINARY PEOPLE -- STRUCK BY BLACK SPHERES -- BECOME EXTRA-ORDINARY! SO MUCH SO THAT NOT EVEN THE JUSTICE SOCIETY OF EARTH-TWO OR THEIR JUSTICE LEAGUE COUNTERPARTS OF EARTH-ONE KNEW HOW TO HANDLE ...

# The SUPER-CRISIS THAT STRUCK EARTH-TWO!

CHINESE BANDIT *HOW CHU* STANDS BEFORE A FIRING SQUAD, SENTENCED TO PAY WITH HIS LIFE FOR HIS CRIMES...

READY...

AIM...

OUT OF THE SKY HURTLES A SMALL BLACK SPHERE...

FIRE!

AN INSTANT BEFORE THE BULLETS REACH THEIR TARGET, THE GLOBE SINKS INTO THE BANDIT'S BODY-- AND...

HYEEE-AGH! THE BULLETS--BOUNCING OFF HIM!

WITH A SNARL OF UTTER FURY AND A BLAST OF AWESOME, RAGING STRENGTH-- HE RIPS LOOSE HIS BONDS...

FOOLS! YOU ARE LIKE STRAW MEN TO *HOW CHU*! I AM MIGHTIER THAN ALL OF YOU--!

IN CHICAGO, U.S.A., STENOGRAPHER CLAIRE MORTON IS ADMIRING A JEWELRY DISPLAY WHEN...

I WONDER IF I'LL EVER BE RICH ENOUGH TO WEAR SUCH GORGEOUS GEMS...

OHHHH! WHAT HIT ME--?

AS THAT EERIE EBONY IS ABSORBED INTO HER BODY...

WHY WAIT? I CAN TAKE ALL THE JEWELS I WANT--RIGHT NOW!

CRASH!

IN LONDON, ENGLAND, BUSINESS MAGNATE HORACE ROWLAND STRIDES TOWARD A BANK WHEN...

IF I PUT ACROSS THAT BUSINESS DEAL, IT'LL MAKE A HANDSOME PROFIT--

EH? THAT BLACK BALL-- ALMOST STRUCK ME--

BANK OF LONDON LTD.

2

ON ALL THE PLANET *EARTH*, FOUR PEOPLE STRUCK AT RANDOM--TURNED INTO SUPER-BEINGS FOR SOME UNKNOWN REASON! AND THIS--IS ONLY THE BEGINNING! FOR IN THE DAYS THAT FOLLOW, HOW CHU LOOTS AS HE WILLS--*CLAIRE MORTON* BECOMES A GEM-GRABBER TO HER HEART'S DELIGHT...

IN KEEPING WITH THEIR ILLEGAL ACTIVITIES, THIS NEW BREED OF VILLAINS HAS ADOPTED COLORFUL COSTUMES TO SUIT THEIR CRIMES...

MONEY-- MONEY-- MONEY! I CAN'T GET ENOUGH OF IT!

NOBODY'LL EVER PLAY FOOTBALL ON THIS FIELD AGAIN!

GATHERED IN ANSWER TO THIS WORLDWIDE CRIMINAL OUTBURST ARE CERTAIN MEMBERS OF THE *JUSTICE SOCIETY OF AMERICA.* YES--THE JUSTICE SOCIETY-- FOR ALL THIS HAS TAKEN PLACE ON *EARTH-TWO*, THAT PARALLEL PLANET OF *EARTH-ONE*, OUT OF WHICH OPERATES ITS COUNTERPART, THE *JUSTICE LEAGUE OF AMERICA!*

ROBIN

HAWKMAN

HOURMAN

MR. TERRIFIC

Wonder Woman

WILDCAT

AT THIS EMERGENCY MEETING, *HAWKMAN* SERVES AS CHAIRMAN...

BEFORE WE GET DOWN TO THE URGENT BUSINESS AT HAND -- I WANT TO WELCOME *ROBIN* AS A NEW MEMBER OF THE *JUSTICE SOCIETY!*

IT'S AN HONOR AND A PRIVILEGE, *HAWKMAN!*

4

NO LONGER THE *"BOY WONDER"*, THE GROWN-UP *ROBIN* ACKNOWLEDGES THE ROUND OF APPLAUSE...

FIRST OF ALL, I WANT TO CONVEY *BATMAN'S* BEST WISHES!

THOUGH HE'S IN SEMI-RETIREMENT,

HE STILL GOES OUT ON SPECIAL CASES--WHICH IS WHAT'S KEEPING HIM FROM ATTENDING THIS MEETING!

*JOHNNY THUNDER* HAS NO SUCH EXCUSE--HE'S *ALWAYS* LATE!

CLAP!  CLAP!  CLAP!

NOW FOR MY OWN--I WANT TO THANK THE *JUSTICE SOCIETY* FOR FULFILLING MY LIFE'S AMBITION TO BE A MEMBER OF SUCH A DISTINGUISHED GROUP! I'LL DO MY BEST TO PROVE WORTHY OF THE HONOR!

YOU'VE JOINED US AT A SUPER-CRISIS, *ROBIN*--

HOW TO HANDLE THIS BLACK SPHERES PUZZLE!

AS FAR AS WE CAN MAKE OUT FROM WHAT WE'VE LEARNED FROM *INTERPOL*-- FOUR GLOBES FELL OUT OF THE SKY AND TURNED FOUR HUMAN BEINGS INTO SUPER-CRIMINALS!

IN SOME MYSTERIOUS MANNER, THESE SPHERES ALTERED THE MENTAL AND PHYSICAL STRUCTURES OF THREE MEN AND A GIRL--

THEN WE'D BETTER GO OUT AND MATCH POWERS WITH THEM! I SUGGEST *MR. TERRIFIC* AND I TAKE ON THAT LONDON BUSINESS-MAN WHO'S MAD OVER MONEY!

IF THERE ARE NO OBJECTIONS, I'D LIKE TO HANDLE *HOW CHU* IN CHINA!

CLAIRE MORTON AND HER JEWELRY CAPERS SEEM MADE FOR ME!

AS *HOURMAN* SWALLOWS THE *MIRACLO* PILL THAT GIVES HIM SUPER-CHARGED ENERGY FOR SIXTY MINUTES, *WONDER WOMAN* TAKES OFF IN HER *ROBOT PLANE*-- *ROBIN* AND *WILDCAT* IN THE *BAT-JET*--AND *HAWKMAN* WINGS IT WITH *MR. TERRIFIC*..

--ENDOWING THEM WITH POWERS ONLY CERTAIN MEMBERS OF THE *JUSTICE SOCIETY* CAN MATCH--

THAT LEAVES US, *ROBIN*! WE'LL TEAM UP TO GO OUT AFTER THAT FORMER BASEBALL STAR WHO'S BEEN SMASHING SPORTS ARENAS!

THAT SUITS ME! I'M A RABID SPORTS FAN AND WOULD LIKE TO PUT AN END TO HIS GAME!

WITHIN AN HOUR, THE *BAT-JET* ARRIVES AT *CORTEZ STADIUM* IN MEXICO...

THE *PAN-AMERICAN* GAMES ARE SCHEDULED TO START HERE TOMORROW, *WILDCAT!*

FROM THE SMASHED STADIUMS BAXTER'S LEFT IN HIS WAKE, I'M BETTING HE'LL SHOW UP HERE NEXT!

LANDING, THE *JUSTICE SOCIETY* DUO BEGINS A SEARCH FOR ITS QUARRY THAT ENDS WHEN...

THERE HE IS -- BLOWING THE WATER OUT OF THE POOL WITH ONE PUFF OF BREATH!

LET'S TAKE THE BIG *BLOWHARD!*

SWOOOSH!

HE'S WAVING AN ARM AT US -- BUT NOT AS A SIGN OF GREETING!

IT'S CAUSING THE GROUND TO RUMBLE BELOW US -- LIKE AN *EARTHQUAKE!*

WELL, LOOK WHO WANTS TO PLAY -- THE CHEERFUL FEARFULS!

YOU WON'T MAKE JOKES WHEN THESE FISTS KNOCK YOU FOR A *GOAL!*

I MAY BE OLDER -- BUT I'M STILL A *PUNSTER* AT HEART!

NOT EVEN IN MY DAYS AS HEAVYWEIGHT CHAMPION OF THE WORLD DID I EVER LAND A HARDER BLOW!

WHAKK!

THUNK!

BUT THE *SMASHING SPORTSMAN* CAN SHAKE OFF KNOCKOUT BLOWS AS A WET DOG SHAKES OFF WATER...

YOU KNOW, I FEEL LET DOWN BY THE *JUSTICE SOCIETY*! THEY SHOULD'VE SENT *SUPERMAN* AFTER ME! OR EVEN *DOCTOR FATE*!

I'LL WIND THIS UP RIGHT NOW!

SCORE ANOTHER SUCCESS FOR THE *SMASHING SPORTSMAN*!

CATAPULTING OUTWARD FROM THE WRECKAGE, THE *MASKED MANHUNTER* HURLS HIS FIST LIKE A PROJECTILE...

YOU AREN'T THE ONLY ONE WHO CAN RIDE WITH A PUNCH, BAXTER!

CAUGHT HIM ON THE FLY!

7

THEN... WHATEVER THAT BLACK SPHERE WAS--IT JUST ABOUT MADE ME *INVINCIBLE!*

I WISH THE *JSA* WOULD SEND *MORE* SUPER-HEROES TO TEST ME! THE WAY I FEEL NOW, I COULD TAKE THEM ALL ON--AND TROUNCE THEM!

*SWAK!*

MEANWHILE, I'VE GOT SOME MORE STADIUM-SMASHING TO DO!

WHILE AN UNCONSCIOUS *ROBIN* AND *WILDCAT* ARE GETTING THEIR LUMPS--*WONDER WOMAN* IS FLYING OVER CHICAGO...

ACCORDING TO MY SHORTWAVE RADIO, THE *GEM GIRL*--AS CLAIRE MORTON NOW CALLS HERSELF--HAS BEEN SPOTTED LOOTING THE AFRICAN DIAMOND COLLECTION IN THE CITY MUSEUM!

AS LONG AS I'M RIGHT OVER THE MUSEUM--I'LL PERSONALLY DROP IN ON HER VIA THE WIND CURRENTS OF THE *WINDY CITY!*

*AH!* REAL COMPETITION AT LAST! HERE'S MY OPPORTUNITY TO DISPLAY MY NEW-FOUND POWERS--THROUGH MY GEMS!

*PEARLS* ARE FANCIED IN GEM-LORE TO HAVE THE ABILITY TO GIVE *LIFE...*

SO I'LL ANIMATE *OLD BONEY* HERE--AND LET *HIM* HANDLE HER!

*MERCIFUL MINERVA*-- THAT DINOSAUR SKELETON'S COME ALIVE!

*SNAP!*

THAT OUGHT TO RATTLE ITS *BONES!*

NOW TO JAIL THAT JEWELED JEZEBEL!

DIAMONDS ARE A GIRL'S BEST FRIEND, *WONDER WOMAN*--

AS THE LOOP OF THE *MAGIC LASSO* SETTLES AROUND THE DARING JEWEL THIEF...

CAUGHT YOU--YOU ARE FORCED TO OBEY ME!

DROP THAT SACK OF STOLEN JEWELS!

A DIAMOND IS REPUTED TO BE A *MAGIC STONE, WONDER WOMAN*--

BUT IT CAN *REALLY* COUNTER THE MAGIC OF YOUR *LARIAT!*

LIKE SO!

GREAT *HERA!* MY LASSO HAS BEEN SLICED INTO SECTIONS!

THAT'S ONLY THE START!

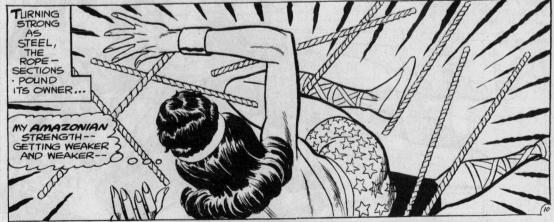

TURNING STRONG AS STEEL, THE ROPE-SECTIONS POUND ITS OWNER...

MY *AMAZONIAN* STRENGTH-- GETTING WEAKER AND WEAKER--

# The SUPER-CRISIS THAT STRUCK EARTH-TWO-- PART 2

THANKS TO YOUR THROWING ME IN AMONG THESE COINS, I'VE MADE CONTACT-CONTROL WITH THEM --

ENABLING ME TO USE THEM AS *GUIDED MISSILES!*

THOSE FLYING COINS-- STOPPING US COLD!

CAN'T MAKE ANY HEADWAY!

HAVING ABSORBED ELECTRICITY FROM THE CLOCK, IT GIVES ME CONTROL OVER ALL THE ELECTRICAL OBJECTS IN THE BANK!

CHANDELIER-- MAKE LIKE A BOMB!

KRRRAAACT!

HA, HA, HA! THESE TWO GREAT *JUSTICE SOCIETY* CRIME-FIGHTERS KNOCKED OUT--AND I'D HARDLY BEGUN TO FIGHT!

15

LIFTING THE TOURING CAR LIKE A TOY...

OUR CAR-- WRECKED!

A SMALL PRICE TO PAY-- TO SAVE OUR GOLD!

KLAA-BLAAK

TIME'S RUNNING OUT ON ME--

I BETTER DOUBLE UP ON MY FIST-- ACTION!

TO HIS INTENSE AMAZEMENT, THE CHINESE BANDIT RISES HIGH INTO THE AIR...

WOW! DID I SOCK HIM THAT HARD?

PREPARE TO DIE, FOREIGN DEVIL!

I MAKE CHOP SUEY OUT OF YOU!

AIEEEE! YOU REAL DEVIL! NO MAN ABLE TO BREAK MY BLADE WITH FIST!

I'M JUST AS TOUGH ON DEFENSE-- AS I AM ON OFFENSE!

SKRIKKK

17

WITH A CRY OF FURY, *HOW CHU* LIFTS AN ARM--ROTATES IT...

NOW I KNOW YOU *DEVIL* -- I USE SPECIAL POWER TO OVERCOME *DEVIL* ! HAI-AAAGH !

THE DEVIL YOU SAY !

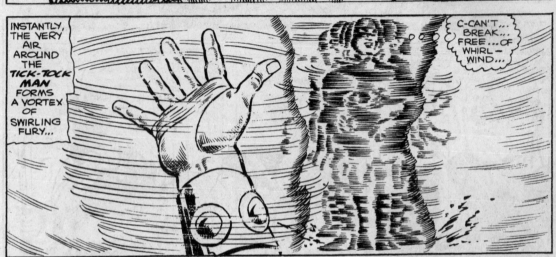

INSTANTLY, THE VERY AIR AROUND THE *TICK-TOCK MAN* FORMS A VORTEX OF SWIRLING FURY...

C-CAN'T... BREAK... FREE... OF WHIRL-WIND...

IT'S BORING ME INTO THE GROUND !

NOT EVEN MY *MIRACLO* PILL CAN HELP ME HERE ...

HOW FAR DOWN... IS HE GOING... TO SEND ME... ?

HA! HA! HA! ANCIENT CHINESE TORTURE ! I LEAVE YOU LIKE THAT-- GO ROB SOMEPLACE ELSE !

AT LEAST HE STOPPED THE WHIRLWIND...

BUT EVEN IF I DO MANAGE TO GET OUT OF HERE --BY THAT TIME, *HOW CHU* WILL BE FAR GONE !

MEANWHILE, IN THE SECRET HEADQUARTERS OF THE *JUSTICE SOCIETY OF AMERICA*-- WHERE *JOHNNY THUNDER*, HAVING ARRIVED TOO LATE TO GO ON ASSIGNMENT, IMPATIENTLY AWAITS THE RETURN OF HIS FELLOW MEMBERS...

WHAT'S KEEPIN' 'EM? WHERE'D THEY GO? MAYBE THEY CAN USE MY HELP?

AT LONG LAST, THE DOOR OPENS AND...

YOU'RE BACK! BUT LOOK AT THE SHAPE YOU'RE IN!

WE'RE LUCKY TO GET BACK HERE ALIVE!

WE TANGLED WITH SUPER-CRIMINALS-- THAT NONE OF US COULD OVERCOME!

MY TIMING WAS WAY OFF!

AFTER THEIR STORIES HAVE BEEN TOLD...

YOU SHOULD'VE WAITED FOR ME! ME AND MY *THUNDERBOLT* WOULD HAVE TROUNCED 'EM!

MAYBE IT'S NOT TOO LATE! I'LL SEND *THUNDERBOLT* OUT AFTER 'EM!

SAY YOU!*

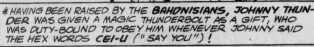

* HAVING BEEN RAISED BY THE *BAHDNISIANS*, JOHNNY THUNDER WAS GIVEN A MAGIC THUNDERBOLT AS A GIFT, WHO WAS DUTY-BOUND TO OBEY HIM WHENEVER JOHNNY SAID THE HEX WORDS *CEI-U* ("SAY YOU")!

*THUNDERBOLT*-- GET OUT THERE AND CAPTURE HORACE ROWLAND, CLAIRE MORTON, MARTIN BAXTER AND *HOW CHU*!

WHAT WAS THAT LAST NAME?

HOW CHU!

GESUNDHEIT!

HALF AN HOUR GOES BY! THEN THE DOOR OPENS AGAIN AND...

*Pant! Pant!* WHAT A BRAWL! I'VE MET MY MATCH! NOT EVEN MY *BAHDNISIAN HEX MAGIC* COULD STOP THOSE SUPER-DUPERS!

HUH? MOVE OVER, JSA-- I'M JOINING THE LOSERS TABLE!

WAIT! I GOT *ANOTHER* IDEA!

OHHHHH--NO!

IF IT CON-CERNS *ME*...

PLEASE-- HAVE *MERCY!*

YOUR NEXT ASSIGNMENT IS NOTHING TO BE AFRAID OF...

SAYS *YOU!*

SAYS *ME*--I MEAN, *SAY YOU*-- GET OVER INTO *EARTH-ONE* AND BRING BACK SOME *JUSTICE LEAGUE* MEMBERS! MAYBE THE *LEAGUE* CAN SUCCEED WHERE THE *SOCIETY* FAILED!

THIS IS NO REFLECTION ON YOU FELLAS, YOU UNDERSTAND! IT'S JUST THAT THE *JLA* MIGHT HAVE A FRESH VIEWPOINT! MAYBE THEY CAN COME UP WITH AN ANGLE WE CAN'T!

IT'S WORTH A TRY!

ANYTHING'S BETTER THAN RESIGNING OURSELVES TO DEFEAT!

*ZWOOOM*

INSTANTLY-- WELL, *ALMOST* INSTANTLY!

HUH? ONLY *SUPERMAN, FLASH, GREEN ARROW* AND *GREEN LANTERN?* WHERE ARE THE OTHERS?

YOU SAID BRING *"SOME"!* TO ME, *SOME* MEANS *FOUR!*

÷ *WHEW* ÷ AS IF WE DIDN'T HAVE ENOUGH TROUBLES WITHOUT *JOHNNY* AND HIS *THUNDERBOLT* COMPLICATING OUR LIVES!

WE'VE GOT TO GET BACK TO OUR OWN *EARTH!*

AND FAST! A *SUPER-CRISIS* HAS STRUCK OUR WORLD!

20

BUT **HOW** DID YOU MANAGE TO FIND OUT?

JUST BECAUSE **HE'S** A **KOOK**, DON'T THINK **I** AM! NATURALLY, BEFORE I STARTED FIGHTING THEM, I FOUND OUT ALL I COULD ABOUT THE CROOKS AND THOSE BLACK SPHERES!

HOLD YOUR **BAHDNISIAN** TONGUE, **THUNDERBOLT!** HMM--DO NOT HOLD IT! GO AHEAD! **SAY YOU**-- TELL US WHAT YOU KNOW!

THE BLACK SPHERES CAME FROM A UNIVERSE IN WHICH THEY EVOLVED--IN **POSITIVE TIME**--TO A PEAK, AT WHICH POINT THEY BECAME THE ULTIMATE IN SUPER-INTELLIGENT LIFE! THEY THEN STARTED TO DEVOLVE RAPIDLY--IN **NEGATIVE TIME**-- LOSING THEIR INTELLIGENCE...

BEGINNING OF TIME

**EVOLUTION**

POSITIVE TIME

**BLACK SPHERE UNIVERSE**

NEGATIVE TIME

DEVOLUTION

PEAK OF EVOLUTION

TO ESCAPE THEIR **DOOM**, THEY SOUGHT OUT ANOTHER UNIVERSE STILL ON **POSITIVE TIME**--OURS--IN ORDER TO MAINTAIN AND EVEN INCREASE THEIR SUPER-POWERS! BECAUSE TIME WAS SHORT, THEY HAD TO HURL THEM- SELVES AT RANDOM INTO OUR UNIVERSE...

...HOPING AT LEAST SOME OF THEM WOULD MAKE CONTACT WITH THE HIGHEST OF ALL EARTH LIFE-FORMS--HUMAN BEINGS--AND BE ABSORBED INTO THEIR BODIES!

BUT ONLY **FOUR** OF THEM MADE THE VITAL CONTACT! THE REMAINDER EVIDENTLY PERISHED!

ON CONTACT WITH A HUMAN, THE "LIFE-FORCE" OF THE BLACK SPHERE WAS ABSORBED BY THE HUMAN, WHERE IT'LL REMAIN SEMI-DORMANT UNTIL IT RECOVERS FROM ITS JOURNEY!

BUT WHAT MADE THE FOUR HUMANS ACT--EVILLY?

22

STRANGELY ENOUGH, THE CHEMICAL UNION OF ALIEN AND HUMAN CAUSED AN EVIL REACTION! THE FOUR HUMANS FOUND THEM-SELVES FORCED TO CARRY OUT THEIR SECRET WISHES IN A CRIMINAL MANNER!

EVENTUALLY, WHEN THE FOUR ALIEN SUPER-BEINGS "AWAKEN," *THEY* WILL BE IN *FULL CONTROL* OF THEIR HUMAN HOSTS!

*WHEW!* IT WAS BAD ENOUGH BEFORE-- NOW IT SEEMS DOUBLY HOPELESS!

WELL, WE HAVE ONE THING GOING FOR US! WE HAVE A *DOUBLE TEAM* TO FIGHT THEM NOW!

WE SHOULD SYMPATHIZE WITH THEIR BATTLE FOR SURVIVAL --

BUT NOT WHEN OUR OWN SURVIVAL IS AT STAKE!

MAN, I SURE WISH I KNEW HOW THIS IS GOING TO TURN OUT!

SO SAY WE ALL, *ROBIN!* BUT TO FIND OUT HOW THE *JUSTICE* HEROES COPE WITH THIS *SUPER-CRISIS,* SEE THE NEXT ISSUE OF *JUSTICE LEAGUE* of *AMERICA!*

25

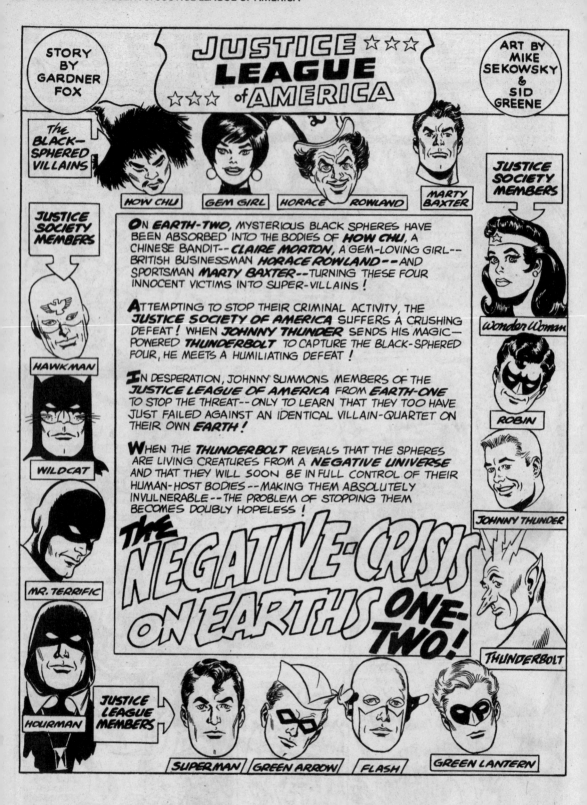

STORY BY GARDNER FOX

JUSTICE ☆☆☆ LEAGUE ☆☆☆ of AMERICA

ART BY MIKE SEKOWSKY & SID GREENE

THE BLACK-SPHERED VILLAINS

HOW CHU

GEM GIRL

HORACE ROWLAND

MARTY BAXTER

JUSTICE SOCIETY MEMBERS

JUSTICE SOCIETY MEMBERS

HAWKMAN

WILDCAT

MR. TERRIFIC

HOURMAN

JUSTICE LEAGUE MEMBERS

Wonder Woman

ROBIN

JOHNNY THUNDER

THUNDERBOLT

On EARTH-TWO, MYSTERIOUS BLACK SPHERES HAVE BEEN ABSORBED INTO THE BODIES OF HOW CHU, A CHINESE BANDIT--CLAIRE MORTON, A GEM-LOVING GIRL-- BRITISH BUSINESSMAN HORACE ROWLAND--AND SPORTSMAN MARTY BAXTER--TURNING THESE FOUR INNOCENT VICTIMS INTO SUPER-VILLAINS!

Attempting TO STOP THEIR CRIMINAL ACTIVITY, THE JUSTICE SOCIETY OF AMERICA SUFFERS A CRUSHING DEFEAT! WHEN JOHNNY THUNDER SENDS HIS MAGIC-POWERED THUNDERBOLT TO CAPTURE THE BLACK-SPHERED FOUR, HE MEETS A HUMILIATING DEFEAT!

In DESPERATION, JOHNNY SUMMONS MEMBERS OF THE JUSTICE LEAGUE OF AMERICA FROM EARTH-ONE TO STOP THE THREAT--ONLY TO LEARN THAT THEY TOO HAVE JUST FAILED AGAINST AN IDENTICAL VILLAIN-QUARTET ON THEIR OWN EARTH!

When THE THUNDERBOLT REVEALS THAT THE SPHERES ARE LIVING CREATURES FROM A NEGATIVE UNIVERSE AND THAT THEY WILL SOON BE IN FULL CONTROL OF THEIR HUMAN-HOST BODIES--MAKING THEM ABSOLUTELY INVULNERABLE--THE PROBLEM OF STOPPING THEM BECOMES DOUBLY HOPELESS!

THE NEGATIVE-CRISIS ON EARTHS ONE-TWO!

SUPERMAN

GREEN ARROW

FLASH

GREEN LANTERN

FACED BY A SEEMINGLY INSOLVABLE PROBLEM, THE MINGLED *JUSTICE SOCIETY-JUSTICE LEAGUE* MEMBERS PONDER THEIR PLIGHT...

IF WE COULDN'T DEFEAT THE FOUR HUMANS WHILE THE BLACK-SPHERE INTELLIGENCES WERE *DORMANT* INSIDE THEM...

THE POSSIBILITY OF BEATING THEM--ASSUMING THERE IS ANY--BECOMES *ZERO* ONCE THE SPHERES "AWAKEN" AND TAKE COMPLETE COMMAND OF THEIR HUMAN-HOST BODIES!

ONE THING'S SURE--STAYING HERE DOING NOTHING--WILL ACCOMPLISH NOTHING!

WITH OUR INCREASED FORCES WE COULD GANG UP ON EACH OF THESE SUPER-VILLAINS!

WHERE WE EACH FAILED ON OUR OWN *EARTHS*, A *JLA-JSA* TEAM-UP MIGHT PROVE TO BE A WINNING COMBINATION--

THE IDEA *SOUNDS* GOOD--BUT WE MUST TAKE INTO ACCOUNT THAT--

--THE THING THAT CAUSED OUR DOWNFALL WAS THE *BLACK SPHERE RADIATION* IN OUR FOES' BODIES! IT'S GROWN EVEN STRONGER BY THIS TIME--WHILE OUR SUPER-POWERS HAVE REMAINED *CONSTANT*!

SURE--WE'D BE BETTER OFF WITH INCREASED SUPER-POWERS--BUT--

BUT--*THAT'S* THE ANSWER!

THAT'S RIGHT--BUT ONLY THE *FOUR* THAT WERE ABSORBED BY THE FOUR HUMAN BODIES REMAINED ALIVE! ALL THE OTHER SPHERES FROM THE NEGATIVE-TIME UNIVERSE DIED OUT! YOU'LL GET NO HELP FROM THEM!

TRUE--BUT HOW ABOUT THE RADIATION THE SPHERES GAVE OFF? MAYBE SOME OF IT STILL EXISTS!

IF WE COULD FIND SOME OF THAT *"NEGATIVE"* RADIATION AND ABSORB IT INTO OUR BODIES...

IT MIGHT PROTECT US FROM THE RADIATED BODIES OF *HOW CHU, HORACE ROWLAND, GEM GIRL* AND *MARTY BAXTER*!

MAYBE IT WOULD EVEN INCREASE OUR OWN SUPER-POWERS!

THUNDERBOLT--YOU SAID A *LOT* OF BLACK SPHERES LANDED ON EARTH!

WE'VE GOT TO WORK FAST! THAT MEANS THE SUPER-SPEEDSTERS AMONG US--*SUPERMAN*, *FLASH*, *WONDER WOMAN* AND *GREEN LANTERN*--MUST GO OUT AND TRY TO LOCATE THE BLACK SPHERE RADIATION--

I COULD FIND IT WITH MY *X-RAY* AND *TELESCOPIC* VISION!

AS SOON AS YOU DO, I'LL MARK THE SPOTS WITH A GREEN MARKER!

WHILE *WONDER WOMAN* AND I RACE ACROSS THE EARTH, COLLECTING IT!

MOMENTS LATER, HIGH IN THE AIR ABOVE *EARTH-TWO*...

LOCK YOUR *POWER RING BEAM* ONTO MY *SUPER-VISION*, GREEN LANTERN--AND WE'LL GET TO WORK!

ON THE GROUND, FAR BELOW THE SPEEDING SUPER-HEROES..

THERE'S *GREEN LANTERN'S* MARKER--SHOWING A DEPOSIT OF BLACK SPHERE RADIATION HERE!

BUT EVEN WHEN THEY EXAMINE THE FIRST RADIATION DEPOSIT..

THE BLACK SPHERE'S SHRIVELED UP--DEAD! ITS RADIATION HAS PETERED OUT!

SAY--WHAT ARE THOSE GLOWING BLACK STREAKS IN THIS ROCK?

IT LOOKS LIKE THE ROCK'S ABSORBED A TRACE OF THE BLACK SPHERE'S RADIATION--AND IT'S STILL ACTIVE!

WE'LL "MINE" THOSE RADIATION STREAKS--

--AND PILE 'EM UP FOR *GREEN LANTERN* TO GATHER UP WITH HIS *POWER RING*!

WE'LL FOLLOW THE SAME PROCEDURE AT THE OTHER MARKERS!

3

WITHIN AN HOUR, A MASS OF RADIOACTIVE MATTER IS BEING POURED INSIDE A HOPPER IN THE *JUSTICE SOCIETY* LABORATORY...

HOW MUCH *"NEGATIVE"* RADIATION DO YOU THINK WE'VE ACCUMULATED, *FLASH?*

ACCORDING TO MY CALCULATIONS, JUST ENOUGH TO FEED IT TO *FOUR* OF OUR MEMBERS!

ONE WORD OF CAUTION! WE KNOW THAT THIS RADIATION MADE THE FOUR HUMANS IT ENTERED--*EVIL*--AGAINST THEIR WILL! THE SAME THING MAY HAPPEN TO WHICH-EVER FOUR MEMBERS ARE CHOSEN TO RECEIVE IT!

IT'S A CALCULATED RISK WE'LL HAVE TO TAKE!

AS A SAFEGUARD, THE REST OF US CAN ACCOMPANY THE IRRADIATED FOUR--SO THAT IF THEY TURN EVIL, WE'LL BE ON HAND TO STOP THEM--IF WE CAN!

IN QUICK-TIME FOUR OF THE MEMBERS ARE ELECTED TO RECEIVE THE RADIATION FROM THE *"NEGATIVE"* UNIVERSE...

HOURMAN AND *WONDER WOMAN* OF *EARTH-TWO*--

*GREEN LANTERN* AND *FLASH* OF *EARTH-ONE!*

BECAUSE THEY'RE ALREADY SUPER-POWERED AND WOULD HAVE A BETTER CHANCE AGAINST THE EVIL FOUR THAT THE REST OF US NON-POWERED ONES!

*SUPERMAN* WOULD HAVE BEEN CHOSEN--BUT HIS BODY IS IMMUNE TO RADIATION!

*WONDER WOMAN,* ALONG WITH *JOHNNY THUNDER* AND THE *THUNDER-BOLT--GREEN LANTERN* AND *WILDCAT* WITH *MR. TERRIFIC--FLASH, HAWKMAN* AND *GREEN ARROW--HOURMAN* WITH *SUPERMAN* AND *ROBIN--*STREAK OFF ACROSS THE WORLD THEY HOPE TO SAVE...

4

SOON, AS THE *HOURMAN-SUPERMAN-ROBIN* TEAM REACH THE CITY OF *ROME*...

...I SEE MARTY BAXTER NOW-- DEMOLISHING THE MOST FAMOUS SPORTS ARENA OF THE ANCIENT WORLD-- THE *COLOSSEUM*!

DO YOUR STUFF, *HOURMAN*!

BUT INSTEAD OF CLASHING WITH THE SPORTS-WRECKER, *HOURMAN* TURNS ON HIS TEAM-MATES AND...

I'M NOT STOPPING BAXTER-- AND NEITHER ARE YOU TWO!

JUST AS WE FEARED! *HOURMAN'S* BEEN INFECTED BY THE "NEGATIVE" RADIATION-- AND HAS BECOME JUST AS EVIL AND ALL-POWERFUL AS THE MAN WE'RE AFTER!

NOW TO FIND OUT WHETHER I CAN DO ANY BETTER AGAINST *HOURMAN* THAN I DID AGAINST MY EVIL-RADIATED FOE BACK ON *EARTH-ONE!*

WHOOMP!

*HOURMAN'S* NEXT SURPRISING MOVE IS TO DIVE GROUNDWARD...

I'LL CUT THE FIGHTING TIME SHORT AGAINST *SUPERMAN* WITH THIS MANEUVER...

WHAT'S HE UP TO? I CAN GO UNDERGROUND AFTER HIM IF THAT'S THE WAY HE WANTS TO PLAY--

BUT FIRST I'D BETTER GRAB *ROBIN* BEFORE HE HITS THE GROUND!

AN INSTANT LATER...

JUST LIKE AN UNDER SURFACE-TO-AIR MISSILE!

5

IT DOESN'T SEEM POSSIBLE! HOURMAN BELTING SUPERMAN AT WILL! AND--SUPERMAN'S FEELING THOSE PUNCHES!

WHAK!

HIS FISTS PUMPING LIKE PILE DRIVERS, THE TICK-TOCK MAN DRIVES THE MAN OF STEEL BEFORE HIM...

SUPERMAN HASN'T THROWN A PUNCH SINCE HOURMAN CAME UP FROM THE GROUND AT HIM!

HE SEEMS TO BE GETTING WEAKER AND WEAKER!

WHACK!

KA-POW!

ONLY ONE ANSWER! WHEN HOURMAN DOVE INTO THE GROUND--HE MUST HAVE SPOTTED A DEPOSIT OF KRYPTONITE, SUPERMAN'S WEAKNESS! HE TOOK A CHUNK IN EACH HAND-- AND IS USING HIS FISTS TO HIDE IT!

I'VE GOT TO GET THAT KRYPTONITE AWAY FROM HOURMAN!

THERE'S A KARATE TRICK TO MAKE A MAN OPEN HIS FINGERS IN REFLEX ACTION! HAVE TO CONNECT JUST RIGHT TO MAKE IT WORK...

HIS MIDDLE FINGERS DOUBLED UP, ROBIN STRIKES WITH ALL THE FORCE HE CAN COMMAND INTO THE CENTER OF HOURMAN'S HAND...

TOUCHÉ! EEYAH!

AS *HOURMAN'S* FINGERS FLY OPEN-- AND TWIN CHUNKS OF *KRYPTONITE* DROP TO THE GROUND...

COME ON, *SUPERMAN!* GET AWAY FROM THAT *KRYPTONITE!*

SOON'S I GET MY STRENGTH BACK, *ROBIN--* WE'LL MAKE ANOTHER TRY AT HIM!

HERE, LEAN ON ME!

THE *TICK-TOCK MAN* TURNS AND ANGLES HIS RUN TOWARD THE NEARBY *TIBER RIVER* ...

HE MUST BE PREPARING ANOTHER SURPRISE MOVE AGAINST US!

AFTER HIM, *ROBIN--* WHILE I GATHER MY SUPERSTRENGTH!

AT THE BANK OF THE RIVER...

GOT TO KEEP *HOURMAN* BUSY TILL *SUPERMAN* CAN PITCH IN--

THAT'S ODD! DESPITE HIS INCREASED SUPER-POWERS, HE'S AVOIDING MY BLOW--WHICH WOULD BE ONLY A POWDERPUFF PUNCH AGAINST HIM!

NEXT, *ROBIN* HURLS HIMSELF FORWARD LIKE A PRO FOOTBALL BLOCKING BACK...

IS THE *GOOD* IN THE *EVIL HOURMAN* TRYING TO CLUE ME INTO SOMETHING BY ACTING THIS WAY?

WHAAM!

YOU'VE DUG YOURSELF A WATERY GRAVE, *ROBIN!*

*ULP!* THE "GOOD" IN *HOURMAN* DIDN'T LAST LONG!

I'M READY TO TAKE ANOTHER CRACK AT *HOURMAN* NOW!

7

UNDER THE *TIBER*...

MY LUNGS-- BURSTING!

NEITHER *HOURMAN* NOR *SUPERMAN* NEED AIR UNDERWATER--BUT *I* DO!

GRIPPED IN A *SUPER-HAMMERLOCK*, THE *TICK-TOCK MAN'S* HANDS FLY APART...

JUST--IN-TIME! GOT TO--HEAD FOR THE SURFACE!

I CAN FEEL *HOURMAN* GETTING *WEAKER!* COULD HIS BEING *UNDERWATER* HAVE SOMETHING TO DO WITH THAT?

MUST BE! I DAZED HIM WITH THAT BLOW!

WHOOMP!

MAYBE A GOOD SWALLOW OF WATER WILL SPEED HIS COLLAPSE!

GLUP! GLUP!

SQUEEZING THE MUSCLES OF HIS JAW--FORCING OPEN HIS MOUTH!

UTTERLY LIMP, *HOURMAN* IS DRAGGED FROM THE WATERS OF THE *TIBER*...

NOW THAT WE KNOW-- THANKS TO *HOUR-MAN*--THAT THE "*NEGATIVE*" RADIATION WITHIN HUMANS MAKES THEM *VULNERABLE TO WATER*-- WE CAN "TAKE" MARTY BAXTER!

8

HIGH ABOVE THE MOUNTAINOUS INTERIOR OF *RED CHINA* WING *HAWKMAN* AND *GREEN ARROW*, WHILE *FLASH* RACES BELOW THEM...

FROM THIS HEIGHT I CAN SPOT *HOW CHU*-- LOOTING THE LOST CITY OF *LOU LAN* OF ITS RARE TREASURES!

I KNEW I WAS CLOSE TO *HOW CHU*--I CAN FEEL HIS RADIATION MINGLING WITH MINE-- SENDING SINISTER THOUGHTS THROUGH ME...

INSTANTLY THE *FASTEST MAN ON EARTH-ONE* RACES AROUND AND AROUND--CREATING A SUDDEN DOWNDRAFT-- SENDING HAWKMAN AND GREEN ARROW PLUMMETING GROUND- WARD...

OUR WORST FEARS HAVE BEEN REALIZED! *FLASH'S* BECOME *EVIL-RADIATED!*

WELL, THAT'S WHY WE TAGGED ALONG --TO STRAIGHTEN *FLASH* OUT!

BRAKING HIS FALL, THE *AERIAL ACE* CATCHES HOLD OF *GREEN ARROW* AND...

IT WON'T BE EASY! *FLASH'S* FASTER THAN EVER-- WE CAN'T EVEN *SEE* HIM!

I CAN'T *SEE* HIM--BUT THERE'S NOTHING WRONG WITH MY *HEARING!* I'LL DO AN ABOUT- FACE AND...

ZZUNK

CONTACT!

KNOCKED FLAT ON HIS BACK BY THE TREMENDOUS IMPACT, THE *SCARLET SPEEDSTER* LIFTS A RIGID FINGER AND...

THE BLACK SPHERE'S RADIATION WITHIN ME HAS GIVEN ME ADDED POWERS--

CONTROL OVER THE VARIOUS GASES IN THE ATMOSPHERE!

HUH? *SMOKE RINGS*-- FORMING LIKE MAGIC!

9

THIS WILL KEEP *HAWKMAN* WRAPPED UP WHILE I GO AFTER *GREEN ARROW*--

*eh?* HE'S TRYING TO GET AN *ARROW-JUMP* ON ME!

I'LL ROTATE HIS ARROWS SO SWIFTLY IN THIS AIR WHIRLPOOL I'M WHIPPING UP-- THE FRICTION WITH THE AIR WILL CAUSE THEIR WOODEN SHAFTS TO BURST INTO FLAMES!

NOW TO TURN THOSE BLAZING ARROWS BACK AT *HAWKMAN* AND *GREEN ARROW*--

GOT TO TURN AWAY THOSE FIRE-STICKS!

A *PROPELLER ARROW* SHOULD HELP *HAWKMAN* OUT OF HIS JAM!

NICE WORK, *GREEN ARROW!* IT'S BLOWING AWAY THE SMOKE RINGS! I CAN FREE MYSELF--

--AND USE MY WINGS TO BLOW THE FIRE-ARROWS OFF COURSE!

NOW--BACK TO ACTION AGAINST *FLASH*--WITH A SERIES OF SURPRISE STRIKES OF OUR OWN!

FIRST OFF-- A *SMOKESCREEN ARROW* TO CONCEAL OUR MOVEMENTS!

10

MOMENTS LATER, OUT OF THE BILLOWING CLOUDS OF SMOKE...

I FEEL LIKE AN *"UNDERCOVER"* AGENT!

AS THE *SCARLET SPEEDSTER* WINDMILLS AWAY THE PROTECTIVE FOG...

DOES G.A. THINK I CAN'T GET UP ENOUGH SPEED TO DART AWAY FROM HIS *ELECTRI-ARROW?*

GREEN ARROW-- DID YOU SEE *THAT?*

*FLASH* DOVE RIGHT IN *FRONT* OF THE ARROW TO AVOID IT-- TAKING A DANGEROUS, UN-NECESSARY RISK! HE COULD HAVE OUTRUN IT BY DASH-ING THROUGH THAT FIELD OF *WISTERIA* BEHIND HIM!

HERE'S MY CHANCE! I CAN'T *"TELL"* THEM HOW TO DEFEAT ME, BUT I CAN *"SHOW"* THEM-- BY THE WAY I AVOID THAT ARROW!

LET'S FIND OUT WHY *FLASH* PREFERRED TO RISK A HIT BY A *SHOCKING ARROW--* RATHER THAN BACK OFF INTO THOSE *CHINESE WISTERIA!*

I'LL BLAST THOSE SHRUBS WITH *EXPLOSI-ARROWS!*

AS THE HUGE WISTERIA PETALS ERUPT INTO THE AIR, *HAWK-MAN'S* WINGS WHIP THEM DOWN AT *THE FLASH*...

BLAAM!

WHEEZE! WHEEZE!

NO WONDER HE DIDN'T GO NEAR THE WISTERIA! HE'S *ALLERGIC* TO IT!

IT'S AFFECTED HIM SO MUCH-- HE CAN'T EVEN USE HIS *SUPER-SPEED!*

11

BUT I *CAN* WORK UP ENOUGH POWER TO "TURN THE TABLES" ON THEM!

;*UHH*; IF ONLY WE HAD-- SOMETHING *YELLOW* TO USE AGAINST HIM!

OF COURSE! HIS RING IS POWER-LESS AGAINST ANYTHING *YELLOW*!

WE'RE IN LUCK, *MR.T*! THIS FIELD IS FILLED WITH *YELLOW* PRIM-ROSES! GRAB A HANDFUL AND WE'LL STOP HIS POWER-BLOWS!

S-SURE--JUST AS SOON AS MY HEAD CLEARS!

AS *WILDCAT* HURLS HIMSELF FORWARD IN FELINE FURY...

I'LL WIPE THAT SMIRK OFF YOUR-- *OHHH!*

*HA! HA! HA!* THANKS TO THAT "*NEGATIVE*" RADIATION WITHIN ME, I'M ABLE TO MODIFY MY *POWER RING* SO THAT IT'S NO LONGER HELPLESS AGAINST ANYTHING *YELLOW*!

;*eh*; NOT THAT CORNY GLOVE GIMMICK AGAIN, *GL*?

MY APOLOGIES, *WILDCAT*! I KNOW I'VE USED IT MORE OFTEN THAN ANY OTHER--BUT I COULDN'T RESIST USING IT AGAINST A BOXING CHAMPION LIKE YOU!

HOW DO YOU LIKE THEM APPLES, FELLA?

*SNAP!*

THAT "*NEGATIVE*" RADIATION IS MAKING ME ACT LIKE A *CAMP*-STYLE *GREEN LANTERN*!

I CAN'T BELIEVE IT--THAT BRANCH HIT *GREEN LANTERN*-- AND *STAGGERED* HIM! HOW'S IT POSSIBLE?

*WHACK!*

I THINK I KNOW, *WILDCAT!*

WHEN THE YELLOW-WEAKNESS WAS REMOVED FROM *GL's* RING--IT WAS COMPENSATED FOR BY GIVING HIM THE WEAKNESS OF OUR *EARTH-TWO GREEN LANTERN*-- WOOD!

*QUICK*, BEFORE HE COMES TO--LET'S ARM OURSELVES WITH WOODEN WEAPONS!

I HATE TO DO THIS TO HIM--

BUT IT'S THE ONLY WAY TO OVERCOME HIM!

*THUNK!*

*WAK!*

THAT DOES IT!

WE'LL HAVE TO CARRY ON WITHOUT *GREEN LANTERN*-- GO AFTER ROWLAND OURSELVES --

--AFTER WE PUT *GREEN LANTERN* IN A WOODEN BOX TO KEEP HIM IN HIS HELPLESS STATE!

16

NOT BY YOURSELF, YOU NINCOMPOOP!

SAY YOU-- COME BACK HERE AND TAKE ME WITH YOU!

ONE EYE-BLINK LATER...

WHERE'S WONDER WOMAN? WHERE'S GEM GIRL?

INSIDE THE SYNDICATE HIDE-OUT--WHERE THE GEMS ARE STORED! GEM GIRL'S AFTER THEM--AND SO'S WONDER WOMAN!

INSIDE THE SYNDICATE LAIR...

FOR AGES, THE MOONSTONE HAS BROUGHT LUCK TO ITS WEARER! AHHH--IT'S WORKING! ASSISTANCE ARRIVES FOR ME!

HOLD IT, WONDER WOMAN! YOU'RE SUPPOSED TO BE AFTER GEM GIRL-- NOT THE GEMS!

THE AMAZON PRINCESS WHIRLS AND...

I'M LOOKING OUT FOR MYSELF --

--WHICH IS MORE THAN I CAN SAY FOR YOU!

GNNNG!

SWATT

SHE KNOCKED JOHNNY COLD! CAN'T DO A THING ABOUT IT TILL HE GIVES ME MY ORDERS--!

18

AT THE FAR END OF THE UNDERGROUND CORRIDOR..

I HAVE YOU NOW, *GEM GIRL!*

IS THAT A BOAST-- OR A THREAT?

A *FACT,* GEM GIRL!

SWOOSH

KRAASH!

UH-OH! JOHNNY'S COMING TO-- REVIVED BY THE WATER!

;Gasp; ;Sputter; SAY YOU, THUNDER-BOLT--USE YOUR MAGIC AGAINST *WONDER WOMAN* TO HOLD HER HELPLESS!

WHILE THESE CHARACTERS ARE FIGHTING EACH OTHER, I'LL ABSCOND WITH THE LOOT!

MY APOLOGIES, PRINCESS-- BUT I'M JUST FOLLOWING *JOHNNY'S* ORDERS!

YOUR MAGIC BOLTS DON'T SCARE ME!

BECAUSE THE *"NEGATIVE"* RADIATION INSIDE ME GIVES ME THE POWER TO HURL YOUR MAGIC RIGHT BACK AT YOU!

SO THAT'S HOW THE FOUR VILLAINS BEAT ME WHEN I WAS SENT OUT AFTER THEM! THEY TURNED MY OWN MAGIC AGAINST ME!

19

YOU'RE NEXT, JOHNNY BOY!

*ULP* I BETTER FAST-TALK MY WAY OUT OF THIS!

**WAPP!**

MAYBE A GOOD LAUGH WILL CLEAR THE AIR!

WONDER WOMAN, DIDYA EVER HEAR THE ONE ABOUT THE LADY WHO RAN FOR A BOTTLE OF VITAMINS WHEN SHE SAW A MAN HIT BY A CAR--

--BECAUSE SHE HEARD VITAMINS WERE GOOD FOR RUN-DOWN PEOPLE?

THE *AMAZING AMAZON* PAUSES--THEN BREAKS OUT INTO A--

*TEE-HEE* THAT WAS AWFUL!

YEAH-- BUT WONDER WOMAN LIKES IT!

MAYBE I CAN BREAK HER UP WITH ANOTHER GAG! I'LL TELL HER THE ONE ABOUT...

...THE BOY WHO WAS OUT CAMPING AND CAME RUNNING BACK SCARED, COMPLAINING OF HAVING SEEN A BLACKSNAKE...

WHEN HE WAS TOLD THAT A BLACKSNAKE ISN'T POISONOUS, THE BOY SAID, "IF HE CAN MAKE ME JUMP OFF A FIFTY-FOOT CLIFF-- HE DOESN'T HAVE TO BE!"

HA! HA! HA!

I'VE GOT HER HELPLESS WITH LAUGHTER!

HA! HA! HA! STOP IT! I CAN'T STAND ANY MORE!

JOKES MUST BE A WEAKNESS OF THE BLACK-SPHERE HUMANS-- NOBODY COULD LAUGH LIKE THAT AT A JOKE--ESPECIALLY SUCH A TERRIBLE ONE!

SAY YOU-- NEVER MIND THE COMMENTS--JUST TIE THAT MAGIC LASSO AROUND WONDER WOMAN--

AND LET'S GO AFTER GEM GIRL SO I CAN JOKE HER INTO SUBMISSION TOO!

20

LEAVING **WONDER WOMAN** HELPLESSLY BOUND WITH HER MAGIC LASSO, THE **THUNDER-BOLT** CARRIES JOHNNY INTO A CRIMINAL HIDE-OUT WHERE...

WHAT A COUP! **GEM GIRL**-- AND THE OTHER THREE BLACK-SPHERE HUMANS ARE HERE!

THEY'VE GATHERED HERE TO DIVVY UP THE EARTH BETWEEN THEM!

HERE'S ANOTHER URGENT BULLETIN, **JOHNNY**-- THE BLACK SPHERES ARE ABOUT TO GAIN COMPLETE CONTROL OF THEIR HOST BODIES!

LEAVE THESE TWO TO ME! I'LL GIVE THEM A GEM-FULL OF KNOCKOUT POWDER!

I'LL SOON HAVE 'EM ROLLING ON THE FLOOR...

THERE WAS THIS LITTLE BOY, SEE--WHO WAS ALWAYS LATE FOR SCHOOL! ONE DAY HIS TEACHER WANTED TO KNOW WHY AND HE SAID--

"BECAUSE OF ALL THE SIGNS THAT SAY: SCHOOL-- GO SLOW!"

TELL 'EM ANOTHER, JOHNNY! MAKE 'EM SO WEAK THEY WON'T BE ABLE TO FIRE MY MAGIC BACK AT ME--AND I CAN USE MY **HEX POWERS** TO DRIVE THE BLACK SPHERES OUT OF THEIR BODIES!

HA, HO!

HO HO

HA HA

DON'T STOP ME IF YOU'VE HEARD THIS! AS A MAN FELL OVERBOARD INTO THE WATER, ONE SHARK SAID TO THE OTHER, "WHAT'S THAT FUNNY, TWO-LEGGED THING?"

AND THE OTHER SHARK SAID, "I'LL BITE!"

**THERE!** I'VE BLASTED THE BLACK SPHERES OUT OF THEM-- AND WITHOUT HOST BODIES TO SUSTAIN THEIR LIFE-- THE ALIENS WILL QUICKLY DIE!

21

SUDDENLY THE DOOR SLAMS OPEN AND...

YOU CAN RELAX, FELLA MEMBERS! THE BLACK SPHERE THREAT HAS BEEN ELIMINATED!

GREAT WORK, *JOHNNY!* NOW HOW ABOUT REMOVING THE NEGATIVE RADIATION FROM *WONDER WOMAN, GREEN LANTERN, FLASH,* AND *HOURMAN?*

THAT'S *YOUR* DEPARTMENT, *THUNDERBOLT!* SAY YOU--

I'M OFF AND RUNNING!

AND AFTER *T-BOLT* RETURNS WITH THE BACK-TO-NORMAL SUPER-HEROES...

*HOURMAN,* I WOULDN'T TELL JOHNNY FOR THE WORLD--BUT WHEN I REALIZED LAUGHTER WAS A WEAKNESS OF THE "NEGATIVE" RADIATION WITHIN ME-- PROBABLY BECAUSE THE BLACK-SPHERE BEINGS HAD NEVER BEEN SUBJECTED TO LAUGHTER--I GIGGLED A LITTLE TO ENCOURAGE HIM TO GO ON TELLING JOKES!

WHEN I REALIZED WATER WAS A WEAK-NESS OF THAT RADIATION, I DELIBERATELY RAN TOWARD THE *TIBER RIVER* WHEN *SUPERMAN* AND *ROBIN* WERE TRYING TO CAPTURE ME!

WE COULDN'T COME RIGHT OUT AND TELL OUR FELLOW-MEMBERS ABOUT OUR VULNERABILITY-- SO I JUMPED IN FRONT OF *GREEN ARROW'S* ARROW TO GIVE HIM A HINT ABOUT MY ALLERGY TO THE WISTERIA BLOSSOMS...

WHICH IS WHY I THREW *WILDCAT* UP INTO THAT TREE-- TO BREAK A BRANCH OFF SO IT WOULD HIT ME!

YES, WHY SPOIL JOHNNY'S TRIUMPH BY TELLING HIM WE HAD THE MEANS OF OVERCOMING THE BLACK-SPHERED HUMANS!

22

WE'LL RECOMMEND THAT THERE NOT BE ANY LEGAL ACTION AGAINST THESE FOUR PEOPLE--THEY COULDN'T HELP ACTING AS THEY DID WITH THE BLACK SPHERES INSIDE THEM!

NOW THAT THE ALIEN SPHERES ARE DEAD, THEY'LL BE THEIR FORMER SELVES AGAIN!

IN THE *JUSTICE SOCIETY* HEADQUARTERS, SOMEWHAT LATER...

NOW WE *JUSTICE LEAGUERS* MUST RETURN TO OUR OWN *EARTH* AND PUT AN END TO THE CRISIS THERE-- USING THE SAME TECHNIQUE!

WHAT ARE YOU DOING, JOHNNY? AREN'T YOU GOING TO SAY GOOD-BYE?

JUST AS SOON AS I WRITE OUT SOME JOKES FOR THE *JUSTICE LEAGUERS*, ROBIN--SO THAT THEY CAN OVERCOME THOSE BLACK SPHERES WITHOUT ANY TROUBLE!

THE END

STORY BY GARDNER FOX

JUSTICE ★★★ LEAGUE ★★★ of AMERICA

ART BY MIKE SEKOWSKY & SID GREENE

ONE MAN IS VERY MUCH LIKE ANOTHER--NO MATTER WHAT THE NAME OF THE GOD HE WORSHIPS--OR THE COLOR OF HIS SKIN. EVERY MAN WANTS HAPPINESS, BE IT WITH A FAMILY OR BY REASON OF FAME AND GLORY.
FOR THIS HAPPINESS, MAN HAS ALWAYS STRIVEN--AND ALWAYS EACH MAN'S WORST ENEMY IS HIS OTHER-SELF--MEN WHO ARE LIKE HIM, BUT SEEMINGLY UNLIKE HIM!

BECAUSE OF MAN'S INHUMANITY TO MAN, MEN HAVE LEARNED TO HATE ONE ANOTHER. FOR THIS HATE IS SOMETHING THAT MUST BE LEARNED! IT DOES NOT COME WITH BIRTH!

# "MAN, THY NAME IS-- BROTHER!"

The Roll Call — FLASH-- GREEN ARROW --HAWKMAN-- SNAPPER CARR

MANY A *JUSTICE LEAGUE* STORY HAS BEGUN WITH THE CHAIRMAN CALLING THE MEETING TO ORDER! THIS PARTICULAR TALE OF HIGH ADVENTURE AND HUMANITY HAS ITS BEGINNINGS AS A NON-EVENTFUL MEETING BREAKS UP...

NO RUSH FOR ME TO FLY ON HOME, *FLASH!* HAWKGIRL'S AWAY ON *THANAGAR*...

MY WIFE'S AWAY ON A NEWSPAPER ASSIGNMENT! NO HURRY FOR ME TO RETURN EITHER...

WHAT'S THAT YOU'RE DOING, *SNAPPER?*

LOOKING OVER SOME RESEARCH MATERIAL FOR A TERM PAPER-- ABOUT BROTHER-HOOD WEEK!

THESE ARE ITEMS I'VE CLIPPED FROM VARIOUS NEWSPAPERS ABOUT CERTAIN PEOPLE WHO FASCINATE ME!

EACH OF THEM IS IN-VOLVED IN SOME SORT OF BROTHERHOOD PROBLEM! I SURE WISH I COULD SPEAK WITH THEM, GET THEIR INSIDE STORIES!

MAYBE I CAN HELP YOU!

HELP *SNAPPER* WITH WHAT, *GREEN ARROW?*

THIS ITEM IS ABOUT AN *APACHE BOY* NAMED *JERRY NIMO* WHO--DESPITE HIGH GRADES AND OUTSTAND-ING ATHLETIC ACHIEVEMENTS--DROPPED OUT OF HIGH SCHOOL IN HIS SENIOR YEAR! COULD BE A BROTHERHOOD ANGLE THERE!

THIS ONE DEALS WITH PROMINENT PHILANTHROPIST *HARVEY YOUNG* ABANDONING HIS PRO-JECT TO AID IMPOVERISHED PEOPLE OF INDIA--BECAUSE OF THE OPPOSITION TO HIS PROGRAM BY THE VERY PEOPLE HE'S TRYING TO HELP!

*YOUNG* ISN'T A QUITTER! WHY WOULD HE GIVE UP THIS WAY?

ASKED WHAT REWARD HE WANTED FOR SAVING THE LIFE OF A WEALTHY GAR-MENTS MANUFACTURER-- *JOEL HARPER*, A YOUNG NEGRO, REQUESTED ONLY-- A JOB!

I'D SURE LIKE TO KNOW WHY--OF ALL THINGS HE *COULD* HAVE HAD--JOEL SETTLED FOR A JOB!

2

OKAY, GREEN ARROW-- WHAT ABOUT THAT OFFER OF HELP?

I'M LEAVING FOR THE SOUTHWEST TO PICK UP A NEW ARROW-CAR! ON THE WAY BACK I COULD SEE THE APACHE BOY, JERRY NIMO, FOR YOU!

I'VE GOT TIME ON MY HANDS--SO I VOLUNTEER TO FLY TO INDIA AND INTERVIEW HARVEY YOUNG!

WHILE I COULD DASH OVER TO METROPOLE CITY WHERE JOEL HARPER WORKS AND GET HIS STORY...

MAN, THAT'S TERRIFIC! I ONLY WISH I COULD GO WITH ONE OF YOU!

WHY NOT? LET'S MAKE IT ODD FINGER WINS SNAPPER!

I GO WITH HAWKMAN!

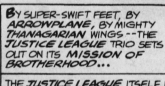

BY SUPER-SWIFT FEET, BY ARROWPLANE, BY MIGHTY THANAGARIAN WINGS--THE JUSTICE LEAGUE TRIO SETS OUT ON ITS MISSION OF BROTHERHOOD...

THE JUSTICE LEAGUE ITSELF IS A GOOD EXAMPLE OF BROTHER-HOOD IN ACTION, SNAPPER!

THAT'S RIGHT! THERE ARE TEN MEMBERS WITH DIFFERENT SUPER-POWERS-- THREE OF WHOM WERE BORN ON PLANETS OTHER THAN EARTH!

YET WHEN EVIL THREATENS WE ALL BAND TOGETHER TO FIGHT INJUSTICE!

AT THIS MOMENT IN METROPOLE CITY, JOEL HARPER IS PUSHING A RACK OF MEN'S WEAR ALONG A STREET IN THE GARMENT DISTRICT WHEN...

HUH? THOSE MEN-- RUNNING FROM THAT BANK!

HELP! ROBBERY--!

NATIONAL BANK

ACTING INSTINCTIVELY, JOEL HURLS HIS CLOTHES RACK IN FRONT OF THE FLEEING BANDITS...

SOME KID--TRYIN' TO BE A HERO!

HE'LL END UP--A DEAD HERO!

VOOMP!

FOUR GUNS LEVEL AT THE HORRIFIED YOUTH AS BYSTANDERS FLEE FOR COVER...

N-NO...

A QUARTET OF GUNS BLAST AS ONE...

HEY! WHERE'D THE KID GO?

HE JUST-- DISAPPEARED!

BLAM!

BLAM!

BLAM!

IN A NEARBY DOORWAY...

FLASH! Y-YOU SAVED ME...?!

STAY HERE, JOEL HARPER!

YOU KNOW ME?

SURE--FROM YOUR PICTURE IN THE NEWSPAPERS! THAT WAS A BRAVE THING YOU DID--BUT I'LL TAKE OVER NOW!

NEXT INSTANT A SCARLET STREAK TAKES OFF LIKE A RUNAWAY LIGHTNING BOLT...

YOU GUYS ARE GOING TO BE GUN-SHY--

FOUR TIMES OVER!

WHAK!

I'LL WIND UP THIS CASE IN A HURRY-- MAKING LIKE A HURRICANE!

WHOOOOOOO

THE CLOTHING-- FLYING ALL OVER US!

WRAPPING AROUND US!

4

I'LL FOLLOW UP THE WINDSTORM WITH A RAIN OF FISTS!

I USED THIS FLARE-GUN TO BLIND THE PEOPLE IN THE BANK WHEN WE ROBBED IT--

I'LL GIVE FLASH THE BUSINESS WITH IT TOO!

OHHHH! THAT FLARE OF LIGHT!

I--CAN'T-- SEE!

NEXT MOMENT... HERE'S MY CHANCE TO RID THE UNDERWORLD OF THAT SUPER-FAST GANGBUSTER!

TARGET-- HEART-- STOP!

BLAM! BLAM! BLAM!

STUNNED EYES WIDEN AS...

HUH? THE BULLETS WENT--RIGHT THROUGH HIM!

I HEARD THE CLICK OF HIS TRIGGER-- KNEW HE WAS GOING TO SHOOT--SO I SIMPLY VIBRATED SO SWIFTLY THE BULLETS PASSED HARMLESSLY THROUGH ME!

I CAN HEAR THEIR FADING-AWAY FOOTBEATS! THEY'RE GETTING AWAY!

JOEL! WHICH WAY'D THEY GO? TELL ME-- I'M BLIND!

NOT ME, FLASH! I NEVER SHOULD HAVE MIXED UP IN THIS--!

5

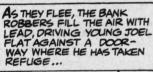

AS THEY FLEE, THE BANK ROBBERS FILL THE AIR WITH LEAD, DRIVING YOUNG JOEL FLAT AGAINST A DOOR-WAY WHERE HE HAS TAKEN REFUGE...

STILL--THE FLASH HELPED ME! AND-- FAIR IS FAIR!

RISKING A DELUGE OF FLYING LEAD, JOEL LEANS FROM HIS HIDING PLACE...

THEY'RE IN A CAR STRAIGHT AHEAD OF YOU, FLASH--PULLING AWAY FROM THE CURB!

THANKS, JOEL!

PING!

PING!

PING!

ARMS WINDMILLING THE AIR SO SWIFTLY THAT THEY BECOME INVISIBLE, THE FASTEST MAN ON EARTH HURTLES FORWARD..

IF I CAN JUST CATCH THEM BROADSIDE ON--I'LL STOP THEM SHORT!

VROOOOM!

THEN--WITH A SHRIEK OF TORTURED TIRE-RUBBER AND METAL, THE GETAWAY CAR TOPPLES OVER...

YOU KNOCKED THE CAR OVER, FLASH--WATCH OUT! THERE'S A GUY TO YOUR NEAR-RIGHT GETTING OUTTA THE CAR!

CRASH!

VROOOOSH!

NE-1652

CAUGHT THIS ONE IN HIS BREAD-BASKET!

CAREFUL, FLASH! ANOTHER CROOK TO YOUR FAR RIGHT-- DRAWING A GUN!

WHAP!

6

TWO MORE OF 'EM PILING OUT OF THE CAR, *FLASH*-- TO YOUR LEFT!

WE GOTTA STOP THAT KID!

HE'S CALLIN' THE SHOTS AGAINST US!

WARNED AGAIN BY THE SNICK OF A GUN-HAMMER BEING PULLED BACK, THE SIGHT-LESS *SCARLET SPEEDSTER* WHIRLS...

CAN'T LET ANY HARM COME TO JOEL!

A FURIOUS SHOULDER-SMASH BY *THE FLASH* AND...

WHUMP

A MOTOR REVS UP--A STOLEN CAR RACES OFF AS...

YOU GOT ONE OF 'EM, *FLASH*-- BUT THE OTHERS ARE GETTING AWAY!

IT'D BE TOO HARD FOLLOW-ING THEM WITHOUT SEE-ING WHERE I'M GOING!

MOMENTS LATER, A VOICE CRACKS WITH RAW FURY AND EXPLOSIVE RAGE...

LOOK AT MY CLOTHES! THEY'RE RUINED!

PUSH-BOY--YOU'RE TO BLAME! WHO TOLD YOU TO GET MIXED UP WITH THOSE CROOKS?

*YOU'RE FIRED!*

BUT, MR. NOSTRAND-- ALL I TRIED TO DO WAS--STOP 'EM!

7

HE FIRED ME, *FLASH*--BECAUSE I'M *COLORED*!

I BETCHA I WOULDN'T HAVE BEEN CANNED-- IF I'D BEEN A *WHITE BOY*!

NO, JOEL--DON'T TALK THAT WAY!

RIGHT NOW HE'S *TOO* EXCITED TO THINK! GIVE HIM TIME TO COOL OFF! WHEN HE REALIZES WHAT A HERO YOU WERE, HE'LL GIVE YOU BACK YOUR JOB!

NOT IN A MILLION YEARS! COLORED BOYS NEVER GET A BREAK!

WOULD YOU BELIEVE I'VE BEEN STUDYIN' UP ON MEN'S CLOTHES AND FASHIONS--DREAMIN' THAT SOME DAY I MIGHT OWN MY OWN BUSINESS?

WHAT A LAUGH-- DREAMS LIKE THAT DON'T COME TRUE-- NOT FOR ME..

JOEL, DON'T FEEL THAT WAY! EVERY-BODY HAS UPS AND DOWNS IN LIFE!

BESIDES, I NEED YOU-- TO BE MY EYES--TO HELP ME CATCH THOSE BANK ROBBERS!

*ME* HELP *YOU*--THE FLASH?! BUT I'M *COLORED*--A *BLACK BOY*--

WHAT'S THAT GOT TO DO WITH IT? YOU'RE A *MAN*--AS *BRAVE* AS THEY COME!

BUT *HOW* CAN I HELP?

YOU SAID YOU'VE STUDIED UP ON MEN'S FASHIONS! BY ANY CHANCE, DID YOU NOTICE IF ANY OF THOSE MEN WORE SOME SORT OF DISTINCTIVE GARMENTS?

WHY, SURE! ONE OF THEM HAD ON A *PIERRE L'ARKIN* SPORTS JACKET!

THAT'S A GOOD START! BUT WHERE DO WE GO FROM THERE?

TO THE ONE STORE IN TOWN WHICH CARRIES THE *PIERRE L'ARKIN* LINE!

SHORTLY, AT AN EXCLUSIVE MEN'S FASHION SHOP...

WHY, YES-- WE SOLD A SPORTS JACKET TO A MAN SUCH AS YOU DESCRIBE ABOUT A WEEK AGO! AND--WE DO HAVE HIS ADDRESS!

JOT DOWN THE ADDRESS, JOEL--AND LET'S BE ON OUR WAY!

8

As they emerge onto the sidewalk...

AHHH...MY EYESIGHT'S COMING BACK! I CAN SEE AGAIN!

THEN YOU--ER-- WON'T BE NEEDING ME!

YOU'LL STAY WITH ME, JOEL! YOU WERE IN AT THE BEGINNING OF THIS-- YOU'RE GOING TO BE IN AT THE END!

BESIDES, I HAVE AN IDEA ABOUT YOU! I'LL TELL YOU ABOUT IT LATER...

Within moments, in a house on the outskirts of METROPOLE CITY...

WHEW! I NEVER TRAVELED SO FAST IN MY LIFE!

THE FLASH AGAIN?!

THE SCARLET SPEEDSTER IS LIKE A FIST-FILLED TORNADO-- HITTING THE CROOKS HERE, THERE, AND EVERY- WHERE...

WHONK

SPANNG

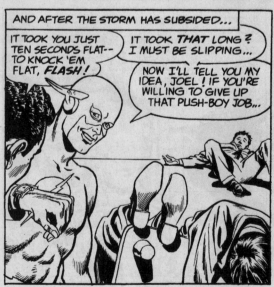

AND AFTER THE STORM HAS SUBSIDED...

IT TOOK YOU JUST TEN SECONDS FLAT-- TO KNOCK 'EM FLAT, FLASH!

IT TOOK THAT LONG? I MUST BE SLIPPING...

NOW I'LL TELL YOU MY IDEA, JOEL! IF YOU'RE WILLING TO GIVE UP THAT PUSH-BOY JOB...

I'D LIKE YOU TO GO TO CENTRAL CITY AND SEE A GOOD FRIEND OF MINE--BARRY ALLEN! HE'LL HELP YOU GET ON THE POLICE FORCE!

I'M CONFIDENT THAT SOME DAY YOU'LL BE A TOP-GRADE POLICEMAN--IF YOU HAVE THE CONFIDENCE AND AMBITION TO MAKE A GO OF IT!

I SURE HAVE--AND YOU KNOW--THIS "BROTHER-HOOD OF MAN" IDEA IS OKAY--

I HELPED YOU--YOU'RE HELPING ME! IF ONLY MORE OF US DIF-FERENTLY COLORED FOLKS WOULD EXTEND HELPING HANDS TO EACH OTHER--WE'D GET ALONG A LOT BETTER!

9

TO THE SOUTHWEST, SOME MINUTES AFTER THE *ARROWCAR* HAS BRAKED TO A STOP NEAR A RAILROAD DESERT DEPOT...

YOU CAN'T TRUST THESE *'PACHE* KIDS!

THEY COME FROM BAD STOCK!

NO! NO! I DIDN'T HAVE ANYTHING TO DO WITH IT!

WHAT'S WRONG HERE?

TEEN BEAT IS THE NEW SCENE!

*GREEN ARROW!* YOU'RE A MEMBER OF THE *JUSTICE LEAGUE*-- SO LET'S HAVE SOME *JUSTICE* AROUND HERE!

THIS *'PACHE* YOUNGSTER WAS WORKING IN LEAGUE WITH SOME CROOKS WHO FLAGGED DOWN THE TRAIN AND ROBBED THE MAIL CAR! GOT AWAY WITH HALF A MILLION DOLLARS!

I TAKE IT YOU'RE JERRY *NIMO!* WHAT'VE YOU GOT TO SAY TO THAT ACCUSATION?

*NIMO* CLAIMS THE CROOKS KNOCKED HIM OUT AND FLAGGED DOWN THE TRAIN!

BUT ONE OF THE BANDITS SAID AS HE RAN OFF, "YOU'LL GET YOURS LATER, KID!" HE'S GUILTY, ALL RIGHT!

IT WAS A *THREAT*-- NOT A PAY-OFF!

NOBODY'S GUILTY-- UNTIL *PROVED* GUILTY!

EXCEPT AN *APACHE!* THEY SAY *APACHE* BLOOD IS--BAD BLOOD! BUT I NEVER SAW THOSE CROOKS BEFORE TODAY!

I BELIEVE YOU, JERRY! MOREOVER, I'M GOING TO GIVE YOU A CHANCE TO PROVE YOUR INNO-CENCE--BY HAVING YOU HELP ME ROUND UP THOSE TRAIN ROBBERS! 10

THEY TOOK OFF IN A STATION-WAGON-- OUT ACROSS THE DESERT!

SEE--THERE ARE THE MARKS OF THEIR TIRES!

I STILL SAY THAT 'PACHE OUGHT TO BE IN JAIL--NOT WALKIN' AROUND FREE!

MOMENTS AFTERWARD, THE *ARROWCAR* RACES ACROSS THE DESERT SANDS...

WE'RE DRIVING ALONG--SUPPOSE YOU TELL ME WHY YOU DROPPED OUT OF HIGH SCHOOL, WHEN YOU WERE DOING SO WELL SCHOLASTICALLY AND ATHLETICALLY?

JERRY--WHILE

BECAUSE I'M AN-- *APACHE!*

EVEN THE *NAVAJO* AND *HOPI* KIDS SCORNED ME!

THEY CALLED ME "*DIRTY 'PACHE*"--"*PACHE PIG*"! THE WHITE BOYS WEREN'T SO BAD--IT WAS MY FELLOW *REDSKINS* WHO MADE MY LIFE SO MISERABLE I COULDN'T TAKE IT!

I COULDN'T CONCENTRATE ON MY STUDIES! SPORTS WEREN'T FUN ANY MORE! I JUST DECIDED TO CHUCK THE WHOLE THING AND COME TO A LONELY SPOT WHERE-- OH-OH!

THE STATION-WAGON TURNED ONTO THIS STATE HIGHWAY!

THEN WE WON'T BE ABLE TO TRACK THE GETAWAY CAR ANY MORE! THOSE TIRE MARKS WON'T SHOW ON THE PAVED ROAD!

NOT THE TIRE MARKS--BUT *SOMETHING ELSE* WILL!

YOU SEE THESE OIL DROPPINGS IN THE SAND?

THEY CAME FROM A LEAKY TRANS-MISSION! THEY APPEAR LIKE BLACK BLOBS IN THE SAND...

ON THE HIGHWAY THOSE BLOBS TAKE DEFINITE SHAPE--LIKE BLACK TEARDROPS--POINTING OUT THE DIRECTION WHICH THE CAR TOOK!

AS THE *ARROWCAR* ROCKETS ALONG THE HIGHWAY...

JERRY, YOU SHOULD BE PROUD OF YOUR *APACHE* HERITAGE!

YOUR ANCESTORS WERE RENOWNED FOR THEIR EXCEPTIONAL TRACKING ABILITY-- AND FOR THEIR EXTRAORDINARY FIGHTING PROWESS, TOO!

YOU MAKE IT SOUND *GOOD* TO BE AN *APACHE*, GREEN ARROW! BUT *I'M* AN EXCEPTION!

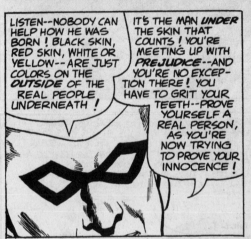

LISTEN--NOBODY CAN HELP HOW HE WAS BORN! BLACK SKIN, RED SKIN, WHITE OR YELLOW--ARE JUST COLORS ON THE *OUTSIDE* OF THE REAL PEOPLE UNDERNEATH!

IT'S THE MAN *UNDER* THE SKIN THAT COUNTS! YOU'RE MEETING UP WITH *PREJUDICE*--AND YOU'RE NO EXCEP- TION THERE! YOU HAVE TO GRIT YOUR TEETH--PROVE YOURSELF A REAL PERSON, AS YOU'RE NOW TRYING TO PROVE YOUR INNOCENCE!

IT'S EASY TO THROW UP YOUR HANDS AND SURRENDER! IT TAKES REAL GUTS TO GRIN AND BEAR IT--AND SHOW YOURSELF A BETTER MAN THAN HE WHO CONDEMNS YOU!

LOOK--THE CROOKS' CAR TURNED OFF THE HIGHWAY ONTO THAT SIDE ROAD!

AS THE *ARROWCAR* STREAKS ALONG THE SIDE ROAD...

DID *APACHE CHIEF* GERONIMO HAVE GUTS? *MANGAS COLORADO?* YOU BET THEY DID-- AGAINST OVERWHELMING ODDS!

BY *GERONIMO'S* SPIRIT-- YOU'VE GIVEN ME NEW HOPE, *GREEN ARROW!* I'M GOING TO MEET MY TROUBLES HEAD-ON... FROM NOW ON ...

SUDDENLY... AT A FORK IN THE ROAD...

A DESERT WIND'S SPRUNG UP-- BLOWING SAND OVER THE OIL SLICKS!

THERE *WOULD* BE A FORK IN THE ROAD HERE! NO WAY OF TELL- ING WHICH ROAD THE CROOKS TOOK!

WHAT ARE YOU UP TO, JERRY?

ONE REASON THE *APACHE* MADE SUCH A GOOD TRACKER IS--HIS SENSE OF SMELL!

I'M TRYING TO SMELL THE OIL BENEATH THE SAND!

SNIFF SNIFF

SNIFF! YES,... THE CAR CAME THIS WAY...THE SMELL OF OIL IS STRONG ENOUGH FOR ME TO DETECT!

HOP IN, JERRY-- AND LET'S GET GOING AGAIN!

TEN MINUTES FURTHER ON...

THERE'S THEIR STATION-WAGON!

YOU'VE DONE YOUR PART, JERRY! I'M GOING IN AFTER THOSE CROOKS ALONE! I DON'T WANT TO RISK YOU GETTING HURT!

A MOMENT LATER, THE *ACE ARCHER* FIRES AN *EXPLOSI-ARROW* AT THE LOCKED FRONT DOOR ...

BA-A BLAMM

13

THEN LIKE A BATTERING RAM, HE HITS THE SHREDDED DOOR-- CRASHING THROUGH WITH BOW-AND-ARROWS TIGHTLY GRIPPED...

FOUR OF THEM--IN HERE!

AND ALL OF THEM--ARMED!

GOT TO ACT FAST--LET FLY WITH MY "CHAIN ARROWS"!

PLUG HIM!

WATCH IT--HE'S TRICKY!

THE TWANG OF A TAUT BOWSTRING--THE WHISTLE OF METAL LINKS IN THEIR LIGHTNING-SWIFT PASSAGE THROUGH THE AIR--AND...

SOMERSAULTING HIS BODY--GREEN ARROW KICKS AT HIS BOW WITH BOTH FEET...

I'VE PRACTICED THIS TRICK SHOT A HUNDRED TIMES ON MY ARROW RANGE...

LET'S HOPE IT PAYS OFF NOW!

THIS SOOT-BALL ARROW IS A NEW ONE! I'VE NEVER TRIED IT OUT IN COMBAT CONDITIONS BEFORE!

GET HIM! DON'T GIVE HIM A CHANCE TO USE ANY MORE TRICKY SHAFTS ON US!

14

THE *SOOT-BALL ARROW* HITS THE WALL AND...

HEYYY! SURROUNDED BY BLACKNESS!

BLOMP!

THE *SOOT-BALL ARROW* DOESN'T SEEM TO DO VERY MUCH -- BUT IT PUTS A STAIN ON THEIR FLESH THAT'LL MAKE IT EASY TO IDENTIFY THEM IF THEY GET AWAY!

BUT I DON'T INTEND TO LET THEM GET AWAY!

FOUR AGAINST ONE ARE LONG ODDS! *GREEN ARROW* TAKES A FIST IN RETURN...

YA'D DO BETTER TA STICK TO YER ARROWS, BOW-BOY!

A VASE CRASHES DOWN ACROSS HIS HEAD EVEN AS A PAIR OF HANDS BATTERS HIM...

THUNK
WAK
THUD

AS HE REELS FLOORWARD, A COPPER-COLORED YOUTH DRIVES BETWEEN *GREEN ARROW* AND THE BANDITS...

I KNOW YOU TOLD ME TO STAY AWAY, *GREEN ARROW*--BUT THESE ARE THE GUYS WHO TRIED TO GET ME IN TROUBLE!

AND MY *APACHE PRIDE* DEMANDS I DO SOME FIGHTING AGAINST THEM!

15

BUT I'M NOT TOO PROUD TO USE A BIT OF *JUDO*--WHICH I'VE BORROWED FROM THE WHITE MAN--WHO IN TURN BORROWED IT FROM THE YELLOW SKINS!

WITH ONLY TWO FOES AGAINST HIM, THE *AMAZING ARCHER* SCORNS TO USE HIS BEWILDERING BOW-SHOTS...

YOU'VE GOT THE CHIN I LOVE TO TOUCH!

KA-LUNK

THAT'S USING THEIR HEADS TO STOP THEM, JERRY!

ONE THING I MUST SAY ABOUT THE *APACHES*, *GREEN ARROW*-- WE NEVER MAKE PUNS!

GREAT WORK, JERRY! YOU'VE PROVED YOUR INNOCENCE--

BUT EVEN BETTER, YOU'VE SHOWN A PRIDE IN YOUR *APACHE* HERITAGE THAT WILL HELP YOU OVERCOME ANY OBSTACLES FROM NOW ON!

I WON'T FAIL YOU...OR MYSELF... *GREEN ARROW!* I'M GOING BACK TO SCHOOL AND MAKE SOMETHING OF MYSELF!

16

IT IS NIGHT TIME WHEN *HAWKMAN* AND *SNAPPER CARR* ARRIVE AT A REMOTE AREA OF *INDIA* NEAR THE *GHAGRA RIVER*...

*SNAPPER*--LOOK BELOW!

THOSE NATIVES HAVE A COUPLE OF WHITE MEN PRISONERS AND ARE ABOUT TO--

JUMP, *SNAPPER!* I'M GOING INTO ACTION-- AND I NEED ROOM TO MOVE!

I'M GOING INTO ACTION MYSELF--EVEN IF *HAWKMAN* DOESN'T EXPECT ME TO!

THE MAN IN THE TORN SHIRT IS *HARVEY YOUNG*--THE PHILANTHROPIST!

I DON'T KNOW WHAT HE DID TO OFFEND THESE PEOPLE--BUT I CAN'T LET THEM KILL HIM!

RESCUED BY-- *HAWKMAN!*

WHAT A STROKE OF LUCK TO HAVE *HIM* TURN UP HERE!

RUN, MEN, RUN!

I C-CAN'T! I HURT MY LEG A COUPLE OF DAYS AGO!

THOSE LANCES-- GOING TO GET US!

17

THEN OUT OF A TREE DROPS...

I'M SURE GLAD THIS WAS A LONG BRANCH!

BY RUNNING OUT ON ITS TIP--MY WEIGHT MADE IT SNAP JUST IN TIME TO SHATTER THOSE LETHAL LANCES!

CRACK! CRACK!

SNAP

I'M TRAPPED!

JUMP, SNAPPER--JUMP FOR IT!

I GUESS I'M NO SUPER-HERO!

FORGET IT, SNAPPER! EVERYBODY "FREEZES" OCCASIONALLY! EVEN PROFESSIONAL BASEBALL PLAYERS SOMETIMES "FREEZE" LIKE THAT WHEN THEY SEE A BALL COMING AT THEIR HEADS!

WITH SNAPPER PERCHED SAFELY ON A ROOFTOP, HAWKMAN SWOOPS ONCE MORE TO THE ATTACK--WHEN...

NO, SAHIB!

WE NO FIGHT YOU ANYMORE!

SAHIB YOUNG CAN LIVE!

WE GO TO FIGHT OUR ENEMIES, THE UTTARS!

I BETTER EXPLAIN, HAWKMAN! THE UTTARS STOLE THE CROPS OVER WHICH THESE BASAS HAVE WORKED FOR A YEAR!

THE BASAS BLAME ME FOR WHAT HAPPENED--AND WERE ABOUT TO KILL ME WHEN YOU SHOWED UP!

18

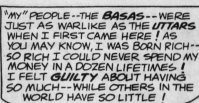

"MY" PEOPLE--THE *BASAS*--WERE JUST AS WARLIKE AS THE *UTTARS* WHEN I FIRST CAME HERE! AS YOU MAY KNOW, I WAS BORN RICH-- SO RICH I COULD NEVER SPEND MY MONEY IN A DOZEN LIFETIMES! I FELT *GUILTY* ABOUT HAVING SO MUCH--WHILE OTHERS IN THE WORLD HAVE SO LITTLE!

SO I DE-CIDED TO DO SOME-THING ABOUT IT!

I MADE MYSELF MY BROTHER'S KEEPER! WITH MY FRIEND *JOE IMLOFF* HERE, I BROUGHT SEEDS AND AGRICULTURAL INSTRUMENTS TO THIS REMOTE AREA IN *INDIA*!

WE PERSUADED THE *BASAS* TO PUT ASIDE THEIR SWORDS AND SPEARS, AND TAKE TO THE HOE AND PLOW INSTEAD!

THE LAND IS GOOD, THE CROPS GREW SWIFTLY--AND *THAT'S* THE TROUBLE!

YES, THAT'S THE REASON WE FAILED--BECAUSE THE CROPS WERE SO GOOD THEY TEMPTED THE *BASAS'* HEREDITARY ENEMIES THE *UTTARS* TO COME AND STEAL THEM!

NOW "MY" PEOPLE PREPARE FOR WAR! FORGOTTEN ARE THE TALKS I GAVE THEM ON THE BROTHER-HOOD OF MAN!

I'VE GOT TO DO WHATEVER'S IN MY POWER TO STOP THIS WAR!

YOU'LL BE SAFE ENOUGH UNTIL I RETURN, MR. YOUNG!

LET'S GO, *SNAPPER!* WE *JUSTICE LEAGUERS* HAVE A JOB TO DO!

THE FIRST RULE OF THE BROTHERHOOD OF MAN IS--THAT PEOPLE MUST LEARN TO LIVE IN PEACE WITH ONE ANOTHER!

NOT ONLY THAT--THEY HAVE TO *RESPECT* EACH OTHER'S CUSTOMS AND BELIEFS!

TO DO THIS--THEY MUST *KNOW* ONE ANOTHER, THEIR HABITS AND CUSTOMS AND BELIEFS!

ABSOLUTELY CORRECT, *SNAPPER!* IF THE PEOPLES OF *EARTH* DID THIS--THERE WOULD BE PEACE--FRIENDLY COOPERATION AMONG NATIONS--HAPPY INTER-MINGLING BETWEEN VARIOUS RACIAL GROUPS!

AND THE WORLD WOULD BE A BETTER PLACE FOR *ALL* OF US!

IN THE VILLAGE OF THE **UTTARS**, A GREAT VICTORY FEAST IS ABOUT TO BE CELEBRATED WHEN...

HEAR ME, UTTARS! ONLY EVIL COMES TO THOSE WHO STEAL FROM THEIR NEIGHBORS!

BEHOLD!

OUT OF THE DARK SKY COMES A RAIN OF RICE...

HARVEY YOUNG PREACHED PEACE TO THE **BASAS**-- BUT NEGLECTED TO DO SO TO THEIR ENEMIES, THE **UTTARS**!

I'LL MAKE UP FOR HIS OVER-SIGHT-- BY "PREACHING" TO THEM IN MY OWN FASHION!

THE FOOD WE STOLE IS PELTING US FROM THE SKY!

OUR GODS ARE ANGRY AT US!

AMIDST THE DOWNPOUR OF RICE--COME HARD PINE-APPLES...

FLEE--LEST THE GODS DROWN US IN RICE--

AND BOMBARD US WITH PINE-APPLES!

FROM THE CONCEALMENT OF A NEARBY ROOFTOP--**SNAPPER** ADDS TO THE CONFUSION BY...

THESE HARD-SHELLED BEANS WILL STING SOME SENSE INTO THEM!

ARMED NOW WITH MELONS, THE **WINGED WONDER** MOVES OVERHEAD AND...

THE FRUITS OF OTHERS' LABOR--SHALL LEAVE A BAD TASTE IN YOUR MOUTHS!

20

ONCE MORE THE *FLYING FURY* SWOOPS ACROSS THE VILLAGE AND...

THIS GRAPEVINE MAKES A PRETTY GOOD LARIAT--STRONG ENOUGH TO LIFT THE *UTTAR* CHIEF OUT OF HIS VILLAGE...

...AND DROP HIM INTO THAT LAKE ...

HE HASN'T SEEN ME-- SO HE AND HIS PEOPLE WILL THINK THE GRAPE- VINE DID IT--WITH THE HELP OF THEIR "GODS"!

SP*LASH*!

AND SO--AS PANIC SPREADS THROUGH THE VILLAGE ...

SPARE US, GODS OF THE FRUITS AND VEGETABLES!

FORGIVE US FOR HAVING OFFENDED!

AND IN THE COLD LAKE WATERS, A TREMBLING CHIEF VOWS...

WE SHALL RETURN WHAT REMAINS OF THE STOLEN FOOD!

EVEN MORE--WE SHALL GIVE GIFTS TO THE *BASAS*--AND ASK THEM TO BE FRIENDS!

21

BUT, AS THE SUN RISES ON THE WOULD-BE PEACEFUL *UTTAR* VILLAGE...

WHAT BAD TIMING!

JUST WHEN I'VE CONVINCED THE *UTTARS* TO RETURN THE STOLEN FOOD--THE *BASAS* APPEAR TO TAKE IT BACK BY FORCE OF ARMS!

MOMENTS LATER, THEIR ARMS LADEN ONLY WITH FOOD--THE WEAPONLESS *UTTARS* CONFRONT THE ARMED AND ANGRY *BASAS*...

WE COME IN PEACE, *BASAS*! WE BRING A GIFT OF FISH!

AND HERE ARE YOUR FRUITS AND VEGETABLES--SUCH AS ARE LEFT OF THEM--WHICH WE RETURN TO YOU!

YOU STOLE OUR FOOD! YOU PAY THE PRICE OF STEALING-- WITH *DEATH*!

I SAY--*NOBODY DIES*!

THE *BASAS* AND THE *UTTARS* SHALL MAKE PEACE--*NOW*!

IT IS A WINGED MESSENGER--

FROM THE *GODS*!

THEN IT IS AGREED! WE SHALL *HUNT* AND *FISH* FOR YOU-- IN EXCHANGE FOR YOUR FRUITS AND VEGETABLES!

YES! TOGETHER WE SHALL LIVE IN PEACE--LIKE BROTHERS!

IF ONLY EVERY MAN--EVERYWHERE-- COULD END HIS TROUBLES IN SUCH A FRIENDLY WAY!

IN THE *BASAS* CAMP, A LITTLE LATER...

SINCE YOU AND *SNAPPER* TOOK A HAND HERE, *HAWKMAN*-- EVERYTHING'S CHANGED! I'M GOING TO STICK WITH IT--AND USING THE *BASAS* AND *UTTARS* AS EXAMPLES--CARRY ON WITH MY MISSION IN LIFE...

FINALLY, BACK IN *JUSTICE LEAGUE* HEADQUARTERS...

*GREEN ARROW* AND I HAVE THE INFORMATION YOU WANT FOR YOUR TERM PAPER, *SNAPPER*! HOW DID YOU AND *HAWKMAN* MAKE OUT?

I'LL TELL YOU--I'VE LEARNED ONE THING FOR SURE! PEOPLE ALL OVER THE WORLD-- NO MATTER WHAT THEIR RELIGION OR THE COLOR OF THEIR SKINS--ARE ALL PRETTY MUCH ALIKE!

THEY ALL HAVE THE SAME BASIC NEEDS--THE SAME FEARS--THE SAME OUTLOOK ON LIFE! EVERY MAN IS A BROTHER TO EVERY OTHER MAN!

WHAT A WORLD IT WILL BE WHEN *MANKIND* IS-- KIND TO MAN!

23

THE END

AS EARTH'S GREATEST SUPER-HEROES ENTER THEIR SECRET SANCTUARY FOR A REGULARLY SCHEDULED MEETING...

WONDER WOMAN, LET ME TELL YOU ABOUT THE SENSATIONAL WAY I USED MY *POWER RING* AGAINST THE *GOLDEN GURUS* OF *GOLISTAN*...

...AND SO I SWOOPED DOWN ON THE CRIMINALS WITH MY WINGS AFLAME...

I WAS DOWN TO MY LAST ARROW, *FLASH*, WHEN I...

HARDLY HAS THE LAST *JUSTICE LEAGUER* TAKEN HIS SEAT WHEN GIGANTIC TEARDROPS MATERIALIZE AROUND FIVE OF THE MEMBERS...

WE'RE BEING ATTACKED!

BY WHOM?

BY WHAT?

HOLD TIGHT! I'LL SMASH THE TEARDROPS WITH MY *POWER RING!*

THEY DISAPPEARED-- EVEN BEFORE MY RING COULD REACH 'EM!

SUPERMAN--FLASH-- WONDER WOMAN-- AQUAMAN-- MARTIAN MANHUNTER! *GONE!*

WHY DID IT HAPPEN ONLY TO *THOSE FIVE?* WHY NOT *ALL* OF US?

AT THIS EXACT MOMENT ON A WORLD FAR REMOVED FROM THE *MILKY WAY GALAXY*...

HERE WE ARE-- WHEREVER *"HERE"* MAY BE!

IT'S ANOTHER PLANET-- AND I, FOR ONE, AM IN *TROUBLE!*

WHAT'S THAT FLATTISH LENS-LIKE OBJECT?

WE'RE FREE--SO LET'S TAKE A CLOSER LOOK!

2

IT IS OUR DESTINY--TO BE ALWAYS *RIGHT* IN WHATEVER WE DO! IT IS UTTERLY *IMPOSSIBLE* FOR US TO DO ANYTHING WRONG!

THUS WHEN THE THOUGHT STRUCK US TO BRING YOU FIVE TO *MARITHANIA*--WE DID SO!

CUT THE COMEDY! THE *REAL* REASON IS THAT YOU'RE EXPECTING TROUBLE AND YOU NEED US TO HELP YOU OUT WITH OUR SUPER-POWERS!

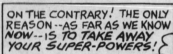

ON THE CONTRARY! THE ONLY REASON--AS FAR AS WE KNOW NOW--IS TO TAKE AWAY YOUR SUPER-POWERS!

YOU'RE NOT *MAN* ENOUGH TO PULL OFF *THAT* TRICK!

THEY MAY BE RIGHT, *WONDER WOMAN!* AFTER ALL, *I'M* THEIR FIRST VICTIM!

BUT-- WHY WE FIVE?

WHAT ABOUT THE REST OF US-- *GREEN LANTERN, BATMAN, HAWKMAN...*

WE'RE SURPRISED THE ANSWER HASN'T ALREADY OCCURRED TO *YOU*--AS IT DID TO *US!*

NOT ONE OF YOU *FIVE EARNED* YOUR SUPER-POWERS!

"YOU, *FLASH*-- WERE THE RECIPIENT OF *SUPER-SPEED* WHEN A LIGHTNING BOLT CAUSED A RACK OF CHEMICALS TO SPLASH OVER YOU..."

"YOU, *SUPERMAN*-- AND YOU, *MARTIAN MANHUNTER*-- RECEIVED YOUR EXTRA-ORDINARY POWERS BY THE ACCIDENT OF *BIRTH* ON THE PLANETS *KRYPTON* AND *MARS*-- AS WELL AS YOU, *AQUAMAN*, IN THE UNDER-WATER WORLD OF *ATLANTIS*..."

4

"WHILE YOU, *WONDER WOMAN*--HAD YOUR GREAT ATTRIBUTES BESTOWED UPON YOU BY THE GODDESS *APHRODITE*..."

AS FOR YOUR ABSENTEE MEMBERS, *GREEN LANTERN* EARNED HIS TITLE BECAUSE OF HIS FEARLESS PROWESS!

WHILE *ATOM*, *BATMAN*, *GREEN ARROW* AND *HAWKMAN* ALL *DEVISED* AND *DEVELOPED* THEIR SPECIAL POWERS AND ABILITIES!

SO BECAUSE YOU DID NOT *EARN* YOUR POWERS, OUR UNERRING WISDOM TELLS US IT IS *RIGHT* THAT WE TAKE THEM AWAY FROM YOU!

YOU'RE CERTAINLY TAKING A LOT FOR GRANTED--INCLUDING THE NOTION THAT WE'LL STAND IDLY BY WHILE YOU'RE MAKING A TRY AT IT!

BELIEVE US WHEN WE SAY--WE'RE DOING THE *RIGHT THING!* IT'LL ALL TURN OUT FOR THE *BEST.!*

BOTH FOR *YOU*--AS WELL AS *US!*

AND JUST *HOW* OR *WHY* WE'RE MOST ANXIOUS TO SEE!

WELL, *THAT'S* A SWITCH, ALL RIGHT.! ANYONE'S WHO'S EVER BROUGHT US TO DIFFERENT PLACES IN THE UNIVERSE...

... AND THEN TRIED TO TAKE AWAY OUR SUPER-POWERS...

... ALWAYS HAD A SINISTER MOTIVE.!

BUT THESE DO-GOODERS CLAIM THEY HAVE NO PLAN TO ROB, INVADE, CONQUER OR GET REVENGE.!

THEY'RE *SO GOOD* TO US, IT SOUNDS-- *IMPOSSIBLE!* SO LET'S DO SOMETHING ABOUT IT.!

5

AND THEN --*SEEING IS BELIEVING!*..

I CAN'T TELEPATH COMMANDS TO ANYTHING, LET ALONE SEA CREATURES!

MY SUPER-SPEED IS GONE!

I'M AS NORMAL AS IF I WERE ON MY NATIVE KRYPTON!

YOU AND ME BOTH, SUPERMAN!

I CAN'T GET MY MAGIC LASSO TO RESPOND!

ANGRILY, THE POWERLESS *JUSTICE LEAGUERS* WHIRL ON THE *IMPOSSIBLES*...

ALL RIGHT, KNOW-IT-ALLS! WHEN DO WE COLLECT OUR BENEFIT INSURANCE?

BETTER YET--WHAT ARE THE CHANCES OF US EVER REGAINING OUR SUPER-POWERS?

ALAS-- WE ARE NOT PROPHETS! ALL WE KNOW IS THAT IT WAS RIGHT FOR THE MACHINE THAT REMOVED YOUR POWERS-- TO BE DESTROYED IN TURN!

SUDDENLY...

BE ASSURED--THAT BECAUSE YOU HAVE LOST YOUR SUPER-POWERS-- ONLY *GOOD* CAN COME-- *HYEAH!*

RECTANGULAR BEAMS--FLASHING IN ON THE *IMPOSSIBLES!*

WHA ZAAAAPP

THE CONTRA-WORLD IS ATTACKING!

THEIR DISONAL BEAMS-- DRAINING US OF LIFE!

THE CONTRAS ARE OUR ANCIENT ENEMIES--WHOM WE DEFEATED AND BANISHED TO A DIFFERENT PLANET-- A MILLION AGES AGO!

NOW THEY HAVE FOUND A WEAPON OUR GUARDING DEVICES WERE UNABLE TO DETECT--AND HAVE RETURNED TO CONQUER US!

WITHOUT US--SHOULD WE BE DESTROYED BY THE CONTRA CREATURES-- THE ENTIRE UNIVERSE WILL BE DOMINATED BY SHEER EVIL!

7

AS THE UNERRING *IMPOSSIBLES* COLLAPSE IN COMAS...

OVER HERE! THEIR *VISISCOPE* IS PICKING UP THE ATTACKING *CONTRAS*!

WE HAVE ONE THING IN OUR FAVOR! THOSE ALIENS DON'T KNOW WE'RE HERE ON *MARITHANIA*--OR THEY WOULD HAVE INCLUDED US IN STAB-IN-THE-BACK ASSAULT.!

FASCINATED EYES STARE AT A COUPLE OF DIMENSIONAL CRAFT AS THEY ZERO IN ON *MARITHANIA*...

DO YOU SUPPOSE THOSE INVADERS CAN ACTUALLY TRAVEL BETWEEN THE MULTI-PLANES OF EXISTENCE?

WE'LL FIND OUT SOON ENOUGH-- WHEN WE GO OUT TO FIGHT THEM--MINUS OUR SUPER-POWERS.!

SAY, AS LONG AS WE'VE LOST OUR SUPER-POWERS-- AT LEAST WE'VE ALSO LOST OUR *WEAKNESSES.!*

MAYBE THAT'LL HELP-- BUT JUST HOW, I CAN'T IMAGINE.!

*FLASH*--LET'S YOU AND I TEAM UP--SEE WHAT SORT OF FIGHT WE CAN PUT UP!

AQUAMAN, MARTIAN MANHUNTER AND MYSELF WILL PUT UP AS GOOD A "NORMAL-POWERED" FIGHT AS WE CAN!

AS THEY COME IN SIGHT OF THE BETWEEN-DIMENSIONS VESSELS, THE DIFFERENT-LOOKING HATCHWAYS OPEN...

TWO SHIPS FROM THE SAME PLACE --AND THEY'RE *BOTH* DIFFERENT?!

MAKES SENSE--IF THEY COME FROM A *CONTRARY* WORLD! EVERYTHING ON THAT WORLD MUST BE *DIFFERENT* FROM ANYTHING ELSE!

TAKE YOUR TARGETS--AND GIVE IT ALL YOU'VE GOT!

8

I MAY NOT BE ABLE TO *TELEPATH*--BUT I CAN STILL SEND THIS "ROCKY MESSAGE" AT THAT WALKING "BRAIN"!

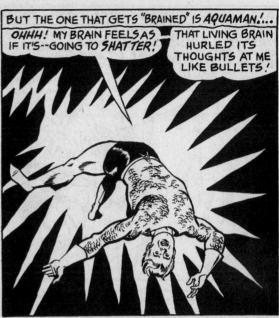

BUT THE ONE THAT GETS "BRAINED" IS *AQUAMAN!*...

*OHHH!* MY BRAIN FEELS AS IF IT'S--GOING TO *SHATTER!*

THAT LIVING BRAIN HURLED ITS THOUGHTS AT ME LIKE BULLETS!

THE *IMPOSSIBLES* WERE RIGHT, *MARTIAN MANHUNTER!* IF--I'D STILL HAD MY TELEPATHIC POWERS--THE BRAIN'S THOUGHTS WOULD HAVE *KILLED* ME!

SO FAR--THE *IMPOSSIBLES DID* DO THE RIGHT THING BY *YOU, AQUAMAN!*

THAT LEAVES IT TO THE TWO OF US, MM-- TO KEEP ON BATTLING!

THE *EX-MAN OF STEEL* AND FORMER *MARTIAN MANHUNTER* RIP LOOSE A LONG TOUGH VINE AND...

IF WE CAN TRIP THIS CRYSTAL ONE UP--

--WE MAY BE ABLE TO *CLOBBER* HIM WITH A WEAPON!

9

DISDAINFULLY--FOR TO THE *CONTRA CRYSTAL CREATURE*, *SUPERMAN* AND *MARTIAN MANHUNTER* ARE NO MORE DANGEROUS THAN BUZZING FLIES...

THAT HURT--AND THAT'S A WORD I DON'T USE TOO OFTEN!

BONK

WHAKK!

WHEW! IF I STILL POSSESSED MY MARTIAN POWERS--THAT BOLT OF FLAME WOULD HAVE FRIZZLED ME TO A CINDER!

CHALK UP ANOTHER GOOD DEED FOR THE IMPOSSIBLES!

TO ONE SIDE, THE NO-LONGER *SCARLET SPEEDSTER* AND THE POWERLESS *PRINCESS OF PARADISE ISLAND* FACE THEIR OWN SPECIAL FOES AS...

PUFF! PUFF! IF ONLY I HAD MY SUPER-SPEED--

HERE COME THE *CONTRAS* FROM THE SECOND SHIP! FOR A STARTER--

LET'S GRAB THIS FLOWER THING AND TWIST IT AROUND THE LIVING NEON-BEING!

RIGHT! TANGLE THEM UP SO BADLY THEY'LL BE UNABLE TO FIRE AT US--WITHOUT DESTROYING EACH OTHER!

THE NEON-MAN GLOWS-- CAUSING THE AIR TO SHIMMER ABOUT *FLASH* AND *WONDER WOMAN*...

OHHH! IT'S MAKING ME VIBRATE AT ULTRA-SPEED-- TWISTING EVERY ATOM IN MY BODY! IF--IF I STILL HAD MY SUPER-SPEED--IT WOULD HAVE *IMPLODED* ME!

DOVE OUT OF THE WAY--JUST IN TIME!

10

THOUGH CHECKED BY THE SUPER-FAST VIBRATION, *FLASH* MANAGES TO COME TO THE *AMAZING AMAZON'S* AID... THAT NEON-FIGURE LOOKS FRAGILE ENOUGH -- TO CRACK UNDER THE BLOW OF THIS FALLING STATUE!

HE WAS SAVED BY THE FLOWER-BEING!

THEY WORK IN TEAMS, TOO!

COPYCATS! WHY DIDN'T YOU COME UP WITH A WEAPON OF YOUR OWN?

KAA-RAASSH

AS IF IN TAUNTING ANSWER, THE FLOWER CREATURE SHOOTS OUT A STREAM OF SEEDS WITH EXPLOSIVE POWER...

ME AND MY BIG MOUTH!

THIS IS LIKE A SHRAPNEL BLAST!

11

BEFORE THE *JUSTICE LEAGUERS* CAN CARRY OUT THEIR ATTACK, CONCENTRIC CIRCLES OF POWER BEAT OUT FROM THE CREATURES OF THE *CONTRA WORLD*...

JUMP FOR IT! THEY'RE SHATTERING THE LENS!

THOSE ALIENS NULLIFY WHAT-EVER WE DO!

THEN WE'VE GOT TO USE OUR THINK-BOXES AND COME UP WITH SOME *NEW* FORM OF ATTACK!

THEY ALL HAVE SUCH CONTRARY WAYS OF FIGHTING-- WE CAN'T COUNT ON ANYTHING!

SHATTERED GLASS AND FRAGMENTS OF SHARP SLIVERS RAIN DOWN AS...

MAYBE THAT'S THEIR *WEAK-NESS* --THEY NEVER DO ANYTHING THE SAME.

*THAT* GIVES ME AN IDEA!

WHEN WE WERE PRYING LOOSE THE *VISISCOPE LENS*-- I FOUND THIS CHUNK OF *KRYPTONITE* HALF-BURIED UNDER THE SURFACE!

IT DOESN'T HARM ME BECAUSE I'VE LOST MY SUPER-POWERS!

WORKING ON THAT PRINCIPLE-- I CAN USE THIS BIT OF MAG-NIFYING GLASS BROKEN OFF THE *VISISCOPE LENS*! TURN MY FORMER WEAKNESS AGAINST *THEM!*

WHAT ABOUT YOU, *AQUAMAN?* YOUR WEAKNESS IS--WAS-- THAT YOU CAN'T BE OUT OF WATER FOR MORE THAN AN HOUR!

TRUE ENOUGH, *SUPERMAN--* AND I'M GOING TO TURN THAT INTO AN *ADVANTAGE!* ONE OF THOSE *CONTRAS* IS MADE TO ORDER FOR AN EXPERIMENT I HAVE IN MIND!

NO MORE TIME FOR TALK! THOSE FIVE NO-GOODERS ARE ABOUT TO KILL THE *IMPOSSIBLES!*

I'M NOT SURE WHICH OF THEM THE *KRYPTON* RADIATION WILL AFFECT --SO I'LL JUST AIM IT IN ALL DIRECTIONS!

13

WITH ITS DEADLY WEAPONS SPLASHING A BARRAGE OF LETHAL RAIN ACROSS THE LANDSCAPE, THE FLOWER-BEING TAKES OFF AFTER THE *MARTIAN MANHUNTER*...

I'VE LOST MY MARTIAN SPEED-- BUT I CAN OUTRUN THAT WALKING LEAF!

WHAT I HAVE TO WATCH OUT FOR ARE HIS PECULIAR POWERS-- NONE OF WHICH IS EVER LIKE ANY OTHER!

OPENING UP A LEAD ON HIS EERIE FOE, THE *MAN FROM MARS* PAUSES TO...

START A FIRE-- AND MAKE MYSELF A TORCH!

SEEMS STRANGE TO BE HANDLING FIRE LIKE THIS-- BUT IT'S THE ONE WEAPON WHICH SHOULD WORK AGAINST A FLOWER-BEING!

RETREATING TO THE OPEN HATCH OF THE DIMENSION SHIP, HE MAKES HIS STAND...

HOPE I CAN REACH HIM WITH THESE FLAMES-- BEFORE HE LAUNCHES HIS ATTACK!

THE *CONTRA*-CREATURE DRIVES A PETALED FLOWER FORWARD-- ROTATING IT WITH THE SPEED AND FORCE OF AN AIRPLANE PROPELLER...

YIIII! NEVER HAD A CHANCE --

FLAT ON HIS BACK, *J'ONN J'ONZZ* SEES HIS NEMESIS STEP INTO THE DIMENSIONAL CRAFT...

CLOSING IN ON ME-- FOR THE KILL!

WHAT CAN I DO TO *STOP* HIM?

15

LUNGING SIDEWAYS, HIS DESPERATELY GROPING HAND FINDS A TREE-BRANCH...

THESE BINS MUST CONTAIN SOIL AND PLANT SAMPLINGS FROM THE VARIOUS PLANETS THESE *CONTRAS* HAVE EXPLORED!

AH! WHEN THOSE PETALS HIT THE WOOD--THEY FLY APART!

SNATCHING UP HANDFULS OF SOIL-- HE FLINGS THEM SAVAGELY...

THE SOIL IS PEBBLY--AND ODDLY FAMILIAR! IT MUST STING LIKE BIRDSHOT AS IT HITS THE TENDER LEAVES AND STALKS OF THAT CREATURE! IT'S DRIVING HIM BACKWARDS...

UNAWARE THAT THE BURNING TORCH IS RIGHT BEHIND HIM, THE FLOWER-BEING BACKTRACKS INTO ITS FLAMES--AND...

EEEARGHH

HE WITHERED AS SOON AS THE FLAMES TOUCHED HIM!

I'VE *WON!* NOT ONLY THAT-- I'VE GAINED A *BONUS* FOR MY EFFORTS!

IN THE MEANTIME, THE *SEA KING* AND *SUPERMAN* HAVE FLED UNTIL THE SALT SMELL OF THE *MARITHANIAN SEA* IS STRONG IN THEIR NOSTRILS. THEN...

DIVE, SUPERMAN!

JUST AS MY BODY COULDN'T DO WITHOUT WATER FOR MORE THAN AN HOUR--SO NO *BRAIN* CAN DO WITHOUT OXYGEN FOR MORE THAN *SIX MINUTES!* *

*EDITOR'S NOTE: IF DEPRIVED OF OXYGEN FOR LONGER THAN SIX MINUTES, THE BRAIN CELLS DIE!

THOSE ELECTRIC EMANATIONS FROM THE BRAIN ARE HITTING THE WATER IN THE FORM OF LIGHTNING BOLTS --AND SINCE WATER IS AN EXCELLENT CONDUCTOR OF ELECTRICITY--THEY'LL KILL BOTH *SUPERMAN* AND ME --UNLESS...

16

WHILE THE ELECTRICAL STORM THE BRAIN IS SENDING OUT IS BUILDING IN INTENSITY, WE'LL LEAVE THE WATER--AND MAKE A LASSO OUT OF THIS SEA WEED, *SUPERMAN!*

WITHIN MOMENTS, THE *MAN OF STEEL* AND *AQUAMAN* HAVE FASHIONED A SEA WEED LASSO AND...

THE *STARFISH OF MARITHANIA* HAS SUCTION DISCS JUST AS DO EARTH'S STARFISH! THOSE DISCS WILL CATCH AND HOLD THE BRAIN--

LONG ENOUGH FOR ME TO YANK IT INTO THE SEA!

AS THE SALT WATERS CLOSE ABOUT THE BRAIN, *AQUAMAN* LENDS HIS HANDS TO THE TASK OF KEEPING IT BELOW THE SURFACE...

IT WON'T DARE RELEASE THE ELECTRIC LIGHTNING AGAIN--IT WOULD ONLY ELECTROCUTE ITSELF!

MINUTES PASS! THE *CONTRA* BRAIN-BEING STRUGGLES DESPERATELY BUT THE MUSCLES DEVELOPED BY YEARS OF SWIMMING ENABLE *AQUAMAN* TO MAINTAIN HIS GRIP...

IT'S BOMBARDING ME WITH MENTAL TELEPATHY WAVES--SO POWERFUL-- IT'S LIKE BEING HIT BY SLEDGE-HAMMERS!

ITS STRUGGLES ARE WEAKENING--GROWING LESS AND LESS AS ITS LACK OF OXYGEN OVERCOMES IT--AND AS IT DOES...SOMETHING WONDERFUL IS HAPPENING TO ME!

EVEN AS *AQUAMAN* AND THE BRAIN DISAPPEAR UNDER THE WATER, *SUPERMAN* FINDS HIMSELF UNDER ATTACK BY THE *NEON-MAN*...

⌇ KOFF ⌇ ⌇ KOFF ⌇

THIS *GREEN KRYPTONITE GAS* WOULD HAVE KILLED ME--HAD I MY SUPER-POWERS! AS IT IS--IT STINGS AND CHOKES ME--MAKING MY EYES WATER!

17

BUT WATERY EYES OR NOT--I CAN STILL SEE WELL ENOUGH TO BELT THAT *CONTRA* WITH THIS CHUNK OF *KRYPTONITE!*

THOSE DARTS HE'S SHOOTING AT ME ARE TRAVELING WITH THE SPEED OF LIGHT--BUT THEY'RE GOING PAST ME INTO THE SKY!

AS THE *EX-MAN OF STEEL* HURLS HIS *KRYPTONITE* GLOBE--A FLASH OF GOLDEN BRILLIANCE AND A HOT WIND SWEEP ACROSS *MARITHANIA*...

THE *KRYPTONITE* RAYS ONLY STUNNED THE MAN OF CRYSTAL IN *EXACTIKON* CITY--BUT I'M HOPING THAT BY *HITTING* THE NEON-MAN WITH IT...

I'LL DO SOME EFFECTIVE DAMAGE!

AS THE GREEN GLOBE MAKES CONTACT...

IT WORKED!

THE *KRYPTONITE* FUSED THE NEON-MAN INTO INERTNESS--TURNED HIM INTO A GLOB! AND--BETTER YET--IS THE INCREDIBLE AFTEREFFECT!

MEANWHILE IN *EXACTIKON CITY, FLASH* AND *WONDER WOMAN* ARE BATTLING FOR THEIR VERY LIVES...

THOSE STREAMERS AND STARS--WHIRLING THE ATOMS OF MY BODY APART!

I CAN'T KEEP DODGING THOSE FIRE-WHEELS FOR-EVER!

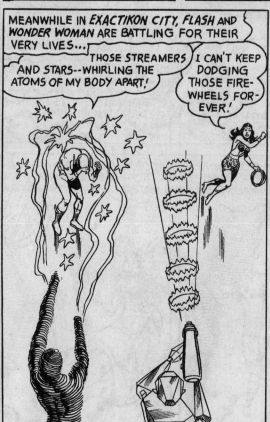

I MAY NOT HAVE MY *SUPER-POWERS*--AND THERE MAY NOT BE ANY *MAGIC* LEFT IN MY *LASSO*...

...BUT I'VE DEVELOPED ENOUGH SKILL WITH THE *LARIAT* OVER THE YEARS TO GET *FLASH* OUT OF THAT EERIE BOMBARDMENT...

18

HE'S FREE!

WONDER WOMAN IS IN NO POSITION TO AVOID THOSE ENERGY BLOCKS HEADING HER WAY!

GOT TO SAVE HER--AS SHE SAVED ME!

HANG ON, *WONDER WOMAN!* ONE GOOD YANK DESERVES ANOTHER!

SUDDENLY--A HOT WIND AND GOLDEN GLOW SWEEP ACROSS THE PLANET...

I DON'T KNOW WHAT'S CAUSED THAT WIND OR YELLOW COLOR TO APPEAR OVER *MARITHANIA*-- BUT THE SHAKING EFFECT IT HAS ON THE SPIRAL CREATURE SUGGESTS--

SUGGESTS *WHAT,* FLASH?

WATCH, WONDER WOMAN!

GREAT HERA! *FLASH* STUMBLED-- FELL DOWN AT THE FEET OF THE *SPIRAL- BEING!*

IT'S SPRAYING CHEMICAL FLUIDS ON *FLASH!* THEY'LL KILL HIM!

19

AS THOSE CHEMICALS BATHE THE FORMER SCARLET SPEEDSTER-- A TREMENDOUS ENERGY-BEAM FROM THE CRYSTAL CREATURE FLASHES THROUGH THEM-- AND SLAMS INTO WONDER WOMAN!...

I DELIBERATELY FELL HERE--PUTTING MYSELF IN POSITION-- TO PRESS THE SPECIAL DEVICE IN MY RING --

OHHHH!

JUST AS I FIGURED! THE SPIRAL CREATURE IS SO WISPY THAT MY RING'S SUCTION DEVICE IS SHRINKING AND DRAWING HIM INTO IT--THE SAME WAY IT DOES TO MY UNIFORM!

WHAT'S HAPPENING TO ME?

EVERYTHING DISAPPEARS BEFORE THE AMAZING AMAZON AS SHE IS THRUST BACKWARD... BACKWARD THROUGH THE MISTS OF TIME...

AS THE CHRONAL MISTS FADE AWAY...

GREAT HERA! I'VE BEEN DISPLACED IN TIME--AND I'M NOW ON THE OTHER SIDE OF THE MACHINE THAT TOOK AWAY OUR SUPER-POWERS!

I FEEL AS POWERLESS-- AS IF I WERE SURROUNDED BY FLAMES!

THAT'S MARTIAN MANHUNTER'S VOICE! THAT MEANS I'M DUE TO LOSE MY SUPER-POWERS NEXT!

20

AS THE SHATTERED PIECES OF CRYSTAL-MAN RAIN DOWN...

FLASH--WATCH YOURSELF! THOSE CRYSTAL FRAGMENTS WILL--*EH?!* YOU'RE VIBRATING THROUGH THEM AT *SUPER-SPEED!*

I'M MY OLD SELF AGAIN TOO!

WHEN THE SPIRAL-BEING DOUSED ME WITH THOSE CHEMICALS, CRYSTAL-MAN FIRED AN ENERGY-BOLT THROUGH THEM--THEREBY DUPLICATING THE VERY PROCESS THAT ORIGINALLY GAVE ME SUPER-SPEED!

NOW THAT YOU AND I HAVE OUR POWERS BACK, *WONDER WOMAN,* WE CAN HELP THE OTHERS--

DON'T BOTHER! I'VE REGAINED MY SUPER-POWERS, AS YOU CAN SEE!

WHEN *NEON-MAN* FIRED THOSE *GREEN* ENERGY DARTS AT ME WITH THE SPEED OF LIGHT--THEY FLEW OUT INTO SPACE AND CRASHED INTO THE RED SUN OF *MARITHANIA* AND TURNED IT INTO A YELLOW ONE!

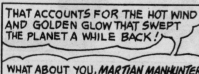

THAT ACCOUNTS FOR THE HOT WIND AND GOLDEN GLOW THAT SWEPT THE PLANET A WHILE BACK!

WHAT ABOUT YOU, *MARTIAN MANHUNTER?* HOW'D YOU RECOVER *YOUR* POWERS?

INSIDE THE *CONTRA* DIMENSIONAL-SHIP, I PICKED UP SOME FAMILIAR, PEBBLY SOIL TO FLING IT AT THE FLOWER-MAN! AS I DID SO, I RECOGNIZED IT AS--DIRT FROM *MARS!*

UPON *CONTACT* WITH MY NATIVE SOIL, I WON BACK MY MARTIAN SUPER-POWERS!

NEXT MOMENT...

IT'S *AQUAMAN!* WHAT IN THE WORLD IS HOLDING YOU UP?

THE TENTACLE OF A GIGANTIC OCTOPUS! WHEN THE BRAIN-BEING INUNDATED MY MIND WITH ITS MENTAL COMMANDS, IT GAVE ME BACK MY TELEPATHIC ABILITY TO COMMUNICATE WITH SEA CREATURES!

22

IN *EXACTIKON CITY*, A LITTLE LATER, AFTER THE THREE *IMPOSSIBLES* HAVE BEEN REVIVED...

YOU SEE? WE TOLD YOU EVERYTHING WE DID WAS FOR THE *BEST!* IF WE HADN'T BROUGHT YOU HERE--AND TAKEN AWAY YOUR SUPER-POWERS...

...*YOU* WOULD HAVE BEEN KILLED--AND SO WOULD *WE!* AND THE *CONTRAS* WOULD HAVE GAINED RUTHLESS CONTROL OF THE UNIVERSE!

AND NOW--BECAUSE WE INSTINCTIVELY KNOW IT'S THE *RIGHT* THING TO DO-- WE ARE RETURNING YOU TO YOUR HEADQUARTERS!

AFTER THE FIVE SUPER-HEROES HAVE RELATED THEIR ADVENTURE ...

*WHEW!* TALK ABOUT "*IMPOSSIBLE*" ADVENTURES--

IT MUST BE TERRIBLE TO BE *RIGHT* ALL THE TIME!

IT TAKES ALL THE SUSPENSE-- ALL THE FUN-- OUT OF LIFE!

OH, I DON'T KNOW! I HAVE SOME EXAMS COMING UP NEXT WEEK AND I'D BE ON *EASY STREET* IF I KNEW ALL MY ANSWERS WERE GOING TO BE *CORRECT!*

23

The End

STORY BY GARDNER FOX

ART BY MIKE SEKOWSKY & SID GREENE

# JUSTICE ☆☆☆ LEAGUE ☆☆☆ of AMERICA

THE REIGNING MONARCH OF THE BEE-WORLD *KORLL* WASN'T SATISFIED TO BE HAILED BY HER SUBJECTS-- *"LONG LIVE QUEEN ZAZZALA!"*
SHE WAS DETERMINED TO LIVE *FOREVER*--AND EQUALLY DETERMINED TO MAKE THE ENTIRE UNIVERSE HER REALM!
TO GAIN HER OBJECTIVE, THE QUEEN BEE NEEDED AN UNBEATABLE ARMY--WHICH LED HER TO *EARTH* AND THE DRAFTING OF THE *JUSTICE LEAGUE OF AMERICA* AS THE--

# WINGED WARRIORS of the IMMORTAL QUEEN!

THE ROLL CALL...

ATOM
AQUAMAN
BATMAN
FLASH
GREEN ARROW
GREEN LANTERN
HAWKMAN
MARTIAN MANHUNTER
SUPERMAN
WONDER WOMAN
AND ☆ SPECIAL GUEST- STAR BATGIRL ☆!

GO FORTH, MY DRONES-- AND CONQUER THE UNIVERSE FOR *QUEEN ZAZZALA THE IMMORTAL!*

A VOICE BELLOWS OUT A CHALLENGE AS MARCO (MARTIAN MANHUNTER) XAVIER SPENDS *NEW YEAR'S EVE* CATCHING UP WITH THE CRIME SYNDICATE KNOWN AS...

*VULTURE!* I KNOW YOU'RE IN THERE! I'M SMASHING MY WAY IN!

DID YOU EVER SEE A DISPLAY OF *MARTIAN SUPER-STRENGTH?* WELL, YOU WON'T SEE IT NOW-- BECAUSE...

GREAT PHOBOS! I CAN'T MOVE!

AT THIS VERY MOMENT, ON THE ROOFTOP OF THE *MIDWAY CITY MUSEUM*...

TIME TO PAY A VISIT TO OUR *THANAGARIAN SPACESHIP* AND--

*HAWKMAN!* HAVEN'T YOU FORGOTTEN SOMETHING? *SPREAD YOUR WINGS!*

HE'S STIFF AS A BOARD!

HE'LL BE KILLED IF HE HITS THE GROUND LIKE THAT!

GOT TO SAVE HIM!

IN MID-OCEAN, ASTRIDE A MIGHTY DOLPHIN, AQUAMAN SENDS OUT HIS *TELEPATHIC COMMANDS...*

TAKE ME TO THAT SMUGGLERS' SHIP, *THAG!*

RAM INTO IT-- AND UPSET THEIR CRIMINAL SCHEMES!

2

AT EXPRESS TRAIN SPEED, MAN AND DOLPHIN RAM THE VESSEL...

CAN'T HOLD ON!

MY NERVOUS SYSTEM PARALYZED-- LOST CONTROL OF MY BODY....!

WHILE AT A NEW YEAR'S EVE PARTY, ALONE WITH THE GIRL HE ADORES, COLONEL STEVE TREVOR CATCHES HER CLOSE AND...

WONDER WOMAN COULDN'T REFUSE ME THIS HAPPY NEW YEAR KISS...

GREAT HERA! STEVE'S KISS-- MAKING ME SWOON...

ANGEL--WHAT IS IT? WHAT'S HAPPENED TO YOU?

I--WISH-- I--KNEW...

THE RINGING IN OF THE NEW YEAR IN IVY TOWN FINDS *THE ATOM* RINGING A PHONE NUMBER...

JEAN'LL BE MAD AS A WET HEN IF I DON'T SHOW UP SOON!

NOW THAT I'VE ROUNDED UP THE *TRUMPETEER* GANG, I'LL TELEPHONE MYSELF BACK TO THE APART- MENT AND...

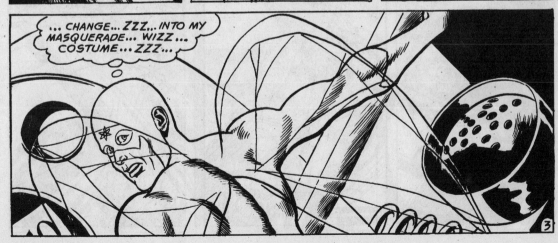

...CHANGE...ZZZ...INTO MY MASQUERADE...WIZZ... COSTUME...ZZZ...

3

SOME DISTANCE FROM *IVY TOWN,* INSIDE A BEEHIVE-SHAPED SPACESHIP...

WHY--OF ALL *FIVE JUSTICE LEAGUE* MEMBERS I BEAMED MY *DRONE ROD* ON--DID ONLY ATOM RESPOND PROPERLY? THE OTHERS BECAME PARALYZED--USELESS TO ME!

ATOM IS WINGING TOWARD ME AS ORDERED! CAN IT BE THAT BECAUSE HE IS *SMALL*--THE DRONE ENERGY WORKED SOLELY ON HIM?

I MUST MAKE AN ADJUSTMENT IN MY ROD--BEFORE I SUMMON THE REMAINING *JUSTICE LEAGUERS* TO ME!

THE FIVE-WAY ENERGY BLAST EXHAUSTED MY ROD! IT'LL NEED RECHARGING!

SOMETIME LATER, IN *GOTHAM CITY*...

BATMAN--BATROPING UP THAT WALL-- AFTER SOME CROOKS!

I'LL BRAKE UP--SEE IF I CAN LEND A HAND!

AS SHE STARES UPWARD, BAT-GIRL'S EYES AND MOUTH WIDEN IN UTTER SHOCK...

BATMAN-- GETTING SMALLER... AND SMALLER...

GROWING A PAIR OF TINY WINGS...

...AND FLYING OFF!

I'D BETTER GET A FIX ON HIM WITH MY MULTI-COLOR TRACKING DEVICE--AND FOLLOW HIM!

AS THE DRONE-LIKE BATMAN WINGS HIS WAY TOWARD THE SPACE-SHIP FROM THE PLANET KORLL...

I THOUGHT I HAD IT BAD! BUT THE SAME THING'S HAPPENED TO GREEN LANTERN-- GREEN ARROW-- SUPERMAN AND FLASH!

WHAT EERIE POWER HAS CAUGHT US IN ITS CLUTCHES?

INSIDE THE SHIP...

QUEEN ZAZZALA THE IMMORTAL WELCOMES HER SHRUNKEN-IN-SIZE DRONES!

THE QUEEN BEE! CALLING HERSELF IMMORTAL!?

I PUT A POWER RING SHEATH AROUND THOSE VIALS THAT HELD THE ELIXIR OF IMMORTALITY!* HOW COULD YOU POSSIBLY HAVE OPENED THEM?

IT TOOK A BIT OF DOING, BELIEVE ME! AFTER REPEATED FAILURES, A WAY OUT OF THE DILEMMA SUDDENLY STRUCK ME!

SINCE PER KAZZ HAD DEVELOPED THE IMMORTALITY ELIXIR, I REASONED HE MIGHT STILL HELP ME DRINK IT-- EVEN THOUGH HE WAS DEAD!

* JUSTICE LEAGUE OF AMERICA #23: "DRONES OF THE QUEEN BEE!"

"ENTERING HIS LABORATORY, I SEARCHED ABOUT UNTIL I FOUND HIS NOTEBOOKS AND BEGAN STUDYING THEM..."

AHH--NOW I'M GETTING SOMEWHERE! PER KAZZ WAS INTERESTED IN GREEN ENERGY BEAMS WHICH HE HAD OBSERVED FROM TIME TO TIME FLASHING THROUGH SPACE...

HE SOON DETERMINED THEY WERE POWER RING BEAMS USED BY GREEN LANTERNS--

"WITH MOUNTING EXCITEMENT, I NOTED HOW PER KAZZ SOUGHT TO OVERCOME THE POWER BEAMS' WEAKNESS TO YELLOW..."

GOOD FOR YOU, PER KAZZ! YOU SOLVED THE PROBLEM--WITH THIS DEVICE THAT ABSORBS POWER RING ENERGY!

IT WILL BE SIMPLE FOR ME NOW TO REMOVE THE POWER SHEATH AROUND THE ELIXIR VIALS--

AND DRINK MYSELF INTO IMMORTALITY!

5

AT LAST! I AM-- QUEEN ZAZZALA THE IMMORTAL!

AND BEFITTING MY NEW STATURE, I WILL INCORPORATE *PER KAZZ'S* POWER FORCE--WITH ITS NON-WEAKNESS FOR YELLOW--INTO MY *MAGNO-NUCLEAR ROD!*

"CAME *THE MOST MAGNIFICENT MOMENT* OF ALL WHEN--"

ROD--FROM THIS TIME ON, YOU SHALL OBEY ONLY THE COMMANDS OF QUEEN ZAZZALA THE IMMORTAL!

I KNOW WHAT YOU'RE THINKING! WHY, SINCE I AM IMMORTAL AND POSSESS THE MIGHTIEST WEAPON EVER CONCEIVED--HAVE I DRAFTED YOU AS MY WINGED WARRIORS!

TO BE BLUNT ABOUT IT--I NEED YOUR HELP TO SAVE ME--FROM A *LIVING DEATH!*

MY *IMMORTALITY* IS GRADUALLY TURNING ME *IMMOBILE!* AT ANY MOMENT I SHALL NOT BE ABLE TO MOVE AT ALL! SUCH IS THE CURSE OF MY IMMORTALITY!

IT IS IMPERATIVE THAT I BECOME *MORTAL* AGAIN--LEAD MY NORMAL LIFE TO THE FULLEST--AS AN *ACTIVE* QUEEN OF THE UNIVERSE!

ONLY YOU--THE WORLD'S GREATEST SUPER-HEROES-- CAN MAKE ME MORTAL AGAIN--!

WHAT MAKES YOU THINK WE'LL COOPERATE, ZAZZALA?

6

BRAVE AS BATGIRL IS--TRICKY AS HER FIGHTING TECHNIQUES ARE--SHE CAN'T COPE WITH A SIX-WAY ONSLAUGHT...

MY SUPER-SPEED VIBRATIONS GIVING HER THE SHAKES!

THAT DOES IT!

MAKE WAY FOR BATGIRL'S DOWNFALL!

TEAMWORK WILL DO IT EVERY TIME!

VERY GOOD, MY DRONES!

PREPARE TO WELCOME TO THE FOLD--A SMALL-SIZE, WINGED BATGIRL!

I DARE NOT RISK GOING TO THOSE THREE PLANETS FOR THE IMMORTALITY ANTIDOTES--LEST I BECOME IMMOBILE BEFORE I OBTAIN THEM ALL!

THEREFORE I'M COMMISSIONING YOU SEVEN TO GO IN MY STEAD!

THUS, SHOULD THE IMMOBILITY BLIGHT SUDDENLY STRIKE ME, YOU WILL HAVE THE MEANS TO RESTORE MY MORTALITY!

MOMENTS LATER, INSIDE THE SPACE-SHIP AS IT ZOOMS OFF EARTH WITH ITS ANTI-DETECTION DEVICES TURNED ON...

HERE ARE YOUR TEAMED-UP ASSIGNMENTS! GREEN LANTERN and ATOM--FETCH THE URN OF IRRILLIUM ON GRAM!

SUPERMAN and FLASH--BRING ME THE THERMOSOLAR SPHERE FROM ISHTHAN!

BATMAN, BATGIRL and GREEN ARROW-- FILL THOSE FLASKS WITH THE POOL LIQUID ON PEREMUNDA!

9

I MUST WARN YOU--EACH MISSION PRESENTS ITS OWN SPECIAL PROBLEM--WHICH MUST BE SOLVED BEFORE YOU CAN SUCCEED!

I HAVE CHOSEN YOUR TEAMS TO GIVE YOU THE BEST POSSIBLE CHANCE TO SUCCEED IN YOUR MISSION--

AND *SUCCEED* YOU MUST!

NOW HOVER UNDER THE TELEPORTATION LENSES THAT WILL BEAM YOU TO YOUR DESTINATIONS--

AS I BRIEF YOU TO THE NATURE OF THE INDIVIDUAL PROBLEMS THAT WILL CONFRONT YOU!

AS THE QUEEN BEE PULLS THE ACTIVATION LEVER OF HER TRANSPORTATIONAL DEVICE...

KNOW THEN, *GREEN LANTERN* AND *ATOM*-- THAT WHEN YOU TAKE THE URN OF *IRRILLIUM* OFF *GRAM*--IT WILL CAUSE THE DESTRUCTION OF THAT WORLD WITH ALL ITS MANY LIFE-FORMS!

GL AND *ATOM* WILL BE HARD-PRESSED TO FIND A WAY OUT OF *THAT* DILEMMA!

I--I WONDER WHAT'S IN STORE FOR THE REST OF US?

JUSTICE LEAGUE of AMERICA

TO ONE SIDE OF THE BATTLING TINY TITAN...

CAME TO JUST IN TIME TO CUSHION MY FALL!

BUT HALF-WAY DOWN...

THAT YELLOW SPEAR-- CUT OFF MY POWER BEAM! GOING TO CRASH-LAND--

WHAT'S THE MATTER WITH ME? FORGOT ALL ABOUT MY BEING WINGED!

CAN'T STOP THOSE YELLOW-GARBED GNOMES DIRECTLY--

13

BUT BY *POWER-RINGING* THE GROUND, I CAN MAKE IT LIFT AND SWELL LIKE OCEAN WAVES--

GIVING ME A CHANCE TO BLAST THEM WITH SHEER FIST-POWER!

*SIDE BY SIDE, THE FIGHTING, FLYING FURIES RIP A PATH THROUGH THE GNOMES OF GRAM...*

THE TEMPLE HOLDING THE URN IS ONLY A FEW FEET AHEAD! GRAB IT, *ATOM*--WHILE I HOLD 'EM OFF!

GOT THE URN--BUT DO WE DARE REMOVE IT FROM *GRAM*--AND BECOME PLANET-WRECKERS?

WHEN I WHIPPED UP THAT MINOR EARTHQUAKE THAT KNOCKED OUR FOES OFF THEIR PINS--THE THOUGHT STRUCK ME THAT WHAT I COULD DO-- I CAN ALSO *UNDO!*

I'M GOING TO STOP THE PLANETARY UPHEAVALS BEFORE THEY CAN DO ANY DAMAGE!

*AS THE TINY TITAN LIFTS THE URN AND HIMSELF INTO THE TRANSPORTATIONAL BEAM, THE GREEN GLADIATOR BLANKETS THE PLANET GRAM WITH THE ENERGIES OF HIS POWER RING...*

THE GROUND'S STARTING TO RUMBLE! POUR IT ON, *GL*--!

TAKING EVERY ERG OF MY WILL POWER TO STOP THIS PLANET FROM BLOWING ITS TOP!

BEADS OF SWEAT STAIN HIS UNIFORM AS HE STRAINS WILL POWER AGAINST DESTRUCTIVE PLANETARY FORCES...

TIDE'S TURNING AGAINST ME!

MUST SUMMON UP WHATEVER RESERVE-POWER'S LEFT IN ME!

THEN... AS THE GLADIATOR COLLAPSES FROM EXHAUSTION...

HE DID IT-- BUT IS IN NO CONDITION TO REALIZE IT!

NOW I KNOW WHY ZAZZALA PICKED US FOR THIS JOB! IT TOOK THE TWO OF US TO PULL IT OFF!

MEANWHILE, ON THE LIFELESS PLANET ISHTHAN, A PUZZLED SUPERMAN AND DUBIOUS FLASH STARE ABOUT THEM...

THERE'S THE HEAT-GLOBE WE'RE HERE TO PICK UP! IT LOOKS LIKE EASY PICKIN'S...

REMEMBER ZAZZALA'S WARNING! SHE SAID IT'D BE TOUGH TO HANDLE!

ON THE ALERT FOR THE UNEXPECTED, THE TWO FASTEST HUMANS IN EXISTENCE WING AT THEIR TARGET...

WE'LL SOON FIND OUT WHAT THE MYSTERY IS ALL ABOUT.

IF IT "ATTACKS", LET ME HANDLE IT, FLASH! I'M THE INVULNERABLE ONE AROUND HERE!

AS THEIR HANDS REACH OUT TO GRAB THE THERMO-SOLAR BALL...

HEY! IT DARTED AWAY FROM US!

GREAT KRYPTON! IT MUST BE EQUIPPED WITH SOME SORT OF BUILT-IN ESCAPE GADGET--THAT AUTOMATICALLY CATAPULTS IT AWAY FROM US--AT SUPER-SPEED!

WE'LL HAVE TO OUTTHINK THIS THING! LET'S ATTACK IT FROM OPPOSITE SIDES!

SPREAD YOUR ARMS WIDE SO IT CAN'T ROLL PAST US!

SWOOSH!

WHAT A TRICKY CUSTOMER--!

IT LEAPED STRAIGHT UP! LEAVING US EMPTY-HANDED AGAIN!

I'LL RACE IN A TIGHT CIRCLE UNDER THE SPHERE, SUPERMAN--

WHILE I TRY TO GRAB IT ON THE WING!

KEEP IT UP THERE WITH AN UPDRAFT OF AIR!

NO GO!

THIS IS WORSE THAN TRYING TO CATCH THE GREASED PIG AT A COUNTY FAIR!

SWISH!

FOR HECTIC MINUTE AFTER ANOTHER, THE SUPER-SPEED-STERS PLAY A LOSING GAME OF TEASE-TAG WITH THE THERMO-SOLAR GLOBE...

16

*PANT! PANT! I'M TOO BEAT--TO KEEP GOING--YOU'LL HAVE TO CARRY ON--BY YOURSELF-- SUPERMAN...*

*WHILE YOU TAKE A BREATHER, LET'S BOTH THINK THIS OUT!*

*HAVE YOU FIGURED OUT A PLAN OF ACTION YET, READER? WELL, WATCH WHAT SUPERMAN AND FLASH COME UP WITH!*

*WE'LL TRY TO HERD THE BALL TOWARD THAT ROCK--!*

*WE'VE GOT TO BE SNEAKY ABOUT THIS-- RACING BACK AND FORTH LIKE SHEEPDOGS WITH A FLOCK OF LAMBS!*

*AT SUPER-SPEED THE CRUSADERS DART BACK AND FORTH UNTIL THEY MANEUVER THE SPHERE INTO POSITION! THEN--*

*NOW-- RUSH IT!*

*IT'S FLEEING--FUSING ITSELF INTO THAT ROCK--JUST AS WE COUNTED ON! IT'S TRAPPED ITSELF!*

*UHH! THAT ROCK IS HOT! TOO HOT FOR ME TO HANDLE!*

*THAT'S WHY ZAZZALA TEAMED US UP-- OUR COMBINED SPEEDS TO CORRAL THAT BALL, AND MY HEATPROOF BODY TO HANDLE IT WHEN ITS HIDING PLACE GOT TOO HOT!*

*ON PEREMUNDA, THE DESTINATION OF THE TELEPORTED BATGIRL, BATMAN AND GREEN ARROW...*

*THERE'LL BE NO PROBLEM GETTING THIS LIQUID INTO OUR FLASKS!*

*THAT'LL COME WHEN WE TAKE IT TO ZAZZALA--FOR THE LIQUID LOSES ITS RADIATION WHEN REMOVED FROM THIS POOL!*

*FIRST THINGS FIRST! LET'S FILL THE FLASKS!*

17

THERE IS AN AIR OF HUSHED EXPECTANCY OVER THE PLANET AS BATGIRL DIPS HER FLASK INTO THE POOL...

I DON'T LIKE THIS EERIE SILENCE! IT'S SORT OF -- THREATENING!

YOUR FEMALE INTUITION IS MAKING YOU IMAGINE THINGS, BATGIRL!

WITH STARTLING SWIFTNESS, A TREE BRANCH WRAPS AROUND THE MASKED MAIDEN, AND SWINGS HER INTO THE AMAZING ARCHER...

FEMALE IMAGINATION, EH?

SWAAAT!

WRITHING PLANT TENTACLES WHIP THE PAIR UPWARD...

GRAB MY LEGS, BATGIRL!

WITH MY FREE ARMS, I'LL FIRE OFF A JET-ARROW!

ZZZIPP

IT'S WHIPPED US FREE! HANG ON!

LIKE PAPER TO THE WALL!

18

BELOW, THE MASKED MANHUNTER STRUGGLES FIERCELY AGAINST THE WRAPAROUND TENTACLES OF ANOTHER TREE...

I WAS TOO FAR AWAY FROM GREEN ARROW TO GRAB HOLD OF HIM!

I'LL HAVE TO FREE MYSELF--MY OWN WAY!

OUT FLASHES THE LASER-GUN FROM HIS UTILITY BELT--ONLY TO HAVE HIS ARM GRIPPED SO TIGHTLY, HE CANNOT MOVE IT!...

THE TREE--CRUSHING ME IN ITS GRIP--! GOT TO TAKE A DESPERATE CHANCE!

HEAR ME, TREE! RELEASE ME-- OR I FIRE MY WEAPON AT THE POOL--

AND DRY IT UP!

NO! NO!

YOU ARE FREE, HUMAN! WE CANNOT SURVIVE WITHOUT THE POOL! BUT HOW DID YOU KNOW--

ON MY OWN WORLD, ALL LIFE DEPENDS ON WATER! I FIGURED THAT THE POOL-- THE ONLY ONE ON THIS WORLD--MUST BE PRECIOUS TO YOU--YOUR VERY LIVES DEPENDING ON IT!

YES--AND JUST AS THE POOL LIQUID'S RADIATION KEEPS US ALIVE--SO OUR RADIATION SUSTAINS THE LIQUID!

AN UNUSUAL SYMBIOSIS--THE MUTUAL LIVING TOGETHER OF TWO SPECIES!

OUT OF THE WAY, BATMAN! MY EXPLOSI-ARROW WILL BLAST THAT TREE-THREAT--

19

HOLD YOUR FIRE, *GREEN ARROW!*

I HAVE BETTER USE FOR YOUR WONDER ARROW--

UP THERE IN THE CLOUDS!

THOSE CLOUDS ARE THUNDER-HEADS--FILLED WITH LIQUID! I HAVE SOME SILVER IODIDE PELLETS IN MY *UTILITY BELT!*...

GOT YOU! WE'LL LOAD THE SILVER IODIDE ONTO MY *EXPLOSI-ARROW* AND SHOOT IT INTO THOSE CLOUDS!

THE "SEEDING" WILL RELEASE THE LIQUID--!

SHORTLY, A WELCOME PHENOMENON ON PEREMUNDA-- *RAIN!*...

IT WILL FORM MANY POOLS OVER THE PLANET--ENABLING US TO SPREAD OUR ROOTS ACROSS *PEREMUNDA!*

WE WILL NOT INTERFERE NOW, HUMANS, AS YOU FILL YOUR FLASKS FROM THE POOL! TO SHOW OUR GRATITUDE, ONE OF OUR PLANTLINGS WILL ACCOMPANY YOU--TO SUSTAIN THE RADIATION IN THE POOL LIQUID!

SOON, THE TRANSPORT BEAMS REUNITE THE JUSTICE LEAGUERS INSIDE THE QUEEN BEE'S SPACE-SHIP...

WE'RE TOO LATE!

*ZAZZALA* HAS BECOME *IMMOBILE!*

LET'S GRAB HER ROD--FREE OURSELVES FROM HER CONTROL!

*BUT*--AS THEY FLY FORWARD...

WE CAN'T REACH HER!

SHE'S STILL PROTECTED BY HER *MAGNO-NUCLEAR ROD!*

IT'LL OBEY ONLY HER COMMANDS!

HOW WILL WE EVER GET OUT OF THIS?

FOLLOW MY LEAD--AND I'LL SHOW YOU!

20

POUR THE *POOL LIQUID* INTO THE *URN*--THAT'S IT!

*SUPERMAN*--GET SET TO DROP THE HEAT-CORE INTO THE LIQUID-FILLED URN!

ONLY BY OBEYING HER COMMANDS TO MAKE *ZAZZALA* MORTAL AGAIN, CAN WE GET PAST HER FORCE-FIELD!

AS SOON AS SHE'S MADE MORTAL--AND MOBILE-- SHE MAY RELEASE HER HOLD ON US--AS A REWARD FOR SUCCESSFULLY COMPLETING OUR MISSION!

ON THE OTHER HAND, *ATOM*--ZAZZALA MAY INSIST ON USING US AS HER WINGED WARRIORS TO CONQUER THE UNIVERSE!

I'VE CONSIDERED THAT POSSIBILITY, *BATGIRL*-- AND AM PREPARED TO COPE WITH IT!

DRINK, *ZAZZALA*, DRINK!

*THE QUEEN BEE STIRS-- HER BODY FLEXES, BECOMES ANIMATED AS SHE TURNS AND ROARS WITH LAUGHTER AT HER DRONES...*

IN MY IMMOBILE STATE, I WAS AWARE OF YOUR EFFORTS TO FREE YOURSELVES FROM MY DOMINATION--

BUT THANKS TO MY FORESIGHTEDNESS, THE ROD COULD OBEY ONLY *MY* COMMANDS!

AND SUBJECT TO MY COMMANDS, YOU SHALL REMAIN!

THAT'S ALL I WANT TO KNOW! TIME FOR ME TO MAKE MY MOVE!

21

THE TINY TITAN CLICKS HIS GLOVE CONTROLS AND...

ATOM--GROWING IN SIZE--APPEARING IN ANOTHER COSTUME?!

AT THE COST OF MY SECRET IDENTITY--BUT IT'S THE ONLY WAY I CAN SAVE THIS CRITICAL SITUATION!

NEXT MOMENT, BEFORE THE QUEEN BEE CAN INTERFERE...

I'LL TAKE THAT ROD, ZAZZALA!

IT WON'T DO YOU ANY GOOD! IT'LL ONLY OBEY *ME*, REMEMBER?

I REMEMBER SOMETHING ELSE! LISTEN--AND WATCH!

YOUR ROD WAS ABLE TO DOMINATE US ONLY IN *SMALL* SIZE--

SO I ENLARGED MYSELF TO RELEASE ITS GRIP ON ME--

AND BECAUSE YOU ORDERED THE ROD TO OBEY ONLY *QUEEN ZAZZALA THE IMMORTAL*--

WE MADE YOU *MORTAL*--SO YOUR HOLD ON IT WOULD NO LONGER APPLY!

NOW THAT I'VE RESTORED THE *JUSTICE LEAGUERS* AND *BATGIRL* TO THEIR NORMAL SHAPES--

I'M ELIMINATING YOU AS A THREAT TO THE UNIVERSE...

BY TURNING YOU *IMMOBILE* AGAIN--

IN WHICH STATE YOU'LL SPEND THE REST OF YOUR MORTAL LIFE!

AFTER QUEEN ZAZZALA HAS BEEN TAKEN TO HER HOME WORLD OF *KORLL* AND THE PLANT TO *PEREMUNDA*--THE CRUSADERS RETURN TO *EARTH*, WHERE ZAZZALA'S ROD IS USED TO REMOVE THE PARALYSIS GRIPPING MARTIAN MANHUNTER, HAWKMAN, AQUAMAN AND WONDER WOMAN...

(22)